Complete Virtual Reality and Augmented Reality Development with Unity

Leverage the power of Unity and become a pro at creating mixed reality applications

Jesse Glover
Jonathan Linowes

BIRMINGHAM - MUMBAI

Complete Virtual Reality and Augmented Reality Development with Unity

Copyright © 2019 Packt Publishing

First Published: April 2019

Production Reference: 1170419

Published by Packt Publishing Ltd.
Livery Place, 35 Livery Street
Birmingham, B3 2PB, U.K.

ISBN 978-1-83864-818-3

www.packtpub.com

mapt.io

Mapt is an online digital library that gives you full access to over 5,000 books and videos, as well as industry-leading tools to help you plan your personal development and advance your career. For more information, please visit our website.

Why Subscribe?

- Spend less time learning and more time coding with practical eBooks and Videos from over 4,000 industry professionals

- Improve your learning with Skill Plans built especially for you

- Get a free eBook or video every month

- Mapt is fully searchable

- Copy and paste, print, and bookmark content

Packt.com

Did you know that Packt offers eBook versions of every book published, with PDF and ePub files available? You can upgrade to the eBook version at www.packt.com and as a print book customer, you are entitled to a discount on the eBook copy. Get in touch with us at customercare@packtpub.com for more details.

At www.packt.com, you can also read a collection of free technical articles, sign up for a range of free newsletters, and receive exclusive discounts and offers on Packt books and eBooks.

Contributors

About the Authors

Jesse Glover is a self-taught software developer and indie game developer who has worked with multiple game engines and has written many tutorials on the subject of game development over the past 8 years. He maintains a YouTube channel dedicated to game development made easy and writes for Zenva in his spare time to teach the ins and outs of game development with Unity, CryEngine, and Unreal Engine, just to name a few. Jesse has also written Unity Programming for Human Beings.

Jonathan Linowes is a founder of Parkerhill Reality Labs, an immersive media indie studio and developer of the BridgeXR toolkit, Power Solitaire VR game, and upcoming Chess Or Die game. He is a VR/AR evangelist, Unity developer, entrepreneur, and teacher. Jonathan has a BFA degree from Syracuse University, an MS degree from the MIT Media Lab, and held technical leadership positions at Autodesk, among other companies. He has authored a number of books and videos by Packt, including Unity Virtual Reality Projects (first edition 2015), Cardboard VR Projects for Android, and Augmented Reality for Developers.

Packt Is Searching for Authors Like You

If you're interested in becoming an author for Packt, please visit `authors.packtpub.com` and apply today. We have worked with thousands of developers and tech professionals, just like you, to help them share their insight with the global tech community. You can make a general application, apply for a specific hot topic that we are recruiting an author for, or submit your own idea.

Table of Contents

Preface

Unity is the leading platform to develop mixed reality experiences because it provides a great pipeline for working with 3D assets.

Using a practical and project-based approach, this Learning Path educates you about the specifics of AR and VR development using Unity 2018 and Unity 3D. You'll learn to integrate, animate, and overlay 3D objects on your camera feed, before moving on to implement sensor-based AR applications. You'll explore various concepts by creating an AR application using Vuforia for both macOS and Windows for Android and iOS devices. Next, you'll learn how to develop VR applications that can be experienced with devices, such as Oculus and Vive. You'll also explore various tools for VR development: gaze-based versus hand controller input, world space UI canvases, locomotion and teleportation, timeline animation, and multiplayer networking.
You'll learn the Unity 3D game engine via the interactive Unity Editor and C# programming.

By the end of this Learning Path, you'll be fully equipped to develop rich, interactive mixed reality experiences using Unity.

Who This Book Is For

If you are a game developer familiar with 3D computer graphics and interested in building your own AR and VR games or applications, then this Learning Path is for you. Any prior experience in Unity and C# will be an advantage. In all, this course teaches you the tools and techniques to develop engaging mixed reality applications.

What This Book Covers

Chapter 1, *Virtually Everything for Everyone*, is an introduction to the new technologies and opportunities in consumer virtual reality in games and non-gaming applications, including an explanation of stereoscopic viewing and head tracking.

Chapter 2, *Content, Objects, and Scale*, introduces the Unity game engine as we build a simple diorama scene and reviews importing 3D content created with other tools such as Blender, Tilt Brush, Google Poly, and Unity EditorXR.

Chapter 3, *VR Build and Run*, helps you set up your system and Unity project to build and run on your target device(s), including SteamVR, Oculus Rift, Windows MR, GearVR, Oculus Go, and Google Daydream.

Chapter 4, *Gaze-Based Control*, explores the relationship between the VR camera and objects in the scene, including 3D cursors and gaze-based ray guns. This chapter also introduces Unity scripting in the C# programming language.

Chapter 5, *Handy Interactables*, looks at user input events using controller buttons and interactable objects, using various software patterns including polling, scriptable objects, Unity events, and interactable components provided with toolkit SDK.

Chapter 6, *World Space UI*, implements many examples of user interface (UI) for VR using a Unity world space canvas, including a heads-up display (HUD), info-bubbles, in-game objects, and a wrist-based menu palette.

Chapter 7, *Locomotion and Comfort*, dives into techniques for moving yourself around a VR scene, looking closely at the Unity first-person character objects and components, locomotion, teleportation, and room-scale VR.

Chapter 8, *Playing with Physics and Fire*, explores the Unity physics engine, physic materials, particle systems, and more C# scripting, as we build a paddle ball game to whack fireballs in time to your favorite music.

Chapter 9, *Animation and VR Storytelling*, builds a complete VR storytelling experience using imported 3D assets and soundtrack, and Unity timelines and animation.

Chapter 10, *What AR is and How to Get Set Up*, explains the processes of installing various SDKs and packages for enabling AR, and building a Hello World example with AR.

Chapter 11, *GIS Fundamentals - The Power of Mapping*, explores the history of GIS, GIS implications in applications and games, and GIS in education.

Chapter 12, *Censored - Various Sensor Data and Plugins*, looks at how to write plugins for Unity in C#, how to write plugins for Unity in C++, how to write plugins for Unity in Objective-C, and how to write plugins for Unity in Java.

Chapter 13, *The Sound of Flowery Prose*, goes into details of the steps for designing an application, looks at conceptualizing the project, and explores how to create an AR application based on the perception of sound.

Chapter 14, *Picture Puzzle - The AR Experience*, helps you design an educational app, learn to use Vuforia, and develop an educational AR application with Vuforia.

Chapter 15, *Fitness for Fun - Tourism and Random Walking*, teaches about Mapbox, integrating Mapbox into Unity, and building a random walk-to-location app prototype.

Chapter 16, *Snap it! Adding Filters to Pictures*, helps you learn about OpenCV, incorporate OpenCV into Unity, build OpenCV from source, and build a facial detection app prototype with OpenCV.

Chapter 17, *To the HoloLens and Beyond*, gives you an insight into the difference between AR and **Mixed Reality** (**MR**), teaches you how to use the Hololens simulator, and gets you to build a basic prototype for MR using the Hololens simulator.

To Get the Most out of This Book

To get the most out of this book, you should have some knowledge of the Unity Editor, UI, and build processes. In addition to this, it is highly advised that you have some skill with C# that is above the beginners' level, as this book does not go into how to write C# code. Lastly, it is suggested that you should have, at the very least, take a look at other programming languages, such as Swift, Objective-C, C, C++, and Java, and are able to get the gist of what is happening with the code that you will encounter in this book at a glance.

The only requirements are basic knowledge of the Unity Game Engine and C#, as they are the primary focuses of this book.

Download the Example Code Files

You can download the example code files for this book from your account at www.packt.com. If you purchased this book elsewhere, you can visit www.packt.com/support and register to have the files emailed directly to you.

You can download the code files by following these steps:

1. Log in or register at www.packt.com.
2. Select the **SUPPORT** tab.
3. Click on **Code Downloads & Errata**.
4. Enter the name of the book in the **Search** box and follow the onscreen instructions.

Once the file is downloaded, please make sure that you unzip or extract the folder using the latest version of:

- WinRAR/7-Zip for Windows
- Zipeg/iZip/UnRarX for Mac
- 7-Zip/PeaZip for Linux

The code bundle for the book is also hosted on GitHub at `https://github.com/PacktPublishing/Complete-Virtual-Reality-and-Augmented-Reality-Development-with-Unity`. In case there's an update to the code, it will be updated on the existing GitHub repository.

We also have other code bundles from our rich catalog of books and videos available at `https://github.com/PacktPublishing/`. Check them out!

Conventions Used

There are a number of text conventions used throughout this book.

`CodeInText`: Indicates code words in text, database table names, folder names, filenames, file extensions, pathnames, dummy URLs, user input, and Twitter handles. Here is an example: "Create a brand new Unity Project. I will call mine `Snap`."

A block of code is set as follows:

```
struct Circle
{
Circle(int x, int y, int radius) : X(x), Y(y), Radius(radius) {}
int X, Y, Radius;
};
```

When we wish to draw your attention to a particular part of a code block, the relevant lines or items are set in bold:

```
extern "C" void __declspec(dllexport) __stdcall  Close()
{
_capture.release();
}
```

Bold: Indicates a new term, an important word, or words that you see onscreen. For example, words in menus or dialog boxes appear in the text like this. Here is an example: "Select **System info** from the **Administration** panel."

Warnings or important notes appear like this.

Tips and tricks appear like this.

Get in Touch

Feedback from our readers is always welcome.

General feedback: If you have questions about any aspect of this book, mention the book title in the subject of your message and email us at customercare@packtpub.com.

Errata: Although we have taken every care to ensure the accuracy of our content, mistakes do happen. If you have found a mistake in this book, we would be grateful if you would report this to us. Please visit www.packt.com/submit-errata, selecting your book, clicking on the Errata Submission Form link, and entering the details.

Piracy: If you come across any illegal copies of our works in any form on the Internet, we would be grateful if you would provide us with the location address or website name. Please contact us at copyright@packt.com with a link to the material.

If you are interested in becoming an author: If there is a topic that you have expertise in and you are interested in either writing or contributing to a book, please visit authors.packtpub.com.

Reviews

Please leave a review. Once you have read and used this book, why not leave a review on the site that you purchased it from? Potential readers can then see and use your unbiased opinion to make purchase decisions, we at Packt can understand what you think about our products, and our authors can see your feedback on their book. Thank you!

For more information about Packt, please visit packt.com.

1
Virtually Everything for Everyone

This virtual reality thing calls into question, what does it mean to
"be somewhere"?
Before cell phones, you would call someone and it would make no sense to
say, "Hey, where are you?" You know where they are, you called their house,
that's where they are.
So then cell phones come around and you start to hear people say, "Hello. Oh, I'm at
Starbucks," because the person on the other end wouldn't necessarily know where you are,
because you became un-tethered from your house for voice communications.
So when I saw a VR demo, I had this vision of coming home and my wife has got the kids
settled down, she has a couple minutes to herself, and she's on the couch wearing goggles
on her face. I come over and tap her on the shoulder, and I'm like, "Hey, where are you?"
It's super weird. The person's sitting right in front of you, but you don't know where they
are.

-Jonathan Stark, mobile expert, and podcaster

Welcome to **virtual reality (VR)**! In this book, we will explore what it takes to create virtual reality experiences on our own. We will take a walk through a series of hands-on projects, step-by-step tutorials, and in-depth discussions using the Unity 3D game engine and other free or open source software. Though the virtual reality technology is rapidly advancing, we'll try to capture the basic principles and techniques that you can use to make your VR games and applications feel immersive and comfortable.

In this first chapter, we will define virtual reality and illustrate how it can be applied not only to games but also many other areas of interest and productivity. This chapter discusses the following topics:

- What is virtual reality?
- Differences between virtual reality and augmented reality
- How VR applications may differ from VR games
- Types of VR experiences
- Technical skills that are necessary for the development of VR

What is virtual reality to you?

Today, we are witnesses to the burgeoning consumer virtual reality, an exciting technology that promises to transform in a fundamental way how we interact with information, our friends, and the world at large.

What is virtual reality? In general, VR is the computer-generated simulation of a 3D environment, which seems very real to the person experiencing it, using special electronic equipment. The objective is to achieve a strong sense of being present in the virtual environment.

Today's consumer tech VR involves wearing an HMD (head-mounted display goggles) to view stereoscopic 3D scenes. You can look around by moving your head, and walk around by using hand controls or motion sensors. You are engaged in a fully immersive experience. It's as if you're really there in some other virtual world. The following image shows me, the author, experiencing an **Oculus Rift Development Kit 2 (DK2)** in 2015:

Virtual reality is not new. It's been here for decades, albeit hidden away in academic research labs and high-end industrial and military facilities. It was big, clunky, and expensive. Ivan Sutherland invented the first HMD in 1965 (see `https://amturing.acm.org/photo/sutherland_3467412.cfm`). It was tethered to the ceiling! In the past, several failed attempts have been made to bring consumer-level virtual reality products to the market.

In 2012, Palmer Luckey, the founder of Oculus VR LLC, gave a demonstration of a makeshift head-mounted VR display to John Carmack, the famed developer of the Doom, Wolfenstein 3D, and Quake classic video games. Together, they ran a successful **Kickstarter** campaign and released a developer kit called **Oculus Rift Development Kit 1 (DK1)** to an enthusiastic community. This caught the attention of investors as well as Mark Zuckerberg, and in March 2014, Facebook bought the company for $2 billion. With no product, no customers, and infinite promise, the money, and attention that it attracted helped fuel a new category of consumer products.

Concurrently, others also working on their own products which were soon introduced to the market, including Steam's HTC VIVE, Google Daydream, Sony PlayStation VR, Samsung Gear VR, Microsoft's immersive Mixed Reality, and more. New innovations and devices that enhance the VR experience continue to be introduced.

Most of the basic research has already been done and the technology is now affordable thanks in large part to the mass adoption of devices that work on mobile technology. There is a huge community of developers with experience in building 3D games and mobile apps. Creative content producers are joining in and the media is talking it up. At last, virtual reality is real!

Say what? *Virtual reality is real?* Ha! If it's virtual, how can it be... Oh, never mind.

Eventually, we will get past the focus on the emerging hardware devices and recognize that *content is king*. The current generation of 3D development software (commercial, free, and open source) that has spawned a plethora of indie, or independent, game developers can also be used to build non-game VR applications.

Though VR finds most of its enthusiasts in the gaming community, the potential applications reach well beyond that. Any business that presently uses 3D modeling and computer graphics will be more effective if it uses VR technology. The sense of immersive presence that is afforded by VR can enhance all common online experiences today, which includes engineering, social networking, shopping, marketing, entertainment, and business development. In the near future, viewing 3D websites with a VR headset may be as common as visiting ordinary flat websites today.

Types of head-mounted displays

Presently, there are two basic categories of HMDs for virtual reality—**desktop VR** and **mobile VR**, although the distinctions are increasingly becoming blurred. Eventually, we might just talk about platforms as we do traditional computing, in terms of the operating system—Windows, Android, or console VR.

Desktop VR

With desktop VR (and console VR), your headset is peripheral to a more powerful computer that processes the heavy graphics. The computer may be a Windows PC, Mac, Linux, or a game console, although Windows is by far the most prominent PC and the PS4 is a bestseller in terms of console VR.

Most likely, the headset is connected to the computer with wires. The game runs on the remote machine and the HMD is a peripheral display device with a motion sensing input. The term *desktop* is an unfortunate misnomer since it's just as likely to be stationed in either a living room or a den.

The **Oculus Rift** (https://www.oculus.com/) is an example of a device where the goggles have an integrated display and sensors. The games run on a separate PC. Other desktop headsets include the **HTC VIVE**, Sony's **PlayStation VR**, and **Microsoft immersive Mixed Reality**.

Desktop VR devices rely on a desktop computer (usually via video and USB cables) for CPU and **graphics processing unit (GPU)** power, where more is better. Please refer to the recommended specification requirements for your specific device.

However, for the purpose of this book, we won't have any heavy rendering in our projects, and you can get by with minimum system specifications.

Mobile VR

Mobile VR originated with **Google Cardboard** (https://vr.google.com/cardboard/), a simple housing device for two lenses and a slot for your mobile phone. The phone's display is used to show the twin stereoscopic views. It has rotational head tracking, but it has no positional tracking. The Cardboard also provides the user with the ability to click or *tap* its side to make selections in a game. The complexity of the imagery is limited because it uses your phone's processor for rendering the views on the phone display screen.

Google Daydream and Samsung GearVR improved the platforms by requiring more performant minimum specifications including greater processing power in the mobile phone. GearVR's headsets include motion sensors to assist the phone device. These devices also introduced a three-**degrees-of-freedom** (**DOF**) hand controller that can be used as a laser pointer within VR experiences.

The next generation of mobile VR devices includes all-in-one headsets, like Oculus Go, with embedded screens and processors, eliminating the need for a separate mobile phone. Newer models may include depth sensors and spatial mapping processors to track the user's location in 3D space.

The bottom line is, the projects in this book will explore features from the high end to the low end of the consumer VR device spectrum. But generally, our projects do not demand a lot of processing power nor do they require high-end VR capability, so you can begin developing for VR on any of these types of devices, including Google Cardboard and an ordinary mobile phone.

 If you are interested in developing VR applications for Google Daydream on Android directly in Java rather than through the Unity game engine, please also refer to another of the author's books, *Cardboard VR Projects for Android* from Packt Publishing (`https://www.packtpub.com/application-development/cardboard-vr-projects-android`).

The difference between virtual reality and augmented reality

It's probably worthwhile to clarify what virtual reality is not.

A sister technology to VR is **augmented reality** (**AR**), which combines computer-generated imagery (CGI) with views of the real world. AR on smartphones has recently garnered widespread interest with the introduction of Apple's ARKit for iOS and Google ARCore for Android. Further, the Vuforia AR toolkit is now integrated directly with the Unity game engine, helping to drive even more adoption of the technology. AR on a mobile device overlays the CGI on top of live video from a camera.

The latest innovations in AR are wearable AR headsets, such as Microsoft's **HoloLens** and **Magic Leap**, which show the computer graphics directly in your field of view. The graphics are not mixed into a video image. If VR headsets are like closed goggles, AR headsets are like translucent sunglasses that combine the real-world light rays with CGI. A challenge for AR is ensuring that the CGI is consistently aligned with and mapped onto the objects in the real-world space and to eliminate latency while moving about so that they (the CGI and objects in the real-world space) stay aligned.

AR holds as much promise as VR for future applications, but it's different. Though AR intends to engage the user within their current surroundings, virtual reality is fully immersive. In AR, you may open your hand and see a log cabin resting in your palm, but in VR, you're transported directly inside the log cabin and you can walk around inside it.

We are also beginning to see hybrid devices that combine features of VR and AR and let you switch between modes.

 If you are interested in developing applications for AR, please also refer to the author's book *Augmented Reality for Developers* from Packt Publishing (https://www.packtpub.com/web-development/augmented-reality-developers).

Applications versus games

Consumer-level virtual reality started with gaming. Video gamers are already accustomed to being engaged in highly interactive hyper-realistic 3D environments. VR just ups the ante.

Gamers are early adopters of high-end graphics technology. Mass production of gaming consoles and PC-based components in the tens of millions and competition between vendors leads to lower prices and higher performance. Game developers follow suit, often pushing the state of the art, squeezing every ounce of performance out of hardware and software. Gamers are a very demanding bunch, and the market has consistently stepped up to keep them satisfied. It's no surprise that many, if not most, of the current wave of VR hardware and software companies, are first targeting the video gaming industry. A majority of the VR apps on the Oculus Store such as Rift (https://www.oculus.com/experiences/rift/), GearVR (https://www.oculus.com/experiences/gear-vr/), and Google Play for Daydream (https://play.google.com/store/search?q=daydreamc=apps hl=en), for example, are games. And of course, the Steam VR platform (http://store.steampowered.com/steamvr) is almost entirely about gaming. Gamers are the most enthusiastic VR advocates and seriously appreciate its potential.

Game developers know that the core of a game is the **game mechanics**, or the rules, which are largely independent of the *skin*, or the thematic topic of the game. Gameplay mechanics can include puzzles, chance, strategy, timing, or muscle memory. VR games can have the same mechanic elements but might need to be adjusted for the virtual environment. For example, a first-person character walking in a console video game is probably going about 1.5 times faster than their actual pace in real life. If this wasn't the case, the player would feel that the game was too slow and boring. Put the same character in a VR scene and they will feel that it is too fast; it could likely make the player feel nauseous. In VR, you want your characters to walk at a normal, earthly pace. Not all video games will map well to VR; it may not be fun to be in the middle of a war zone when you're actually there.

That said, virtual reality is also being applied in areas other than gaming. Though games will remain important, non-gaming applications will eventually overshadow them. These applications may differ from games in a number of ways, with the most significant having much less emphasis on game mechanics and more emphasis on either the experience itself or application-specific goals. Of course, this doesn't preclude some game mechanics. For example, the application may be specifically designed to train the user in a specific skill. Sometimes, the **gamification** of a business or personal application makes it more fun and effective in driving the desired behavior through competition.

In general, non-gaming VR applications are less about winning and more about the experience itself.

Here are a few examples of the kinds of non-gaming applications that people are working on:

- **Travel and tourism**: Visit faraway places without leaving your home. Visit art museums in Paris, New York, and Tokyo in one afternoon. Take a walk on Mars. You can even enjoy Holi, the spring festival of colors, in India while sitting in your wintery cabin in Vermont.
- **Mechanical engineering and industrial design**: Computer-aided design software such as AutoCAD and SOLIDWORKS pioneered three-dimensional modeling, simulation, and visualization. With VR, engineers and designers can directly experience the end product before it's actually built and play with what-if scenarios at a very low cost. Consider iterating a new automobile design. How does it look? How does it perform? How does it appear when sitting in the driver's seat?

- **Architecture and civil engineering**: Architects and engineers have always constructed scale models of their designs, if only to pitch the ideas to clients and investors or, more importantly, to validate the many assumptions about the design. Presently, modeling and rendering software is commonly used to build virtual models from architectural plans. With VR, the conversations with stakeholders can be so much more confident. Other personnel, such as the interior designers, HVAC, and electrical engineers, can be brought into the process sooner.

- **Real estate**: Real estate agents have been quick adopters of the internet and visualization technology to attract buyers and close sales. Real estate search websites were some of the first successful uses of the web. Online panoramic video walkthroughs of for-sale properties are commonplace today. With VR, I can be in New York and find a place to live in Los Angeles.

- **Medicine**: The potential of VR for health and medicine may literally be a matter of life and death. Every day, hospitals use MRI and other scanning devices to produce models of our bones and organs that are used for medical diagnosis and possibly pre-operative planning. Using VR to enhance visualization and measurement will provide a more intuitive analysis. Virtual reality is also being used for the simulation of surgery to train medical students.

- **Mental health**: Virtual reality experiences have been shown to be effective in a therapeutic context for the treatment of **post-traumatic stress disorder** (**PTSD**) in what's called **exposure therapy**, where the patient, guided by a trained therapist, confronts their traumatic memories through the retelling of the experience. Similarly, VR is being used to treat arachnophobia (fear of spiders) and the fear of flying.

- **Education**: The educational opportunities for VR are almost too obvious to mention. One of the first successful VR experiences is **Titans of Space**, which lets you explore the solar system first-hand. In science, history, arts, and mathematics, VR will help students of all ages because, as they say, field trips are much more effective than textbooks.

- **Training**: Toyota has demonstrated a VR simulation of drivers' education to teach teenagers about the risks of distracted driving. In another project, vocational students got to experience the operating of cranes and other heavy construction equipment. Training for first responders, the police, and fire and rescue workers can be enhanced with VR by presenting highly risky situations and alternative virtual scenarios. The **National Football League** (**NFL**) and college teams are looking to VR for athletic training.

- **Entertainment and journalism**: Virtually attend rock concerts and sporting events. Watch music videos Erotica. Re-experience news events as if you were personally present. Enjoy 360-degree cinematic experiences. The art of storytelling will be transformed by virtual reality.

Wow, that's quite a list! This is just the low-hanging fruit.

The purpose of this book is not to dive too deeply into any of these applications. Rather, I hope that this survey helps stimulate your thinking and provides an idea of how virtual reality has the potential to be virtually anything for everyone.

How virtual reality really works

So, what is it about VR that's got everyone so excited? With your headset on, you experience synthetic scenes. It appears 3D, it feels 3D, and maybe you even have a sense of actually being there inside the virtual world. The strikingly obvious thing is: VR looks and feels *really cool!* But why?

Immersion and *presence* are the two words used to describe the quality of a VR experience. The Holy Grail is to increase both to the point where it seems so real, you forget you're in a virtual world. *Immersion* is the result of emulating the sensory input that your body receives (visual, auditory, motor, and so on). This can be explained technically. *Presence* is the visceral feeling that you get being transported there—a deep emotional or intuitive feeling. You could say that immersion is the science of VR and presence is art. And that, my friend, is cool.

A number of different technologies and techniques come together to make the VR experience work, which can be separated into two basic areas:

- 3D viewing
- Head-pose tracking

In other words, displays and sensors, like those built into today's mobile devices, are a big reason why VR is possible and affordable today.

Suppose the VR system knows exactly where your head is positioned at any given moment in time. Suppose that it can immediately render and display the 3D scene for this precise viewpoint stereoscopically. Then, wherever and whenever you move, you'll see the virtual scene exactly as you should. You will have a nearly perfect visual VR experience. That's basically it. *Ta-dah!*

Well, not so fast. Literally.

Stereoscopic 3D viewing

Split-screen stereography was discovered not long after the invention of photography, like the popular stereograph viewer from 1876 shown in the following picture (B.W. Kilborn & Co, Littleton, New Hampshire; see `http://en.wikipedia.org/wiki/Benjamin_W._Kilburn`). A stereo photograph has separate views for the left and right eyes, which are slightly offset to create parallax. This fools the brain into thinking that it's a truly three-dimensional view. The device contains separate lenses for each eye, which let you easily focus on the photo close up:

Similarly, rendering these side-by-side stereo views is the first job of the VR-enabled camera in Unity.

Let's say that you're wearing a VR headset and you're holding your head very still so that the image looks frozen. It still appears better than a simple stereograph. Why?

The old-fashioned stereograph has relatively small twin images rectangularly bound. When your eye is focused on the center of the view, the 3D effect is convincing, but you will see the boundaries of the view. Move your eyes around (even with your head still), and any remaining sense of immersion is totally lost. You're just an observer on the outside peering into a diorama.

Now, consider what a VR screen looks like without the headset (see the following screenshot):

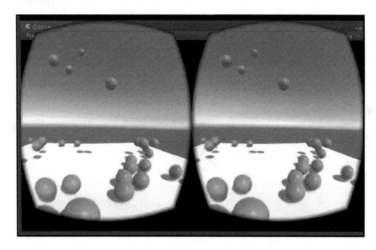

The first thing that you will notice is that each eye has a barrel-shaped view. Why is that? The headset lens is a very wide-angle lens. So, when you look through it, you have a nice wide field of view. In fact, it is so wide (and tall), it distorts the image (**pincushion effect**). The graphics software SDK does an inverse of that distortion (**barrel distortion**) so that it looks correct to us through the lenses. This is referred to as an **ocular distortion correction**. The result is an apparent **field of view** (**FOV**) that is wide enough to include a lot more of your peripheral vision. For example, the Oculus Rift has a FOV of about 100 degrees.

Also, of course, the view angle from each eye is slightly offset, comparable to the distance between your eyes or the **Inter Pupillary Distance** (**IPD**). IPD is used to calculate the parallax and can vary from one person to the next. (The Oculus Configuration Utility comes with a utility to measure and configure your IPD. Alternatively, you can ask your eye doctor for an accurate measurement.)

It might be less obvious, but if you look closer at the VR screen, you will see color separations, as you'd get from a color printer whose print head is not aligned properly. This is intentional. Light passing through a lens is refracted at different angles based on the wavelength of the light. Again, the rendering software does an inverse of the color separation so that it looks correct to us. This is referred to as a **chromatic aberration correction**. It helps make the image look really crisp.

The resolution of the screen is also important to get a convincing view. If it's too low-res, you'll see the pixels, or what some refer to as a **screen-door effect**. The pixel width and height of the display is an oft-quoted specification when comparing the HMDs, but the **pixels per inch** (**PPI**) value may be more important. Other innovations in display technology such as **pixel smearing** and **foveated rendering** (showing higher-resolution details exactly where the eyeball is looking) will also help reduce the screen-door effect.

When experiencing a 3D scene in VR, you must also consider the **frames per second** (**FPS**). If the FPS is too slow, the animation will look choppy. Things that affect FPS include the GPU performance and the complexity of the Unity scene (the number of polygons and lighting calculations), among other factors. *This is compounded in VR because you need to draw the scene twice, once for each eye.* Technology innovations, such as GPUs optimized for VR, frame interpolation, and other techniques will improve the frame rates. For us, developers, performance-tuning techniques in Unity, such as those used by mobile game developers, can be applied in VR. These techniques and optics help make the 3D scene appear realistic.

Sound is also very important—more important than many people realize. VR should be experienced while wearing stereo headphones. In fact, when the audio is done well but the graphics are pretty crappy, you can still have a great experience. We see this a lot in TV and cinema. The same holds true in VR. Binaural audio gives each ear its own stereo *view* of a sound source in such a way that your brain imagines its location in 3D space. No special listening devices are needed. Regular headphones will work (speakers will not). For example, put on your headphones and visit the *Virtual Barber Shop* at `https://www.youtube.com/watch?v=IUDTlvagjJA`. True 3D audio provides an even more realistic spatial audio rendering, where sounds bounce off nearby walls and can be occluded by obstacles in the scene to enhance the first-person experience and realism.

Lastly, the VR headset should fit your head and face comfortably so that it's easy to forget that you're wearing it, and it should block out light from the real environment around you.

Head tracking

So, we have a nice 3D picture that is viewable in a comfortable VR headset with a wide field of view. If this was it and you moved your head, it'd feel like you had a diorama box stuck to your face. Move your head and the box moves along with it, and this is much like holding the antique stereograph device or the childhood **View-Master**. Fortunately, VR is so much better.

The VR headset has a motion sensor (IMU) inside that detects spatial acceleration and rotation rates on all three axes, providing what's called the **six degrees of freedom**. This is the same technology that is commonly found in mobile phones and some console game controllers. Mounted on your headset, when you move your head, the current viewpoint is calculated and used when the next frame's image is drawn. This is referred to as **motion detection**.

The previous generation of mobile motion sensors was good enough for us to play mobile games on a phone, but for VR, it's not accurate enough. These inaccuracies (rounding errors) accumulate over time, as the sensor is sampled thousands of times per second and one may eventually lose track of where they were in the real world. This *drift* was a major shortfall of the older, phone-based Google Cardboard VR. It could sense your head's motion, but it lost track of your head's orientation. The current generation of phones, such as Google Pixel and Samsung Galaxy, which conform to the Daydream specifications, have upgraded sensors.

High-end HMDs account for drift with a separate *positional tracking* mechanism. The Oculus Rift does this with *inside-out positional tracking*, where an array of (invisible) infrared LEDs on the HMD are read by an external optical sensor (infrared camera) to determine your position. You need to remain within the *view* of the camera for the head tracking to work.

Alternatively, the Steam VR VIVE Lighthouse technology does outside-in positional tracking, where two or more dumb laser emitters are placed in the room (much like the lasers in a barcode reader at the grocery checkout), and an optical sensor on the headset reads the rays to determine your position.

Windows MR headsets use no external sensors or cameras. Rather, there are integrated cameras and sensors to perform spatial mapping of the local environment around you, in order to locate and track your position in the real-world 3D space.

Either way, the primary purpose is to accurately find the position of your head and other similarly equipped devices, such as handheld controllers.

Together, the position, tilt, and the forward direction of your head—or the *head pose*—are used by the graphics software to redraw the 3D scene from this vantage point. Graphics engines such as Unity are really good at this.

Now, let's say that the screen is getting updated at 90 FPS, and you're moving your head. The software determines the head pose, renders the 3D view, and draws it on the HMD screen. However, you're still moving your head. So, by the time it's displayed, the image is a little out of date with respect to your current position. This is called **latency**, and it can make you feel nauseous.

Motion sickness caused by latency in VR occurs when you're moving your head and your brain expects the world around you to change exactly in sync. Any perceptible delay can make you uncomfortable, to say the least.

Latency can be measured as the time from reading a motion sensor to rendering the corresponding image, or the *sensor-to-pixel* delay. According to Oculus's John Carmack:

> *A total latency of 50 milliseconds will feel responsive, but still noticeable laggy. 20 milliseconds or less will provide the minimum level of latency deemed acceptable.*

There are a number of very clever strategies that can be used to implement latency compensation. The details are outside the scope of this book and inevitably will change as device manufacturers improve on the technology. One of these strategies is what Oculus calls the **timewarp**, which tries to guess where your head will be by the time the rendering is done and uses that future head pose instead of the actual detected one. All of this is handled in the SDK, so as a Unity developer, you do not have to deal with it directly.

Meanwhile, as VR developers, we need to be aware of latency as well as the other causes of motion sickness. Latency can be reduced via the faster rendering of each frame (keeping the recommended FPS). This can be achieved by discouraging your head from moving too quickly and using other techniques to make yourself feel grounded and comfortable.

Another thing that the Rift does to improve head tracking and realism is that it uses a skeletal representation of the neck so that all the rotations that it receives are mapped more accurately to the head rotation. For example, looking down at your lap creates a small forward translation since it knows it's impossible to rotate one's head downwards on the spot.

Other than head tracking, stereography, and 3D audio, virtual reality experiences can be enhanced with body tracking, hand tracking (and gesture recognition), locomotion tracking (for example, VR treadmills), and controllers with haptic feedback. The goal of all of this is to increase your sense of immersion and presence in the virtual world.

Types of VR experiences

There is not just one kind of virtual reality experience. In fact, there are many. Consider the following types of virtual reality experiences:

- **Diorama**: In the simplest case, we build a 3D scene. You're observing from a third-person perspective. Your eye is the camera. Actually, each eye is a separate camera that gives you a stereographic view. You can look around.

- **First-person experience**: This time, you're immersed in the scene as a freely moving avatar. Using an input controller (keyboard, game controller, or some other technique), you can walk around and explore the virtual scene.

- **Interactive virtual environment**: This is like the first-person experience, but it has an additional feature—while you are in the scene, you can interact with the objects in it. Physics is at play. Objects may respond to you. You may be given specific goals to achieve and challenges with the game mechanics. You might even earn points and keep score.

- **3D content creation**: In VR, create content that can be experienced in VR. **Google Tilt Brush** is one of the first blockbuster experiences, as is **Oculus Medium** and **Google Blocks** and others. Unity is working on **EditorXR** for Unity developers to work on their projects directly in the VR scene.

- **Riding on rails**: In this kind of experience, you're seated and being transported through the environment (or the environment changes around you). For example, you can ride a rollercoaster via this virtual reality experience. However, it may not necessarily be an extreme thrill ride. It can be a simple real estate walk-through or even a slow, easy, and meditative experience.

- **360-degree media**: Think panoramic images taken with **GoPro** on steroids that are projected on the inside of a sphere. You're positioned at the center of the sphere and can look all around. Some purists don't consider this *real* virtual reality, because you're seeing a projection and not a model rendering. However, it can provide an effective sense of presence.

- **Social VR**: When multiple players enter the same VR space and can see and speak with each other's avatars, it becomes a remarkable social experience.

In this book, we will implement a number of projects that demonstrate how to build each of these types of VR experience. For brevity, we'll need to keep it pure and simple, with suggestions for areas for further investigation.

Technical skills that are important to VR

Each chapter of the book introduces new technical skills and concepts that are important if you wish to build your own virtual reality applications. You will learn about the following in this book:

- **World scale**: When building for a VR experience, attention to the 3D space and scale is important. One unit in Unity is usually equal to one meter in the virtual world.

- **First-person controls**: There are various techniques that can be used to control the movement of your avatar (first-person camera), gaze-based selection, tracked hand input controllers, and head movements.
- **User interface controls**: Unlike conventional video (and mobile) games, all user interface components are in world coordinates in VR, not screen coordinates. We'll explore ways to present notices, buttons, selectors, and other **user interface (UI)** controls to the users so that they can interact and make selections.
- **Physics and gravity**: Critical to the sense of presence and immersion in VR is the physics and gravity of the world. We'll use the Unity physics engine to our advantage.
- **Animations**: Moving objects within the scene is called *animation*—duh! It can either be along predefined paths or it may use AI (artificial intelligence) scripting that follows a logical algorithm in response to events in the environment.
- **Multi-user services**: Real-time networking and multi-user games are not easy to implement, but online services make it easy without you having to be a computer engineer.
- **Build, run and optimize**: Different HMDs use different developer kits SDK and assets to build applications that target a specific device. We'll consider techniques that let you use a single interface for multiple devices. Understanding the rendering pipeline and how to optimize performance is a critical skill for VR development.

We will write scripts in the C# language and use features of Unity as and when they are needed to get things done.

However, there are technical areas that we will not cover, such as realistic rendering, shaders, materials, and lighting. We will not go into modeling techniques, terrains, or humanoid animations. We also won't discuss game mechanics, dynamics, and strategies. All of these are very important topics that may be necessary for you to learn (or for someone in your team), in addition to this book, to build complete, successful and immersive VR applications.

Summary

In this chapter, we looked at virtual reality and realized that it can mean a lot of things to different people and can have different applications. There's no single definition, and it's a moving target. We are not alone, as everyone's still trying to figure it out. The fact is that virtual reality is a new medium that will take years, if not decades, to reach its potential.

VR is not just for games; it can be a game changer for many different applications. We identified over a dozen. There are different kinds of VR experiences, which we'll explore in the projects in this book.

VR headsets can be divided into those that require a separate processing unit (such as a desktop PC or a console) that runs with a powerful GPU and the ones that use your mobile technologies for processing.

We're all pioneers living at an exciting time. Because you're reading this book, you're one, too. Whatever happens next is literally up to you. *The best way to predict the future is to invent it.*

So, let's get to it!

In the next chapter, we'll jump right into Unity and create our first 3D scene and learn about world coordinates, scaling, and importing 3D assets. Then, in Chapter 3, *VR Build and Run*, we'll build and run it on a VR headset, and we'll discuss how virtual reality really works.

Content, Objects, and Scale 2

You may remember building a diorama project for school from a shoebox as a child. We're going to make one today, using Unity. Let's assemble our first scene, which is composed of simple geometric objects. Along the way, we'll talk a lot about **world scale**. Then we'll explore various 3D content creation tools that developers and artists use for assets imported into Unity. In this chapter, we will discuss the following topics:

- A short introduction to the Unity 3D game engine
- Creating a simple diorama in Unity
- Making some measuring tools, including a unit cube and a grid projector
- Using **Blender** to create a cube with texture maps and importing it into Unity
- Using Google Tilt Brush to create a 3D sketch and importing it into Unity via Google Poly
- Using the experimental Unity EditorXR tools for editing scenes directly in VR

Getting started with Unity

If you don't have the Unity 3D game engine application installed on your PC yet, do that now! The full-featured **Personal Edition** is free and runs on both Windows and Mac. To get Unity, go to `https://store.unity.com/`, select the version that you want, click on **Download Installer**, and continue following the instructions. This book assumes you have version 2017.2 or later of Unity.

For you beginners out there, we're going to take this first section nice and slow, with more hand-holding than what you'll get later on in the book. Furthermore, even if you already know Unity and have developed your own games, it may be worthwhile to revisit the fundamental concepts, since the rules are sometimes different when designing for virtual reality.

Creating a new Unity project

Let's create a new Unity project named `VR_is_Awesome`, or whatever you'd like.

To create a new Unity project, launch Unity from your operating system and the **Open** dialog box will appear. From this dialog box, select **New**, which opens a **New Project** dialog box, as shown in the following screenshot:

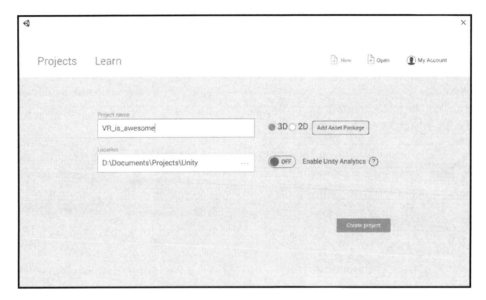

Fill in the name of your project and verify that the folder location is what you want. Ensure that **3D** is selected (on the right). There is no need to add any extra asset packages at this time, as we'll bring them in later if we need them. Click on **Create project**.

 Unity 2018 introduced the Unity Hub tool for managing multiple Unity versions and projects. If you are using Unity Hub, you can choose the "3D" template, or one of the newer VR render pipeline templates for your project.

The Unity editor

Your new project opens in the Unity editor, as shown in the following screenshot (where I arranged the window panels in a custom layout to facilitate this discussion and labeled the visible panels):

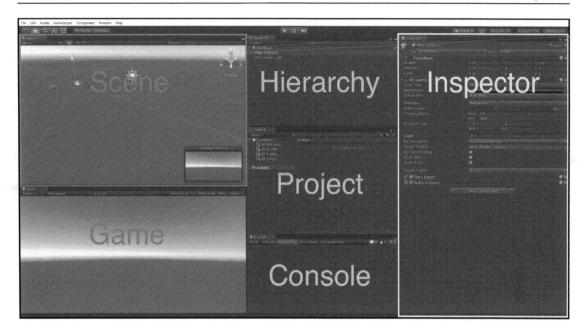

The Unity editor consists of a number of non-overlapping windows, or *panels*, which may be subdivided into *panes*. Here's a brief explanation of each panel that is shown in the preceding layout image (your layout may be different):

- The **Scene** panel on the upper left-hand side (highlighted) is where you can visually compose the 3D space of the current scene, including the placement of objects.
- Below the **Scene** panel is the **Game** view (lower left-hand side), which shows the actual game camera view (presently, it is empty with an ambient sky). When in **Play Mode**, your game runs in this panel.
- In the center, we have arranged the **Hierarchy**, **Project**, and **Console** panels (from the top to the bottom, respectively).
- The **Hierarchy** panel provides a tree view of all the *objects* in the current scene.
- The **Project** panel contains all the *reusable assets* for the project, including the ones imported as well as those that you'll create along the way.
- The **Console** panel shows messages from Unity, including *warnings and errors* from code scripts.
- On the right-hand side is the **Inspector** panel (highlighted), which contains the properties of the currently selected object. (Objects are selected by clicking on them in the **Scene**, **Hierarchy**, or the **Project** panel). The **Inspector** panel has separate panes for each component of the object.

- At the top is the main menu bar (on a Mac, this will be at the top of your screen, not at the top of the Unity window). There's a toolbar area with various controls that we'll use later on, including the **Play** (triangle icon) button that starts **Play** mode.

From the main menu bar's **Window** menu, you can open additional panels as needed. The editor's user interface is configurable. Each panel can be rearranged, resized, and tabbed by grabbing one of the panel tabs and dragging it. Go ahead, try it! On the upper right-hand side is a **Layout** selector that lets you either choose between various default layouts or save your own preferences.

The default world space

A default empty Unity scene consists of the **Main Camera** object and a single **Directional Light** object, as listed in the **Hierarchy** panel and depicted in the **Scene** panel. The **Scene** panel also shows a perspective of an infinite reference ground plane grid, like a piece of graph paper with nothing on it yet. The grid spans across the x (red) and z (blue) axes. The y-axis (green) is up.

An easy way to remember the Gizmo axes colors is by keeping in mind that R-G-B corresponds to *X-Y-Z*.

The **Inspector** panel shows the details of the currently selected item. Select the **Directional Light** with your mouse, either from the **Hierarchy** list or within the scene itself, and look at the **Inspector** panel for each of the properties and components associated with the object, including its transform. An object's transform specifies its position, rotation, and scale in the 3D world space. For example, position (0, 3, 0) is 3 units above (in the *Y* direction) the center of the ground plane (*X* = 0, *Z* = 0). A rotation of (50, 330, 0) means that it's rotated 50 degrees around the x-axis and 330 degrees around the y-axis. As you'll see, you can change an object's transforms numerically here or directly with the mouse in the **Scene** panel.

Similarly, if you click on the **Main Camera**, it may be located at the (0, 1, -10) position with no rotation. That is, it's pointed straight ahead, towards the positive *Z* direction.

When you select the **Main Camera**, as shown in the preceding editor screenshot, a **Camera Preview** inset is added to the **Scene** panel, which shows the view that the camera presently sees. (If the **Game** tab is open, you'll see the same view there too). Presently, the view is empty and the reference grid does not get rendered, but a foggy horizon is discernible, with the grey ground plane below and the blue default ambient **Skybox** above.

Creating a simple diorama

Now, we will add a few objects to the scene to set up the environment, including a unit cube, a flat plane, a red ball, and a photographic backdrop. Here is a photograph of a physical mock-up of the diorama we will build in VR:

Adding a cube

Let's add the first object to the scene: a unit-sized cube.

Within the **Hierarchy** panel, use the **Create** menu and choose **3D Object** | **Cube**. The same selection can also be found in the main menu bar's **GameObject** drop-down menu.

A default white cube is added to the scene, centered on the ground plane at the (0, 0, 0) position, with no rotation, and a scale of one, as you can see in the **Inspector** panel. This is the **Reset** setting, which can be found in the object's **Transform** component of the **Inspector** panel.

The **Reset** values of the **Transform** component are **Position** (0, 0, 0), **Rotation** (0, 0, 0), and **Scale** (1, 1, 1).

If for some reason your cube has other Transform values, set these in the **Inspector** panel or locate the small *gear* icon in the upper right-hand side of the **Inspector** panel's **Transform** component, click on it, and select **Reset**.

This cube has the dimensions of one unit on each side. As we'll see later, one unit in Unity corresponds to one meter in world coordinates. Its local center is the center of the cube.

Adding a plane

Now, let's add a ground plane object into the scene.

In the **Hierarchy** panel, click on the **Create** menu (or main **GameObject** menu) and choose **3D Object** | **Plane**.

A default white plane is added to the scene, centered on the ground plane at **Position** (0, 0, 0). (If necessary, select **Reset** from the **Inspector** panel's **Transform** component's *gear* icon). Rename it to GroundPlane.

Note that at a scale of (1, 1, 1), Unity's plane object actually measures 10 by 10 units in X and Z. In other words, the size of GroundPlane is 10 by 10 units and its transform's Scale is 1.

The cube is centered at **Position** (0, 0, 0), just like the ground plane. However, maybe it doesn't look like it to you. The **Scene** panel may show a **Perspective** projection that renders 3D scenes onto a 2D image. The **Perspective** distortion makes the cube not seem centered on the ground plane, but it is. Count the grid lines on either side of the cube. As you'll see, when it is viewed in VR and you're actually standing in the scene, it won't look distorted at all. This is shown in the following screenshot:

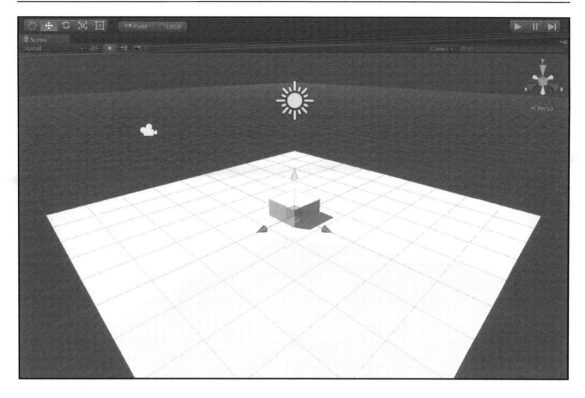

The cube is submerged in the ground plane because its local origin is at its geometric center—it measures 1 by 1 by 1 and its middle point is (0.5, 0.5, 0.5). This might sound obvious, but it is possible for the origin of a model to not be its geometric center (such as one of its corners). The **Transform** component's position is the world space location of the object's local origin. Let's move the cube as follows:

1. Move the cube onto the surface of the ground plane—in the **Inspector** panel, set its **Y** position to 0.5: **Position** (0, 0.5, 0).
2. Let's rotate the cube a bit around the y-axis. Enter 20 into its **Y** rotation: **Rotation** (0, 0.5, 0).

Note the direction in which it rotates. That's 20 degrees clockwise. Using your left hand, give a thumbs-up gesture. See the direction your fingers are pointing? Unity uses a left-handed coordinate system. (There is no standard for the coordinate system *handedness*. Some software uses left-handedness, others use right-handedness).

Unity uses a left-handed coordinate system. And the y-axis is up.

Adding a sphere and some material

Next, let's add a sphere. Select **GameObject** | **3D Object** | **Sphere** from the menu.

Like the cube, the sphere has a radius of 1.0, with its origin at the center. (If necessary, select **Reset** from the **Inspector** panel **Transform** component's *gear* icon). It's hard to see the sphere as it is embedded in the cube. We need to move the sphere's position.

This time, let's use the **Scene** panel's **Gizmos** component to move the object. In the **Scene** view, you can select graphical controls, or Gizmos, to manipulate the objects transforms, as illustrated in the following screenshot from the Unity documentation (http://docs.unity3d.com/Manual/PositioningGameObjects.html):

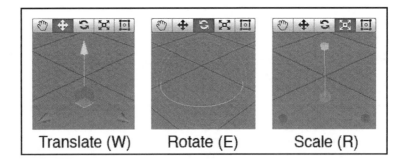

In the **Scene** panel, with the sphere selected, make sure that the **Translate** tool is active (second icon on the top-left icon toolbar) and use the arrows of the *x*, *y*, and *z*-axes to position it. I left mine at **Position** (1.6, 0.75, −1.75).

A **Gizmo** is a graphical control that lets you manipulate the parameters of an object or a view. Gizmos have to grab points or handle that you can click and drag with the mouse.

Before we go much further, let's save our work as follows:

1. From the main menu bar, select **File | Save Scene As...** and name it Diorama.
2. Also, navigate to **File | Save Project** for good measure. Note that in the **Project** panel, the new scene object was saved in the top-level **Assets** folder.

Let's add some color to the scene by making a couple of colored materials and applying them to our objects. Follow these steps:

1. In the **Project** panel, select the top-level **Assets** folder and select **Create | Folder**. Rename the folder to Materials.
2. With the Materials folder selected, select **Create | Material** and rename it to Red Material.
3. In the **Inspector** panel, click the white rectangle to the right of **Albedo**, which opens the **Color** panel. Choose a nice juicy red.
4. Repeat the preceding steps to make a Blue Material too.
5. Select a **Sphere** from the **Hierarchy** (or **Scene**) panel.
6. Drag the Red Material from the **Project** panel into the **Inspector** panel for the sphere. The sphere should now look red.
7. Select **Cube** from the **Scene** (or **Hierarchy**) panel.
8. This time, drag the Blue Material from the Project panel into the scene and drop it onto the cube. It should now look blue.

Save your scene and save the project. Here's what my scene looks like now (yours might be a little different, but that's OK):

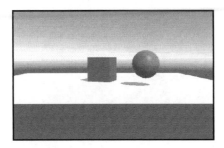

 Note that we're using the folders in the Project panel /Assets/ directory to organize our stuff.

Changing the scene view

You can change the scene view any time in a number of ways, and this varies depending on whether you have a mouse with three buttons, or two-buttons, or Mac with only one button. Read up on it in the Unity manual, which can be found at `http://docs.unity3d.com/Manual/SceneViewNavigation.html`, to find out what works for you.

In general, combinations of left/right mouse clicks with the *Shift + Ctrl + Alt* keys will let you perform the following actions:

- Drag the camera around.
- Orbit the camera around the current pivot point.
- Zoom in and out.
- Press *Alt* and right-click to swing the current eye orbit up, down, left, and right.
- When the **Hand** tool is selected (in the upper-left icon bar), the right mouse button moves the eye. The middle-click of the mouse does a similar thing.

In the upper right-hand side of the **Scene** panel, you have the **Scene View** Gizmo, which depicts the current scene view orientation as shown in the following screenshot. It may indicate, for example, a **Perspective** view, with **x** extending back to the left and **z** extending back to the right:

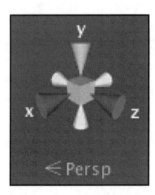

You can change the view to look directly along any of the three axes by clicking on the corresponding colored cone as shown in the following screenshot. Clicking on the small cube in the center changes the **Perspective** view to the **Orthographic** (non-distorted) view:

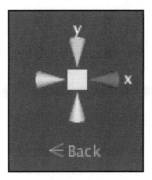

Before moving on, let's first align the scene view with the **Main Camera** direction. You may recall me saying that the default camera orientation, (0, 0, 0), is looking down the positive z-direction (back to front). Follow the following steps:

1. Click on the white z cone on the Scene View Gizmo to adjust the view from the **Back** (back direction), looking forward.
2. Also, use the Hand tool (or the middle mouse button) to slide the view up a tad.

Now, when you select the **Main Camera** component (from the **Hierarchy** panel), you will see that the **Scene** view is roughly similar to the **Camera Preview**, looking in the same direction. (See the screen capture image shown in the following section for what the scene and preview look like with this view direction after we add the photo.)

For a full list of Unity shortcut hotkeys, see `https://docs.unity3d.com/ Manual/UnityHotkeys.html`.

Adding a photo

Now, let's add a photo for the big-screen backdrop of our diorama.

In computer graphics, an image that is mapped onto an object is called a **texture**. While objects are represented in the **x**, **y**, and **z** world coordinates, textures are said to be in the U, V coordinates (such as pixels). We'll see that textures and UV maps can have their own scaling issues. Follow the following steps:

1. Create a plane by navigating to **GameObject** | **3D Object** | **Plane** and rename it `PhotoPlane`.

2. Reset the plane's transform. In the **Inspector** panel, find the *gear* icon on the upper right-hand side of the **Transform** panel. Click on this icon and select **Reset**.

3. Next, rotate it by 90 degrees around the z-axis (set its **Transform** component's **Rotation** value of **z** to -90). That's *minus 90*. So, it's standing up, perpendicular to the ground.

4. Rotate it by 90 degrees around the y-axis so that its front is facing us.

5. Move it to the end of the ground plane at **Position** value of **z** = 5 and above, at **Position** value of **y** = 5 (you may recall that the ground plane is 10 x 10 units).

6. Choose any photo from your computer to paste on this photo plane using Windows Explorer or Mac Finder. (Alternatively, you can use the `GrandCanyon.jpg` image that comes with this book).

7. In the **Project** panel, select the top-level **Assets** folder and navigate to **Create** | **Folder**. Rename the folder to `Textures`.

8. Drag the photo file into the `Assets/Textures` folder. It should automatically import as a texture object. Alternatively, you can right-click on the **Assets** folder, select **Import New Asset...**, and import the picture.

Select the new image **Texture** in the **Project** panel and review its settings in the **Inspector** panel. For Unity's rendering purposes, even if the original photo was rectangular, the texture is square now (for example, 2048 x 2048) and looks squished. When you map it onto a square-shaped face, it will be squished there too. Let's perform the following steps:

1. Drag the photo texture from the **Project** panel onto the photo plane (in the **Scene** panel).

    Oops! In my case, the picture is rotated sideways—yours, too?

2. Select `PhotoPlane` (the photo plane) and set the **Transform** component's **Rotation** value of **X** to 90 degrees.

OK, it's upright, but still squished. Let's fix this. Check the original resolution of your photo and determine its aspect ratio. My `Grand Canyon` image was 2576 x 1932. When you divide its width by its height, you get the 0.75 ratio.

3. In Unity, set the `PhotoPlane` plane **Transform** component's **Scale** value of **Z** to `0.75`.

   Because its scale origin is the center, we also have to move it back down a bit.

4. Set the **Position** value of **y** to `3.75`.

 Why 3.75? The height started at 10. So, we scaled it to 7.5. The scaling of objects is relative to their origin. So now, the half of the height is 3.75. We want to position the center of the backdrop 3.5 unit above the ground plane.

We have the size and position set up, but the photo looks washed out. That's because the ambient lighting in the scene is affecting it. You might want to keep it that way, especially as you build more sophisticated lighting models and materials in your scenes. But for now, we'll un-light it.

With `PhotoPlane` selected, note that the photo's **Texture** component in the **Inspector** panel has its default **Shader** component set as **Standard**. Change it to **Unlit | Texture**.

Here's what mine looks like; yours should be similar:

There! That looks pretty good. Save your scene and project.

 You may notice that Planes are only visible from their front. All surfaces in computer graphics have a front-facing direction (normal vector). The view camera must be towards the front face or else the object will not be rendered. This is a performance optimization. If you require a *plane* with faces on both sides, use a Cube scaled thinly, or two separate Planes facing away from each other.

Notice that if you check your Materials folder now, you'll find that Unity has automatically created a `GrandCanyon.mat` material for you that uses the `GrandCanyon.jpg` texture.

Coloring the ground plane

If you want to change the ground plane color, create a new material (in the **Project** panel), name it `Ground`, and drag it onto the ground plane. Then, change its **Albedo** color. I suggest using the dropper (icon) to pick an earth tone from the image in your photo plane.

Measurement tools

We've created a Unity scene, added a few primitive 3D objects, and created a couple of basic textures, including a photograph. Along the way, we learned about positioning and transforming objects in Unity's 3D world space. The problem is that the actual size of stuff in your scene is not always obvious. You could be zoomed up or you may be using either a **Perspective** or **Orthographic** view, or other features that affect the apparent size. Let's look at ways to deal with the scale.

Keeping a unit cube handy

I suggest keeping a unit cube handy in your **Hierarchy** panel. When it's not needed, just disable it (uncheck the checkbox in the top left-hand side of the **Inspector** panel). It can be used like a measuring stick, or rather, a measuring block when needed. I use one to estimate actual world sizes of objects, distances between objects, heights, and elevations, and so forth. Let's do it now.

Create a unit cube, name it `Unit Cube`, and place it somewhere out of the way for now, such as **Position** (-2, 0.5, -2).

Leave it enabled for the time being.

Using a Grid Projector

I want to tell you about the **Grid Projector**, a handy tool that is used to visualize a scale in any Unity scene. It's one of the **Standard Assets** in the **Effects** package. So, you may need to import it into your project. To import, perform the following steps:

1. Select **Assets** in the main menu bar and then navigate to **Import Package | Effects**.
2. The **Import** dialog box pops up, containing a list of all the things that can get imported. Then select **Import**.

 If you cannot find the `Effects` package to import, you may not have installed `Standard Assets` when you installed Unity. To get them now, you will need to run the `UnityDownloadAssistant` again as described at the beginning of this chapter (and it may already be in your `Downloads` folder).

Now, we'll add a projector to the scene, as follows:

1. Find the Grid Projector prefab located in the **Project** panel by navigating to the `Assets/Standard Assets/Effects/Projectors/Prefabs` folder.
2. Drag a copy of the Grid Projector into your scene. Set the **y** value of the **Position** to 5 so that it's above the ground plane.

The default Grid Projector is facing downward (**Rotation** value of x = 90), which is usually what we want. In the **Scene** view, you can see the Orthographic projection rays. A Unity doc (`http://docs.unity3d.com/Manual/class-Projector.html`) explains a Projector as follows:

A Projector allows you to project a Material onto all objects that intersect its frustum.

This means that the objects intersected by the projection rays will receive the projected material.

In this case, as you'd expect, the projector material (also named `GridProjector`) has a *grid* texture, which simply looks like a crosshair. (See for yourself, in the `Assets/.../Projectors/Textures/Grid` object).

By default, the projector shines the grid pattern as a light on the surface that it illuminates. In our scene, the `GroundPlane` plane is a light color. So, the grid may not show up. Now, follow the following steps:

With Grid Projector selected in the **Hierarchy** panel, locate the `GridProjector` material component in the **Inspector** panel and change its **Shader** from **Projector/Light** to **Projector/Multiply**.

It now paints the white gridlines black. To get a better feel of what's going on, change the scene view to a **Top** view orientation, as follows:

1. Click the green y cone on the **Scene View Gizmo** in the upper right-hand side of the **View** panel.
2. Also, click the little cube at the center of the Gizmo to change from the **Perspective** to the **Orthographic** (flattened) view.

You should now be looking straight down onto the ground plane. With the Grid Projector selected (make sure that the Translate tool is active, which is the second icon in the top-left icon toolbar), you can grab the **Translate Gizmo** attached to the **Projector** and move it from side to side. The grid line will move accordingly. You might leave it at **Position** (-2.5, 5, -0.5) and avoid the projector Gizmo blocking the directional light.

At this point, the built-in view reference grid might be confusing. So, turn it off in the following way:

1. In the **Scene** view panel, click on **Gizmos** (the menu with this name, which has options to control your Gizmos) and uncheck **Show Grid**.

   OK, so what does this get us? We can see that the default grid size measures half the edge of the unit cube. In **Inspector**, the Projector component's **Orthographic** size value is 0.25.

2. Change the Projector's **Orthographic** size value from 0.25 to 0.5.
3. Save the scene and the project.

Now we have a one-unit grid that can be turned on and projected onto the scene any time it is needed.

Let's leave it on for now because it looks kind of cool, as you can see in the following screenshot:

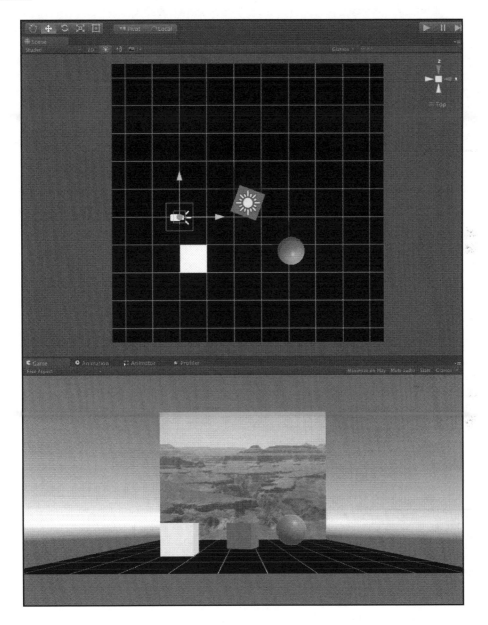

Measuring the Ethan character

How big is an avatar? Unity comes with a third-person character named `Ethan`. Let's add him to our scene. He's one of the `Standard Assets` in the `Characters` package. So, you may need to import that into your project.

To import, perform the following steps:

1. Select **Assets** in the main menu bar and then navigate to **Import Package | Characters**.
2. The **Import** dialog box pops up, containing a list of all the things that can get imported. Click **All** and then **Import**. The `ThirdPersonController` is a prefab (pre-built asset) located in the **Project** panel. This can be found by navigating to the `Assets/Standard Assets/Characters/ThirdPersonCharacter/Prefabs` folder.
3. Drag a copy of `ThirdPersonController` into your scene. The exact **x** and **z** positions don't matter, but set **y** to `0` so that the character named `Ethan` is standing on `GroundPlane`. I left mine at (`2.2, 0, 0.75`).

Let's try it out:

1. Click on the *Play* icon at the top of the Unity window in the center, to start your game. Use the *W*, *A*, *S*, and *D* keys to move him around. *Run, Ethan! Run!*
2. Click on the *Play* icon again to stop the game and return to edit mode.

So, how big is Ethan? According to Google search, the average height of a human male is 5 foot 6 inches, or 1.68 meters (in the USA, the average adult male is more like 5' 10" or 1.77 meters tall). Let's see how tall Ethan is when compared to these:

- Slide the unit cube next to Ethan using the Translate Gizmo

  Alright, he's about 1.6 times its height

- Scale the unit cube's height (**y**) to 1.6 and center its **y** position to 0.8

Look again. As illustrated in the following screenshot, he's not quite 1.6. So, Ethan is a little shorter than the average male (unless you include his pointy hairdo). Swinging my view around, I'm looking Ethan right in the face, and by further adjusting the cube, the eye level is about 1.4 meters. Make a note of this:

1. Restore the unit cube's **Scale** (1,1,1) and **Position** (−2, 0.5, −2)
2. Save the scene and the project

The following screenshot shows the comparison of the unit cube and Ethan:

Using third-party content

So far we have shown you how to use Unity and be productive creating a scene, but with pretty simple content. Inherently, Unity is not a 3D modeling or asset creation tool. Rather (as the name *Unity* suggests), it's a unified platform for pulling together content from a variety of sources to assemble and program a game or experience involving animation, physics, rendering effects, and so on. If you are a 3D artist you may know how to create content in other programs like Blender, 3D Studio Max, or Maya. If not, you can find a plethora of models on the web.

One terrific source is the **Unity Asset Store** (https://www.assetstore.unity3d.com/en/). Many asset packs are free, especially starter ones, with possible paid upgrades if you want more. If you are looking for a few things to get your learning and experimental projects going, here are some of my free favorites:

- Nature Starter Kit 1 and 2 (https://assetstore.unity.com/packages/3d/environments/nature-starter-kit-1-49962)
- Wispy Skybox (https://assetstore.unity.com/packages/2d/textures-materials/sky/wispy-skybox-21737)

- Planet Earth Free (`https://assetstore.unity.com/packages/3d/environments/sci-fi/planet-earth-free-23399`)
- Seamless Texture Pack (`https://assetstore.unity.com/packages/2d/textures-materials/seamless-texture-pack-21934`)
- And of course, Cute Snowman (`https://assetstore.unity.com/packages/3d/props/cute-snowman-12477`)

 In addition to 3D models, the Asset Store contains an amazing amalgamation of development tools, add-ons, audio, and more. The Asset Store, its active community of developers, and its huge amount of content is one of the things that has made Unity so successful.

The Asset Store is available directly within the Unity Editor. To access it, choose **Window | Asset Store** and begin exploring.

To add assets to your project using the Asset Store for example, simply find one and select **Download**, then choose **Import** to add it to your `Project Assets` folder. Asset packs often come with example scenes you can open to exploring how it looks and works. After that, locate its `Prefab` folder and simply drag any prefabs into your own scene. An example is shown here:

Furthermore, there are many sites for sharing 3D models, both free and for a fee. Some are oriented towards higher-end 3D CAD for engineers. Others cater to 3D printing enthusiasts. No matter. Just be sure to look for FBX or OBJ file formats of the model so they can be imported into Unity. Some of the more popular resource sites include:

- 3D CAD Browser: `https://www.3dcadbrowser.com/`
- BlenderSwap: `http://www.blendswap.com/`
- CG Trader: `https://www.cgtrader.com/`
- Free3D: `https://free3d.com/`
- Google Poly: `https://poly.google.com/`
- Microsoft Remix 3D: `https://www.remix3d.com`
- Sketchfab: `https://sketchfab.com`
- TurboSquid: `http://www.turbosquid.com/`

We will use *Google Poly* later in this chapter.

Creating 3D content with Blender

Unity offers some basic geometric shapes, but when it comes to more complex models, you'll need to go beyond Unity. As we discussed, the Unity **Asset Store** and many sites have tons of amazing models. Where do they come from? Will you run into problems while importing them into Unity?

I know that this book is about Unity, but we're going on a short side adventure right now. We're going to use Blender (version 2.7x), a free and open source 3D animation suite (`http://www.blender.org/`), to make a model and then import it into Unity. Grab a coffee and strap yourself in!

The plan is not to build anything very fancy right now. We'll just make a cube and a simple texture map. The purpose of this exercise is to find out how well a one-unit cube in Blender imports with the same scale and orientation into Unity.

Feel free to skip this section or try a similar experiment using your favorite modeling software (`https://en.wikipedia.org/wiki/List_of_3D_modeling_software`). If you prefer not to follow along or run into problems, a copy of the completed files created in this topic is available in the download package for this book.

An introduction to Blender

Open the Blender application. Dismiss the opening splash screen. You will be in the Blender editor, which is similar to what's shown in the following screenshot:

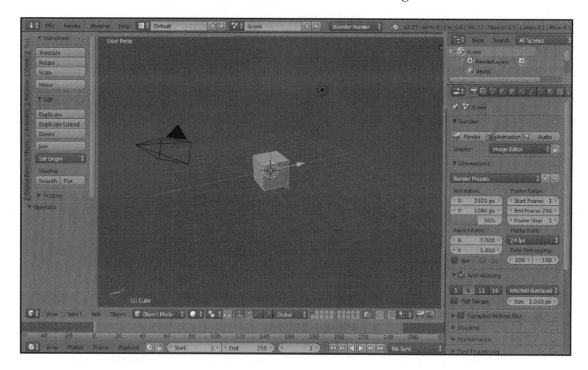

Like Unity, Blender consists of a number of non-overlapping windows, and their layout can be customized to suit your needs. However, the Blender interface can be more daunting, in part because it integrates a number of different editors that can be opened at the same time, in their own panels.

It's helpful to realize that the default view, as shown in the preceding screenshot, contains five different editors!

The most obvious editor is the large **3D View**, which I highlighted with a (red) rectangle. This is where you can view, move, and organize the objects in your Blender scene.

The following are the other editors that are opened:

- The **Info editor**, which can be seen along the top edge of the app, has global menus and information about the application
- The **Timeline editor**, which is present along the bottom edge of the app, is for animations
- The **Outliner editor**, on the upper right-hand side, has a hierarchical view of the objects in your scene
- The **Properties editor**, which can be seen to the right below the Outliner, is a powerful panel that lets you see and modify many properties of the objects in the scene

Each editor can have multiple panes. Let's consider the 3D View editor:

- The large area in the middle is the **3D Viewport**, where you can view, move, and organize the objects in your Blender scene.
- Just below the 3D Viewport is the editor **Header**, which is called so although it's at the bottom in this case. The Header is a row of menus and tools that provide great control over the editor, including view selectors, edit modes, transform manipulators and layer management.
- On the left-hand side is the **Tool Shelf** containing various editing tools that can be applied to the currently selected object, which can be organized into tabbed groups. The **Tool Shelf** can be toggled open or closed by grabbing and sliding its edge or by pressing the key *T*.
- The 3D Viewport also has a **Properties** pane, which may be hidden by default and can be toggled open or closed by pressing the key *N*. It provides the property settings for the currently selected object.

In the upcoming instructions, we will ask you to change the **Interaction Mode** of the 3D View editor, say between the **Edit Mode** and **Texture Paint** mode. This is selected in the Header, as shown in the following screenshot:

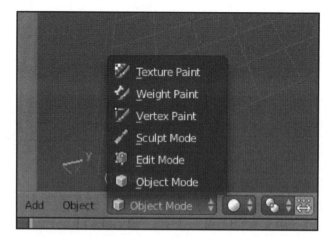

The other editors also have the Header panes. The Info editor (at the top of the app) is only a Header! The outliner and Properties editors (on the right) have their Headers at the top of their panel rather than at the bottom.

Once you recognize this layout, it doesn't look so crowded and confusing.

The Properties editor Header has a wide set of icons, which act like tabs, to select the group of properties presented in the rest of the panel. Hovering your mouse over the icon (like any of the UI widgets here) will show a tooltip with a better hint in regards to what it's for. It's pictured in the following images (in a couple of pages) when we get to use it.

The Blender layout is very flexible. You can even change a panel from one editor to another. At the far left of each Header is the **Editor Type** selector. When you click on it, you can see all the options.

In addition to the plethora of things that you can click on in the Blender interface, you can use just about any command using a keyboard shortcut. If you forget where to find a selection, press the space bar and type in your best guess of the command name that you're looking for. It just might pop up!

The following is a screenshot showing the **Editor Type** selector available in Blender:

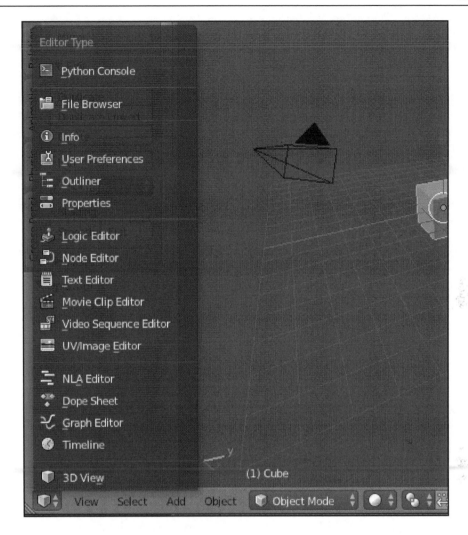

A unit cube

Now, let's build a unit cube in Blender.

The default scene may already have objects, including a cube, camera, and a light source, as shown earlier in the default Blender window. (Your startup settings may be different since that can be configured.)

If your startup scene does *not* contain a unit cube, create one, as follows:

1. Make sure that the scene is empty by deleting whatever is in it (right-click to select, *X* on the keyboard to delete).
2. Set the 3D cursor to the origin (0,0,0) using *Shift + S* (opens the **Snap** options list) | **Cursor To Center**.
3. In the left **Tool Shelf** panel, choose the **Create** tab and under **Mesh** select **Cube** to add a cube.

OK, now we're all on the same page.

Note that in Blender, the reference grid extends in the x and y axes, and z is up (unlike Unity, where the y-axis is up).

Furthermore, note that the default cube in Blender has a size of (2, 2, 2). We want a unit cube sitting on the ground plane at the origin. For this, follow the following steps:

1. Open the Properties pane with the keyboard *N* key
2. Navigate to **Transform** | **Scale** and set **X**, **Y**, **Z** to (0.5, 0.5, 0.5)
3. Navigate to **Transform** | **Location** and set **Z** to 0.5
4. Press the *N* key again to hide the pane
5. You can zoom in using the scroll wheel of the mouse

For our purposes, also ensure that the current renderer is **Blender Render** (in the drop-down selector on the Info editor—at the top of the app window in the center).

UV Texture image

Let's paint the faces of our cube. 3D computer models in Unity are defined by *meshes*—a set of Vector3 points connected with edges, forming triangular-shaped facets. When building a model in Blender, you can unwrap a mesh into a flattened 2D configuration to define the mapping of texture pixels to the corresponding areas on the mesh surface (UV coordinates). The result is called a UV Texture image.

We will create a **UV Texture image** for our cube, as follows:

1. Go into **Edit Mode** using the Interaction Mode selector in the bottom Header bar.
2. Select *all* (press the *A* key on the keyboard twice) to make sure that all the faces are selected.
3. In the left **Tool Shelf** panel, select the **Shading/UVs** tab.
4. Under **UV Mapping** click on **Unwrap**, select **Smart UV Project** from the drop-down list, accept the default values, and click on **OK** (the result, shown in the following screenshot, also shows what the unwrapped cube looks like).
5. Now, go into the **Texture Paint** mode using the Interaction Mode selector in the bottom Header bar again.
6. We need to define a *paint slot* for our material. Click on **Add Paint Slot**, select **Diffuse Color**, name it CubeFaces, and press **OK**.

We can now start painting directly on the cube. Paint the front face first, as follows:

1. Make a smaller brush. In the left **Tool Shelf** panel, in the **Tools** tab, navigate to **Brush** | **Radius** and enter 8 px.
2. It may be easier to work in an orthographic view. From the menu bar at the bottom, navigate to **View** | **View Persp/Ortho**.
3. Then, navigate to **View** | **Front**.
4. You can zoom in or out using the mouse scroll wheel if needed.
5. With your best handwriting, write the word Front using the left-click of the mouse and draw.
6. Now, the back face.
7. From the menu bar at the bottom, navigate to **View** | **Back** and select this face with a right-click.
8. With your best handwriting, write Back.

Repeat the above process for the left, right, top, and bottom faces. If at some point it's not painting, make sure that there's a current face selected. Try right-clicking on the face to reselect it. The result should look something like this (shown side by side both in the **3D View** editor with an orthographic perspective and in the **UV/Image Editor**):

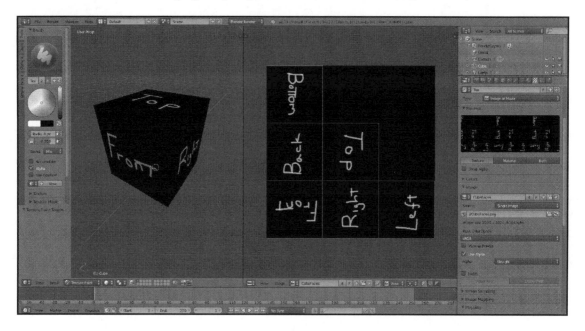

Now, we need to save the texture image and set up its properties, as follows:

1. Change the current **Editor Type** to **UV/Image Editor** using the selector on the far left of the Header at the bottom of the **3D View** editor.

2. Click on the **Browse Image to be linked** selector icon (just towards the left of the **+** icon) and choose CubeFaces from the list.

3. The Image menu item on the menu bar at the bottom now has an asterisk (**Image***) indicating that there's an unsaved image. Click on it, select **Save As Image**, and save it as CubeFaces.png. Use a folder outside the Unity project.

4. On the right-hand side, in the Properties editor panel, find the long row of icons in its Header and select the **Texture** one (third from the last.) It may be hidden if the panel isn't wide enough; you can scroll down with your mouse to show it, as shown in the following screenshot:

5. Within the Texture properties, change **Type** to **Image or Movie**.
6. Then, in the **Image** group of properties, click on the **Browse Image to be Linked** selector icon (as shown in the following screenshot) and choose CubeFaces:

7. You should see the labeled faces texture image in the **Preview** window.

Good! Let's save the Blender model, as follows:

1. Select **File** from the top main menu bar in the Info editor and click on **Save** (or press *Ctrl + S*).
2. Use the same folder as the one where you saved the texture image.
3. Name it UprightCube.blend and click on **Save Blender File**.

We should now have two files in a folder, UprightCube.blend and CubeFaces.png. I use a folder named Models/ in the root of my Unity project.

We recommend you then export the model as FBX format. This is a standard format for Unity. (Unity can import Blend files but may require you always have Blender installed on the same system). Use **File** | **Export** | **FBX** to save the .fbx version.

Wow, that was a lot. Don't worry if you didn't get it all. Blender can be daunting. However, Unity needs models. You can always download someone else's models from the Unity **Asset Store** and other 3D model sharing sites, or you can learn to make your own. Haha! Seriously, it's a good thing to start to learn. Actually, with VR, it's gotten a lot easier as we'll show you later in this chapter.

Importing into Unity

Back in Unity, we now want to import both the files, `UprightCube.fbx` and `CubeFaces.png`, one at a time, as follows:

1. In the **Project** panel, select the top-level **Assets** folder, navigate to **Create | Folder**, and rename the folder to `Models`.
2. An easy way to import files into Unity is to just drag and drop the `.fbx` (or `.blend`) file from the Windows Explorer (or Mac Finder) window into the **Project** panel **Assets/Models** folder and drag and drop the `.png` file into the **Assets/Textures** folder (or you can use **Assets | Import New Asset...** from the main menu bar).
3. Add `UprightCube` to the scene by dragging it from the **Assets/Models** folder where it was just imported into the **Scene** view.
4. Set its position so that it's away from the other objects. I left mine at **Position** (`2.6`, `2.2`, `-3`).
5. Drag the `CubeFaces` texture from the **Assets/Textures** folder into the **Scene** view, hovering over the just added `UprightCube` so that it receives the texture, and drop the texture onto the cube.

The scene should now look something like this:

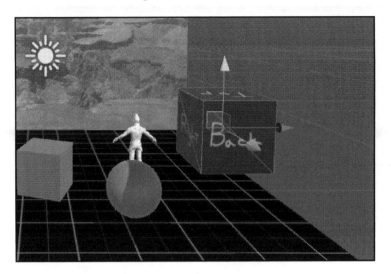

A few observations

The back of the cube is facing us. Is that a mistake? Actually, it makes sense since the current viewpoint is looking forward. So, we should see the back of the cube. If you didn't notice already, the same goes for Ethan. It also seems like the cube has a one-unit dimension.

However, on closer examination, in the cube's **Inspector** panel, you'll see it imported with the scale that we gave it in Blender (0.5, 0.5, 0.5). Also, it has an **X** rotation of -90 (minus 90). Thus, if we reset the transform, that is, the scale to (1,1,1), it'll be 2 units in our world space and tipped over (so, don't reset it).

There's not much that we can do to compensate for the rotational adjustment without going back to Blender. But the scale can be adjusted in the model's Import Settings (in Inspector).

Blender's default up direction is **Z**, while Unity's is **Y**. Importing with a -90 **X** rotation adjusts for that. An imported scale can be adjusted in the object's **Inspector** panel's **Import Settings**.

We have more control when it comes to exporting FBX from Blender. As shown in the screenshot, during Export you can customize the settings, for example, making **Y** the up axis and **Z** the forward one and setting the scale factor for import:

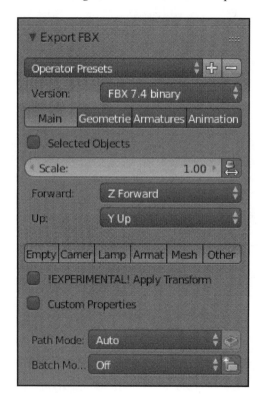

Before ending the preceding process, select `UprightCube` from the **Hierarchy** panel and drag it into the **Project** panel's **Assets** folder. (You may consider making an **Assets/Prefabs** subfolder and placing it into that.) This makes it a reusable prefab, texture image and all.

There are some important lessons in this exercise (other than having learned a little bit about Blender) that apply to any 3D Unity project, including the VR ones. Normally, you will be importing models that are much more complex than a cube. You will likely run into issues related to data conversion, scale, orientation, and UV texture images that might be confusing at best. If this happens, try to break the problem into smaller, more isolated scenarios. Do little tests to gain insight into how applications exchange data and to help you understand which parameter tweaks might be necessary.

Creating 3D content in VR

In addition to traditional 3D modeling software like Blender (and ZBrush, 3D Studio Max, Maya, and so on) there is a new generation of 3D design apps that let you to directly create inside VR. After all, it's pretty awkward trying to use an inherently 2D desktop screen with a 2D mouse to form, sculpt, assemble, and manipulate 3D models. If only it could be more like real-life sculpture and construction. So, why not just do it directly in 3D? In VR!

Like other digital platforms, we can categorize VR apps into ones that present an experience, ones where you interact to engage with the environment, and ones where you actually create content, for yourself or for sharing. An example of the latter and one of the first to be widely successful is Google Tilt Brush (`https://www.tiltbrush.com/`) where you paint in 3D. This is one of my favorite go-to apps when introducing VR to family and friends. Tilt Brush lets you paint in 3D in virtual reality.

Other VR 3D with sculpting and painting tools, to name just a few, include:

- **Google Blocks**: Low poly modeling (`https://vr.google.com/blocks/`)
- **Oculus Medium**: Sculpt, model, paint in VR (`https://www.oculus.com/medium/`)
- **Oculus Quill**: A VR illustration tool (`https://www.facebook.com/QuillApp/`)
- **Kudon**: Surface and volume sculpting (`http://store.steampowered.com/app/479010/Kodon/`)
- **MasterpieceVR**: VR sculpting and painting (`https://www.masterpievr.com/`)
- **Microsoft Paint 3D**: Easy 3D sculpting and painting bundled free with Windows (`https://www.microsoft.com/en-us/store/p/paint-3d/9nblggh5fv99`)

Making stuff and playing with it in VR is creative and fun, but to be useful and productive, you need to be able to share your creations outside of the app. Most VR sculpting tools let you export the models to share on the Internet, export in FBX file format, for example and import them into Unity. There are two different workflows to do this:

- **Export/Import**: In the first workflow you make a model and export it to a compatible format, like FBX. This is akin to traditional 3D software like we did with Blender.
- **Publish/Import**: The second workflow is to upload it to a sharing service and subsequently download and install it into your Unity project.

In this section, we will use a Tilt Brush as an example. Suppose you have Google Tilt Brush and a compatible VR rig. Further, suppose you have a creation you'd like to integrate with your VR app with Unity. Let's walk through each workflow process.

I opened Tilt Brush in VR and created a masterpiece using the Paper ribbon brush. I call it *TiltBox*, consistent with the cube theme we're using in this chapter. I know, it's beautiful.

 The Tilt Brush features and user interface presented here (at the time of writing) are considered by Google to be in beta or experimental and are subject to change by the time you read this.

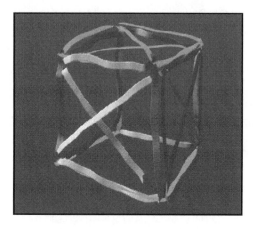

Exporting and importing Tilt Brush models

We are going to export our model as FBX and then import it into Unity. This is an advanced topic so if you're new to Unity you may want to skip this topic for now and look at the *Publishing and importing with Google Poly* section instead.

In Tilt Brush, to export, go to the **Save** panel and choose the **More Options...** | **Labs** | **Export** menu. (Note the location of the **Export** option may change in a future release.)

The default folder where your files are saved in Windows is `Documents/Tilt Brush/Exports/[DrawingName]/`. If you turn your right-hand controller around you'll discover an Info panel on the back, which is a message console that reports the actual pathname of the drawing on your system, as shown here:

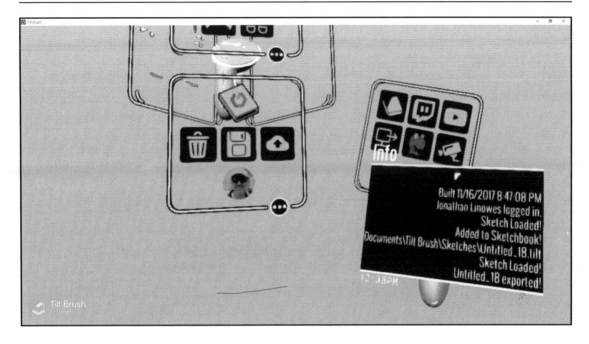

The folder will contain several files, including the `.fbx` of the model and the `.png`'s of the brush textures (not used, as the Tilt Brush Toolkit also provides them).

To import into Unity you need the Tilt Brush Toolkit Unity package. The Google Poly package includes the toolkit (install from the Asset Store as described in the next topic). Or install it directly from GitHub, as follows:

1. Go to `https://github.com/googlevr/tilt-brush-toolkit` and use the download link for `tiltbrush-UnitySDK-vNN.N.N.unitypackage` (via `https://github.com/googlevr/tilt-brush-toolkit/releases`)
2. Import the toolkit in Unity using **Assets** | **Import Package** | **Custom Package...**, then press **Import**

You'll find that the toolkit includes assets for rendering brushes.

There is also a `README` file in the `Exports` folder with details about your Tilt Brush version and export capabilities, including how to use the `CFG` file for tweaking various options for advanced users.

Now we can import the drawing's FBX:

1. Drag the FBX file into your Project Assets (or use **Assets** | **Import New Asset...**).
2. Ignore any materials created by the import; we will use those provided in the toolkit. You can disable this in the model's Import settings **Materials** | **Import Materials** uncheck, and then click **Apply**.
3. You can now drag the model to your scene.
4. Locate the brush material for your sketch in `Assets/TiltBrush/Assets/Brushes/`. In our case, the sketch uses Paper brush strokes, located in the `Basic/Paper/` subfolder.
5. Drag the material onto your sketch strokes as needed.

Your scene now contains your Tilt Brush sketch. For more advanced features including audio reactive features, animations, and VR teleportation, please refer to the Tilt Brush documentation and example scenes.

That was not too difficult although a bit tedious. Other 3D modeling apps require a similar process to export models and import into Unity.

Publishing and importing using Google Poly

Fortunately, Google has made things a whole lot easier with the introduction of Google Poly (`https://poly.google.com/`) as a place to publish, browse, and download free 3D objects created with Google Tilt Brush and Google Blocks (and other apps that create OBJ files with materials).

I don't mean to sound like a Google fanboy, but let's stick to the Tilt Brush theme. Within Tilt Brush, it is very easy to publish your sketches to Google Poly with the click of a button. And importing Poly models into Unity is equally easy with the Poly Toolkit Unity package available on the Asset Store. Let's go through it:

 Poly is not just for Unity developers. Google provides SDK for access from many platforms. See `https://developers.google.com/poly/`.

1. Within Tilt Brush, first, ensure that you are logged into your Google account (**My Profile**).
2. On the Save menu panel, choose the cloud upload option, as shown. This will upload your sketch to Poly.

3. Then complete the publishing step in your browser (out of VR), and press **Publish**.

 Note that Poly Toolkit includes the Tilt Brush Toolkit. If you already imported the Tilt Brush toolkit into your project from the previous section, we suggest you delete it (and the third-party folders) first before importing Poly to avoid conflict.

In Unity:

1. Open the Asset Store panel (**Window | Asset Store**)
2. Search for `Poly Toolkit`, then **Download** and **Import** the Poly Toolkit asset package into your project (`https://assetstore.unity.com/packages/templates/systems/poly-toolkit-104464`)
3. Note that the toolkit installs a new Poly menu in the Unity menu bar. Choose **Poly | Browse Assets...** to open the Poly browser panel, as shown:

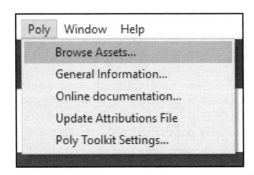

4. This panel can be docked in the Unity editor by dragging its tab
5. Before you can browse your own uploads, you must sign in using the Sign In button in the upper right
6. Then, in the Poly Toolkit panel's **Show** selection, choose **Your Uploads**
7. Locate the model you wish to import. Its page includes a number of import options, including scaling and recentering the model transform
8. Choose **Import Into Project**
9. By default, it will import the model into the `Project Assets/Poly/Assets/` folder as a prefab
10. Drag the model's prefab from the folder into your scene

That's it. You now have a world of 3D models at your fingertips: ones you created and published on Poly and others you've discovered on Poly, the Unity Asset store, or the plethora of other 3D model sites you can explore.

Editing Unity in VR with EditorXR

In this chapter, we have learned about the Unity Editor—a tool for creating 3D scenes and projects on a 2D computer screen. We also learned a bit about Blender—a tool for creating 3D assets on at 2D computer screen. Then we progressed to the new generation of 3D asset creation tools in virtual reality including Tilt Brush and Poly. Now we'll explore creating VR scenes directly in virtual reality too!

Unity EditorXR (EXR) is a new experimental feature of Unity (at time of writing) where you can edit your 3D scenes directly in VR rather than on your 2D monitor. In this section, we may be getting ahead of ourselves in more ways than one. This is both an advanced topic and an experimental one. If you are just getting started with VR, or if you are just getting started with Unity, you may want to skip this topic for now and come back at a later time.

EXR is an advanced topic because it assumes you are comfortable with using the Unity Editor windows, are used to thinking in 3D, and are somewhat experienced in working with 3D assets. It also assumes you have a VR rig with tracking hand controllers, like Oculus Rift and HTC Vive. You will need a powerful PC with a high-end graphics card if you hope to have any chance of a smooth, comfortable experience. And last but not least, some of EXR's user interaction conventions take some learning and getting used to.

Despite that, EXR is a pretty sweet project that you could start using today to be productive. Especially if you're not afraid of software that is experimental. This also means that the UI we describe in this book is certainly subject to change. (For example, at this moment in time the package is being rebranded from EditorVR to EditorXR and EXR). Current links to information include:

- Getting started presentation: `https://docs.google.com/presentation/d/1THBAjLV267NVvZop9VLuUSNx1R2hyp8USgOc8110Nv8/edit#slide=id.g1e97811ad3_2_17`
- Getting started documentation: `https://docs.google.com/document/d/1xWunGC3NJoDRBBz44gxpMUAh3SmedtNK12LqACyy2L0/edit#heading=h.9hlhay6ebu98`
- EditorXR community forum: `https://forum.unity3d.com/forums/editorvr.126/`
- GitHub repository: `https://github.com/Unity-Technologies/EditorVR`

Another reason EXR is an advanced topic this early in this book is that we need to enable VR in our project, a topic we do not get to until the next chapter. But we'll walk you through it now quickly without a lot of explanation.

Setting up EditorXR

To get started using EXR in your projects, download and install the Unity package. By the time you read this, it may already be bundled with the Unity Download Assistant or available in the Asset Store:

1. Download the EditorXR Unity package (`https://github.com/Unity-Technologies/EditorXR/releases`).
2. Import it into your project (**Assets | Import Package | Custom Package...**).
3. If you are using a version earlier than Unity 2018, download and import Text Mesh Pro from the Asset Store (`https://assetstore.unity.com/packages/essentials/beta-projects/textmesh-pro-84126`), a free asset from Unity Technologies.
4. If you are using VIVE, download and import the SteamVR Plugin from the Asset Store (`https://www.assetstore.unity3d.com/en/#!/content/32647`).
5. If you are using Oculus Rift with Touch controllers, download and import the Oculus Utilities for Unity (`https://developer3.oculus.com/downloads/`).
6. Set up your default VR platform in Player Settings (**Edit | Project Settings | Player**). Find the XR Settings section (at bottom of the Inspector panel) and check the Virtual Reality Supported checkbox.
7. Add the Virtual Reality SDKs for Oculus and/or OpenVR.
8. If you are using Oculus Rift with touch controllers, make sure the Oculus one comes first, as shown:

When you're ready to launch into EXR:

1. Select **Windows | EditorXR**
2. If necessary, press Toggle Device View to make the VR view active
3. Then put on your headset

Now you can access much of the same editing features found in Unity Editor but within VR.

Using EditorXR

The user interaction in EXR is similar to Google Tilt Brush. One hand holds your menu palette and the other picks functions from it. Like a boxy glove, you can change menus with the flick of your thumb to rotate menu box faces. That's the starting point but EXR is ever more complex, as it needs to provide the rich set of Unity Editor features in your virtual workspace, compounded with the need to navigate the scene, organize your editor panels, and of course edit your scene game objects. We encourage you to watch a few demo videos before jumping in.

The hand controller selectors implement an innovative, simultaneous combination of laser pointers for picking distant objects and grabbing (via a *selection cone*) for objects within reach, as illustrated here:

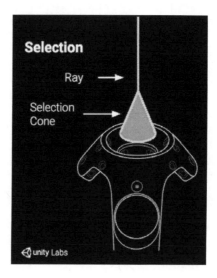

To manipulate objects, EXR has implemented robust 3D versions of the familiar scene editor widgets in the 2D Editor. They're really quite powerful and easy to use.

Without going into much further detail, here are the key features in EXR editor:

- **Selection**: Robust use of the hand controller thumbpad/stick, buttons, trigger, and grib
- **Menus**: Boxed glove menu panels, radial menu, shortcuts, and tools to organize panels in 3D
- **Navigation**: Move throughout your scene as you work, fly and blink modes, rotate in place, scale the world, use a mini-world view
- **Workspaces**: Correspond to windows in the 2D editor, for Project, Hierarchy, Inspector, Console, Profile, and more, can be opened and placed in the VR work area
- Other features include locked objects, snapping,

The following diagram shows how the manipulator Gizmo can be used for direct manipulation of the currently selected object, in conjunction with the radial menu on your controller, to switch tools:

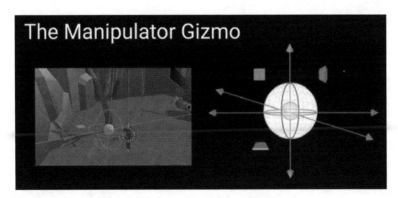

Perhaps one of the more challenging things to learn in EXR is what each of the hand controls does as they switch meaning depending on the current context. The following diagram shows the controller guides for the VIVE:

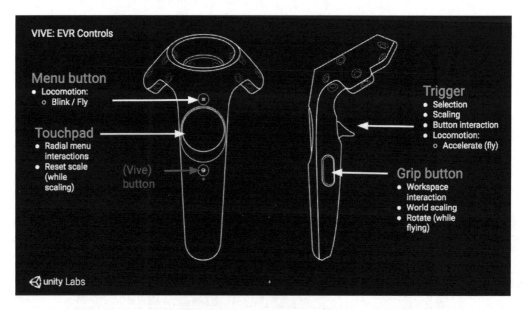

Controller guides for the Oculus touch are shown here:

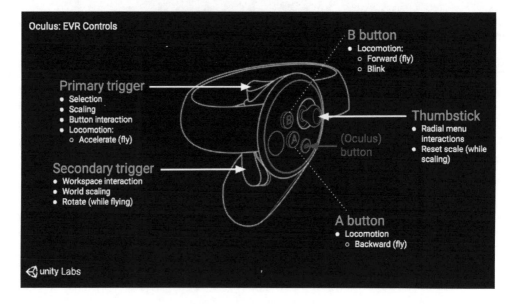

To wrap up this topic, you can even use Google Poly to find objects and insert them into your scene in VR. An example of the third-party extensions of the EditorXR interface and API, the Poly workspace is available in VR. If you have the Poly Toolkit installed (as discussed) and you are using EditorXR, then Poly is one of the available workspaces. Open it to browse and add 3D models from the cloud into your scene, as shown:

 To learn more about EditorXR and Google Poly see this debut blog post by Matt Schoen of Unity Labs: https://blogs.unity3d.com/2017/11/30/ learn-how-googles-poly-works-with-unity-editorxr/. As a side note, Schoen is a friend and the co-author of another book from Packt, *Cardboard VR Projects for Android* (2016): https://www.packtpub.com/ application-development/cardboard-vr-projects-android.

Summary

In this chapter, we built a simple diorama, became more acquainted with the Unity editor, and learned about the importance of world scale in designing your scenes, including several in-game tools to help us work with scaling and positioning.

We then emphasized that Unity is not so much an asset creation tool. Developers typically use tools outside of Unity and then import their models. We introduced you to the free and open source Blender modeling app as well as Google Tilt Brush and showed you how to export assets and then import them into Unity, including cloud services like Google Poly.

One of the really cool things about developing for VR is how quickly things are changing. It's the burgeoning of a new industry, a new media, and new paradigms evolve year to year as VR comes into its own. New devices are being introduced every quarter. Unity is updated every month. New software tools are released every week. There are new things to do and learn every day. Of course, this can also be very frustrating. My advice is to not let this get to you, and rather embrace it.

One key to this is to continuously try new things. That's what we tried to usher you through in this chapter. Come up with an idea, then see if you can get it to work. Try out new software. Learn a new Unity feature. Do things one at a time so you don't become overwhelmed. Of course, that's what this book is about. The journey is a continuous and adventurous one.

In the next chapter, we'll set up your development system and Unity settings to build and run the project to play in your VR headset.

3
VR Build and Run

Yeah well, this is cool and everything, but where's my VR? I WANT MY VR!

Hold on kid, we're getting there.

In this chapter, we are going to set up your system and configure your project to build and run with a virtual reality **head-mounted display (HMD)**. We will be discussing the following topics:

- The levels of VR device integration software
- Enabling virtual reality for your platform
- Using device-specific camera rigs in your project
- Setting up your development machine to build and run VR projects from Unity

This chapter is very nuts and bolts. Although Unity aims to provide a unified platform for *create once, build many*, you are always going to need to do some system setup, project configuration, and include object components for your specific target devices. After the first couple of topics in this chapter, you can jump to the section(s) that most concern you and your target devices. This chapter includes cookbook instructions for the following:

- Building for SteamVR
- Building for Oculus Rift
- Building for Windows immersive MR
- Setting up for Android devices
- Building for GearVR and Oculus Go
- Building for Google VR
- Setting up for iOS devices

Unity VR Support and Toolkits

Generally, as a developer, you spend your time working on your project scene. As we did for the diorama in the previous chapter, you'll add objects, attach materials, write scripts, and so on. When you build and run your project, the scene is rendered on a VR device and responds in real time to head and hand motions. The following diagram summarizes this Unity system VR architecture:

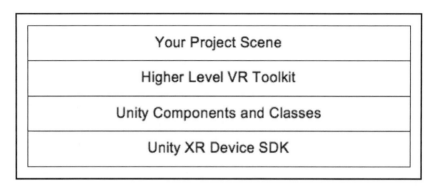

Within your scene, you may include a camera rig and other higher-level toolkit prefabs and components. All device manufacturers provide toolkits that are tuned to their specific devices. At a minimum, this includes the Unity Camera component for rendering the VR scene. It probably also includes a whole suite of prefabs and components, some required and some optional, which really help you create interactive, responsive, and comfortable VR experiences. We will go into detail throughout this chapter on how to set up your scene with these specific devices.

Unity has a growing library of built-in classes and components to support VR—what they call *XR*—and also to include augmented reality. Some are platform specific. But some are device independent. These include stereo rendering, input tracking, and audio spatializers, to name a few. For details, see the Unity Manual pages for `UnityEngine.XR` and `UnityEngine.SpatialTracking` (`https://docs.unity3d.com/ScriptReference/30_search.html?q=xr`).

At the lower level, any Unity project that runs on VR must set up the **XR Player Settings** with **Virtual Reality Supported**, and identify the specific low-level SDK the application should be used to drive the VR device. We will go into detail throughout this chapter on how to set up your project for specific devices.

So, as you can see, Unity is sandwiched between the app-level toolkit components and the device-level SDK. It provides a device-independent glue between device-specific API, tools, and optimizations.

 Strategically, the team at Unity Technologies is dedicated to delivering a unified development platform for 2D, 3D, VR, and AR games and apps. Important new components are under development at Unity (and may already be available by the time you read this book) including the VR Foundation Toolkit and new input system. These are not covered in this book.

Before jumping in, let's understand the possible ways to integrate our Unity project with virtual reality devices. Software for the integration of applications with VR hardware spans a spectrum, from built-in support and device-specific interfaces to device-independent and platform- independent ones. So, let's consider your options.

Unity's built-in VR support

In general, your Unity project must include a camera object that can render stereoscopic views, one for each eye on the VR headset. Since Unity 5.1, support for VR headsets has been built into Unity for various devices across several platforms.

You can simply use a standard camera component, like the one attached to the default `Main Camera` when you create a new scene. As we'll see, you can have **Virtual Reality Supported** enabled in **XR Player Settings** for Unity to render stereoscopic camera views and run your project on a VR headset (HMD). In **Player Settings**, you then choose which specific virtual reality SDK(s) to use when the project is built. The SDK talks to the device runtime drivers and underlying hardware. Unity's support for VR devices is collected in the XR class, and is documented as follows:

- **XR Settings**: Global XR-related settings including a list of supported devices in the build, and eye textures for the loaded device. See `https://docs.unity3d.com/ScriptReference/XR.XRSettings.html`.
- **XR Device**: Query the capabilities of the current device such as the refresh rate and tracking space type. See `https://docs.unity3d.com/ScriptReference/XR.XRDevice.html`.
- **XR Input Tracking**: Access the VR positional tracking data including the position and rotation of individual *nodes*. See `https://docs.unity3d.com/ScriptReference/XR.InputTracking.html`.

Input controller buttons, triggers, touchpads, and thumbsticks can also map generically to Unity's Input system. For example, the OpenVR hand controller mappings can be found here: `https://docs.unity3d.com/Manual/OpenVRControllers.html`.

Device-specific toolkits

While built-in VR support may be sufficient to get started, you are advised to also install the device-specific Unity package provided by the manufacturer. The device-specific interface will provide prefab objects, lots of useful custom scripts, shaders, and other important optimizations that directly take advantage of the features of the underlying runtime and hardware. The toolkits ordinarily include example scenes, prefabs, components, and documentation to guide you. Toolkits include:

- **SteamVR Plugin**: Steam's SteamVR toolkit (`https://assetstore.unity.com/packages/tools/steamvr-plugin-32647`) was originally released for HTC VIVE only. It now has support for several VR devices and runtimes that have positional-tracked left and right-hand controllers. This includes Oculus Rift and Windows Immersive MR. You build your project using the OpenVR SDK and the final executable program will decide at runtime which type of hardware you have attached to your PC and run that app on that device. This way, you don't need different versions of your app for VIVE, Rift, and IMR devices.
- **Oculus Integration Toolkit**: The Oculus Integration plugin for Unity (`https://assetstore.unity.com/packages/tools/integration/oculus-integration-82022`) supports Oculus VR devices including Rift, GearVR, and GO. In addition to the Touch hand controllers, it supports Oculus Avatar, Spatial Audio, and network Rooms SDK.
- **Windows Mixed Reality Toolkit**: The Windows MRTK plugin (`https://github.com/Microsoft/MixedRealityToolkit-Unity`) supports VR and AR devices in the Windows 10 UWP Mixed Reality family, including immersive HMD (like those from Acer, HP, and others) as well as the wearable HoloLens augmented reality headset.
- **Google VR SDK for Unity**: The GVR SDK for Unity plugin (`https://github.com/googlevr/gvr-unity-sdk/releases`) provides support for user input, controllers, and rendering for both Google Daydream and simpler Google Cardboard environments.

When you set up your VR projects in Unity, you will probably install one or more of these toolkits. We walk you through this later in this chapter.

Application toolkits

If you require more device independence plus higher-level interactive features, consider the open source **Virtual Reality ToolKit** (**VRTK**) at `https://assetstore.unity.com/packages/tools/vrtk-virtual-reality-toolkit-vr-toolkit-64131` and **NewtonVR** (`https://github.com/TomorrowTodayLabs/NewtonVR`). These Unity plugins provide a framework for developing VR applications with support for multiple platforms, locomotion, interactions, and UI controls. NewtonVR focuses mostly on *physics interactions*. VRTK is built on top of the Unity built-in VR support plus the device-specific prefabs, so it's not *instead of* but is a wrapper on top of those SDKs.

It is worth mentioning at this point that Unity is working on its own toolkit, the **XR Foundation Toolkit** (**XRFT**) at `https://blogs.unity3d.com/2017/02/28/updates-from-unitys-gdc-2017-keynote/` which will include:

- Cross-platform controller input
- Customizable physics systems
- AR/VR-specific shaders and camera fades
- Object snapping and building systems
- Developer debugging and profiling tools
- All major AR and VR hardware systems

Web and JavaScript-based VR

Important JavaScript APIs are being built directly into major web browsers, including special builds of Firefox, Chrome, Microsoft Edge, and other browsers like those from Oculus and Samsung for GearVR.

WebVR, for example, is like **WebGL** (the 2D and 3D graphics markup API for the web), adding VR rendering and hardware support. While Unity presently has support for WebGL, it does not support building VR apps for WebVR (yet). But we hope to see this happen one day soon.

The promise of Internet-based WebVR is exciting. The internet is the greatest content distribution system in the history of the world. The ability to build and distribute VR content just as easily as web pages will be revolutionary.

As we know, browsers run on just about any platform. So, if you target your game to WebVR or a similar framework, you don't even need to know the user's operating system, let alone which VR hardware they're using! That's the idea anyway. Some of the tools and frameworks to watch include:

- **WebVR** (http://webvr.info/)
- **A-Frame** (https://aframe.io/)
- **Primrose** (https://www.primrosevr.com/)
- **ReactVR** (https://facebook.github.io/react-vr/)

3D worlds

There are a number of third-party 3D world platforms that provide multi-user social experiences in shared virtual spaces. You can chat with other players, move between rooms through *portals*, and even build complex interactions and games without having to be an expert. For examples of 3D virtual worlds, check out the following:

- **VRChat**: http://vrchat.net/
- **AltspaceVR**: http://altvr.com/
- **High Fidelity**: https://highfidelity.com/

While these platforms may have their own tools for building rooms and interactions, in particular, VRChat lets you develop 3D spaces and avatars in Unity. Then you export them using their SDK and load them into VRChat for you and others to share the virtual spaces you created over the internet in a real-time social VR experience.

Enabling Virtual Reality for your platform

The diorama scene we created in the previous chapter was a 3D scene using the Unity default `Main Camera`. As we saw, when you pressed **Play** in the Unity Editor you had the scene running in the **Game** window on your 2D computer monitor. The steps for setting up your project to run in VR include:

- Set the target platform for your project builds
- Enable Virtual Reality in the XR Player Settings in Unity and set the VR SDK

- Import the device toolkit for your target device into your project (optional but recommended) and use the prescribed prefabs instead of the default `Main Camera`
- Install the system tool required to build your target device
- Ensure your device's operating system is enabled for development
- Ensure your device's VR runtime is set up and running

If you are not sure, use the table to determine the target platform, virtual reality SDK, and Unity package to use for your VR device:

Device	Target Platform	VR SDK	Unity Package
HTC VIVE	Standalone	OpenVR	SteamVR Plugin
Oculus Rift	Standalone	OpenVR	SteamVR Plugin
Oculus Rift	Standalone	Oculus	Oculus Integration
Windows IMR	Universal Windows Platform	Windows Mixed Reality	Mixed Reality Toolkit Unity
GearVR/GO	Android	Oculus	Oculus Integration
Daydream	Android	Daydream	Google VR SDK for Unity and Daydream Elements
Cardboard	Android	Cardboard	Google VR SDK for Unity
Cardboard	iOS	Cardboard	Google VR SDK for Unity

Links to the Unity packages for various integration toolkits are listed as follows:

- SteamVR Plugin: `https://assetstore.unity.com/packages/tools/steamvr-plugin-32647`
- Oculus Integration: `https://assetstore.unity.com/packages/tools/integration/oculus-integration-82022`
- MixedRealityToolkit-Unity: `https://github.com/Microsoft/MixedRealityToolkit-Unity`
- Google VR SDK for Unity: `https://github.com/googlevr/gvr-unity-sdk/releases`
- Google Daydream Elements: `https://github.com/googlevr/daydream-elements/releases`

Now, let's configure the project for your specific VR headset.

 As you know, installation and setup details are subject to change. We recommend you double-check with the current Unity manual and your device's Unity interface documentation for the latest instructions and links.

Setting your target platform

New Unity projects normally default to targeting standalone desktop platforms. If this works for you, you do not need to change anything. Let's see:

1. Open the Build Settings window (**File** | **Build Settings...**) and review the Platform list
2. Choose your target platform. For example:
    - If you're building for Oculus Rift or HTC VIVE, for example, choose **PC**, **Mac & Linux Standalone**
    - If you're building for Windows MR, choose **Universal Windows Platform**
    - If you are building for Google Daydream on Android, choose **Android**
    - If you are building for Google Cardboard on iOS, choose **iOS**
3. Then press **Switch Platform**

Setting your XR SDK

When your project is built with **Virtual Reality Supported** enabled in **Player Settings**, it renders stereoscopic camera views and runs on an HMD:

1. Go into Player Settings (**Edit** | **Project Settings** | **Player**).
2. In the Inspector window, find the **XR** Settings at the bottom and check the **Virtual Reality Supported** checkbox.
3. Choose the **Virtual Reality SDK** you will require for your target device. Refer to the previous table.

Depending on the target platform you are using, the Virtual Reality SDKs available in your Unity installation will vary. If your target VR is shown, then you're good to go. You can add others by pressing the (**+**) button in the list, and remove ones pressing the (**-**) button.

For example, the following screenshot shows the Virtual Reality SDKs selected for the Standalone platform. With Virtual Reality Supported enabled, the app will use Oculus SDK if it can. If the app cannot initialize the Oculus SDK at runtime, it will then try the OpenVR SDK.

At this point, by pressing **Play** in the Unity Editor you may be able to preview your scene in VR. Different platforms support Play mode in different ways. Some do not support Editor previews at all.

Installing your device toolkit

Next, install your device-specific Unity package. If the toolkit is available in the Unity Asset Store, use the following steps:

1. Within Unity, open the Asset Store window (**Window** | **Asset Store**)
2. Search for the package you want to install
3. On the asset's page, press **Download**, and then click on **Install** to install the files in your `Project Assets/` folder

If you downloaded the package from the web separately, use the following steps:

1. Within Unity, select **Assets** | **Import Package** | **Custom Package**
2. Navigate to the folder containing the `.unitypackage` file you downloaded
3. Press **Open** and then click on **Install** to install the files into your `Project Assets/` folder

Feel free to explore the package contents files. Try opening and trying out any sample scenes included. And become familiar with any prefab objects (in a `Prefabs/` folder) that might be useful to you later in the book.

Creating the MeMyselfEye player prefab

Most VR toolkits provide a preconfigured player camera rig as a prefab that you can insert into your scene. This rig replaces the default `Main Camera`. For this book, since we do not know which particular devices and platforms you are targeting, we will make our own camera rig. Let's called it `MeMyselfEye` (hey, this is VR!). This will be helpful later on, and it will simplify our conversations in this book, since different VR devices may use different camera assets. *Like an empty vessel for your VR soul...*

We will reuse this `MeMyselfEye` prefab in chapters throughout the book as a convenient generic VR camera asset in our projects.

A **prefab** is a reusable (prefabricated) object retained in your project's Assets folder that can be added one or more times into project scenes. Let's create the object using the following steps:

1. Open Unity and the project from the last chapter. Then, open the diorama scene by navigating to **File** | **Open Scene** (or double-click on the scene object in the **Project** panel, under **Assets**).
2. From the main menu bar, navigate to **GameObject** | **Create Empty**.
3. Rename the object `MeMyselfEye`.
4. Ensure it has a reset transform (in its **Inspector** window's **Transform** pane, choose the **gear icon** in upper-right and select **Reset**).
5. In the **Hierarchy** panel, drag the `Main Camera` object into `MeMyselfEye` so that it's a child object.
6. With the `Main Camera` object selected, reset its transform values (in the **Transform** panel, in the upper-right section, click on the *gear icon* and select **Reset**).
7. Then position yourself near the middle of the scene. Select `MeMyselfEye` again and set its **Position** (0, 0, -1.5).
8. On some VR devices, the player height is determined by the device calibration and sensors, that is, your height in real life, so leave the `Main Camera`'s Y-**Position** at 0.
9. On other VR devices, especially ones with no positional tracking, you need to specify the camera height. Select the `Main Camera` (or more specifically, the game object that has the Camera component on it) and set its **Position** (0, 1.4, 0)

The **Game** view should show that we're inside the scene. If you recall the Ethan experiment that we did earlier, I picked a Y-position of 1.4 so that we'll be at about the eye level with Ethan.

Now, let's save this as a reusable prefabricated object, or *prefab*, in the **Project** panel, under **Assets** so that we can use it again in the other scenes in the other chapters of this book:

1. In **Project** panel, under **Assets**, select the top-level `Assets` folder, right-click and navigate to **Create | Folder**. Rename the folder `Prefabs`.
2. Drag the `MeMyselfEye` prefab into the **Project** panel, under the `Assets/Prefabs` folder to create a prefab.

Your hierarchy with the prefab is shown here:

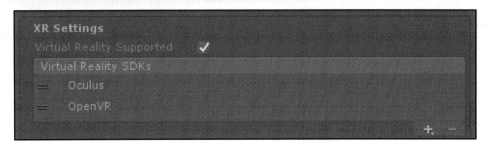

Now we will continue the discussion on how to build your project, on a per-platform basis. Please skip to the topic appropriate for your setup.

If you want to try your projects on multiple platforms, say VIVE (Windows) and Daydream (Android), consider making separate prefabs for each target device, for example, `MeMyselfEye-SteamVR`, `MeMyselfEye-GVR`, and so on and then swap them in and out as needed.

Building for SteamVR

To target your app to use *HTC VIVE* you will use the *OpenVR SDK*. This SDK also supports Oculus Rift with Touch controllers, and **Windows Immersive Mixed Reality (IMR)** devices:

1. Configure your Unity **Build Settings** to target the **Standalone** platform.
2. In **Player Settings**, under **XR Settings**, set Virtual Reality to Enabled
3. Ensure **OpenVR** is at the top of the **Virtual Reality SDKs** list.
4. Download and **Install** the SteamVR Plugin from the Asset Store, as instructed previously.

5. When you install **SteamVR** you may be prompted to accept recommended changes to your project settings. Unless you know better, we recommend you accept them.

Now we will add the SteamVR camera rig to the `MeMyselfEye` object in our scene:

1. Look in your **Project** window; under the `Assets` folder, you should have a folder named `SteamVR`.
2. Within that is a subfolder called `Prefabs`. Drag the prefab named `[CameraRig]` from the `Assets/SteamVR/Prefabs/` folder into your hierarchy. Place it as a child object of `MeMyselfEye`.
3. If necessary, reset its **Transform** to **Position** (0, 0, 0).
4. Disable the `Main Camera` object, also under `MeMyselfEye`; you can disable objects by unchecking the enable checkbox in the top-left of its Inspector window. Alternatively, you can just delete the `Main Camera` object.
5. Save the prefab by selecting `MeMyselfEye` in Hierarchy, then press its **Apply** button in the Inspector.

Note that the SteamVR camera rig Y position should be set to 0 as it will use the real-life height of the player to set the camera height in real time.

To test it out, make sure that the VR device is properly connected and turned on. You should have the SteamVR app opened on the Windows desktop. Click on the game **Play** button at the top-center of the Unity Editor. Put on the headset, and it should be awesome! Within VR, you can look all around—left, right, up, down, and behind you. You can lean over and lean in. Using the hand controller's thumb pad, you can make Ethan walk, run, and jump just like we did earlier.

Now you can build your game as a separate executable app using the following steps. Most likely, you've done this before, at least for non-VR apps. It's pretty much the same:

1. From the main menu bar, navigate to **File | Build Settings...**
2. If the current scene is not already in the **Scenes to Build** list, press **Add Open Scenes.**
3. Click on **Build** and set its name to `Diorama`.
4. I like to keep my builds in a subdirectory named `Build`; create one if you want to.
5. Click on **Save**.

An executable will be created in your Build folder. Run `Diorama` as you would do for any executable application: double-click on it.

 For more information on Unity support for OpenVR, see `https://docs.unity3d.com/Manual/VRDevices-OpenVR.html`.

Building for Oculus Rift

To build for Oculus Rift you can use OpenVR. But if you plan to publish in the Oculus Store and/or use Oculus-specific SDK for other high-value features offered in the Oculus ecosystem, you will need to build to the Oculus SDK, as follows:

1. Configure your Unity **Build Settings** to target the **Standalone** platform
2. In **Player Settings**, under **XR Settings**, set **Virtual Reality Enabled**
3. Ensure **Oculus** is at the top of the **Virtual Reality SDKs** list.
4. Download and **Install** the Oculus Integration package from the Asset Store, as instructed previously

Now we will add the OVR camera rig to the `MeMyselfEye` object in our scene:

1. Look in your Project window, under the *Assets* folder you should have a folder named *OVR*.
2. Within that is a subfolder called `Prefabs`. Drag the prefab named `OVRCameraRig` from the `Assets/OVR/Prefabs/` folder into your Hierarchy. Place it as a child object of `MeMyselfEye`.
3. Set its Y position to 1.6 by setting its **Transform** to **Position** to (0, 1.6, 0).
4. Disable the `Main Camera` object, also under `MeMyselfEye`. You can disable objects by unchecking the enable checkbox in the top-left of its Inspector window. Alternatively, you can just delete the `Main Camera` object.
5. Save the prefab by selecting `MeMyselfEye` in Hierarchy, then press its **Apply** button in the Inspector.

Note that the OVR camera rig should be set to your desired height (1.6 in this case), which will be accommodated at runtime based on the height you configured in the Oculus runtime device configuration.

To test it out, make sure that the VR device is properly connected and turned on. You should have the Oculus runtime app opened on the Windows desktop. Click on the game **Play** button at the top-center of the Unity Editor. Put on the headset, and it should be awesome! Within VR, you can look all around—left, right, up, down, and behind you. You can lean over and lean in. Using the hand controller's thumbstick, you can make Ethan walk, run, and jump just like we did earlier.

Note that the Oculus package installs helpful menu items on the Unity Editor menu bar. We won't go into details here, and they are subject to change. We encourage you to explore the options and shortcuts they provide. See the screenshot:

To include Oculus Dash support, you must use Oculus OVR version 1.19 or later (included with Unity 2017.3 or later). Then:

1. In **Player Settings, XR** panel, unfold the **Oculus SDK** for additional settings
2. Check the **Shared Depth Buffer** checkbox
3. Check the **Dash Support** checkbox:

 For more information on Oculus Dash support in Unity, see `https://developer.oculus.com/documentation/unity/latest/concepts/unity-dash/`.

Now you can build your game as a separate executable app using the following steps. Most likely, you've done this before, at least for non-VR apps. It's pretty much the same:

1. From the main menu bar, navigate to **File | Build Settings...**
2. If the current scene is not already in the **Scenes to Build** list, press **Add Open Scenes**
3. Click on **Build** and set its name to `Diorama`
4. I like to keep my builds in a subdirectory named `Build`; create one if you want to
5. Click on **Save**

An executable will be created in your `Build` folder. Run `Diorama` as you would do for any executable application: double-click on it.

 For more information on Unity support for Oculus, see `https://developer.oculus.com/documentation/unity/latest/concepts/book-unity-gsg/`.

Building for Windows Immersive MR

Microsoft's 3D media **Mixed Reality** strategy is to support the spectrum of devices and applications from virtual reality to augmented reality. This book and our projects are about VR. At the other end is the Microsoft HoloLens wearable AR device. The MixedRealityToolkit-Unity package that we will use includes support for both immersive MR headsets and HoloLens.

To allow your app to use a **Windows immersive Mixed Reality (IMR)** headset, you will use the Window Mixed Reality SDK, as follows:

1. Configure your Unity **Build Settings** to target the **Universal Windows Platform** platform.
2. In **Player Settings**, under **XR Settings**, set **Virtual Reality Enabled**
3. Ensure **Windows Mixed Reality** is at the top of the **Virtual Reality SDKs** list.
4. Download and install the **Mixed Reality Toolkit Unity**, as instructed previously.
5. We also recommend you install its sister examples unity package from the same location.

Now we will add the `MixedRealityCamera` rig to the `MeMyselfEye` object in our scene:

1. Look in your Project window; under the `Assets` folder, you should have a folder named `HoloToolkit` (or `MixedRealityToolkit`).
2. Within that is a subfolder called `Prefabs`. Drag the prefab named `MixedRealityCameraParent` from the `Assets/HoloToolkit/Prefabs/` folder into your Hierarchy. Place it as a child object of `MeMyselfEye`.
3. If necessary, reset its **Transform** to **Position** (0, 0, 0).
4. Disable the `Main Camera` object, also under `MeMyselfEye`. You can disable objects by unchecking the enable checkbox in the top-left of its Inspector window. Alternatively, you can just delete the `Main Camera` object.
5. Save the prefab by selecting `MeMyselfEye` in Hierarchy, then press its **Apply** button in the Inspector.

Note that the `MixedRealityCameraParent` rig y position should be set to 0 as it will use the real-life height of the player to set the camera height in real time.

To test it out, make sure that the VR device is properly connected and turned on. You should have the MR Portal app opened in the Windows desktop. Click on the game **Play** button at the top-center of the Unity Editor. Put on the headset, and it should be awesome! Within VR, you can look all around—left, right, up, down, and behind you. You can lean over and lean in. Using the hand controller's thumb pad, you can make Ethan walk, run, and jump just like we did earlier.

Setting up Windows 10 Developer mode

For Windows MR, you must be developing on Windows 10, with Developer mode enabled. To set Developer mode:

1. Go to **Action Center** | **All Settings** | **Update & Security** | **For Developers**.
2. Select **Developer mode**, as shown:

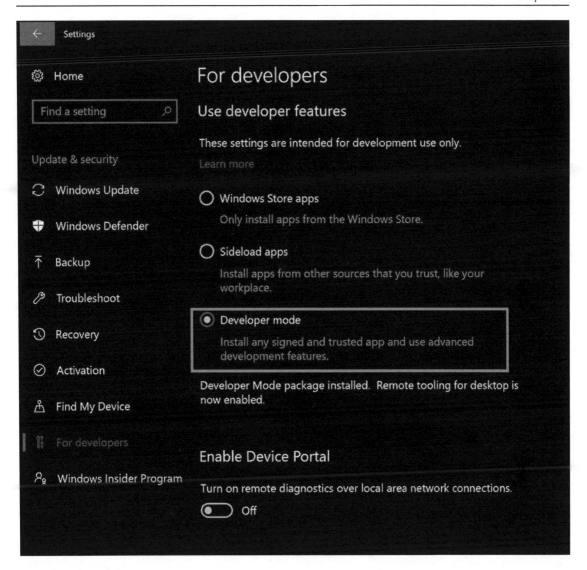

Installing UWP support in Visual Studio

When you install Unity, you have the option to install *Microsoft Visual Studio Tools for Unity* as the default script editor. It's a great editor and debugging environment. However, this edition installed with Unity is not a full version of Visual Studio. To target your build as a separate UWP app, you will need to use a full version of Visual Studio.

Visual Studio is a powerful **integrated developer environment** (IDE) for all kinds of projects. When we build for UWP from Unity we will actually build a Visual Studio-ready project folder that you can then open in VS to complete the compile, build and deploy process, to run the app on your device.

Visual Studio comes in three editions, *Community*, *Professional*, and *Enterprise*; any of these are sufficient for us. The Community version is *free* and can be downloaded from here: https://www.visualstudio.com/vs/.

Once the installer is downloaded, open it to choose which components to install. Under the **Workloads** tab we have selected:

- **Universal Windows Platform development**
- **Game development with Unity**

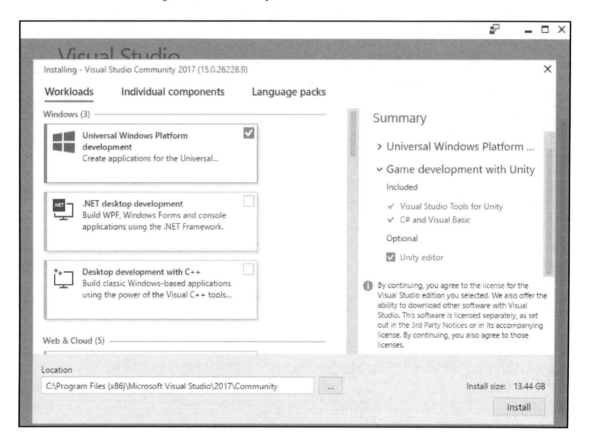

Also, select the **Game development with Unity** options, as follows:

We can now go into Unity. First, we should make sure Unity knows we're using Visual Studio:

1. Go to **Edit | Preferences**
2. In the **External Tools** tab, make sure **Visual Studio** is selected as your **External Script Editor**, like so:

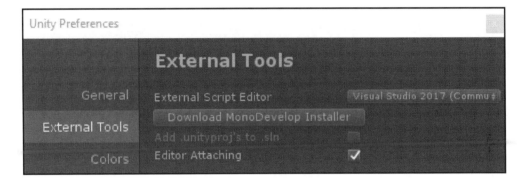

UWP build

Now, you can build your game as a separate executable app using the following steps:

1. From the main menu bar, navigate to **File | Build Settings...**
2. If the current scene is not already in the **Scenes to Build** list, press **Add Open Scenes**

3. On the right side of the dialog are options:
   - **Target Device: PC**
   - **Build Type: D3D**
   - **SDK: Latest Installed** (for example, 10.0.16299.0)
4. Click on **Build** and set its name
5. I like to keep my builds in a subdirectory named Build; create one if you want to
6. Click on **Save**

Note that the Mixed Reality ToolKit provides shortcuts to these and other settings and services, as shown:

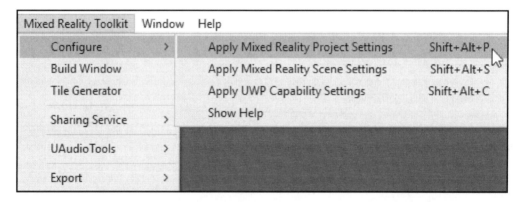

Now open the project in Visual Studio:

1. An easy way is to navigate to the Build folder in File Explorer and look for the `.sln` file for the project (SLN is the Microsoft VS *solution* file). Double-click it to open the project in Visual Studio.
2. Choose the solution configuration: **Debug, Master** or **Release.**
3. Set the target to **x64.**
4. Press **Play Local Machine** to build the solution.

For more information on Unity support for Windows Mixed Reality, see `https://github.com/Microsoft/MixedRealityToolkit-Unity`, including the link to the Getting Started page.

Setting up for Android devices

To develop VR apps that will run on Google Daydream, Cardboard, GearVR, Oculus GO, or other Android devices, we will need to set up a development machine for Android development.

This section will help you set up your Windows PC or Mac. The requirements are not specific to virtual reality; these are the same steps required by anyone building any Android app from Unity. The process is also well documented elsewhere, including the Unity documentation at `https://docs.unity3d.com/Manual/android-sdksetup.html`.

The steps include:

- Install Java Development Kit
- Install Android SDK
- Install USB device drivers and debugging
- Configure the Unity External Tools
- Configure the Unity Player Settings for Android

OK, let's get going.

Installing the Java Development Kit (JDK)

You may already have Java installed on your machine. You can check by opening a terminal window and running the command `java-version`. If you do not have Java or need to upgrade, follow the steps:

1. Browse on over to the Java SE Downloads web page at `http://www.oracle.com/technetwork/java/javase/downloads/index.html` and get it. Look for the **JDK** button icon, which takes you to the downloads page.
2. Choose the package for your system. For example, for Windows choose **Windows x64**. After the file downloads, open it and follow the installation instructions.
3. Make a note of the installation directory for later reference.
4. Once installed, open a fresh terminal window and run `java -version` once more to verify.

Whether you just installed the JDK or it was already there, please make a note of its location on your disk. You will need to tell Unity this information in a later step.

On Windows, the path is probably something like Windows: `C:\Program Files\Java\jdk1.8.0_111\bin`.

If you can't find it, open Windows Explorer, navigate to the `\Program Files` folder, look for **Java**, and drill down until you see its **bin** directory, as the following screenshot shows:

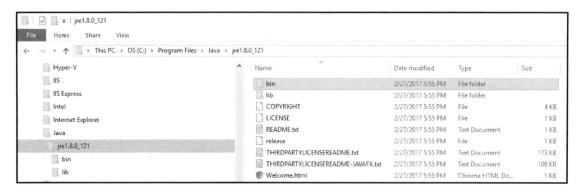

On OS X, the path is probably something like:
`/Library/Java/JavaVirtualMachines/jdk1.8.0_121.jdk/Contents/Home`.

If you can't find it, from a terminal window, run the following command:
`/usr/libexec/java_home`.

Installing Android SDK

You also need to install the Android SDK. Specifically, you need the **Android SDK Manager**. This is available by itself as a command-line tool or part of the full Android Studio IDE. If you can afford the disk space I recommend just installing Android Studio, as it provides a nice graphical interface for SDK Manager.

To install Android Studio IDE, go to `https://developer.android.com/studio/install.html` and click Download Android Studio. When the download is done, open it and follow the installation instructions.

You will be prompted for the locations of the Android Studio IDE and the SDK. You can accept the default locations or change them. Please make a note of the SDK path location; you will need to tell Unity this information in a later step:

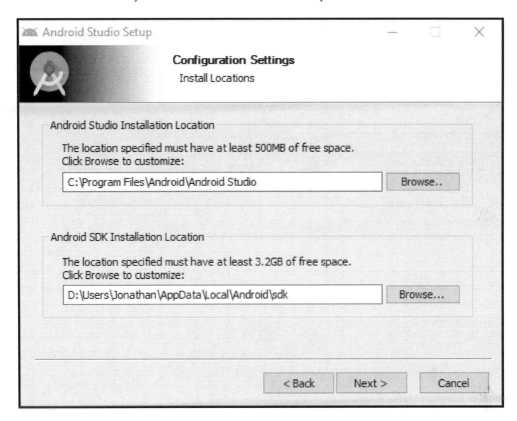

Personally, I have more room on my `D:` drive so I installed the app into `D:\Programs\Android\Android Studio`. And I like to keep the SDK near the Android Studio program files, as it's easier to find again that way, so I change the Android SDK Installation Location to `D:\Programs\Android\sdk`.

Via Command Line Tools

Unity really only needs the command-line tools to build projects for Android. If you prefer, you can install just that package and save disk space. Scroll to the section named **Get just the command line tools** at the bottom of the downloads page. Select the package for your platform:

Get just the command line tools

If you do not need Android Studio, you can download the basic Android command line tools below. You can use the included sdkmanager to download other SDK packages.

These tools are included in Android Studio.

Platform	SDK tools package	Size	SHA-1 checksum
Windows	tools_r25.2.3-windows.zip	292 MB (306,745,639 bytes)	b965decb234ed793eb9574bad8791c50ca574173
Mac	tools_r25.2.3-macosx.zip	191 MB (200,496,727 bytes)	0e88c0bdb8f8ee85cce248580173e033a1bbc9cb
Linux	tools_r25.2.3-linux.zip	264 MB (277,861,433 bytes)	aafe7f28ac51549784efc2f3bdfc620be8a08213

See the SDK tools release notes.

This is a ZIP file; uncompress it to a folder and please remember its location. As mentioned, on Windows I like to use `D:\Programs\Android\sdk`. This will contain `tools` subfolder.

The ZIP is only the tools, not the actual SDK. Use the `sdkmanager` to download the packages you'll need. See `https://developer.android.com/studio/command-line/sdkmanager.html` for details.

To list the installed and available packages, run `sdkmanager --list`. You can install multiple packages by listing them in quotes, delimited with a semicolon as follows:

```
sdkmanager "platforms;android-25"
```

As of writing, the minimum Android API levels are as follows (check the current documentation for changes):

Cardboard: API Level 19 (Android 4.4 *KitKat*)
GearVR: API Level 21 (Android 5.0 *Lollipop*)
Daydream: API Level 24 (Android 7.0 *Nougat*)

About your Android SDK root path location

If you already had Android installed, or if you forget where the SDK is installed, you can find the root path by opening the SDK Manager GUI. While Android Studio is open, navigate to the main menu and **Tools** | **Android** | **SDK Manager**. You can find the path near the top:

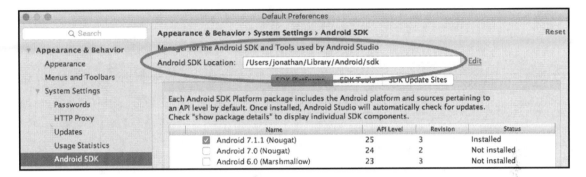

On Windows, the path is probably something like:

- Windows: `C:\Program Files\Android\sdk`, or `C:/Users/Yourname/AppData/Local/Android/Sdk`

On OS X, the path is probably something like:

- OS X: `/Users/Yourname/Library/Android/sdk`

Installing USB device debugging and connection

The next step is to enable USB debugging on your Android device. This is part of the **Developer Options** in your Android **Settings**. But Developer Options may not be visible and has to be enabled:

1. Find the **Build number** property in **Settings** | **About** on the device. Depending on your device you may even need to drill down another level or two (such as **Settings** | **About** | **Software Information** | **More** | **Build number**).
2. Now for the magic incantation. Tap on the build number seven times. It'll count down until the **Developer Options** are enabled, and will now appear as another choice in the Settings.
3. Go to **Settings** | **Developer** options, find **USB debugging**, and enable it.
4. Now connect the device to your development machine via USB cable.

The Android device may automatically be recognized. If you are prompted to update the drivers, you can do this through the Windows Device Manager.

On Windows, if the device is not recognized, you may need to download the Google USB Driver. You can do this through the SDK Manager, under the SDK Tools tab. For more information see `https://developer.android.com/studio/run/win-usb.html`. The following screenshot, for example, shows the SDK Manager's SDK Tools tab with the Google USB Driver selected:

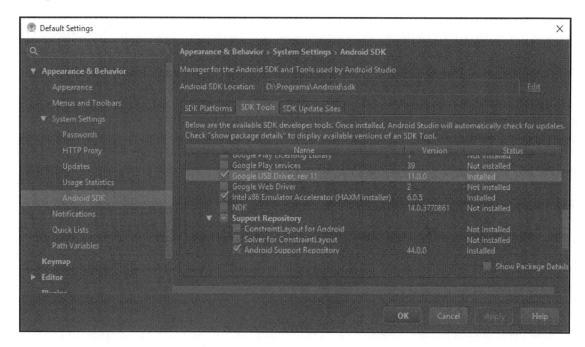

Great job so far!

Configuring the Unity External Tools

Armed with all the stuff we need and the paths to the tools we installed, we can now go back into Unity. We need to tell Unity where to find all the Java and Android stuff. Note that if you skip this step, then Unity will prompt you for the folders when building the app:

1. On Windows, navigate to the main menu and to **Edit | Preferences**, then select the **External Tools** tab on the left. On OS X it's in **Unity | Preferences**.
2. In the **Android SDK** text slot, paste the path of your Android SDK.

3. In the **Java JDK** text slot, paste the path of your Java JDK.

The Unity Preferences with my SDK and JDK are shown here:

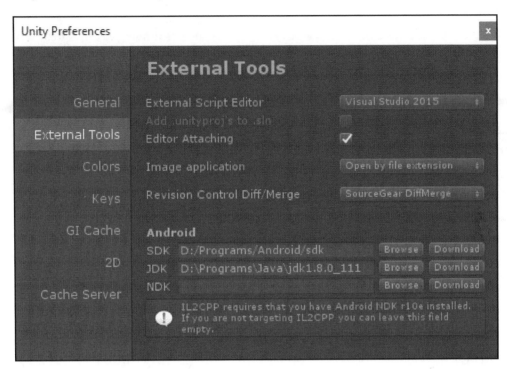

Configuring Unity Player Settings for Android

We now will configure your Unity project to build for Android. First, ensure **Android** is your target platform in **Build Settings**. Unity provides a great deal of support for Android, including configuration and optimization for runtime features and the capabilities of mobile devices. These options can be found in **Player Settings**. We only need to set a couple of them now. The minimum required to build our demo project are Bundle Identifier and Minimum API Level:

1. In Unity, navigate to **File** | **Build Settings** and examine the **Platform** pane.
2. If Android is not presently selected, select it now and press **Switch Platform.**
3. If you have the **Build Settings** window open, press the **Player Settings...** button. Or, you can get there from the main menu and **Edit** | **Project Settings** | **Player**.

4. Look across at the **Inspector** panel, which now contains the Player Settings.
5. Find the **Other Settings** group of parameters, and click the header bar (if it's not already opened) to find the **Identification** variables
6. Set the **Bundle Identifier** to a unique name for your product that resembles a traditional Java package name. An ID is required for all Android apps. Typically it is in the format `com.CompanyName.ProductName`. It must be unique on the target device, and eventually, unique in the Google Play store. You can choose whatever name you want.
7. Set a **Minimum API Level** for your target platform (as listed earlier).

Again, there are many other options in the Player Settings but we can use their defaults for now.

Building for GearVR and Oculus Go

To build for Samsung GearVR and Oculus Go mobile devices, you will use the Oculus SDK. These are both Android-based devices so you must set up your development machine for Android development as described previously (Oculus Go is binary and compatible with GearVR). Then complete the following steps in Unity:

1. Configure your Unity **Build Settings** to target the **Android** platform.
2. In `Player Settings`, under **XR Settings**, set **Virtual Reality Enabled**
3. Ensure **Oculus** is at the top of the **Virtual Reality SDKs** list.
4. Download and **Install** the Oculus Integration package from the Asset Store, as instructed previously.

Now we will add the OVR camera rig to the MeMyselfEye object in our scene. These steps are like the Standalone Oculus Rift setup described previously. In this case, you can use the same MeMyselfEye prefab for both Rift and GearVR.

1. Look in your Project window; under the *Assets* folder, you should have a folder named OVR.
2. Within that is a subfolder called `Prefabs`. Drag the prefab named `OVRCameraRig` from the `Assets/OVR/Prefabs/` folder into your Hierarchy. Place it as a child object of `MeMyselfEye`.
3. Set its height to 1.6 by setting its **Transform** to **Position** to (0, 1.6, 0).

4. Disable the `Main Camera` object also under `MeMyselfEye`. You can disable objects by unchecking the enable-checkbox in the top-left of its Inspector window. Alternatively, you can just delete the `Main Camera` object.

5. Save the prefab by selecting `MeMyselfEye` in Hierarchy, then press its **Apply** button in the Inspector.

Now, you can build your game as a separate executable app using the following steps:

1. From the main menu bar, navigate to **File | Build Settings...**
2. If the current scene is not already in the **Scenes to Build** list, press **Add Open Scenes**
3. Click on **Build and Run** and set its name to `Diorama`
4. I like to keep my builds in a subdirectory named Build; create one if you want to.
5. Click on **Save**

An Android APK file will be created in your Build folder and uploaded to your attached Android device.

 For more information on Unity support for Oculus SDK, see `https://docs.unity3d.com/Manual/VRDevices-Oculus.html`.

Building for Google VR

The Google VR SDK supports both Daydream and Cardboard. **Daydream** is the higher-end version limited to faster, more capable Daydream-ready Android phones. **Cardboard** is lower end and supported on many more mobile devices including Apple iOS iPhones. You can build projects in Unity that target both.

Google Daydream

To build for *Google Daydream* on mobile Android devices, you will use the Daydream SDK. You must set up your development machine for Android development as described above. Then complete the following steps:

1. Configure your Unity **Build Settings** to target the **Android** platform
2. In **Player Settings**, under **XR Settings**, set **Virtual Reality Enabled**

3. Ensure **Daydream** is at the top of the **Virtual Reality SDKs** list

4. Download and **Install** the Google VR SDK package, as instructed previously

We will now build the `MeMyselfEye` camera rig for our scene. At the present time, the best example we have is the **GVRDemo** example scene provided with the Google VR SDK (can be found in the `Assets/GoogleVR/Demos/Scenes/` folder):

1. In your scene Hierarchy, create an empty game object under the `MeMyselfEye` (select the `MeMyselfEye` object, right-click, select **Create Empty**). Name it `MyGvrRig`.

2. Set its height to 1.6 by setting its **Transform** to **Position** to (0, 1.6, 0).

3. From the Project folders, locate the provided prefabs (`Assets/GoogleVR/Prefabs`).

4. Drag a copy of each of the following prefabs from the Project folder to Hierarchy as a child of `MyGvrRig`:
   - Headset/GvrHeadset
   - Controllers/GvrControllerMain
   - EventSystem/GvrEventSystem
   - GvrEditorEmulator
   - GvrInstantPreviewMain

5. Leave the `Main Camera` object under `MeMyselfEye` and enable it. The GoogleVR uses the existing `Main Camera` object.

6. Save the prefab by selecting `MeMyselfEye` in Hierarchy, then press its **Apply** button in the Inspector.

The `GvrHeadset` is a VR camera properties manager. The `GvrControllerMain` provides support for the Daydream 3DOF hand controller. We will use `GvrEventSystem` in later chapters; it provides a drop-in replacement for Unity's Event System object. The `GvrEditorEmulator` is not actually part of your app but enables previewing your scene in the Unity Editor when you press Play. Likewise, adding `GvrInstantPreviewMain` lets you preview your app on your phone when you press Play in the editor.

These are the prefabs that we know we're going to want to use. Certainly, go ahead and explore the other prefabs provided in the SDK. See `https://developers.google.com/vr/unity/reference/`.

We also recommend you take a look at Google Daydream Elements which provides additional demos and scripts "for developing high-quality VR experiences." We introduce this in the next chapter. See `https://developers.google.com/vr/elements/overview`.

When you're ready, you can build your game as a separate executable app using the following steps:

1. From the main menu bar, navigate to **File | Build Settings...**.
2. If the current scene is not already in the **Scenes to Build** list, press **Add Open Scenes**.
3. Click on **Build and Run** and set its name to `Diorama`.
4. I like to keep my builds in a subdirectory named Build; create one if you want to.
5. Click on **Save**.

An Android APK file will be created in your Build folder and uploaded to your attached Android phone.

Google Cardboard

Building for Google Cardboard is similar but simpler than Daydream. Also, Cardboard apps can run on iPhones. You must set up your development machine for Android development as described. Or if you're developing for iOS, see the next section for details. Then set up your project as follows:

1. Configure your Unity Build Settings to target **Android** or **iOS** platform.
2. In Player Settings, under **XR Settings**, set **Virtual Reality Enabled**, and
3. Ensure Cardboard is in the **Virtual Reality SDKs** list.
4. Download and **Install** the Google VR SDK package, as instructed previously.

We will now build the `MeMyselfEye` camera rig for our scene.

1. In your scene Hierarchy, create an empty game object under the `MeMyselfEye` (select the `MeMyselfEye` object, right-click, select **Create Empty**). Name it `MyGvrRig`.
2. Set its height to 1.6 by setting its **Transform** to **Position** to (0, 1.6, 0).
3. From the Project folders, locate the provided prefabs (`Assets/GoogleVR/Prefabs`).

4. Drag a copy of each of the following prefabs from the Project folder to Hierarchy as a child of MyGvrRig:
   - Headset/GvrHeadset
   - GvrEditorEmulator
5. Leave the `Main Camera` object under `MeMyselfEye` and enable it. The GoogleVR uses the existing `Main Camera` object.
6. Save the prefab by selecting `MeMyselfEye` in Hierarchy, then press its **Apply** button in the Inspector

When you're ready, you can build your game as a separate executable app using the following steps:

1. From the main menu bar, navigate to **File** | **Build Settings....**
2. If the current scene is not already in the **Scenes to Build** list, press **Add Open Scenes**.
3. Click on **Build and Run** and set its name to `Diorama`.
4. I like to keep my builds in a subdirectory named Build; create one if you want to.
5. Click on **Save**.

An Android APK file will be created in your Build folder and uploaded to your attached Android phone.

Google VR Play Mode

When your project is configured for Google VR (Daydream or Cardboard), and you press Play in Unity can you preview the scene and use keyboard keys to emulate device motion:

- Use *Alt* + mouse-move to pan and tilt forward or backwards.
- Use *Ctrl* + mouse-move to tilt your head from side to side.
- Use *Shift* + mouse control the Daydream hand controller (Daydream only).
- Click the mouse to select.

For more details, see `https://developers.google.com/vr/unity/get-started`.

With Daydream, you also have the option to use Instant Preview which allows you to test your VR app instantly on your device. Follow the instructions in the Google VR docs (`https://developers.google.com/vr/tools/instant-preview`) to set up your project and device to take advantage of this feature.

For more information on Unity support for Google VR SDK for Daydream, see `https://docs.unity3d.com/Manual/VRDevices-GoogleVR.html`.

Setting up for iOS devices

This section will help set up your Mac for iOS development from Unity for iPhones. The requirements are not specific to virtual reality; these are the same steps required by anyone building any iOS app from Unity. The process is also well documented elsewhere, including the Unity documentation at `https://docs.unity3d.com/Manual/iphone-GettingStarted.html`.

A requirement of Apple's closed ecosystem is you must use a Mac as your development machine to develop for iOS. That's just the way it is. The upside is the setup process is very straightforward.

At the time of writing, the only VR apps that will run on iOS are Google Cardboard.

The steps include:

- Have an Apple ID
- Install Xcode
- Configure the Unity Player Settings for iOS
- Build And Run

OK, let's take a bite of this apple.

Have an Apple ID

To develop for iOS you need a Mac computer to develop on, and an Apple ID to log into the App Store. This will permit you to build iOS apps that run on your personal device.

It is also recommended that you have an Apple Developer account. It costs $99 USD per year but is your admission ticket to the tools and services including setup provisioning profiles needed to share and test your app on other devices. You can find out more about the Apple Developer Program here: `https://developer.apple.com/programs/`.

Install Xcode

Xcode is the all-in-one toolkit for developing for any Apple devices. It is free to download from the Mac App Store here: `https://itunes.apple.com/gb/app/xcode/id497799835?mt=12`. Beware: it is quite big (over 4.5 GB as of writing). Download it, open the downloaded `dmg` file, and follow the installation instructions.

Configuring the Unity Player Settings for iOS

We now will configure your Unity project to build for iOS. First, ensure *iOS* is your target platform in Build Settings. Unity provides a great deal of support for iOS, including configuration and optimization for runtime features and the capabilities of mobile devices. These options can be found in Player Settings. We only need to set a couple of them now (the minimum required to build our projects):

1. In Unity, navigate to **File** | **Build Settings** and examine the **Platform** pane. If iOS is not presently selected, select it now and press **Switch Platform**.
2. If you have the **Build Settings** window open, press the **Player Settings...** button. Or, you can get there from the main menu: **Edit** | **Project Settings** | **Player**. Look across at the Inspector panel, which now contains the Player Settings.
3. Find the **Other Settings** group of parameters, and click the header bar (if it's not already opened) to find the Identification variables.
4. Set the **Bundle Identifier** to a unique name for your product that resembles a traditional Java package name. An ID is required for all iOS apps. Typically, it is in the format `com.CompanyName.ProductName`. It must be unique on the target device, and eventually, unique in the App Store. You can choose whatever name you want.
5. Set the **Automatic Signing Team ID** to your Signing Team setup in Xcode, and check the **Automatically Sign** checkbox.

 To configure your Apple ID with Xcode, in Xcode go to **Preferences** | **Accounts** and add an Apple ID by tapping **+**.

Build And Run

Xcode consists of an **integrated development environment** (**IDE**) that hosts your Xcode projects. When you build for iOS from Unity, it doesn't actually build an iOS executable. Rather, Unity builds an Xcode-ready project folder that you then open in Xcode to complete the compile, build, and deploy process, and to run the app on your device. Let's go!

1. Be sure your device is turned on, connected, and you grant permission for the Mac to access.
2. In the Build Settings, press the **Build And Run** button to begin building.
3. You will be prompted for a name and location of the build files. We recommend you create a new folder in your project root named `Build` and specify the file or subfolder name under that, as needed.

If all goes well, Unity will create an Xcode project and open it in Xcode. It will attempt to build the app, and if successful, upload it to your device. You now have a running VR app on your device you can show off to your friends and family!

Summary

In this chapter, we helped you set up your system for VR development and built your project for your target platform and devices. We discussed the different levels of device integration software and then installed software that was appropriate for your target VR device onto your development machine and asset packages into your Unity project. While we have summarized the steps, all of these steps are well documented on the device manufacturers sites and in the Unity manual and we encourage you to look at all the relevant documentation.

At this point, you should be able to preview your VR scene in Unity Editor's Play mode. And you should be able to build and run your project and install and run it as a binary directly on your device.

In the next chapter, we'll work more on the diorama scene and explore techniques to control objects in virtual reality. From a third-person perspective, we'll interact with objects in the scene (Ethan, the zombie) and implement look-based control.

4
Gaze-Based Control

Right now, our diorama is a third-person virtual reality experience. When you go into it, you're like an observer or a third-person camera. Sure, you can look around and add controls that let you move the camera's viewpoint. However, any action in the scene is from a third-person perspective.

In this chapter, we'll pretty much stay in the third-person mode, but we'll get a little more personally involved. We will explore techniques that can be used to control objects in your virtual world by looking and staring. Our character, Ethan, will be under your control, responding to where you look. Furthermore, we'll start programming the Unity scripts. Along the way, we will discuss the following topics:

- Adding **AI** (short for **artificial intelligence**) and **NavMesh** to our third-person character, Ethan
- Unity programming in C#
- Using our gaze to move a 3D cursor
- Shooting and killing Ethan, the zombie, to good effect

Most intros to Unity development tip-toe you through the easy stuff and maybe never even get to the more interesting, although more complex, things. We're going to mix things up in this chapter, throwing you into a few different 3D graphics topics, some a little advanced. If it's new to you, think of this as a survey tutorial. Nonetheless, we go through it step by step so you should be able to follow along and have a lot of fun too!

Ethan, the walker

Gaming is a common application of virtual reality. So, we might as well start out from there, too! We are going to give our character, Ethan, a life of his own. Well, sort of (or not), because he's going to become a zombie!

We left off at the diorama, with Ethan hanging out. You can make him run around the scene if you have a hand controller with a thumbstick or touchpad, but that is not guaranteed on some VR devices. In fact, if you're viewing the scene with a Google Cardboard, it's pretty unlikely that you'll have a handheld controller (notwithstanding the Bluetooth game controllers). In the next chapter, Chapter 5, *Handy Interactables*, we will go into handheld input controllers. For now, we will consider another way to make him move around, using the direction of your gaze while wearing your VR headset.

Before we attempt this, we'll first transform Ethan into a zombie and have him walk around aimlessly without any user control. We'll do this by giving him some AI and writing a script that sends him to random target locations.

AI controllers and *NavMesh* are somewhat advanced topics in Unity, but we're going to throw you into it just for fun. Besides, it's not as scary as zombies.

Artificially intelligent Ethan

To start, we want to replace the ThirdPersonController prefab that we used initially with Unity's AI character, AIThirdPersonController, using the following steps. Unity uses the word *artificial intelligence* loosely to mean *script-driven*. Perform the following steps:

1. Open the Unity project from the previous chapters with the Diorama scene, and have the Characters package imported from Standard Assets.

2. In the **Project** panel, open the Standard Assets/Characters/ThirdPersonCharacter/Prefabs folder and drag AIThirdPersonController into the scene. Name it Ethan.

3. In the **Hierarchy** panel (or in **Scene**), select the previous ThirdPersonController, (the old Ethan). Then, in the **Inspector** panel's **Transform** pane, choose the *gear* icon on the upper right of the **Transform** pane and select **Copy Component**.

4. Select the new Ethan object (from the **Hierarchy** panel or **Scene**). Then, in the **Inspector** panel's **Transform** pane, choose the *gear* icon and select **Paste Component Values**.

5. Now, you can delete the old Ethan object by selecting it from the **Hierarchy** panel, right-clicking to open options, and clicking on **Delete**.

If you cannot find the `Characters` package to import, you may not have installed `Standard Assets` when you installed Unity. To get them now, you will need to run the `UnityDownloadAssistant` again as described at the beginning of `Chapter 2`, *Content, Objects, and Scale* (and it may already be in your Downloads folder).

Note that this controller has a `NavMesh Agent` component and an `AICharacterControl` script. The NavMesh Agent has parameters for how Ethan will move around the scene. The `AICharacterControl` script takes a target object where Ethan will walk to. Let's populate that, as follows:

1. Add an empty game object to the **Hierarchy** panel, and rename it `WalkTarget`.
2. Reset its **Transform** values to position (0,0,0) (using the gear icon in upper-right of the Transform pane).
3. Select Ethan and drag `WalkTarget` into the **Target** property in the **Inspector** panel's **AI Character Control** pane, as shown here:

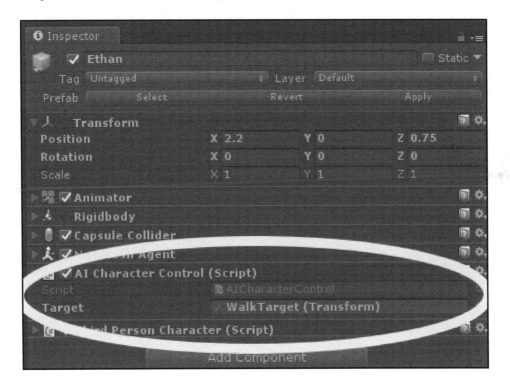

At this point, we have an AI character in the scene (`Ethan`), an empty game object that will be used as a navigation target (`WalkTarget`) initially in the center of our scene, and we told the AI Character Controller to use this target object. When we run the game, wherever `WalkTarget` is, Ethan will go there. But not yet.

The NavMesh bakery

Ethan cannot just go walking around without being told where he's allowed to roam! We need to define a *NavMesh*-a simplified geometrical plane that enables a character to plot its path around obstacles.

In our scene, Ethan is an agent. Where he's allowed to walk is the *navmesh*. Note that he has a **NavMesh Agent** component and an `AICharacterControl` script. The NavMesh Agent has parameters for how Ethan will move around the scene.

Create a `NavMesh` by first identifying the objects in the scene that affect navigation by marking them **Navigation Static**, and then baking the NavMesh, as follows:

1. Select the **Navigation** panel. If it's not already a tab in your editor, open the **Navigation** window from the main menu by navigating to **Window | Navigation**.
2. Select its **Object** tab.
3. Select the **Ground Plane** in **Hierarchy**, then in the **Navigation** window's Object pane, check the **Navigation Static** checkbox. (Alternatively, you can use the object's Inspector window Static dropdown list.)
4. Repeat step 3 for each of the objects that should get in his way: the cubes and the sphere. An example is shown for the sphere.
5. In the Navigation window, select the **Bake** tab, and click on the **Bake** button at the bottom of the panel:

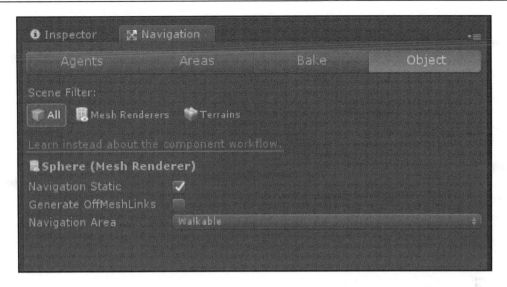

The **Scene** view should now show a blue overlay where the NavMesh is defined, as shown in the following screenshot:

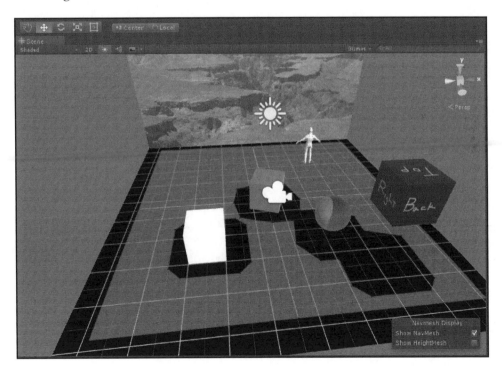

Let's test this out. Ensure that the **Game** panel's **Maximize on Play** is deselected. Click on the *Play* mode button (the triangle at the top of editor). In the **Hierarchy** panel, select the WalkTarget object and ensure that the Translate gizmo is active in the **Scene** panel (press the W key on keyboard). Now, drag the red (**x**) and/or the blue (**z**) arrow handles on the WalkTarget object to move it around the floor plane. As you do, Ethan should follow! Click on *Play* again to stop **Play Mode**.

A random walker in the town

Now, we'll write a script that moves the WalkTarget object to random places.

Writing scripts is an important part of developing with Unity. If you've done anything more that tinker with Unity, you've probably already written at least some scripts. We're going to use the C# programming language.

 If you are new to programming, don't panic! We provide a more detailed introduction to Unity scripting at the end of this chapter. You can skip to that now and come back, or just follow along.

For this first script, we'll take it slow. We will attach the script to the WalkTarget object, as follows:

1. Select the WalkTarget object in the **Hierarchy** panel or the **Scene** view.
2. In its **Inspector** panel, click on the **Add Component** button.
3. Select **New Script** (you many need to scroll down to find it).
4. Name it RandomPosition.
5. Ensure that the **C Sharp** language is selected.
6. Click on **Create and Add**.
7. This should create a script component on the WalkTarget object. Double-click on the RandomPosition script in the slot to the right of **Script** in the **Inspector** pane to open it in your code editor.

The RandomPosition script

We want to move the WalkTarget object to a random location so that Ethan will head in that direction, wait a few seconds, and move the WalkTarget object again. That way, he'll appear to be wandering around aimlessly. We can do this with a script. Rather than developing the script incrementally, I'm presenting the finished version first, and we'll go through it line by line. The RandomPosition.cs script looks like this:

```
using UnityEngine;
using System.Collections;

public class RandomPosition : MonoBehaviour {

  void Start () {
    StartCoroutine (RePositionWithDelay());
  }

  IEnumerator RePositionWithDelay() {
    while (true) {
      SetRandomPosition();
      yield return new WaitForSeconds (5);
    }
  }

  void SetRandomPosition() {
    float x = Random.Range (-5.0f, 5.0f);
    float z = Random.Range (-5.0f, 5.0f);
    Debug.Log ("X,Z: " + x.ToString("F2") + ", " +
      z.ToString("F2"));
    transform.position = new Vector3 (x, 0.0f, z);
  }
}
```

This script defines a MonoBehaviour sub-class named RandomPosition. The first thing we do when defining the class is declare any variables that we'll be using. A variable is a placeholder for a value. The value can be initialized here or assigned elsewhere, just as long as it has a value before the script uses it.

The meat of the script is further down, the function named SetRandomPosition(). Let's see what that does.

If you recall, the `GroundPlane` plane is 10 units square, with the origin in the middle. So, any (x, z) location on the plane will be within a range from –5 to 5 along each axis. The line `float x = Random.Range (-5.0f, 5.0f)` picks a random value within the given range and assigns it to a new `float x` variable. We do the same thing to get a random **z** value. (Usually, I discourage *hardcoding* constant values like this instead of using variables, but I'm keeping things simple for illustration purposes.)

The line `Debug.Log ("X,Z: " + x.ToString("F2") + ", " + z.ToString("F2"))` prints the x and z values in the **Console** panel when the game is running. It'll output something like `X, Z: 2.33, -4.02` because `ToString("F2")` says round up to two decimal places. Note that we're using plus signs to combine the parts of the output string together.

We actually move the target to the given location with the line `transform.position = new Vector3 (x, 0.0f, z);`. We're setting the transform position of the object that this script is attached to. In Unity, values that have an X, Y, and Z are represented by the `Vector3` objects. So, we create a new one with the x and z values that we generated. We give `y=0` so that it sits on `GroundPlane`.

Each `MonoBehaviour` class has a built-in variable called `this`, which refers to the object that the script is attached to. That is, when the script is a component of an object and appears in its **Inspector** panel, the script can refer to its object as `this`. In fact, `this` is so obvious, if you want to call functions on the `this` object, you don't even need to say it. We could have said `this.transform.position = ...`, but the `this` object is implied and is normally omitted. On the other hand, if you had a variable for some other object (for example, `GameObject that;`), then you'd need to say that when you set its position, like `that.transform.position = ...`.

The last mysterious bit is how we handle time delays in Unity, using co-routines. This is a somewhat advanced coding technique, but very handy. In our case, the transform position should get changed once every five seconds. It's solved in several parts:

1. In the `Start()` function, there's the line `StartCoroutine (RePositionWithDelay());`. A **co-routine** is a piece of code that runs separately from the function from which it was called. So, this line kicks off the `RePositionWithDelay()` function in a co-routine.
2. Inside that, there's a `while (true)` loop, which as you might guess, runs forever (as long as the game is running).
3. It calls the `SetRandomPosition()` function, which actually repositions the object.

4. Then, at the bottom of this loop, we do a `yield return new WaitForSeconds (5);` statement, which basically says to Unity, *hey, go do what you want for five seconds and then come back here so that I can go through my loop again.*

5. For all of this to work, the `RePositionWithDelay` co-routine must be declared as the `IEnumerator` type (because the documentation says so).

This co-routine/yield mechanism, although an advanced programming topic, is a common pattern in time-sliced programs such as Unity.

Our script should be saved to a file named `RandomPosition.cs`.

We are now good to go. In the Unity editor, click on *Play*. Ethan is running from one place to another like a madman!

"Zombie-ize" Ethan!

OK, that's pretty random. Let's adjust the NavMesh steering parameters to slow him down to a nice zombie-like pace. For that, perform the following steps:

1. Select `Ethan` in the **Hierarchy** panel

2. Navigate to **Inspector** | **Nav Mesh Agent** | **Steering** and set the following:
    - **Speed**: `0.3`
    - **Angular Speed**: `60`
    - **Acceleration**: `2`

Play again. He has slowed down. That's better.

One more finishing touch: let's turn him into a zombie. I have a texture image named `EthanZombie.png` that will help (included with this book). Perform the following steps:

1. From the **Assets** tab on the main menu, select **Import New Asset...**. Navigate to the files folder with the assets that came with this book.

2. Select the `EthanZombie.png` file.

3. Click on **Import**. For tidiness, ensure that it resides in the `Assets/Textures` folder. (Alternatively, you can just drag and drop the file from Windows Explorer into the **Project** panel Assets/Textures folder.)

4. In the **Hierarchy** panel, unfold the `Ethan` object (click on the triangle) and select `EthanBody`.

5. In the `Inspector` panel, unfold the `EthanGray` shader by clicking on the triangle icon to the left of **Shader**.

6. Select the `EthanZombie` texture from the `Project Assets/Textures` folder.

7. Drag it onto the **Albedo** texture map. It's a small square just to the left of the **Albedo** label under **Main Maps**.

8. In the **Hierarchy** panel, select `EthanGlasses` and uncheck it to disable glasses in the **Inspector** panel. After all, zombies don't need glasses!

His portrait is featured below. *What'd you say? That's not a scary enough zombie??* Well, maybe he's just recently turned. Go ahead and make a better one yourself. Use Blender, Gimp, or Photoshop and paint your own (or even import a whole different zombie humanoid model to replace `EthanBody` itself):

Now, build the project and try it in VR.

We're looking from a third-person perspective. You can look around and watch what's going on. It's kind of fun, and it's pretty interesting. And it's passive. Let's get more active.

Go where I'm looking

In this next script, instead of being random, we'll send Ethan to wherever we look. In Unity, this is accomplished by using **ray casting.** It's like shooting a ray from the camera and seeing what it hits (for more information, visit `http://docs.unity3d.com/Manual/CameraRays.html`).

We're going to create a new script, which will be attached to `WalkTarget` like before, as follows:

1. Select the `WalkTarget` object in the **Hierarchy** panel or the **Scene** view.
2. In its **Inspector** panel, click on the **Add Component** button.
3. Select **New Script**.
4. Name it `LookMoveTo`.
5. Ensure that the **C Sharp** language is selected.
6. Click on **Create** and **Add**.

This should create a script component on the `WalkTarget` object. Double-click on it to open it in your code editor.

> This `LookMoveTo` script replaces the `RandomPosition` one we created before. Disable the `RandomPosition` component of `WalkTarget` before proceeding.

The LookMoveTo script

In our script, each time `Update()` is called, we'll read where the camera is pointing (by using its transform position and rotation), cast a ray in that direction, and ask Unity to tell us where it hits the ground plane. Then, we'll use this location to set the `WalkTarget` object's position.

Here's the full `LookMoveTo.cs` script:

```
using UnityEngine;
using System.Collections;

public class LookMoveTo : MonoBehaviour {
  public GameObject ground;

  void Update () {
    Transform camera = Camera.main.transform;
    Ray ray;
    RaycastHit hit;
    GameObject hitObject;

    Debug.DrawRay (camera.position,
      camera.rotation * Vector3.forward * 100.0f);

    ray = new Ray (camera.position,
```

```
            camera.rotation * Vector3.forward);
        if (Physics.Raycast (ray, out hit)) {
          hitObject = hit.collider.gameObject;
          if (hitObject == ground) {
            Debug.Log ("Hit (x,y,z): " + hit.point.ToString("F2"));
            transform.position = hit.point;
          }
        }
      }

  }
```

Let's go through the script a bit at a time.

```
    public GameObject ground;
```

The first thing the script does is declare a variable for the GroundPlane object. Since it's public, we can use the Unity editor to assign the actual object:

```
    void Update () {
      Transform camera = Camera.main.transform;
      Ray ray;
      RaycastHit hit;
      GameObject hitObject;
```

Inside Update(), we define a few local variables, camera, ray, hit, and hitObject, which have datatypes that are required by the Unity functions that we're going to use.

Camera.main is the current active camera object (that is, tagged as MainCamera). We get its current transform, which will be assigned to the camera variable:

```
      ray = new Ray (camera.position,
        camera.rotation * Vector3.forward);
```

Ignoring the handy Debug statements for a moment, we first determine the ray from the camera using new Ray().

A **ray** can be defined by a starting position in the **x**, y, and z space and a direction vector. A **direction vector** can be defined as the relative offsets from a 3D starting point to some other point in space. The forward direction, where **z** is positive, is (0, 0, 1). Unity will do the math for us. So, if we take a unit vector (Vector3.forward), multiply it by a three-axis rotation (camera.rotation), and scale it by a length (100.0f), we'll get a ray pointing in the same direction as the camera, measuring 100 units long:

```
    if (Physics.Raycast (ray, out hit)) {
```

Then, we cast the ray and see if it hit anything. If so, the `hit` variable will now contain more details about what was hit, including the specific object in `hit.collider.gameObject`. (The `out` keyword means that the `hit` variable value is filled in by the `Physics.Raycast()` function.)

```
if (hitObject == ground) {
    transform.position = hit.point;
}
```

We check whether the ray hit the `GroundPlane` object and if so, we'll assign that as the position to move the `WalkTarget` object to the `hit` location.

> The ==compare operator should not to be confused with =, which is the assignment operator.

This script contains two `Debug` statements, which are a useful way to monitor what's going on while a script is running in Play Mode. `Debug.DrawRay()` will draw the given ray in the **Scene** view so that you can actually see it, and `Debug.Log()` will dump the current hit position to the console if and when there's a hit.

Save the script, switch into the Unity editor, and perform the following steps:

1. With `WalkTarget` selected, in the `Inspector` panel, the `LookMoveTo` script component now has a field for the `GroundPlane` object.
2. From the **Hierarchy** panel, select and drag the `GroundPlane` game object onto the **Ground** field.

Save the scene. The script pane looks like this:

Then, click the *Play* button. Ethan should follow our gaze (at his own pace).

In projects with more than a few objects with colliders, in order to optimize the performance of your raycast, it is advised to place the objects on a specific layer (for example, named "Raycast") and then add that layer mask to the Raycast call. For example, if "Raycast" is layer 5, `int layerMask = 1 << 5`, then `Physics.Raycast(ray, out hit, maxDistance, layerMask);`. See https://docs.unity3d.com/ScriptReference/Physics.Raycast.html and https://docs.unity3d.com/Manual/Layers.html for details and examples.

Adding a feedback cursor

Given it's not always obvious where your gaze is hitting the ground plane, we'll now add a cursor to the scene. It's really easy because what we've been doing is moving around an invisible, empty `WalkTarget` object. If we give it a mesh by using the following steps, it'll be visible:

1. In the **Hierarchy** panel, select the `WalkTarget` object.
2. Right-click on the mouse and navigate to **3D Object | Cylinder**. This will create a cylindrical object parented by `WalkTarget`. (Alternatively, you can use the **GameObject** tab on the main menu bar, and then drag and drop the object onto `WalkTarget`.)
3. Ensure that we're starting with the reset values of transform by clicking on **Reset** from the *gear* icon menu in the **Transform** pane.
4. Select the new cylinder and in its **Inspector** panel, change the **Scale** to (0.4, 0.05, 0.4). This will create a flat disk with a diameter of 0.4.
5. Disable its **Capsule Collider** by unchecking that checkbox.
6. As a performance optimization, in **Mesh Renderer** you can also disable **Cast Shadows**, **Receive Shadows**, **Use Light Probes**, and **Reflection Probes**.

Now, try to play again. The cursor disk follows our gaze.

If you want, decorate the disk better with a colored material. Better yet, find an appropriate texture. For example, we used a grid texture in `Chapter 2`, *Content, Objects, and Scale*, for the `GridProjector` file (`Standard Assets/Effects/Projectors/Textures/Grid.psd`). The `CircleCrossHair.png` file is provided with the files for this book. Drop the texture onto the cylinder cursor. When you do, set its **Shader** to **Standard**.

Observing through obstacles

In this project, we got Ethan to follow where we're looking by moving the `WalkTarget` object to a position on the ground plane determined by raycasting from the camera and seeing where it intersected that plane.

You may have noticed that the cursor seems to get *stuck* when we slide our gaze over the cube and sphere. That's because the **physics engine** has determined which object is hit first, never getting to the ground plane. In our script, we have the conditional statement `if (hitObject == ground)` before moving `WalkTarget`. Without it, the cursor would float over any object in 3D space where the cast ray hits something. Sometimes, that's interesting, but in our case, it is not. We want to keep the cursor on the ground. However now, if the ray hits something other than the ground, it doesn't get repositioned and seems *stuck*. Can you think of a way around it? Here's a hint: look up `Physics.RaycastAll`. Alright, I'll show you. Replace the body of `Update()` with the following code:

```
Transform camera = Camera.main.transform;
Ray ray;
RaycastHit[] hits;
GameObject hitObject;
Debug.DrawRay (camera.position, camera.rotation *
   Vector3.forward * 100.0f);
ray = new Ray (camera.position, camera.rotation *
   Vector3.forward);
hits = Physics.RaycastAll (ray);
for (int i = 0; i < hits.Length; i++) {
  RaycastHit hit = hits [i];
  hitObject = hit.collider.gameObject;
  if (hitObject == ground) {
    Debug.Log ("Hit (x,y,z): " +
       hit.point.ToString("F2"));
    transform.position = hit.point;
  }
}
```

On calling `RaycastAll`, we get back a list, or an array, of hits. Then, we loop through each one looking for a ground hit anywhere along the path of the ray vector. Now our cursor will trace along the ground, whether or not there's another object in between.

 Extra challenge: Another more efficient solution is to use the *layer system*. Create a new layer, assign it to the plane, and pass it as an argument to `Physics.raycast()`. Can you see why that's much more efficient?

If looks could kill

We got this far. We might as well try to kill Ethan (haha!). Here are the specifications for this new feature:

- Looking at Ethan hits him with our line-of-sight raygun
- Sparks are emitted when the gun hits its target
- After 3 seconds of being hit, Ethan is killed
- When he's killed, Ethan explodes (we get a point) and then he respawns at a new location

The KillTarget script

This time, we'll attach the script to a new empty `GameController` object by performing the following steps:

1. Create an empty game object and name it `GameController`.
2. Attach a new C# script to it, using **Add Component**, named `KillTarget`.
3. Open the script in MonoDevelop.

Here's the completed `KillTarget.cs` script:

```
using UnityEngine;
using System.Collections;

public class KillTarget : MonoBehaviour {
  public GameObject target;
  public ParticleSystem hitEffect;
  public GameObject killEffect;
  public float timeToSelect = 3.0f;
  public int score;

  private float countDown;

  void Start () {
    score = 0;
    countDown = timeToSelect;
  }

void Update () {
    Transform camera = Camera.main.transform;
    Ray ray = new Ray (camera.position, camera.rotation *
      Vector3.forward);
```

```
    RaycastHit hit;
    if (Physics.Raycast (ray, out hit) && (hit.collider.gameObject
        == target)) {
      if (countDown > 0.0f) {
        // on target
        countDown -= Time.deltaTime;
        // print (countDown);
        hitEffect.transform.position = hit.point;
        hitEffect.Play ();
      } else {
        // killed
        Instantiate( killEffect, target.transform.position,
            target.transform.rotation );
        score += 1;
        countDown = timeToSelect;
        SetRandomPosition();
      }
    } else {
      // reset
      countDown = timeToSelect;
      hitEffect.Stop ();
    }
  }

  void SetRandomPosition() {
    float x = Random.Range (-5.0f, 5.0f);
    float z = Random.Range (-5.0f, 5.0f);
    target.transform.position = new Vector3 (x, 0.0f, z);
  }
}
```

Let's go through this. First, we declare a number of public variables, as follows:

```
public GameObject target;
public ParticleSystem hitEffect;
public GameObject killEffect;
public float timeToSelect = 3.0f;
public int score;
```

Like we did in the previous LookMoveTo script, our target will be Ethan. We're also adding a hitEffect particle emitter, a killEffect explosion, and a start value for the countdown timer, timeToSelect. Lastly, we'll keep track of our kills in the score variable.

The Start () method, which is called at the start of the gameplay, initializes the score to zero and sets the countDown timer to its starting value.

Then, in the `Update()` method, like in the `LookMoveTo` script, we cast a ray from the camera and check whether it hits our target, Ethan. When it does, we check the `countDown` timer.

If the timer is still counting, we decrement its value by the amount of time that's gone by since the last time `Update()` was called, using `Time.deltaTime`, and make sure that `hitEffect` is emitting at the hit point.

If the ray is still on its target and the timer is done counting down, Ethan is killed. We explode, bump up the score by one, reset the timer to its starting value, and move (respawn) Ethan to a random new location.

For an explosion, we'll use one of Unity's standard assets found in the `ParticleSystems` package. To activate it, `killEffect` should be set to the prefab named `Explosion`. Then, the script *instantiates* it. In other words, it makes it an object in the scene (at a specified transform), which kicks off its awesome scripts and effects.

Lastly, if the ray did not hit Ethan, we reset the counter and turn off the particles.

Save the script and go into the Unity Editor.

 Extra challenge: Refactor the script to use co-routines to manage the delay timing, like we did in the `RandomPosition` script at the start of this chapter.

Adding particle effects

Now, to populate the `public` variables, we will perform the following steps:

1. First, we need the `ParticleSystems` package that comes with Unity standard assets. If you do not have them, navigate to **Assets | Import Package | ParticleSystems**, choose **All**, and then click on **Import**.
2. Select `GameController` from the **Hierarchy** panel and go to the **Kill Target (Script)** pane in the **Inspector** panel.
3. Drag the `Ethan` object from the **Hierarchy** panel onto the **Target** field.
4. From the main menu bar, navigate to **GameObject | Effects | Particle System** and name it `SparkEmitter`.

5. Reselect `GameController` and drag `SparkEmitter` onto the **Hit Effect** field.

6. In the **Project** panel, find the `Explosion` prefab in `Assets/Standard Assets/ParticleSystems/Prefabs` and drag the `Explosion` prefab onto the **Kill Effect** field.

The script pane looks like the following screenshot:

We created a default particle system that will be used as the spark emitter. We need to set that up to our liking. I'll get you started, and you can play with it as you desire, as follows:

1. Select `SparkEmitter` from the **Hierarchy** panel.

2. And in its **Inspector** panel, under **Particle System**, set the following values:
   - **Start Size**: `0.15`
   - **Start Color**: pick a red/orange color
   - **Start Lifetime**: `0.3`
   - **Max Particles**: `50`

3. Under **Emission**, set **Rate over Time**: `100`

4. Under **Shape**, set **Shape**: **Sphere** and **Radius**: `0.01`

Here's what my **Scene** view looks like as I run Play Mode and zap Ethan in the chest:

When Ethan is shot, the `hitEffect` particle system is activated. After 3 seconds (or whatever value you set in the `TimeToSelect` variable), his *health* is depleted, the explosion effect is instantiated, the score is incremented, and he respawns at a new location. In `Chapter 6`, *World Space UI*, we'll see how we can show the current score to the player.

Cleaning up

One last thing before we're done: let's clean up the `Assets` folder a bit and move all the scripts into an `Assets/Scripts/` subfolder. Select the Project Assets folder in Project, create a folder, name it Scripts, and drag all your scripts into it.

Short intro to Unity C# programming

As we just saw, Unity does a lot of things: it manages objects, renders them, animates them, calculates the physics of those objects, and so on. Unity itself is a program. It's made of code. Probably a lot of good code written by some very smart people. This internal Unity code can be accessed by you, the game developer, through the Unity Editor point-and-click interface that we've already been using. Within the Unity Editor, scripts are manifested as configurable components. However, it's also made more directly accessible to you through the Unity scripting API.

API (short for **Application Programming Interface**), refers to published software functions that you can access from your own scripts. Unity's API is very rich and nicely designed. That's one reason why people have written amazing applications and plugin add-ons for Unity.

There are many programming languages in the world. Unity has chosen to support the C# language from Microsoft. Computer languages have a specific syntax that must be obeyed. Otherwise, the computer will not understand your script. In Unity, script errors (and warnings) appear in the **Console** panel of the editor as well as in the bottom footer of the app window.

The default script editor for Unity is an integrated development environment, or an IDE, called **MonoDevelop**. You can configure a different editor or an IDE if you want, such as Microsoft's Visual Studio. MonoDevelop has some nice features such as autocompletion and pop-up help that understand the Unity documentation. C# scripts are text files that are named with a .cs extension.

In a Unity C# script, some of the words and symbols are a part of the C# language itself, some come from the Microsoft .NET Framework, and others are provided by the Unity API. And then there's the code that you write.

An empty default Unity C# script looks like this:

```
using UnityEngine;
using System.Collections;

public class RandomPosition : MonoBehaviour {

    // Use this for initialization
    void Start () {

    }

    // Update is called once per frame
    void Update () {

    }
}
```

Let's dissect it.

The first two lines indicate that this script needs some other stuff to run. The `using` keyword belongs to the C# language. The line using `UnityEngine` says that we'll be using the `UnityEngine` API. The line using `System.Collections` says that we also might use a library of functions named `Collections` to access lists of objects.

In C#, each line of code ends with a semicolon. Double slashes (`//`) indicate comments in the code, and anything from there to the end of that line will be ignored.

This Unity script defines a class named `RandomPosition`. **Classes** are like code templates with their own properties (variables) and behavior (functions). Classes derived from the `MonoBehaviour` base class are recognized by Unity and used when your game runs. For example, in the first script we wrote at the top of this chapter, the line public class `RandomPosition` : `MonoBehaviour` basically says *we are defining a new public class named* `RandomPosition`," *which inherits all the abilities of the* `MonoBehaviour` *Unity base class*, including the capabilities of the `Start()` and `Update()` functions. The body of the class is enclosed in a pair of curly braces (`{ }`).

When something is `public`, it can be seen by other code outside this specific script file. When it's `private`, it can only be referenced within this file. We want Unity to see the `RandomPosition` class.

Classes define variables and functions. A **variable** holds data values of a specific type, such as `float`, `int`, `boolean`, `GameObject`, `Vector3`, and so on. **Functions** implement logic (step-by-step instructions). Functions can receive *arguments*-variables enclosed in a parenthesis used by its code-and can return new values when it's done.

Numeric `float` constants, such as `5.0f`, require an `f` at the end in C# to ensure that the data type is a *simple* floating point value and not a *double-precision* floating point value.

Unity will automatically call some special functions if you've defined them `Start()` and `Update()` are two examples. Empty versions of these are provided in the default C# script. The datatype in front of a function indicates the type of value returned. `Start()` and `Update()` do not return values, so they're `void`.

Each `Start()` function from all `MonoBehaviour` scripts in your game is called before the gameplay begins. It's a good place for data initialization. All the `Update()` functions are called during each time slice, or frame, while the game is running. This is where most of the action lies.

Once you've written or modified a script in the MonoDevelop or Visual Studio editor, save it. Then, switch to the Unity Editor window. Unity will automatically recognize that the script has changed and will reimport it. If errors are found, it will report them right away in the **Console** panel.

This is just a cursory introduction to Unity programming. As we work through the projects in this book, I will explain additional bits as they're introduced.

Summary

In this chapter, we explored the relationship between the VR camera and objects in the scene. We first made Ethan (the zombie) walk randomly around the scene and enabled him to move by using a NavMesh, but then we directed his wanderings using a 3D cursor on the **x**, **z** ground plane. This cursor follows our gaze as we look around the scene in virtual reality. Lastly, we also used our gaze to shoot a ray at Ethan, causing him to lose health and eventually explode.

These look-based techniques can be used in non-VR games, but in VR, it's very common and almost essential. We'll be using them more in the later chapters of this book too.

In the next chapter, we will use our hands to interact with the virtual scene. We will learn about Unity Input events, as well as input systems for SteamVR, Oculus, and Windows Mixed Reality, to name a few. As this can get complicated, we'll write our own VR input event system to keep our application independent of the specific VR devices.

Handy Interactables

5

You're in a virtual world with all this cool stuff; it is our nature to try to reach out and touch something. While gaze-based selection, as we saw in the previous chapter, is a good first step for interacting with virtual scenes, most people intuitively want to use their hands. Most VR devices provide a hand controller to select, grab, and interact with virtual objects in the scene.

In this chapter, we introduce practices for capturing user input in Unity, illustrating how to use them in a simple VR scene. Everyone loves balloons, so in this project we will make balloons. We may even pop a few. We will continue from the previous chapter, using C# programming for basic scripting, and explore several software design patterns for user input. We will discuss the following topics:

- Polling for input device data
- Using scriptable data objects for storing and retrieving input state
- Invoking and subscribing to input events
- Using interactable components provided with device-specific Unity packages

An important lesson we will learn in this chapter is there is not just one way to handle user input for your VR application. There isn't even one *best way*. Unity includes several mechanisms for handling user input and, in general, messaging between objects. VR device manufacturers provide their own input controller objects and scripts for their SDK.

Furthermore, VR manufacturers and others offer convenient framework toolkits with higher-level components and prefabs. We recommend you become familiar with the toolkits provided for your target device. Study the demo scenes to see how the components work and their recommended practices, as we will do at the end of this chapter.

That said, in this chapter we will start with the very simple button press input, and progress from there, showing various design patterns. You won't always want to roll your own, but you should have an understanding of how things work.

Setting up the scene

To begin our exploration of input mechanisms, let's set up our scene. The plan is to let players create balloons. Everyone loves balloons!

For this scene, you could start with a new scene (**File | New Scene**) and then add the **MyMyselfEye** prefab we built in the previous chapter. Instead, I've decided to start with the Diorama scene created in the previous chapter, and remove all but the GroundPlane and PhotoPlane, as follows:

1. Open the **Diorama** scene
2. Remove all the objects, except for **MyMyselfEye, Directional Light, GroundPlane** and **PhotoPlane**
3. Position the **MeMyselfEye** at the scene origin, **Position** (0, 0, 0)
4. Select **File | Save Scene As** and give it a name, such as "Balloons"

Creating a balloon

For the balloon, you can simply use a standard Unity sphere 3D primitive if you choose. Or you can find an object in the Unity Asset Store or elsewhere. We are using a low poly balloon object that we found on Google Poly (`https://poly.google.com/view/a01Rp51l-L3`) and which is provided with the download files for this chapter.

Either way, please parent the object so its origin (pivot point) is at the bottom, as follows:

1. In **Hierarchy**, create an empty object (**Create | Create Empty**) and name it "Balloon".
2. Reset its transform (**Transform | gear-icon | Reset**), then **Position** it at (0, 1, 1).
3. Drag the balloon prefab into the Hierarchy as a child object of Balloon (mine is found in the `Assets/Poly/Assets/` folder).
4. If you do not have a balloon model, use a sphere (**Create | 3D Object | Sphere**). And add a material, like the "Blue Material" we created in the previous chapter.
5. Set the child object's **Position** to (0, 0.5, 0) so its origin (pivot point) is at its bottom when referenced from the parent.

The scene should look something like this:

Making it a prefab

Our intent is to instantiate new balloons from a prefab when your player presses a button on their controller. And when the button is released, the balloon gets released and it floats away.

Let's scale and position the balloon initially in the scene at a starting size and workable distance. We will also give it some physics properties by adding a `RigidBody` component:

> We discuss RigidBodies and Unity physics in more detail in `Chapter 8`, *Playing with Physics and Fire*.

1. Select your Balloon object in **Hierarchy**
2. In **Inspector**, set its **Transform Scale** to (0.1, 0.1, 0.1)

3. Set its **Position** to (0, 1, 1)
4. Use **Add Component** to add a **Rigid Body**
5. Uncheck the **Use Gravity** checkbox

My balloon object now has the following properties:

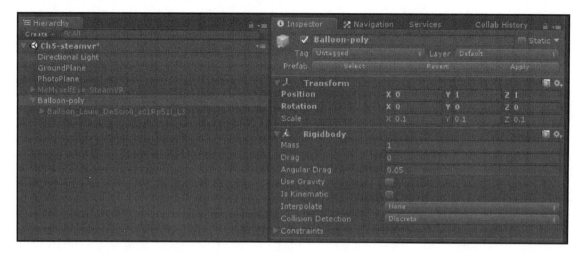

Make it a prefab as follows:

1. Drag the balloon object into your `Prefabs/` folder to make it a prefab object
2. Delete the original balloon object from your Hierarchy

Okay. Now let's play around with controller buttons.

 If you ever want to modify a prefab, drag an instance of it back into the scene. Make the changes you want. Then, use the **Apply** button to save the changes back onto the prefab of the object. Delete the temporary instance from the Hierarchy if it's no longer needed in the scene.

Basic button input

Unity includes a standard Input Manager for accessing traditional game controller, keyboard, mouse, and mobile touchscreen input. This can include specific button presses, joystick axes, and the device accelerometer, for example. It also supports input from VR and AR systems.

The Input Manager provides an abstraction layer over the physical input devices. For example, you can reference logical inputs, such as the `Fire1` button, which is mapped to a physical button. The mappings for your project can be set up and modified in **Edit** | **Project Settings** | **Input**.

> For a general overview and details of Unity Input Manager, see `https://docs.unity3d.com/Manual/ConventionalGameInput.html`. For scripting the Input class, see `https://docs.unity3d.com/ScriptReference/Input.html`. Input mapping for various VR devices can be found at `https://docs.unity3d.com/Manual/vr-input.html`.

Let's take a look. To start, we will write a test script to get a specific button state and see how the Unity Input class works. A common logical button is the one named "Fire1." Let's see which button your input device uses for "Fire1."

Using the Fire1 button

We will now write a script, `MyInputController`, to detect when your user has pressed the `Fire1` button. Add the script to your `MeMyselfEye` object as follows:

1. In **Hierarchy**, select the **MyMyselfEye** object
2. In **Inspector**, click **Add Component**, then **New Script**
3. Name it `MyInputController` and press **Create And Add**
4. Double-click the `MyInputController` script to open it for editing

Edit the script as follows:

```
public class MyInputController : MonoBehaviour
{
  void Update ()
  {
    ButtonTest ();
  }

  private void ButtonTest ()
  {
    string msg = null;

    if (Input.GetButtonDown("Fire1"))
      msg = "Fire1 down";

    if (Input.GetButtonUp("Fire1"))
      msg = "Fire1 up";
```

```
        if (msg != null)
            Debug.Log("Input: " + msg);
    }
}
```

In this script, in each frame Update, we call a private function, `ButtonTest`. This function builds a message string named `msg` that reports whether the `Fire1` button has just been pressed down or released. The call to `Input.GetButtonDown("Fire1")`, for example, will return a Boolean (true or false) value, which we check in the `if` statement. When either of these situations are true, the `msg` string is not empty (null) and gets printed to the Unity Console window:

1. Press **Play** in the Unity editor to run the scene
2. When you press the Fire1 button on your input controller, you will see the **Input: Fire1 down** message as output
3. When you release the Fire1 button, you will see the **Input: Fire1 up** message, as shown here:

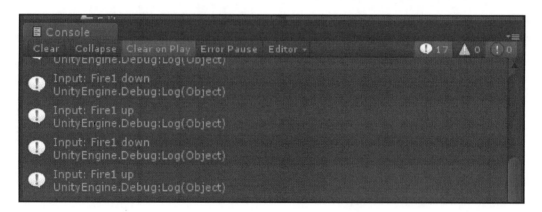

You can use even use this script to identify which physical button on your input controller maps to the logical `Fire1` button. Using OpenVR, for example, `Fire1` is triggered with the menu button on a Vive controller or the **B** button on the Oculus Touch controller ("Button.Two") as shown on the Unity Input System Mappings section in the Input for OpenVR Controllers page of the Unity manual (`https://docs.unity3d.com/Manual/OpenVRControllers.html`). Feel free to experiment with using other logical input names, and/or modifying the mappings using the Input project settings (**Edit | Project Settings | Input**).

Instead of using Unity logical inputs, it is also common to access the device directly through SDK components. Let's look into that in the next section.

OpenVR trigger button

If you have a VR device supported by OpenVR (HTC Vive, Oculus Rift, or Windows MR), let's modify the `ButtonTest` function to check for a pull and release of the trigger button.

To implement this, we need to provide our script with the specific input component that we want to query. In OpenVR, this is represented by the `SteamVR_TrackedObject` component, as shown in the following variation of our script:

```
public class MyInputController : MonoBehaviour
{
  public SteamVR_TrackedObject rightHand;

  private SteamVR_Controller.Device device;

  void Update ()
  {
    ButtonTest();
  }

  private void ButtonTest()
  {
    string msg = null;

    // SteamVR
    device = SteamVR_Controller.Input((int)rightHand.index);
    if (device != null &&
      device.GetPressDown(SteamVR_Controller.ButtonMask.Trigger))
    {
      msg = "Trigger press";
      device.TriggerHapticPulse(700);
    }
    if (device != null &&
      device.GetPressUp(SteamVR_Controller.ButtonMask.Trigger))
    {
      msg = "Trigger release";
    }

    if (msg != null)
      Debug.Log("Input: " + msg);
  }
}
```

After saving this script, we need to populate the `rightHand` variable:

1. In Unity, select **MeMyselfEye** so you can see the **My Input Controller** in the **Inspector**
2. In the **Hierarchy**, unfold the **[CameraRig]** object
3. Click the **Controller (Right)** child object and drag it onto the **My Input Controller**'s Right-Hand slot in the **Inspector**

Given the `rightHand` object, we reference its `SteamVR_TrackedObject` component directly. In the `ButtonTest` function, we get the *device* data using the right hand's device ID (`rightHand.index`) and check specifically for the trigger press status. As a bonus, I've shown you how to also provide a haptic buzz pulse on the device when the trigger is pressed.

Now when you press **Play**, pulling the controller trigger will be recognized.

Using the SDK components like this, you can access other inputs specific to the device not supported by the Unity Input Manager. The trigger on some controllers are not just pressed/unpressed but can return a percentage of the press, represented as a value between 0.0 and 1.0. Another example is the touch-sensitive grips, buttons, and thumb pad on the Oculus Touch controllers and other controllers.

 Try modifying the script to recognize the controller `Grip` button instead, or other inputs. Hint: try *SteamVR_Controller.ButtonMask.Grip*.

Daydream controller clicks

Google Daydream VR on Android may not respond, by default, to `Fire1` events. The following code shows how to access controller clicks directly:

```
private void ButtonTest()
{
  string msg = null;

  if (GvrControllerInput.ClickButtonDown)
    msg = "Button down";
  if (GvrControllerInput.ClickButtonUp)
    msg = "Button up";
```

```
    if (msg != null)
      Debug.Log("Input: " + msg);
  }
}
```

In this case, we call the `GvrControllerInput` class static functions `ClickButtonDown` and `ClickButtonUp`. There is no need to identify a specific controller object because `GvrControllerInput` is a *singleton*. That is why we're guaranteed to have only one instance of it in the scene, so we can reference its data directly. This makes sense because on Daydream there will only be one hand controller, whereas on OpenVR there will be two.

Polling for clicks

The simplest way to obtain user input is just *get* the current data from an input component. We've already seen this using the Input class and VR SDK. Presently, we will write our own input component that maps the Unity (or SDK) input to our own simple API in `MyInputController`. Then, we'll write a `BalloonController` that polls the input, as illustrated:

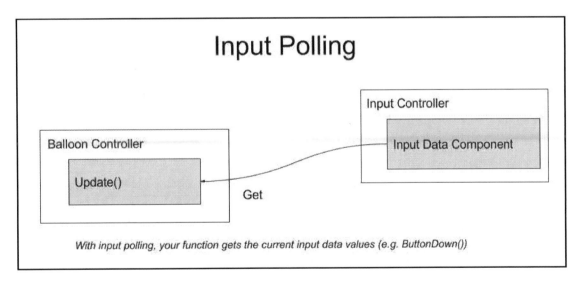

With input polling, your function gets the current input data values (e.g. ButtonDown())

Our own button interface functions

You may recall that the `MeMyselfEye` player rig may have device-specific toolkit child objects for a particular VR SDK. The version for OpenVR, for example, has their **[CameraRig]** prefab. The version for Daydream has the Daydream **Player** prefab. It makes sense to add our `MyInputController` component to `MeMyselfEye`, as it may make device-specific SDK calls. In this way, should you want to maintain camera rig prefabs for a variety of platforms, and swap them in and out as you build the project for a different VR target, the API that is exposed to the rest of your application will be consistent and independent of the specific device toolkit.

Our input controller will expose two custom API Functions, `ButtonDown` and `ButtonUp`. The implementation of these functions will be hidden from the components that call them. For example, we could write it to handle `Fire1` button presses as first but later change it to use a trigger press instead, or make a version for Daydream that does not use `Fire1`. Let's update the `MyInputController` by adding the following code:

```
public bool ButtonDown()
{
   return Input.GetButtonDown("Fire1");
}

public bool ButtonUp()
{
   return Input.GetButtonUp("Fire1");
}
```

Or you can modify the preceding code to use the button interface that works for you. For example, for Daydream you might use this instead:

```
public bool ButtonDown()
{
   return GvrControllerInput.ClickButtonDown;
}

public bool ButtonUp()
{
   return GvrControllerInput.ClickButtonUp;
}
```

Now, we'll use our little `ButtonUp`/`ButtonDown` input API.

Creating and releasing balloons

Let's now create a `BalloonController` that will be the application component that creates and controls balloons. It will reference our `MyInputController`. Follow these steps:

1. In **Hierarchy**, create an empty game object, reset its Transform, and name it `BalloonController`
2. Create a new script on the object named `BalloonController` and open it for editing as follows:

```
public class BalloonController : MonoBehaviour
{
  public GameObject meMyselfEye;

  private MyInputController inputController;

  void Start ()
  {
    inputController =
meMyselfEye.GetComponent<MyInputController>();
  }

  void Update ()
  {
    if (inputController.ButtonDown())
    {
      NewBalloon()
    }
    else if (inputController.ButtonUp())
    {
      ReleaseBalloon();
    }
    // else while button is still pressed, grow it
  }
```

This is the skeleton of the controller. Given a reference to the `MeMyselfEye` object, the `Start()` function gets its `MyInputController` component and assigns it to the `inputController` variable.

`Update()` is called each frame while your game is running. It will call `inputController.ButtonDown` or `ButtonUp` to see if the user has changed their input, and in response, either create or release a balloon. We'll write the functions next.

Note that we've also included a placeholder (as a comment) where we'll add the `GrowBalloon` function too.

Given the balloon prefab, the `BalloonController` can create new instances of it in our scene, by calling the Unity `Instantiate` function. Add the following `public` variable declaration at the top of your controller class for the balloon prefab:

```
public GameObject balloonPrefab;
```

And add a `private` variable to hold the current instance of the balloon:

```
private GameObject balloon;
```

Now, the `NewBalloon` function, which is called when the player presses the button, references the prefab and instantiates it as follows:

```
private void NewBalloon()
{
  balloon = Instantiate(balloonPrefab);
}
```

The `ReleaseBalloon` function is called when the player releases the button. It will apply a gentle upward force on the balloon so it floats skyward. We'll define a floatStrength variable and apply it to the object's RigidBody (the Unity physics engine and RigidBodies are explained in a later chapter):

```
public float floatStrength = 20f;
```

And,

```
private void ReleaseBalloon()
{
  balloon.GetComponent<Rigidbody>().AddForce(Vector3.up * floatStrength);
  balloon = null;
}
```

Notice that we also clear the balloon variable (setting it to null), getting it ready for the next button press.

Save the file and in Unity:

1. Drag the **MeMyselfEye** object from **Hierarchy** onto the BalloonController's **Me Myself Eye** slot in **Inspector**
2. Drag the **Ballon** prefab from the Project's `Assets` folder onto the BalloonController's **Balloon Prefab** slot in **Inspector**

When you're ready, press **Play**. Inside VR, when you press the `Fire1` button (or whichever you programmed), a new balloon is instantiated. When you release it, the balloon floats upwards. In the following game window, I have pressed the button multiple times in succession, creating a series of balloons:

Here is the Hierarchy of the same game state, showing the cloned balloons in the **Hierarchy** (my prefab's name is `Balloon-poly`):

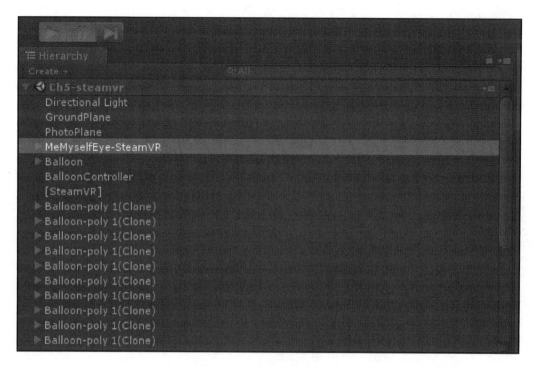

Inflating a balloon while pressed

The next thing we want to do is inflate the balloon while you're still holding the button. We can do this by checking whether there's a current balloon instance from a button press, and modifying its scale each update by a specified grow rate. Let's define that first, to grow by 150% each second the button is held down (1.5 times):

```
public float growRate = 1.5f;
```

Now, modify the Update function with a third `else if` condition as follows:

```
else if (balloon != null)
{
  GrowBalloon();
}
```

And add the `GrowBalloon` function like this:

```
private void GrowBalloon()
{
   balloon.transform.localScale += balloon.transform.localScale * growRate
* Time.deltaTime;
}
```

The `GrowBalloon` function will modify the balloon's local scale by a percentage of its current size. `growRate` is the rate of growth per second. So, we multiply that by the current fraction of a second in this frame (`Time.deltaTime`).

Press **Play** in Unity. When you press the controller button, you'll create a balloon, which continues to inflate until you release the button. Then the balloon floats up. Wow, that's actually pretty fun!

Next, we're going to refactor our code to use a different software pattern for getting user input, using scriptable objects.

No one writes code without expecting to change it. Programming is a dynamic art as you rethink how to do things, as requirements grow, and problems get fixed. Sometimes, these changes are not necessarily to add a new feature or fix a bug but to make the code cleaner, easier to use, and easier to maintain. This is called **refactoring** when you change or rewrite parts of a program but do not necessarily change how the feature works from the player's perspective.

Using scriptable objects for input

In this example, we will further decouple our application from the underlying input device using a technique called **scriptable objects.** These are data objects used for holding information such as game state, player preferences, or any other data that is not necessarily graphical. Scriptable objects are instantiated during runtime, much like MonoBehaviour ones, but do not live in the Hierarchy, have no Transform, nor other physics and rendering behaviors.

It's useful to think of scriptable objects as *data containers* in your projects.

In the previous implementation, BalloonController requires a reference to the MeMyselfEye object to use its MyInputController component. Although the input controller component does separate you from the underlying SDK calls, if you modify your application to use a different MeMyselfEye (for example, from OpenVR to Daydream), you will need to find and replace all references to one MeMyselfEye in the scene and replace them with the new one. Here's will have the input controller populate a scriptable object, and then our BalloonController reference that object for the data, as illustrated here:

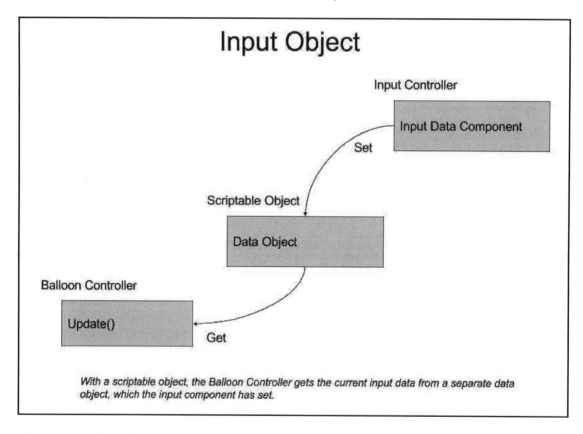

With a scriptable object, the Balloon Controller gets the current input data from a separate data object, which the input component has set.

The process of implementing scriptable objects is a little more involved than game objects with components. But not much. Let's go!

Keep in mind this is just one example of how to use scriptable objects and serves as an introduction to this powerful design pattern in Unity.

Creating the scriptable object

In this example, our object will just have one variable, for the current button action. We'll say the button can have one of three possible values: PressedDown, ReleasedUp, or None. We'll define the action as having occurred current during the current Update, then it's cleared to None. That is, rather than record the current button state (for example, is pressed), we are capturing the current button action (was just pressed), to be consistent with other examples in this chapter.

It's useful to keep scriptable objects in their own folder in the Project Assets:

1. In the **Project** window, create a new folder under *Assets* named ScriptableObjects
2. In the new folder, right-click and select **Create | C# Script**
3. Name the script MyInputAction
4. Then, open the MyInputAction.cs script for editing

Edit the MyInputAction.cs script as follows:

```
[CreateAssetMenu(menuName = "My Objects/Input Action")]
public class MyInputAction : ScriptableObject {
    public enum ButtonAction { None, PressedDown, ReleasedUp };
    public ButtonAction buttonAction;
}
```

Rather than inheriting from MonoBehaviour, we will define the class as a ScriptableObject. We represent the action using an enum to restrict its possible values to the selection list.

"The **enum** keyword is used to declare an enumeration, a distinct type that consists of a set of named constants called the enumerator list." - https://docs.microsoft.com/en-us/dotnet/csharp/language-reference/keywords/enum

Notice the first line of the preceding script. We provide a *property attribute* which generates a menu item in the Unity Editor for our object. Since scriptable objects are not added to the scene Hierarchy, we need a way to create them in the project. Using this attribute makes it easy, as follows:

1. Save the script and return to Unity.
2. In the Unity editor main menu, navigate to **Assets | Create**.
3. You will see a new item, **My Objects**, with a submenu with an item **Input Action**, as directed in the `CreateAssetsMenu` property attribute in our script. The menu is shown next.
4. Choose **Input Action** to create an instance. By default, it will be created in the currently selected Project Assets folder. So if you have the `ScriptableObjects` folder open, it will be created there.
5. Rename the object `My Input Action Data`.

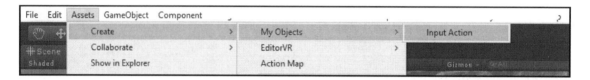

If you select the new `My Input Action Data` object in your `ScriptableObjects/` folder, you can see its properties in the **Inspector**. In the following screen capture, I have clicked the **Button Action** drop-down list to reveal the possible enum values we've specified in our code:

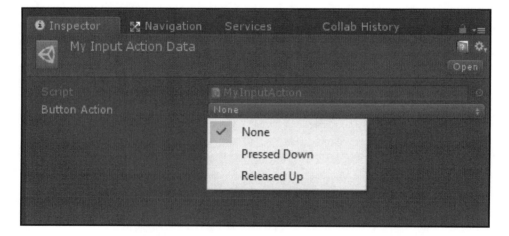

Populating the input action object

The next step is to change `MyInputController.cs` to populate the input data object, using a reference to the object, as follows:

```
public MyInputAction myInput;

void Update ()
{
  if (ButtonDown())
  {
    myInput.buttonAction = MyInputAction.ButtonAction.PressedDown;
  } else if (ButtonUp())
  {
    myInput.buttonAction = MyInputAction.ButtonAction.ReleasedUp;
  } else
  {
    myInput.buttonAction = MyInputAction.ButtonAction.None;
  }
}
```

The script uses its own `ButtonDown` and `ButtonUp` functions to set the `buttonAction` as appropriate. These could even be changed from *public* to *private* to further encapsulate it.

Save the script. Then in Unity:

1. Select **MeMyselfEye** object in Hierarchy
2. Find the **My Input Action Data** object in your `ScriptableObjects` folder
3. Drag it onto the **My Input** slot of the **My Input Controller (Script)** component, as shown here for my Steam version of `MeMyselfEye`:

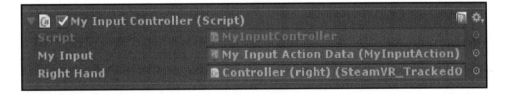

Accessing the input action object

Now the `BalloonController` can access the input data object rather than `MeMyselfEye`. Otherwise is very similar and a simple refactor. Modify `BalloonController.cs` as follows.

First, we can remove any references to `MeMyselfEye` in the `BalloonController`, including the public variable and the entire `Start()` function (we do not need the `GetComponent<MyInputController>`).

Add a variable for the input data object:

```
public MyInputAction myInput;
```

And reference it in the `Update` conditions:

```
void Update()
{
  if (myInput.buttonAction == MyInputAction.ButtonAction.PressedDown)
  {
    NewBalloon();
  }
  else if (myInput.buttonAction == MyInputAction.ButtonAction.ReleasedUp)
  {
    ReleaseBalloon();
  }
  else if (balloon != null)
  {
   GrowBalloon();
  }
}
```

Save the script. Then in Unity, as we did previously for `MyInputController`:

1. Select the **BalloonController** object in **Hierarchy**
2. Find the **My Input Action Data** object in your `ScriptableObjects` folder
3. Drag it onto the **My Input** slot of the **Balloon Controller** component

Press **Play**. The app should work just like before. Press the button to create a balloon, hold the button to inflate it, and release the button to release the balloon.

Simulation testing with scriptable objects

An interesting advantage of this architecture is how it facilitates testing. Having completely decoupled our application objects from the input device, we can simulate input actions without actually using physical input controllers. For example, try this:

1. Select **MeMyselfEye** in **Hierarchy**. Then in **Inspector**, temporarily disable the **My Input Controller** component by unchecking its checkbox.
2. Select the **My Input Action Data** object in the Project `ScriptableObjects/` folder
3. Press **Play.**
4. While the game is running, in **Inspector**, change the **Button Action** from **None** to **PressedDown.**
5. The **BalloonController** thinks a **PressedDown** action has occurred. It creates a new balloon and begins inflating it.
6. In **Inspector**, change the **Input Action** to **PressedUp**.
7. The **BalloonController** sees a **PressedUp** action has occurred and releases the current balloon.

When you're done testing, don't forget to re-enable the input controller component!

This kind of manual setup of object states for development and testing can be very helpful, especially as your project grows and gets more complex.

Using Unity events for input

The third software pattern we will explore using Unity Events. Events allow decoupling of the source of the event from the consumer of the event. Basically, events are a messaging system where one object triggers an event. Any other objects in the project can listen for the event. It can subscribe a specific function to be called when the event occurs.

You can set this up using drag-and-drop via the Unity Inspector. Or you can subscribe listener functions in scripts. In this example, we will minimize the scripting involved, and use the Unity editor to subscribe to events.

Events are a very rich topic and we can only introduce them here. For more information on using Unity Events, there are a lot of good references online, including the Unity tutorials `https://unity3d.com/learn/tutorials/topics/scripting/events` and `https://unity3d.com/learn/tutorials/topics/scripting/events-creating-simple-messaging-system`.

The following diagram illustrates the relationship between our input controller, which invokes events, and the balloon controller, which subscribes to the events:

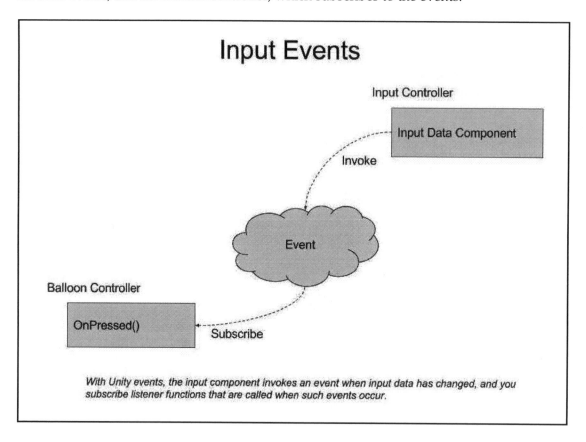

With Unity events, the input component invokes an event when input data has changed, and you subscribe listener functions that are called when such events occur.

It's important to note that, unlike normal events, these events do not need to be unsubscribed.

 If you are a developer and familiar with .NET, it may help to know that Unity Events are delegates. As explained in the Unity Manual, "UnityEvents can be added to any MonoBehaviour and are executed from code like a standard .net delegate. When a UnityEvent is added to a MonoBehaviour it appears in the Inspector and persistent callbacks can be added."

Invoking our input action events

To implement our example using events, we'll first have the `MyInputController` trigger events when a button is pressed and another event when the button is released.

First, at the top of the script we need to declare that we are using the Unity event API. The we declare the two UnityEvents we will invoke. The `Update()` function only needs to invoke one event or the other as they happen.

The entire `MyInputController.cs` is as follows:

```
using UnityEngine;
using UnityEngine.Events;

public class MyInputController : MonoBehaviour
{
  public UnityEvent ButtonDownEvent;
  public UnityEvent ButtonUpEvent;

  void Update()
  {
    if (ButtonDown())
      ButtonDownEvent.Invoke();
    else if (ButtonUp())
      ButtonUpEvent.Invoke();
  }

  private bool ButtonDown()
  {
    return Input.GetButtonDown("Fire1");
  }

  private bool ButtonUp()
  {
    return Input.GetButtonUp("Fire1");
```

```
    }
  }
```

That's it for this side of the equation.

Subscribing to input events

Using events, `BalloonController` does not need to check for input actions each frame
Update. All that conditional logic can be bypassed. Instead, we'll drag and drop the
components to subscribe them to events. The `Update` function now only needs to grow the
balloon if it's already instantiated.

The entire `BalloonController.cs` now looks like this. Aside from being less code, please
note that we changed the `NewBalloon` and `ReleaseBalloon` functions from `private` to
`public` so we can reference them in the Inspector:

```
public class BalloonController : MonoBehaviour
{
  public GameObject balloonPrefab;
  public float floatStrength = 20f;
  public float growRate = 1.5f;

  private GameObject balloon;

 void Update()
 {
   if (balloon != null)
     GrowBalloon();
 }

 public void NewBalloon()
 {
   balloon = Instantiate(balloonPrefab);
 }

 public void ReleaseBalloon()
 {
   balloon.GetComponent<Rigidbody>().AddForce(Vector3.up * floatStrength);
   balloon = null;
 }

 private void GrowBalloon()
 {
   balloon.transform.localScale += balloon.transform.localScale * growRate
 * Time.deltaTime;
```

```
        }
    }
```

To wire up the input events to our balloon controller:

1. Select **MeMyselfEye** and look at its **Inspector** window
2. You will see the **My Input Controller** component now has two event lists, as we declared in its script
3. On the **Button Down Event** list, press the + in the lower-right to create a new item.
4. Drag the **BalloonController** from **Hierarchy** into the empty Object slot
5. In the function select list, choose **BalloonController | NewBalloon**

Repeat the process for the Button Up Event as follows:

1. On the **Button Up Event** list, press the + in the lower-right to create a new item
2. Drag the **BalloonController** from **Hierarchy** into the empty Object slot
3. In the function select list, choose **BalloonController | ReleaseBalloon**

The component should now look like this:

Now when you press **Play** and press a button, the input controller invokes an event. The *NewBalloon* function is listening for these events and gets called. Likewise for the Button Up event.

This wiring can also be done entirely with scripting. We will not go into it here. As a developer, we more often are "users" of event systems set up by others. As your experience grows, you may find yourself implementing your own custom events.

 For another detailed example of using Unity Events for user interface, consider *Augmented Reality for Developers*, a Unity projects book from Packt Publishing co-authored by the author of this book, Jonathan Linowes, and Krystian Babilinski.

Really using your hands

The last couple of things we'll explore in the chapter involve getting your hands even more into virtual reality. In addition to buttons and touch pads, VR hand controllers can be tracked in 3D space along with your head. PC- and console-based VR, such as Rift, Vive, MR, and PSVR, are really very good at this, with full positionally tracked hand controllers for both left and right hands. Lower-end mobile VR, such as Daydream, has a single hand controller with limited tracking, but better than nothing.

To start, we'll take advantage of positional tracking by simply parenting the balloon to your hand model. On VR, without actual positional tracking, like Daydream, the location of your hand controller is approximated by the SDK software, but useful enough.

Parenting balloons to your hand

Suppose when you press the button, rather than creating the new balloon at a fixed position in space, it spawns and grows from your hand position. One way to accomplish this is to make the balloon instance a child of your hand controller object.

The BalloonController will need to know which hand pressed the button and parent the balloon to that controller object. Specifically, we'll pass the hand Game Object to the NewBalloon function as follows:

```
public void NewBalloon(GameObject parentHand)
{
  if (balloon == null)
  {
    balloon = Instantiate(balloonPrefab);
    balloon.transform.SetParent(parentHand.transform);
    balloon.transform.localPosition = Vector3.zero;
  }
}
```

Note that in this function we added an extra test for (`balloon == null`), just to make sure we haven't called `NewBalloon` twice in a row without releasing the first one yet.

Like before, we instantiate a new balloon from the prefab.

Then, we set its parent to the `parentHand` object. This is comparable to dragging one object to become a child of another in the Hierarchy. The parent-child relationships between game objects are handled by the built-in *Transform* component so the API functions are on the transform.

Lastly, we reset the local position of the balloon. If you recall, the prefab was positioned at (0, 1, 1) or something like that. As a child of the hand, we want it attached directly at the pivot point of the hand model. (Alternatively, you could offset the balloon origin to a different attachment point as needed.)

Worth noting, there are variations of the *Instantiate* function that let you specify the parent and transforms all in one call. See `https://docs.unity3d.com/ScriptReference/Object.Instantiate.html`.

Likewise, the `ReleaseBalloon` detaches the balloon from the hand before send it on its way, as follows:

```
public void ReleaseBalloon()
{
   if (balloon != null)
   {
     balloon.transform.parent = null;
     balloon.GetComponent<Rigidbody>().AddForce(Vector3.up *
floatStrength);
   }
   balloon = null;
}
```

How do we pass the hand game object to NewBalloon? Assuming your project is presently using the Unity Events we setup in the previous topic, it's very easy. In **Inspector** we need to update the **Button Down Event** function, since it now requires the game object argument:

1. In Unity editor, select the **MeMyselfEye** object
2. In the **Button Down Event** list, the function may now say something like `Missing BalloonController.NewBalloon`
3. Select the **function** dropdown and choose **BalloonController |
NewBalloon(GameObject)**

4. Unfold the **MeMyselfEye** object in **Hierarchy** and look for the hand model, then drag it onto the empty Game Object slot

5. If you are using OpenVR, the hand will be called **Controller (right)**

6. If you are using Daydream, the hand will be called **GvrControllerPointer**

Here is a screenshot of me generating a bunch of balloons flying "over" the Grand Canyon, fun!

Popping balloons

To be honest, it's really hard to think about creating balloons without also wanting to pop them! For fun, let's do a quick implementation. You can come up with your own ideas how to improve on it.

The Unity physics engine can detect when two object collide. To do this, each object must have a *Collider* component attached. You can then have the collision trigger an event. And we can subscribe that event to make something else happen, like play an explosion effect. This gets set up on the balloon prefab. So when two balloons collide, they'll explode. Let's do that:

1. Drag a copy of your Balloon prefab from Project `Assets prefabs` folder into the scene **Hierarchy.**
2. Select **Add Component | Physics | Sphere Collider**.
3. To scale and center the collider into position, click the **Edit Collider** icon in its component.
4. In the **Scene** window, the green collider outline has small anchor points you can click to edit. Note that the *Alt* key pins the center position and *Shift* locks the scale ratio.
5. Or, you can edit the **Center** and **Radius** values directly. I like **Radius** 0.25 and **Center** (0, 0.25, 0) on my balloon.

Now, we will add a script to handle the collision events.

1. **Add Component** to create a new C# script,
2. Name it `Poppable`
3. And open it for editing

The `Poppable` script will provide a callback function for `OnCollisionEnter` events. When another object with a collider enters this object's collider, our function will get called. At that point, we'll call `PopBalloon` which instantiates the explosion and destroys the balloon:

```
public class Poppable : MonoBehaviour
{
 public GameObject popEffect;

 void OnCollisionEnter(Collision collision)
 {
   PopBalloon();
 }

 private void PopBalloon()
 {
   Instantiate(popEffect, transform.position, transform.rotation);
   Destroy(gameObject);
 }
}
```

You can see that the OnCollisionEnter gets a Collision argument with information including what game object collided with it. We will ignore this here but you might explore it more: https://docs.unity3d.com/ScriptReference/Collision.html.

Save the script. Now, back in Unity:

1. Select a particle system prefab from **Project** Assets, such as Assets/Standard Assets/ParticleSystems/Prefabs/Explosion (this is the one we used to kill Ethan in Chapter 4, *Gaze-Based Control*)
2. Drag the **effects** prefab onto the Poppable's Pop Effect slot
3. Save these changes back to the prefab by pressing **Apply**
4. You can now delete the **Balloon** from the **Hierarchy**

Alright, let's try it. Press **Play**. Create a balloon. Then, reach out and push the button again so a new balloon collides with that one. Does it explode? Yikes!

Interactable items

Directly interacting with objects in VR, such as grabbing items and using them to perform other actions, is a bit more complex. And, it can be tricky to get right. So it doesn't make sense, especially in this book, to grow our own interaction system. Unfortunately, there is not a single standard toolkit either. But, there are more than a few very good toolkits you can use, albeit most are specific to individual target platforms.

Generally, the architecture is similar among these solutions:

- Provides prefabs for the player camera rig
- Camera rig includes objects for your hands, including input controller components
- Hand objects include components that trigger events when interactions occur
- An interactable component is added to any objects in the scene that can be interacted with using input events
- Additional components and options extend the interactable behaviors

Toolkits will include a number of demo scenes which provide rich examples how to use the particular toolkit. Often, it is more informative to study the demos to see how to use the toolkits than the actual documentation.

In this section, we introduce a grabbing and throwing mechanic using two toolkits, the *SteamVR InteractionSystem* and the *Daydream VR Elements*. The technique is similar for other platforms.

 For Oculus SDK (without OpenVR), you will need to integrate the Oculus Avatar SDK. Also, here's a quick video showing how to add an OVR Grabber component to your OVRCameraRig controllers: https://www. youtube.com/watch?v=sxvKGVDmYfY.

Interactables using SteamVR Interaction System

The SteamVR Unity package includes an Interaction System, originally developed and used for minigames and scenes from Steam's impressive demo VR application, *The Lab* (http:// store.steampowered.com/app/450390/The_Lab/). It can be found in the Assets/SteamVR/InteractionSystem/ folder. We recommend you explore the example scenes, prefabs, and scripts.

The Interaction System includes its own **Player** camera rig which replaces the default **[CameraRig]** we have been using. The Player hierarchy is shown here:

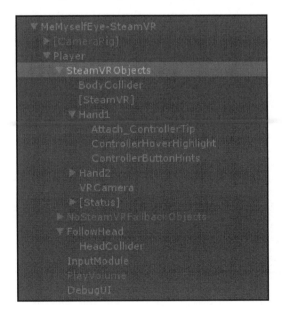

It includes a *VRCamera*, two hands (*Hand1* and *Hand2*), and other useful objects. Each hand includes an attach point (*Attach_ControllerTip*), a hover highlight (*ControllerHoverHighlight*), and a tooltips object (*ControllerButtonHints*).

1. Locate the **Player** prefab in `SteamVR/InteractionSystem/Core/Prefabs` and drag it as a child of **MyMyselfEye** in your scene **Hierarchy**
2. Delete or disable the **[CameraRig]** object

For compatibility with the current scene, we also need to update the **NewBalloon** argument in **Button Down Event**:

1. Unfold the **Player** object in **Hierarchy** so you can see the **Hand1** and **Hand2** objects
2. Select the **MeMyselfEye** in **Hierarchy**
3. Drag **Hand2** (or **Hand1**) from **Hierarchy** onto the **GameObject** argument slot in the **Button Down Event** on the **My Input Controller** component

Next, for interactable objects there is a large collection of components available. Review the `SteamVR/InteractionSystem/Core/Scripts` folder contents. We will use the *Throwable* one.

First, lets try this on a basic Cube. Then, we'll make the balloons grabbable and throwable too:

1. In Hierarchy, create a cube (**Create | 3D Object | Cube**).
2. Scale and position it within reaching distance of the Player. For example, **Scale** (0.3, 0.3, 0.3) and **Position** (-0.25, 1.3, -0.25) may work.
3. With the Cube selected, **Add Component** `Throwable` from the Interaction System.
4. Notice this will automatically add other required components, including the base Interactable and a RigidBody.
5. On the **RigidBody** component, uncheck the **Use Gravity** checkbox, so it hangs in the air rather than falling to the ground when you play.

Now when you press **Play**, reach out to the Cube so your controller penetrates (collides) it. Then, using the Trigger on your controller, grab the Cube and throw it *outta here*!

To make the balloons throwable, we modify the prefab:

1. Drag a copy of the **Balloon** prefab from the **Project** window into the scene **Hierarchy**
2. **Add Component** the Steam **Throwable**
3. Press **Apply** to save the prefab
4. And delete the Balloon from the Hierarchy

Press **Play**. Press the **Fire1** button to create and inflate a balloon. Release it. Then, grab it with the trigger. Throw the balloon. If you implemented the *Poppable* explosion earlier, it'll even explode like a projectile when it hits something, like the ground or the photo plane!

Interactables using Daydream VR Elements

The base GoogleVR package does not include interactables, but you can find them in the Daydream Elements package. This package is a collection of demo scenes, components, and prefabs for using Daydream VR from the engineers at Google. To get the package:

1. Visit the Daydream Elements' Github Releases page at `https://github.com/googlevr/daydream-elements/releases`
2. Download `DaydreamElements.unitypackage`
3. Import it into your project using **Assets** | **Import Package** | **Custom Package...**

The package includes a prefab named `ObjectManipulationPointer` which is a drop-in replacement for the `GvrControllerPointer` we have been using:

1. In **Hierarchy**, unfold your **MeMyselfEye** and drill down to the **Player** object
2. Select **GvrControllerPointer** and disable it in Inspector
3. In the **Project** window, navigate to the `Assets/DaydreamElements/Elements/ObjectManipulationDemo/Prefabs/UI/` folder
4. Drag the **ObjectManipulationPointer** prefab into **Hierarchy** as a sibling of **GvrControllerPointer**

For compatibility with the current scene, we also need to update the **NewBalloon** argument in **Button Down Event**:

1. Select the **MeMyselfEye** in **Hierarchy**
2. Drag **ObjectManipulationPointer** from **Hierarchy** onto the **GameObject** argument slot in the **Button Down Event** on the **My Input Controller** component

Next, for interactable objects we add a `MoveablePhysicsObject` component, found in `Assets/DaydreamElements/Elements/ObjectManipulationDemo/Scripts/`.

 Additional information on Daydream Elements object manipulation can be found at `https://developers.google.com/vr/elements/object-manipulation`.

First, let's try this on a basic Cube. Then, we'll make the balloons grabbable and throwable too:

1. In **Hierarchy**, create a cube (**Create | 3D Object | Cube**).
2. Scale and position it within reaching distance of the Player. For example, **Scale** (0.25, 0.25, 0.25) and **Position** (-0.4, 0.75, -0.3) may work.
3. With the Cube selected, **Add Component** `MoveablePhysicsObject`.
4. Notice this will automatically add a `RigidBody` component if not present.
5. On the `RigidBody` component, uncheck the **Use Gravity** checkbox, so it hangs in the air rather than falling to the ground when you play.

Now when you press **Play**, use your controller so its laser beam hits the cube. Then, press the clicker button on your controller to grab it. Move it around and press again to release it.

Since the app is presently using the same button to create new balloons and manipulate the laser pointer, we get a balloon each time we use the button. Consider that a bug in your application. We will leave this as an exercise for you to implement the logic, for example, to tell *MyInputController* to not invoke events if the *MoveablePhysicsObject* is busy moving something.

 Hint: you could add a script component to Cube that checks the MoveablePhysicsObject state and disables MyInputController actions when the object is Selected. This is not well documented but look at the source code for MoveablePhysicsObjects.cs and its base class, BaseInteractiveObjects.cs.

To make the balloons throwable, we modify the prefab:

1. Drag a copy of the **Balloon** prefab from the **Project** window into the scene **Hierarchy**
2. **Add Component** the **MoveablePhysicsObject**
3. Click **Apply** to save the prefab
4. And delete the Balloon from Hierarchy

Press **Play**. Press the button to create and inflate a balloon. Release it. Then, try to grab it with the laser pointer. If you implemented the *Poppable* explosion earlier, it'll even explode like a projectile when it hits something!

Summary

In this chapter, we explored a variety of software patterns for handling user input for your VR projects. The player uses a controller button to create, inflate, and release balloons into the scene. First, we tried the standard Input class for detecting logical button clicks, like the "Fire1" button, and then learned how to access device-specific SDK input, such as the OpenVR trigger button with haptic feedback.

In our scene, we implemented a simple input component for polling the button actions. Then, we refactored the code to use scriptable objects to hold the input action data. In the third implementation, we used Unity Events to message input actions to listening components. We also enhanced the scene to attach the balloon to your virtual hand position, and added the ability to pop the balloons as explosive projectiles! Lastly, we used an interactable framework (for SteamVR and Daydream) to implement grabbing and throwing mechanics, using components provided in given toolkits rather than attempting to write our own.

In the next chapter, we will further explore user interactions, using the Unity UI (user interface) system for implementing information canvases, buttons, and other UI controls.

World Space UI 6

In the previous chapter, we discovered how to interact with game objects in the world space scene. Not only can these objects can be balls and toys, or tools and weapons, but they can be buttons you interact with and other user interface widgets. Furthermore, Unity includes a user interface canvas system for building menus and other UI.

Graphical user interface (GUI) or just UI, usually refers to on-screen two-dimensional graphics, which overlay the main gameplay and present information to the user with status messages, gauges, and input controls such as menus, buttons, sliders, and so on.

In Unity, UI elements always reside on a **canvas**. The Unity manual describes the `canvas` component as follows:

> *The* `canvas` *component represents the abstract space in which the UI is laid out and rendered. All UI elements must be children of a* `GameObject` *that has a* `canvas` *component attached.*

In conventional video games, UI objects are usually rendered in a **screen space** canvas as an overlay. The screen space UI is analogous to a piece of cardboard pasted on your TV or monitor, overlaying the game action behind it.

However, that doesn't work in VR. If you attempt to use screen space for UI in virtual reality, you'll run into issues. Since there are two stereographic cameras, you need separate views for each eye. While conventional games may co-opt the edges of the screen for UI, *virtual reality has no screen edges*!

Instead, in VR, we use various approaches that place the user interface elements in **World Space** rather than screen space. In this chapter, I characterize a number of these types. We'll define these types in detail and show you examples of them throughout this chapter:

- **Visor heads-up display**: In a visor **heads-up display (HUD)**, the user interface canvas appears at the same spot in front of your eyes regardless of your head movement

- **Reticle cursors**: Similar to visor HUD, a crosshair or a pointer cursor is used to choose things in the scene
- **Windshield HUD**: This is a pop-up panel floating in 3D space like a windshield in a cockpit
- **Game element UI**: The canvas is in the scene as a part of the gameplay, like a scoreboard in a stadium
- **Info bubble**: This is a UI message that is attached to objects in the scene, like a thought bubble hovering over a character's head
- **In-game dashboard**: This is a control panel that is a part of the gameplay, usually at waist or desk height
- **Wrist-based menu palette**: With two-handed input controllers, one hand can hold a menu palette while the other makes selections and uses the selected tool

The differences in these UI techniques basically comes down to where and when you display the canvas and how the user interacts with it. In this chapter, we're going to try each of these in turn. Along the way, we'll also continue to explore user input with head movement and gestures as well as button clicks.

 Note that some of the exercises in this chapter use the scene completed in Chapter 4, *Gaze-Based Control*, but are separate and not directly required by the other chapters in this book. If you decide to skip any of it or not save your work, that's OK.

Studying VR design principles

Before we get into the implementation details, I would like to introduce the topic of designing 3D user interfaces and VR experiences. A lot of work has been done over the past few decades, and more so in the past few years.

With consumer VR devices so readily available, and powerful development tools like Unity, it's not surprising there are many people inventing and trying new things, innovating continuously, and producing really excellent VR experiences. You are probably one of them. But the context of today's VR is not a vacuum. There is a history of research and development that feeds into present-day work. The book *3D User Interfaces: Theory and Practice* (Bowman et al), for example, is a classic academic survey of 3D user interaction for consumer, industrial, and scientific applications and research. Originally published in 2004, the second edition was published in 2017 (LaViola et al) and is an up-to-date review of academic theory and practical principles.

Current writings for VR design are more accessible. An easy to read but practical introduction to VR user experience design is the Medium article *Get started with VR: user experience design* (`https://medium.com/vrinflux-dot-com/get-started-with-vr-user-experience-design-974486cf9d18`) by Adrienne Hunter, co-creator of the popular VR physics package, NewtonVR. She identifies some important core principles, including It's like theatre in the round, drawing attention with to objects, lighting, and audio cues, and designing space for height and accessibility.

Another great article is *Practical VR: A Design Cheat Sheet* (`https://virtualrealitypop.com/practical-vr-ce80427e8e9d`). This is intended to be a living primer with VR design guidelines, process, tools and other resources the author intends to maintain and update.

One of my favorite studies of design for VR is the *VR Interface Design Pre-Visualization Methods* produced by Mike Algers as a grad student in 2015. His inspiring video at `https://vimeo.com/141330081` presents an easily digestible thesis of design principles, especially for seated VR experiences, based on established ergonomics of workspaces and visual perception. We'll use some of these ideas in this chapter. Algers also explores button design for VR, mockup workflows, and concepts for VR operating system design. (Algers presently works in the Google VR development group.)

In his thesis, Algers establishes a set of comfort zones radially around the user's first-person location, as shown:

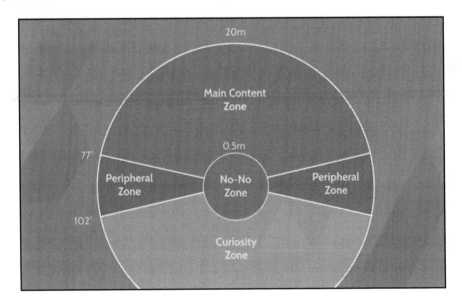

Anything closer than **0.5 m** is too close for comfort; you might have to cross your eyes just to focus and follow objects at that range. Beyond **20 m** is too far way to have meaningful interactions, and is also too far for depth perception with parallax. Your **Peripheral Zones** (77–102 degrees) should not contain primary content and interactions but can have secondary ones. Behind you he calls the **Curiosity Zone**, you'd need to stretch (or swivel your chair or turn around) to see what's going on there so it'd better be important yet not imperative. The **Main Content Zone** is your normal workspace. Then, accounting for arm reach (forward, up, and down) and other normal human movement in a workspace, Algers defines the optimal virtual work zone for seated VR experience as shown:

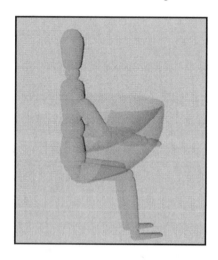

For standing and room-scale VR, the workspace is different. When standing, it may be much easier (and expected) to be able to turn around to access things all around you. With room-scale, you can walk around (and jump, duck, and crawl, for that matter). Alex Schwartz and Devin Reimer of Owlchemy Labs (since acquired by Google), in their talk at Oculus Connect 2 (`https://www.youtube.com/watch?v=hjc7AJwZ4DI`), discuss the challenges of designing standing VR experiences for their popular Job Simulator, including accommodation for real-world ergonomics and varied height experiences.

Some other great resources on designing for virtual reality include:

- Oculus's series of articles on VR design best practices, including on user input (`https://developer.oculus.com/design/latest/concepts/bp-userinput/`) which includes recommendations on movement, button mapping, menus, and using your hands in VR.

- Leap Motion (we do not cover its hand-recognition technology in this book) has some great writings on VR design, which can be found at `https://developer.leapmotion.com/explorations`, including very good articles on interactive design (`http://blog.leapmotion.com/building-blocks-deep-dive-leap-motion-interactive-design/`) and user Interface Design (`http://blog.leapmotion.com/beyond-flatland-user-interface-design-vr/`).
- Google has produced a number of seminal examples, including *Daydream Labs: Lessons Learned from VR Prototyping - Google I/O 2016* (`https://www.youtube.com/watch?v=lGUmTQgbiAY`) and Daydream Elements (`https://developers.google.com/vr/elements/overview`).

Of course, this just scratches the surface; more is being published every day. Google it. A curated, living list of resources on user Interface Design and user experience in virtual reality can be found at The UX of VR site (`https://www.uxofvr.com/`).

Have fun reading and watching videos. Meanwhile, let's get back to work. It's time to implement some VR UI ourselves.

A reusable default canvas

Unity's UI canvas provides lots of options and parameters to accommodate the kinds of graphical layout flexibility that we have come to expect not only in games but also from a web and mobile apps. With this flexibility comes additional complexity. To make our examples in this chapter easier, we'll first build a reusable prefab canvas that has our preferred default settings.

Create a new canvas and change its **Render Mode** to **world space** as follows:

1. Navigate to **GameObject | UI | Canvas**
2. Rename the canvas as `DefaultCanvas`
3. Set **Render Mode** to **World Space**

The **Rect Transform** component defines the grid system on the canvas itself, like the lines on a piece of graph paper. It is used for the placement of UI elements on the canvas. Set it to a convenient `640 x 480`, with a `0.75` aspect ratio. The `Rect Transform` component's width and height are different from the world space size of the canvas in our scene. Let's configure the `Rect Transform` component using the following steps:

1. In `Rect Transform`, set the **Width** to `640` and the **Height** to `480`.

2. In **Scale**, set **X**, **Y**, **Z** to (0.00135, 0.00135, 0.00135). This is the size for one of our pixels in world space units.

3. Now, position the canvas centered on the ground plane one unit above (0.325 is half of 0.75). In **Rect Transform**, set **Pos X**, **Pos Y**, **Pos Z** to (0, 1.325, 0).

Next, we will add an empty Image element (with a white background) to help us visualize the otherwise transparent canvas and provide an opaque background for the canvas when we need one (we can also use a Panel UI element):

1. With DefaultCanvas selected, navigate to **GameObject** | **UI** | **Image** (ensure that it's created as a child of DefaultCanvas; if not, move it under DefaultCanvas).

2. With the **Image** selected, on the upper left of its **Rect Transform** pane, there is an **anchor presets** button (shown in the following screenshot). Selecting it opens the **anchor presets** dialog box. Press and hold the *Alt* key to see the **stretch** and **position** options and choose the one in the bottom-right corner (**stretch-stretch**). Now, the (blank) image is stretched to fill the canvas:

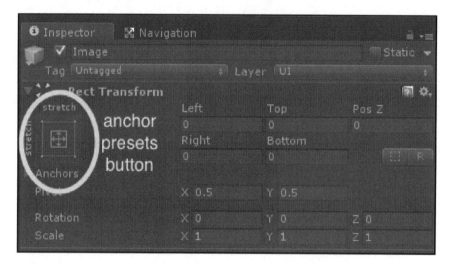

3. Double-check your **Image** settings based on the default properties for the `Image` child of the `DefaultCanvas` as shown in the following screenshot:

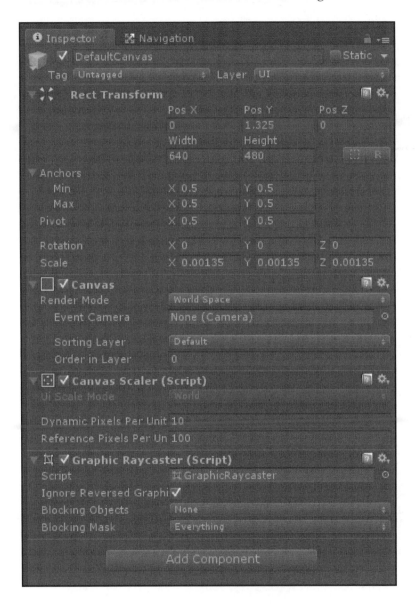

Add a `Text` element with useful default settings, as follows:

1. With `DefaultCanvas` selected, navigate to **GameObject | UI | Text** (ensure that it's created as a child of `DefaultCanvas` (if not, move it under `DefaultCanvas`). The words `New Text` should appear on the canvas.
2. With the **Text** selected, set **Alignment** to **Center Align** and **Middle Align** and set **Vertical Overflow** to **Overflow**. Set the **Scale** to (4, 4, 4).
3. Set its **anchor presets** button to (**stretch - stretch**) using the widget on the upper left of its **Rect Transform** pane.
4. Double-check your **Text** settings based on the default properties for the `Text` child of the `DefaultCanvas` as shown in the following screenshot:

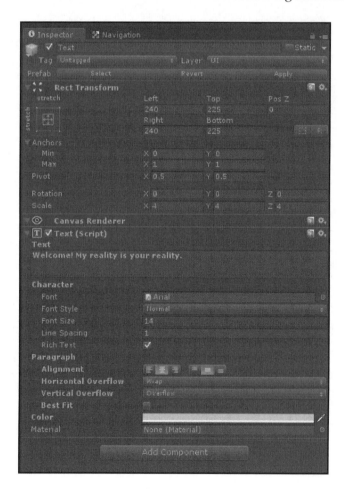

Increase the pixel resolution to give cleaner text fonts by keeping DefaultCanvas selected and setting the **Canvas Scaler | Dynamic Pixels Per Unit** to 10.

Finally, save your work as a prefab asset that you can reuse throughout the chapter in the following manner:

1. If necessary, in **Project Assets**, create a new folder named Prefabs.
2. Drag the DefaultCanvas object into the Project Assets/Prefabs folder to create a prefab.
3. Delete the DefaultCanvas instance in the **Hierarchy** panel now.

OK, glad we got that out of the way! Now we can use the DefaultCanvas prefab with different VR user interfaces.

 A canvas has a Rect Transform component, which defines the grid system on the canvas itself, like the lines on a piece of graph paper. It is used for the placement of UI elements on the canvas. This is different from the size and position of a canvas object in world space.

Visor HUD

A heads-up display, or HUD, is a floating canvas in your field of view that overlays the gameplay scene. In VR vernacular, there are two variations of HUDs. I'll call these variations the *visor HUD* and the *windshield HUD*. This section looks at the first one.

In visor HUD, the UI canvas is attached to the camera. It doesn't appear to respond to your head movement. When you move your head, it appears to be *stuck to your face*. Let's look at a nicer way of visualizing it. Suppose you're wearing a helmet with a visor, and the UI appears projected onto the surface of that visor. There may be contexts where this is OK in virtual reality, but it is likely to break the sense of immersion. So, it should generally only be used either when the visor is a part of the gameplay, or if the intent is to take you out of the scene, such as the utility menus for the hardware or the system.

Let's make a visor HUD with a welcome message as follows, and see for ourselves how it feels:

1. In the **Hierarchy** panel, unfold the MeMyselfEye object and then drill down to the Main Camera object (for OpenVR that might be [CameraRig]/Camera (head); for Daydream, it may be Player/Main Camera/).

2. From the **Project** panel, drag the `DefaultCanvas` prefab onto the camera object so that it becomes a child of it.

3. In the **Hierarchy** panel, with the canvas selected, rename the canvas to `VisorCanvas`.

4. In the **Inspector** panel for the canvas, change the `Rect Transform` component's **Pos X**, **Pos Y**, **Pos Z** to (0, 0, 1).

5. Unfold `VisorCanvas` and select the child `Text` object.

6. In the **Inspector** panel, change the text from **Default Text** to **Welcome! My reality is your reality**. (You can enter line breaks in the input text area.)

7. Change the text color to something bright, such as green.

8. Disable the `Image` object so that only the text shows by unchecking its **Enable** checkbox in **Inspector**.

9. Save the scene, and try it in VR.

Here's a capture of the Rift screen with the `VisorCanvas`:

In VR, when you move your head around, the text follows along as if it's attached to a visor in front of your face.

> A visor HUD canvas and reticle cursor canvas are set as a child object of the camera.

Now, go ahead and either disable `VisorCanvas` or just delete it (in the **Hierarchy** panel, right-click on it and click on **Delete**) because we're going to display the welcome message in a different way in a later section. Next, we'll look at a different application of this technique.

The reticle cursor

A variant of the visor HUD that is essential in first-person shooter games is a *reticle* or crosshair cursor. The analogy here is that you're looking through a gun-sight or an eyepiece (rather than a visor) and your head movement is moving in unison with the gun or turret itself. You can do this with a regular game object (for example, Quad + texture image), but this chapter is about UI. So, let's use our canvas, as follows:

1. Find your **Main Camera** object in the **Hierarchy** panel as we did previously.
2. From the **Project** panel, drag the `DefaultCanvas` prefab onto the camera object so that it becomes a child of the camera. Name it `ReticleCursor`.
3. Set the **Rect Transform** component's **Pos X**, **Pos Y**, **Pos Z** to (0, 0, 1).
4. Delete its child objects: `Image` and `Text`. This will *break* the prefab association; that's OK.
5. Add a raw image child by selecting it from the main menu bar, navigating through **GameObject | UI | Raw Image** and making sure that it's a child of `ReticleCursor`.
6. In the **Raw Image** panel's **Rect Transform**, set **Pos X**, **Pos Y**, **Pos Z** to (0, 0, 0) and the **Width** and **Height** to (22, 22). Then, choose a noticeable **Color** such as red in the **Raw Image (Script)** properties.
7. Save the scene and try it in VR.

If you'd like a nicer-looking reticle, in the **Raw Image (Script)** properties, populate the **Texture** field with a cursor image. For example, click on the tiny *circle* icon on the far right of the **Texture** field. This opens the **Select Texture** dialog. Find and select a suitable one, such as the `Crosshair` image. (A copy of `Crosshair.gif` is included with this book.) Just be sure to change the **Width** and **Height** to the size of your image (`Crosshair.gif` is 22 x 22 in size) and ensure that the **Anchor** is set to **middle-center**.

We set the canvas position **Pos Z** to `1.0` so that the reticle floats in front of you at a 1-meter distance. A fixed distance cursor is fine in many UI situations, like when you're picking something from a flat canvas that is also at a fixed distance from you.

However, this is world space. If another object is between you and the reticle, the reticle will be obfuscated.

Also, if you look at something much farther away, you'll refocus your eyes and have trouble viewing the cursor at the same time. To emphasize this problem, try moving the cursor closer. For example, if you change the **Pos Z** of the `ReticleCursor` to `0.5` or less, you might have to go cross-eyed to see it! To compensate for these issues, we can ray cast and move the cursor to the actual distance of the object that you're looking at, resizing the cursor accordingly so that it appears to stay the same size. Here's a cheap version of this idea:

1. With `ReticleCursor` selected, click on **Add Component** | **New Script**, name it `CursorPositioner` and click on **Create** and **Add**.
2. Open the script in MonoDevelop by double-clicking on the name.

Here's the `CursorPositioner.cs` script:

```
using UnityEngine;
using UnityEngine.EventSystems;
using System.Collections;

public class CursorPositioner : MonoBehaviour {
  private float defaultPosZ;

  void Start () {
    defaultPosZ = transform.localPosition.z;
  }

  void Update () {
    Transform camera = Camera.main.transform;
    Ray ray = new Ray (camera.position, camera.rotation *
      Vector3.forward);
    RaycastHit hit;
    if (Physics.Raycast (ray, out hit)) {
```

```
    if (hit.distance <= defaultPosZ) {
      transform.localPosition = new Vector3(0, 0, hit.distance);
    } else {
      transform.localPosition = new Vector3(0, 0, defaultPosZ);
    }
  }
 }
}
```

The **Rect Transform** component's **Pos Z** is found in the script in
`transform.localPosition`. This script changes it to `hit.distance` if it's less than the
given **Pos Z**. Now, you can also move the reticle to a more comfortable distance, such as
Pos Z = 2.

An excellent tutorial by `@eVRydayVR` shows how to implement both
distance and size compensated world space reticles. You can visit `https:/`
`/www.youtube.com/watch?v=LLKYbwNnKDg`, which is a video titled *Oculus
Rift DK2 - Unity Tutorial: Reticle.*

We just implemented our own cursor reticle, but many VR SDKs now also provide cursors.
For example, in Google VR, the `GvrReticlePointer.cs` script is a more thorough
implementation. Another example, the Oculus OVR package, includes a `Cursor_Timer`
prefab you can use as a Loading... indicator cursor.

The windshield HUD

The term *heads-up display*, or HUD, originates from its use in aircrafts, where a pilot is able
to view information with their head positioned in such a way that they are looking forward
rather down at their instrument panels. Owing to this usage, I'll refer it as *windshield HUD*.
Like visor HUD, the information panel overlays the gameplay, but it isn't attached to your
head. Instead, you can think of it as being attached to your seat while you are in a cockpit
or at the dentist.

A visor HUD is like the UI canvas—it is attached to your head. A
windshield HUD is like it's attached to a glass dome around you.

Let's create a simple windshield HUD by performing the following steps:

1. From the **Project** panel, drag the `DefaultCanvas` prefab onto the `MeMyselfEye` object in the **Hierarchy** panel so that it becomes an immediate child of `MeMyselfEye` (not under the camera this time).
2. Rename it to `WindshieldCanvas`.
3. With `WindshieldCanvas` selected, set the **Rect Transform** component's **Pos X**, **Pos Y**, **Pos Z** to (0, 1.4, 1).
4. Now, we'll set the **Text** component. With **Text** under `WindshieldCanvas` selected, change the text to **Welcome! My reality is your reality**. Also, change the color to something bright, such as green.
5. This time, we'll make the panel translucent. Select the image from **Image** under `WindshieldCanvas` and select its color swatch. Then in the **Color** dialog, modify the `Alpha ("A")` channel from 255 to about 115.

That's pretty straightforward. When you view it in VR, the canvas starts out just in front of you, but as you look around, its position seems to remain stationary and relative to the other objects in the scene, as shown in the following screenshot:

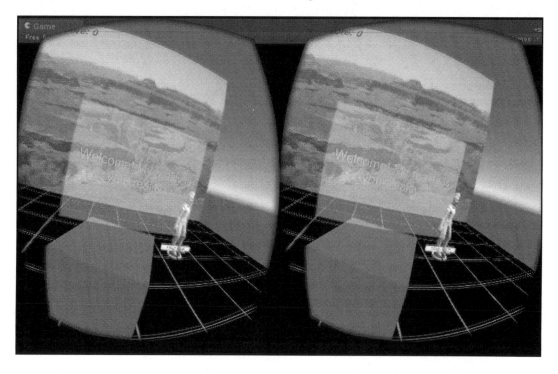

As we'll see in the next chapter, `Chapter 7`, *Locomotion and Comfort*, when a first-person character moves through the scene, the HUD canvas will stay in front of you, at the same relative position to your body object, `MeMyselfEye`. You can try it now in the editor:

1. Select `MeMyselfEye` in **Hierarchy**.

2. Press **Play**.

3. Then in the **Scene** window, using the **Move gizmo**, move the `MeMyselfEye` position. In VR, you'll see the HUD follows along like it's part of your body or a spaceship's cockpit.

> You might have realized that it's possible for objects in the scene to obfuscate the HUD panel since they're all occupying the same world space. If you need to prevent this, you have to ensure that the canvas is always rendered last so that it appears in front of any other objects regardless of its position in 3D space. In a conventional monoscopic game, you can do this by adding a second camera for the UI and changing its render priority. In stereoscopic VR, you have to accomplish this differently, possibly by writing a custom shader for your UI object or doing per-layer occlusion culling. This is an advanced topic; see the *World Space canvas on top of everything?* discussion thread for details: `https://answers.unity.com/questions/878667/world-space-canvas-on-top-of-everything.html`.

A variant of this HUD is to turn the canvas so that it's always facing you, while its position in 3D space is fixed. See the *Info bubble* section of this chapter to learn how to code this.

For kicks, let's write a script that removes the welcome message canvas after 15 seconds, as follows:

1. With `WindshieldCanvas` selected, click on **Add Component | New Script**, name the script as `DestroyTimeout`, and click on **Create** and **Add**.
2. Open the script in MonoDevelop.

Here's the `DestroyTimeout.cs` script:

```
using UnityEngine;

public class DestroyTimeout : MonoBehaviour
{
    public float timer = 15f;

    void Start ()
```

```
    {
      Destroy (gameObject, timer);
    }
  }
```

The `WindshieldCanvas` will disappear after the timer runs out when the game starts up.

> A windshield HUD canvas is set as a child object of the first-person avatar, a sibling object of the camera.

In this example, we start to move further towards a first-person experience. Imagine sitting in a car or the cockpit of an aircraft. The HUD is projected on the windshield in front of you, but you're free to move your head to look around. In the scene's **Hierarchy** panel, there's a first-person object (`MeMyselfEye`) that contains the camera rig, possibly your avatar body, and the other furnishings surrounding you. When the vehicle moves in the game, the entire cockpit moves in unison, including the camera rig and the windshield.

The game element UI

When Ethan gets killed in the Diorama scene from Chapter 4, *Gaze-Based Control*, the score value in the `GameController` object's `KillTarget` script is updated, but we don't show the current score to the player (set up in that chapter). We'll do this now, adding a scoreboard into the scene at the top-left corner of the backdrop `PhotoPlane` image:

1. From the **Project** panel, drag the `DefaultCanvas` prefab directly into the **Scene** view
2. Rename it `ScoreBoard`
3. With `ScoreBoard` selected, set the **Rect Transform** component's **Pos X, Pos Y, Pos Z** to (-2.8, 7, 4.9) and the **Width** and **Height** to (3000, 480)
4. With **Text** under `ScoreBoard` selected, set the **Font Size** to 100 and choose a noticeable color such as red for the **Text**
5. Enter the **Score: 0** sample string for **Text**
6. Disable **Image** under `ScoreBoard` by unchecking the **Enable** check box or deleting it

We have added another canvas to the scene, sized and placed it where we want, and formatted the text for display. It should look like this:

Now, we need to update the KillTarget.cs script, as follows:

- We may be using the UnityEngine UI classes:

    ```
    using UnityEngine.UI;
    ```

- Add a public variable for scoreText:

    ```
    public Text scoreText;
    ```

- Add a line to Start() to initialize the score text:

    ```
    scoreText.text = "Score: 0";
    ```

- And add a line to Update() to change the score text when the score changes:

    ```
    score += 1;
    scoreText.text = "Score: " + score;
    ```

After saving the script file, go back into the Unity editor, select GameController in the **Hierarchy** panel, and then drag and drop the **Text** object under ScoreBoard from **Hierarchy** onto the **Score Text** field in **Kill Target (Script)**.

Run the scene in VR. Each time you kill Ethan (by staring at him), your score will be updated on the ScoreBoard on the upper left of PhotoPlane.

A game element UI canvas is a part of the scene like any other game object.

This was an example of using an object that's a part of the scene for information display. Our example is pretty simplistic. You might want to make a nicer modeled scoreboard, like the one you'd see in a stadium or something. The point is, it's a part of the scene and to see the message you might have to actually turn your head and, well, look at it.

Using TextMeshPro

To make a billboard glow like a neon sign, you can use TextMesh Pro which presently comes included free with Unity. For instance:

1. With `ScoreBoard` selected in Hierarchy, create a new `TextMesh` text element (right-click **UI | TextMeshPro - Text**).
2. This replaces our standard UI text element, so disable the `Text` object.
3. On the TMP text, set its **Font Asset** to **Bangers SDF**.
4. For its **Material Preset**, use **Bangers SDF Glow**.
5. Scroll to **Glow** settings to adjust the colors and other settings as you desire.

You can even write a script that cyclically modifies the glow settings to make a flashing, glowing sign!

If you choose to try this, be sure to update the GameController's `KillTarget` script to use the TMP object rather than the UI one. Modify `KillTarget.cs` as follows:

We may be using the UnityEngine TextMesh Pro classes:

```
using TMP;
```

Replace the data type of the `scoreText` variable with `TMP_Text`:

```
public TMP_Text scoreText;
```

Drag the TMP text item onto the slot in the Inspector. The rest of the script is unchanged since `TMP_Text` has a `text` property just as the UI text one has.

TextMesh Pro is a great tool for text formatting and layout in Unity. It is a replacement for Unity's UI Text, with added advanced text rendering, custom shaders, typographic controls such as paragraph spacing and kerning, and a lot more. It was a third-party plugin and is now included free with Unity. Documentation can be found here: `http://digitalnativestudios.com/textmeshpro/docs/`.

Here is a screenshot of the scoreboard text using a glow effect with TextMesh Pro and its Inspector settings:

Info bubble

In a comic book, when a character says something, it's shown in a *speech bubble*. In many online social VR worlds, participants are represented by avatars and, hovering above someone's avatar, their name is displayed. I'll call this type of user interface an *info bubble*.

Info bubbles are located in world space at a specific 3D position, but the canvas should always be facing the camera. We can ensure this with a script.

In this example, we'll display the **X**, **Z** location of the `WalkTarget` object (set up in Chapter 4, *Gaze-Based Control*), controlled by the `LookMoveTo.cs` script. To add the info bubble, perform the following steps:

1. From the **Project** window, drag the `DefaultCanvas` prefab directly into the **Hierarchy** window so that it's a child of `WalkTarget`.
2. Rename it to `InfoBubble`.
3. With `InfoBubble` selected, set the **Rect Transform** component's **Pos X**, **Pos Y**, **Pos Z** to (0, 0.2, 0).
4. With **Text** under `InfoBubble` selected, set the **Rect Transform** component's **Pos X**, **Pos Y**, **Pos Z** to (0, 0, 0) and **Right** and **Bottom** to 0, 0.
5. With **Image** under `InfoBubble` selected, set **Scale** to (0.7, 0.2, 1).
6. Enter the X:00.00, Z:00.00 sample string for **Text**.

Verify that the canvas and text look roughly the right size and position and adjust the text as you please. (In my scene, there's a cube at the origin so I temporarily disable it to see the WalkTarget also at the origin.)

Now, we will modify the `LookMoveTo.cs` script to show the current `WalkTarget` **X**, **Z** position. Open the script in the MonoDevelop editor and add the following code:

```
using UnityEngine;
using UnityEngine.UI;

public class LookMoveTo : MonoBehaviour
{
  public GameObject ground;
  public Transform infoBubble;

  private Text infoText;

  void Start ()
  {
    if (infoBubble != null)
    {
      infoText = infoBubble.Find ("Text").GetComponent<Text> ();
    }
  }

  void Update ()
  {
    Transform camera = Camera.main.transform;
    Ray ray;
    RaycastHit[] hits;
```

```
GameObject hitObject;

ray = new Ray (camera.position, camera.rotation * Vector3.forward);
hits = Physics.RaycastAll (ray);
for (int i=0; i < hits.Length; i++)
{
  RaycastHit hit = hits [i];
  hitObject = hit.collider.gameObject;
  if (hitObject == ground)
  {
    if (infoBubble != null)
    {
      infoText.text = "X: " + hit.point.x.ToString("F2") +
                      "Z: " + hit.point.z.ToString("F2");

      infoBubble.LookAt(camera.position);
      infoBubble.Rotate (0, 180f, 0);
    }
    transform.position = hit.point;
  }
}
```

The line `using UnityEngine.UI;` states that this script will need access to the Unity UI API. We defined a `public Transform infoBubble` variable, which will be set to the `WalkTarget/InfoBubble` object. We also defined a `private Text infoText` variable, which gets set to the `InfoBubble` object's **Text** object. The script assumes that the given `InfoBubble` has a child **Text** UI object.

Unfortunately, the overuse of the word *text* can be confusing. The `infoText` *text* object has a *text* component, which has a *text* string property! You can see what I mean in Unity editor. If you examine the Inspector panel while `InfoBubble/Text` is selected, you'll see that it contains a **Text (Script)** component, which has a **Text** field. This **Text** field is where we write our messages. So in `Setup()`, we find the `WalkTarget/InfoBubble/Text` object, assigning the **Text** object to `infoText`, and then in `Update()`, we set the string value of `infoText.text` so that the score is shown on the bubble canvas.

Also, in `Update()`, we transformed the `infoBubble` canvas so that it's always facing us using `infoBubble.LookAt()` and passing it the camera position. The result of `LookAt()` has the canvas facing away from us. So, we also need to rotate it around the *y* axis by 180 degrees.

Save the script and drag the `InfoBubble` object from **Hierarchy** onto the **Info Bubble** slot in the **Look Move To (Script)** component. If you don't assign the `InfoBubble` canvas, the script will still run because we test for `null` objects before we reference them.

 An info bubble UI canvas is attached to other game objects, moving when they move and always facing the camera (like a billboard).

Run the scene in VR and you'll see that `WalkTarget` has a little info bubble telling us about its **X**, **Z** position.

 Extra challenge: Want to try something else? Implement a health meter bar for Ethan. Use the `countDown` variable in the `KillTarget` script to determine his percentage of health and to display a health meter (horizontal bar) above his head when it's not at 100 percent.

Info bubbles are useful when you need to display UI messages that belong to specific objects in the scene and may move in concert with the objects.

An in-game dashboard with input events

An in-game dashboard or control panel is a UI display that is integrated into the game itself. A typical scenario is an automobile or a spaceship, where you are seated in a cockpit. At waist level (desk level) is a panel with a set of controls, gauges, information displays, and so on. Dashboards generally feel more natural in a seated VR experience.

A few pages back, we discussed windshield HUDs. Dashboards are pretty much the same thing. One difference is that the dashboard may be more obviously part of the level environment and not simply an auxiliary information display or a menu.

In fact, dashboards can be a very effective mechanism to control VR motion sickness. Researchers have found that when a VR user has a better sense of being grounded and has a consistent *horizon line* in view, he's much less likely to experience nausea while moving around a virtual space. In contrast, being a floating one-dimensional eyeball with no sense of self or grounding is asking for trouble! (See the *Oculus Best Practices* for this, and other great tips, by visiting
`https://developer.oculus.com/documentation/intro-vr/latest/concepts/bp_intro/`).

In this example, we'll make a simple dashboard with Start/Stop buttons. For now, the buttons will operate a water hose in the scene to help fend off the zombies. (*Why not?*) Like other examples in this chapter, this project uses the scene created in `Chapter 4`, *Gaze-Based Control*.

This project is a bit more complicated than you might expect. However, if you've ever had to build anything in Minecraft, you know that even the simple things may require assembling multiple parts. Here's what we will do:

- Create a dashboard canvas with two functional buttons—Start and Stop
- Add a water hose to the scene and wire it to the buttons
- Write a simple version of the script that activates the buttons
- Highlight a button by looking at it
- Improve the script to activate the button only if it's highlighted

So let's get to it.

Creating a dashboard with buttons

First, let's create a dashboard with a Start and a Stop button, as follows:

1. From the **Project** window, drag the `DefaultCanvas` prefab onto the `MeMyselfEye` object in the **Hierarchy** panel so that it becomes a child.
2. Rename it to `Dashboard`.
3. With `Dashboard` selected, set the **Rect Transform** component's **Pos X, Pos Y, Pos Z** to (0, 0.6, 0.6) and its **Rotation** to (60, 0, 0). Feel free to adjust the position for a preferred comfort zone and your specific VR device camera rig.
4. Disable or delete the **Text** child object of `Dashboard`.

This places the dashboard 1 m below your eyes and a little out in front.

For a *work-in-progress* look, if you'd like, I've included an image sketch of a vehicle dashboard that you can use, as follows:

1. Import the `DashboardSketch.png` file into your **Project** (such as the `Assets/Textures` folder).
2. Add a new **GameObject | UI | Raw Image** as a child of `Dashboard`.
3. Drag the `DashboardSketch` texture from the **Project** panel onto the **Texture** field of the **Raw Image** component.

4. Set its **Rect Transform** component's **Pos X, Pos Y, Pos Z** to (0,0,0), **Width** to 140, and **Height** to 105.

5. It should be **Anchored** at **middle-center** (0.5,0.5) in **X**, **Y**, and **Pivot**, with **Rotation** (0,0,0).

6. Set **Scale** to (4.5,4.5,4.5).

Next, we will add the Start and Stop buttons. They can go anywhere you'd like on the canvas, but the sketch has two nice spaces predefined for them:

1. Add a new **GameObject** | **UI** | **Button** as a new child of Dashboard. Name it StartButton.

2. Set its **Rect Transform** component's **X**, **Y**, **Z** to (−48, 117, 0), the **Width** and **Height** to (60, 60), and **Anchored** to **center-middle** (0.5). No **Rotation** and **Scale** of 1.

3. In the button's **Image (Script)** component pane, for **Source Image**, click on the tiny circle on the far right to open the **Select Sprite** picker and choose ButtonAcceleratorUpSprite (which you may have imported into the Assets/Standard Assets/CrossPlatformInput/Sprites folder).

4. In the button's **Button (Script)** component pane, for the **Normal Color**, I used RGB (89,154,43) and set **Highlighted Color** to (105, 255, 0).

5. Similarly, create another button named StopButton with the **Rect Transform** component's **X**, **Y**, **Z** (52, 118, 0) and set the **Width** and **Height** to (60, 60). For **Source Image**, select ButtonBrakeOverSprite, then choose the **Normal Color** (236, 141, 141) and **Highlighted Color** (235, 45, 0).

The result should look like this:

One last thing. If you're using the `ReticleCursor` that was created earlier in this chapter with the `CursorPositioner.cs` script, we want the dashboard itself to have a collider for the script. We can achieve this by performing the following steps:

1. With `Dashboard` selected, right-click for options, and navigate to **3D Object | Plane**.
2. Set its **Position** to (0,0,0), **Rotation** to (270,0,0), and **Scale** to (64,1,48).
3. Disable its **Mesh Renderer** (but leave its **Mesh Collider** enabled).

Now the dashboard has a plane child that isn't rendered, but its collider will be detected when `CursorPositioner` does its ray cast. We do this to see your gaze on this dashboard panel rather than the ground below even when not looking directly at a button.

Having a single toggle button with pressed and released states might be better than separate **Start** and **Stop** buttons. When you're done with this chapter, go ahead and figure out how to do it!

We just created a world space canvas that should appear in VR at waist or desk level. We decorated it with a dashboard sketch and added two UI buttons. Now, we'll wire up the buttons to specific events.

Linking the water hose to the buttons

Let's first give the buttons something to do, such as the action of turning on a water hose. If we aim it strategically, it might even fend off rogue zombies. Coincidentally, the Unity **Particle Systems** under **Standard Assets** which we imported earlier has a water hose that we can use. Add it to the scene as follows:

1. If you haven't done so already, import the **Particle Systems** standard asset from the main menu bar by navigating to **Assets | Import Package | ParticleSystems**.
2. In the **Project** window, find the `Assets/Standard Assets/Particle Systems/Prefabs/Hose` prefab and drag it into the **Hierarchy** window.
3. Set its **Transform** component's **X, Y, Z** to (-3, 0, 1.5) and **Rotation** to (340, 87, 0).
4. Ensure that **Hose** is enabled (check its **Enable** checkbox).
5. Unfold the **Hose** in **Hierarchy** so that you can see its child **WaterShower** particle system. Select it.
6. In **Inspector**, in the **Particle System** properties pane, look for **Play On Awake** and uncheck it.

Note that the **Hose** object in **Hierarchy** has a `WaterShower` child object. This is the actual particle system that we will control with the buttons. It should start as *off*.

The **Hose** prefab itself comes with mouse-driven script that we don't want to use, so disable it as follows:

1. With **Hose** selected, disable (uncheck) its **Hose (Script)**.
2. Also, disable (uncheck) the **Simple Mouse Rotator (Script)** component.

Now we will wire up `StartButton` to the **WaterShower** particle system by telling the buttons to listen for the `OnClick()` events, as follows:

1. Unfold the **Hose** in **Hierarchy** so that you can see its child **WaterShower** particle system.
2. In **Hierarchy**, select `StartButton` (under `MeMyselfEye/Dashboard`).
3. Note that in the **Inspector,** the **On Click()** pane of the `Button` component is empty. Click on the *Plus* (**+**) icon on the lower right of that pane to reveal a new field labeled **None (Object)**.
4. Drag the **WaterShower** particle system from **Hierarchy** onto the **None (Object)** field.
5. Its function selector, the default value, is **No Function**. Change it to **ParticleSystem | Play()**.

OK. The steps are similar for the `StopButton`, as follows:

1. In **Hierarchy**, select `StopButton`.
2. Click on the *Plus* (**+**) icon on the lower right of it's **On Click()** pane.
3. Drag the **WaterShower** from **Hierarchy** onto the **None (Object)** field.
4. Its function selector, the default value, is **No Function**. Change it to **ParticleSystem | Stop()**.

The Start and Stop buttons *listen for* `OnClick()` *events*, and when one comes, it will call the **WaterShower** particle system's `Play()` and `Stop()` functions respectively. To make it work, we need to press the buttons.

Activating buttons from the script

Before we give the user a way to press the buttons, let's see how we can do this from a script. Create a new script on `GameController`, as follows:

1. With `GameController` selected in Hierarchy, press **Add Component** | **New Script** to create a script named `ButtonExecuteTest`.
2. Open the script in MonoDevelop.

In the following script, we turn the hose on and off in five-second intervals, as follows:

```
using UnityEngine;
using UnityEngine.UI;

public class ButtonExecuteTest : MonoBehaviour
{
  public Button startButton;
  public Button stopButton;

  private bool isOn = false;
  private float timer = 5.0f;
  void Update ()
  {
    timer -= Time.deltaTime;
    if (timer < 0.0f)
    {
      isOn = !isOn;
      timer = 5.0f;

      if (isOn)
      {
        stopButton.onClick.Invoke();
      } else
      {
        startButton.onClick.Invoke();
      }
    }
  }
}
```

The script manages a Boolean `isOn` value, which says if the hose is on or off. And it has a timer which counts down from 5 seconds on each update. We use the `private` keyword for variables that are only used within this script, whereas the `public` ones can be viewed and modified via the Unity editor and other scripts. For `startButton` and `stopButton`, you'll drag and drop them in the Unity editor.

In this script, we use the `UnityEngine.UI`. As we saw in the previous chapter, *Events* are a way for different components to talk to one another. When an event occurs, such as a button press, a function in another script may get called. In our case, we're going to trigger an event corresponding to the start button press, and another corresponding to the stop button press, as we set up in the Inspector.

Save the script and click on **Play**. The hose should turn on and off every five seconds.

Now that we have tested the event system connection between the button clicks and the hose, we can disable this script before moving on to the next one:

1. With `GameController` selected,
2. Disable the `ButtonExecuteTest` component by unchecking its **Enable** checkbox, or remove the component.

 Breaking down a complex feature into bite-sized pieces and testing them separately is an excellent implementation strategy.

Look to highlight a button

Meanwhile, let's detect when the user is looking at a button and highlight it. Although **Button** is a Unity UI object, it needs to be detected with a ray cast. There may be other ways to accomplish this, as discussed later in this chapter, but here we will add a game object sphere to each button and cast a ray to detect it. First, add the spheres by performing the following steps:

1. In the **Hierarchy** panel, select `StartButton` (under `MeMyselfEye/Dashboard`), right-click for options and navigate to **3D Object | Sphere**.
2. Set its **Transform** component's **Scale** to (52, 52, 52) so that it fits the button size.
3. Disable the sphere's **Mesh Renderer** by unchecking the **Mesh Renderer** checkbox.

Also, repeat these steps for `StopButton`. A shortcut is to duplicate the sphere, as follows:

1. Right-click the Sphere and choose **Duplicate**.
2. Drag the duplicated item (`Sphere (1)`) into `StopButton`.
3. Reset it **Position** to (0,0,0).

Now, create a new script on `StartButton`, as follows:

1. With `StartButton` selected, navigate to **Add Component** | **New Script** to create a script named `RespondToGaze`.
2. Open the script for editing.

In the following `RespondToGaze.cs` script, we tell the button to become highlighted when you look at it, using the child Sphere object's collider:

```
using UnityEngine;
using UnityEngine.UI;

public class RespondtoGaze : MonoBehaviour
{
  public bool highlight = true;
  private Button button;
  private bool isSelected;

  void Start ()
  {
    button = GetComponent<Button>();
  }

  void Update ()
  {
    isSelected = false;
    Transform camera = Camera.main.transform;
    Ray ray = new Ray(camera.position, camera.rotation * Vector3.forward);
    RaycastHit hit;
    if (Physics.Raycast (ray, out hit) &&
        (hit.transform.parent != null) &&
        (hit.transform.parent.gameObject == gameObject)
    {
      isSelected = true;
    }

    if (isSelected)
    {
      if (highlight)
        button.Select();
    }
    else {
UnityEngine.EventSystems.EventSystem.current.SetSelectedGameObject(null);
    }
  }
}
```

In this script, on each update, we cast a ray from the camera. If it hits this button's sphere collider, then the hit object's parent should be this button. So (after checking that the hit object has a parent), we compare the parent gameObject to this button's gameObject.

If the gaze has selected this button, we trigger the button's **Select** to make it highlight. The highlighting is done within Unity's `EventSystem`. While the EventSystem has all this implemented for mouse clicks and screen touches, we have to manually tell the button it's been selected by calling `button.Select()`.

Unhighlighting the button is not so obvious. The EventSystem maintains a currently selected object across your runtime scene. We clear it by passing null to `SetSelectedGameObject()`.

Save the script and *Play*. When you gaze at a button, it should highlight, and when you gaze away from it, it should remove the highlight.

This is also an example of a reusable component script. We just wrote and tested it for the StartButton. We can use the same script for the StopButton:

1. Select the **StopButton** from the **Hierarchy**.
2. Drag the **RespondToGaze** script from the **Project Assets** onto the button, or
3. Select **Add Component** | **Scripts** | **RespondToGaze**.

Test the project one more time. Both buttons should highlight when you gaze at them.

 If you are using Google VR for Cardboard or Daydream, you can include the `GvrEventSystem` prefab in your scene. Then this `RespondToGaze` script becomes unnecessary and redundant. The `Daydream` component already supports gaze-based select, highlight, and clicking with the input controller. But I encourage you to follow along with this project nonetheless to experience how this functionality can be implemented. If so, temporarily disable `GvrEventSystem` in your scene.

Looking and then clicking to select

To be a functional dashboard, the buttons should operate when they're clicked. In Chapter 5, *Handy Interactables*, we explored the Unity Input system, including the "Fire1" event and other hand controller buttons. You may want to review that now. And choose which code snippet you want to use, if not the basic `Input.GetButtonDown("Fire1")`.

The changes to make to the `RespondToGaze.cs` script are pretty simple. At top of the class, add the following public variables:

```
public bool clicker = true;
public string inputButton = "Fire1";
```

At the bottom of `Update()`, make the following changes:

```
...
if (isSelected)
{
  if (highlight)
      button.Select();
  if (clicker && InputGetButtonDown("Fire1"))
      button.onClick.Invoke();
}
```

When the controller `"Fire1"` button is pressed, it will trigger a click of the UI button.

The component gives you the option to enable highlights and/or clicking with the input controller. You can also choose the logical input button that will trigger the click events.

We now have an in-game dashboard with buttons that respond to user input, which controls the behavior of an object (water hose) in the scene.

Looking and starting to select

Instead of using a clicker, we can use a time-based selection to click on the button. To make this work, we'll keep a countdown timer while staring at a button, much like the one that we used to kill Ethan in the previous chapter.

Change the `RespondToGaze.cs` script. At top of the class, add the following variables:

```
public bool timedClick = true;
public float delay = 2.0f;

private float timer = 0f;
```

In `Update()`, make the following changes:

```
...
  if (isSelected)
  {
    if (highlight)
        button.Select();
    if (clicker && Input.GetButtonDown("Fire1"))
```

```
        button.onClick.Invoke();
    if (timedClick)
    {
      timer += Time.deltaTime;
      if (timer >= delay)
        button.onClick.Invoke();
  }
  else {
UnityEngine.EventSystems.EventSystem.current.SetSelectedGameObject(null);
    timer = 0f;
  }
```

Now, not only will a button click get involved on `Input.GetButtonDown`, but also if you gaze at the button long enough (when `timedClick` is `true`). We begin a timer when the button is selected (highlighted) and count up. When the timer expires the click event is invoked. If the button is deselected before then, the timer is reset to zero.

Does it work for you? Woohoo!

So this was a relatively complex project. The goal was to create a dashboard with buttons that turn a hose on and off. We broke it down into discrete steps, added the objects and components a step at a time, and tested each step to make sure that it worked as expected before moving on. If you tried to implement this all at once or blew through it without testing, things can (and will) go wrong, and it'll be much harder to figure out where the problem cropped up.

Extra challenge: This feature can be further enhanced for different purposes. For example, it can be used to give the user the information that the countdown is running, perhaps by animating a spinner cursor. Also, further feedback can be given when the click event is executed. For example, the Button UI object has a Transition option called Animation that might be helpful. Also, consider audio cues.

Pointing and clicking with VR components

As we have seen, while Unity provides UI elements such as canvas text, buttons, and other controls that are specially tuned for conventional screen space UI and mobile app, using them in World Space and tying them together with VR user input can get pretty involved. World space interactions assume some physics, colliders, and ray casts to detect interaction events.

Fortunately, VR device-specific toolkits may provide components that take care of some of this work already. As we saw in previous chapters, device manufacturers provide toolkits built atop their Unity SDK with convenient scripts, prefabs, and demo scenes that illustrate how to use them.

In this case, we're looking for components that let you design scenes using Unity UI elements on canvas, take advantage of all their EventSystem interactivity goodness, use world space 3D models, and input controllers or laster pointers. For example, consider these:

- Oculus Rift and GearVR: OVRInputModule; see `https://developer.oculus.com/blog/unitys-ui-system-in-vr/`
- SteamVR: Steam InteractionSystem; see the `/Assets/SteamVR/InteractionSystem/` folder after installing the SteamVR package
- Daydream:
- VRTK open source toolkit: `https://github.com/thestonefox/VRTK`

Lastly, you might consider purchasing a package from the Unity Asset Store. The Curved UI package ($25), for example, lets you make VR-ready curved canvases and supports Vive, Oculus Touch, Daydream controllers, and gaze input, as depicted:

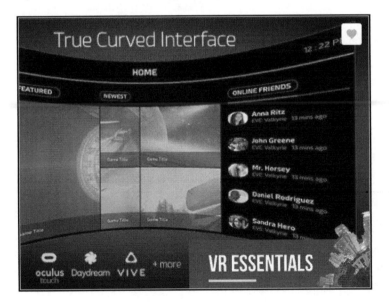

Using Unity UI and SteamVR

We introduced the SteamVR InteractionSystem in Chapter 5, *Handy Interactables*. It is intended as an example of how to use the SteamVR SDK but includes some very useful components and demo scenes. Using the Interaction System, it's very easy to convert your Dashboard into a control panel you can operate directly with your positionally tracked hand controllers.

The Interaction System includes its own `Player` camera rig which replaces the default `[CameraRig]` we have been using. It includes a VRCamera, two hands (Hand1 and Hand2), and other useful objects.

1. Locate the `Assets/SteamVR/InteractionSystem/Core/Prefabs` folder in the **Project** window
2. Drag the `Player` prefab as a child of `MyMyselfEye` into your scene **Hierarchy**
3. Delete or disable the `[CameraRig]` object

To make the `StartButton` and `StopButton` interactable, add the `Interactable` component. Also add the UI `Element` component to handle **OnHandClick** events, as follows:

1. Select the `StartButton` object in **Hierarchy** (child of `Dashboard`).
2. In **Inspector**, select **Add Component | Scripts | Valve.VR.InteractionSystem | Interactable** (tip: use the **Search** field for "Interactable").
3. Select **Add Component | Scripts | Valve.VR.InteractionSystem | UI Element**.
4. In **Inspector** on the **UI Element** component, press the "+" to add an **On Hand Click** handler.
5. Drag the `WaterShower` particle system (child of `Hose` object) from **Hierarchy** onto the **GameObject** field, like we did for the standard **Button OnClick** event.
6. Select the **ParticleSystem | Play()** function.
7. Optionally, disable the `RespondToGaze` component.

Similarly, repeat these steps for the `StopButton`, but choose function **ParticleSystem | Stop()**.

You may also need to move the `Dashboard` closer to yourself so the buttons are within comfortable reach when you're in VR. When you press **Play** you can now reach to touch a button; it highlights. Pull the trigger to press it, as shown in the screenshot, and it turns on the hose:

Using Unity UI and Daydream

Let's now take a look at how to do this on a mobile VR device using Google Daydream. In this case, we won't actually reach out and press the button but use the 3DOF hand controller laser pointer. The solution is as simple as replacing the `GvrReticlePointer` (if you had been using it) with a `GvrControllerPointer`.

1. Under your MeMyselfEye `GVR Camera Rig/ Player / Main Camera /`, if there is a GvrReticlePointer, disable it.
2. Locate the GvrControllerPointer in the `GoogleVR/Prefabs/Controller/` folder.
3. Drag the prefab under Player (as a sibling of Main Camera).

Then set up the Dashboard canvas to accept raycasts:

1. Select the Dashboard object in Hierarchy.
2. Add the GvrPointerGraphicRaycaster component.

Press Play. You can now use the Daydream controller to press the buttons.

Explore the component options for the GvrControllerPointer, its child Laser object, and other Gvr object provided with the package. There are some pretty interesting and useful configurations available, including settings for laser color, end color, and max distance. There's even a checkbox to Draw Debug Rays in the Editor Scene window during Play mode.

Building a wrist-based menu palette

Some VR applications, designed for two-handed setups such as Oculus Rift, HTC Vive, and Windows MR, give you a virtual menu palette attached to one wrist while the other hand selects buttons or items from it. Let's see how that is done. *This scenario will assume you have a two-hand controller VR system.* We'll describe it using the SteamVR camera rig, involving attaching the controls to your left hand and selecting them with your right.

Converting our dashboard control panel into a wrist palette is not too difficult. We just need to scale it appropriately and attach it to the hand controller.

Given you've built the scene up to the point described in the previous *Using Unity UI and SteamVR* section, including the SteamVR `Player` rig (instead of `[CameraRig]`), we'll duplicate and repurpose the `Dashboard` to use it on your left wrist:

1. In Hierarchy, right-click the Dashboard and Duplicate.
2. Rename the new one to "Palette".
3. Disable the old Dashboard.
4. Drag the Palette as a child of the Player/Hand1 object.

Now we'll modify the Palette graphics as follows. Feel free to change for what works for you:

1. On the Palette itself, set its Pos X,Y,Z to (0, 0.1, -0.1); Rotation to (90, -150, -115); Scale (X,Y,Z) to 0.0005;
2. Unfold the Palette and disable or delete the Raw Image object.
3. Enable the Image child object (if it's missing, create a new Image with Anchor Presets to stretch-stretch).
4. Set the Image Scale (X, Y, Z) to 0.5.
5. Set the Image Color Alpha to 75 so it's translucent.
6. Enable the Text child object. Set its Rect Transform Top to 100, Font Size to 18, and Text to "Hose".
7. Move the StartButton Pos Y to 0.
8. Move the StopButton Pos Y to 0.

That's it! All of the click wiring we set up for the Dashboard works without change. Shown here is a screenshot of using the Palette attached to the left-hand controller, and selecting the start button on it with the right-hand controller:

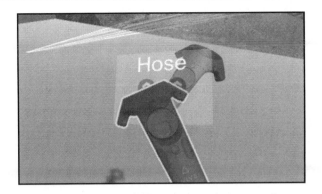

Naturally, the palette can be extended with other buttons and input controls. If you had multiple panels arranged as the sides of the cube (like the TiltBrush menu), you could use the thumb pad to scroll or rotate between the various menus. And that's how it's done.

Summary

In Unity, user interfaces that are based on a canvas object and the event system include buttons, text, images, sliders, and input fields, which can be assembled and wired to objects in the scene.

In this chapter, we took a close look at various world space UI techniques and how they can be used in virtual reality projects. We considered ways in which UI for VR differs from UI for conventional video games and desktop applications. Also, we implemented over a half-dozen of them, demonstrating how each can be constructed, coded, and used in your own projects. Our C# scripting got a little more advanced, probing deeper into the Unity Engine API and modular coding techniques.

You now have a broader vocabulary to approach UI in your VR projects. Some of the examples in this chapter can be directly applicable in your own work. However, not all need to be home-grown. VR UI tools are increasingly being provided in VR headset SDKs, open source VR middleware projects, and third-party Unity Assets Store packages.

In the next chapter, we will add a first-person character controller to our scene. We'll learn about avatars and methods to control navigation in VR so that we can comfortably move around inside the virtual world. Also, we'll learn about managing one of the negative aspects of virtual reality experiences—VR motion sickness.

Locomotion and Comfort

7

Up to this point in this book, the player's point-of-view camera has been stationary. In this chapter, we'll start to move around as we consider various techniques for locomotion and teleportation. First, we'll dig deeper into the Unity standard character components, and then we move ourselves into a controllable first-person character and explore techniques to move around in the virtual world. We'll also discuss practices for managing motion sickness and sense of self within VR.

In this chapter, we will discuss the following topics:

- Unity's character objects and components
- Glide locomotion
- Comfort mode locomotion
- Teleportation
- Issues around VR motion sickness

 Note that the projects in this chapter are separate and not directly required by the other chapters in this book. If you decide to skip any of it or not save your work, that's OK.

Understanding Unity characters

A first-person character is such a key asset in a VR project that we really should understand its components inside out. So, before we go about building one for our project, it would be a good idea to take a close look at the built-in components and standard assets that Unity provides.

Unity components

As you probably know, each Unity game object contains a set of associated **components**. Unity includes many types of built-in components, which you can see by browsing the **Component** menu in the main menu bar. Each component adds properties and behaviors to the object that it belongs to. A component's properties are accessible via the Unity editor's **Inspector** panel and scripts. A script attached to a game object is also a type of a component and may have properties that you can set in the **Inspector** panel.

The component types used to implement first-person characters include the **Camera**, **Character Controller**, and/or **Rigidbody**, and various scripts. Let's review each of these standard components.

The Camera component

The Camera component specifies the viewing parameters that are used to render the scene on each frame update. Any object with a Camera component is considered a camera object. Naturally, we've been using a camera in our scenes since we started, and we've been accessing it in the scripts that we've written.

A stereographic VR camera object renders two views, one for each eye. In VR, the camera controller scripts read data from the headset's motion sensors and positional tracking to determine the current head pose (position, direction, and rotation) and set the camera's transform appropriately.

The Rigidbody component

When you add a Rigidbody component to any Unity game object, it will benefit from the calculations that are performed by the **physics engine**. Rigidbody components have parameters for gravity, mass, and drag, among others. During gameplay, the physics engine calculates each rigid object's *momentum* (mass, speed, and direction).

Rigid objects interact with other rigid objects. For example, if they collide, they'll bounce off each other and the parameters of the interaction can be controlled with a **physic material** with properties such as friction and bounciness factors.

Rigidbodies can be flagged as *kinematic*, which is usually only used when the object is driven by animation or scripts. Collisions will not affect kinematic objects, but they will still affect the motion of other rigidbodies. It's mostly used when objects are chained together with *joints*, like the ones connecting a humanoid's bones or a swinging pendulum.

Any rigid object, given a child camera object, becomes a rigid first-person character. Then, you can add scripts to handle user input to move, jump, look around, and so on.

The Character Controller component

Like a Rigidbody, the **Character Controller** (**CC**) is used for *collision detection* and *character movement*. It needs scripts to handle the user input to move, jump, and look around, too. However, it doesn't automatically have the physics built in.

The CC component is specifically designed for character objects because characters in a game often are not really expected to behave the same as other physics-based objects. It can be used instead of, or in addition to, a Rigidbody.

The CC component has a built-in **Capsule Collider** behavior to detect collisions. However, it doesn't automatically use the physics engine to *respond* to the collision.

For example, if a CC object hits a rigid object such as a wall, it will just stop. It won't bounce. If a rigid object, such as a flying brick, hits a CC object, the brick will get deflected (bounce) based on its own properties, but the CC object will not be affected. Of course, if you want to include behavior like this on the CC object, you can program that in your own scripts.

The CC component does have an especially good support for one force in its scripting API-*gravity*. Built-in parameters are specifically related to keeping the object's feet on the ground. For example, the **Step Offset** parameter defines how tall a step the character can hop onto rather than being an obstacle that blocks his way. Similarly, the **Slope Limit** parameter says how big an incline is too steep and whether it should be treated like a wall. In your scripts, you can use the `Move()` method and the `IsGrounded` variable to implement character behavior.

Unless you script it, a CC object has no momentum and can stop on a dime. It feels very precise, but this could also lead to a jerky movement. The opposite is true for Rigidbody objects, which feel more fluid because they have momentum, acceleration/deceleration, and obey the laws of physics. In VR, we'd ideally like some combination of the two, if we use it at all.

Using physics to move yourself through a VR scene is not always best. As we'll see, alternative locomotion techniques may not use physics at all, such as *teleportation*.

Unity Standard Assets

The **Characters** package in Unity **Standard Assets** comes with a number of third- and first-person character prefab objects. These prefab objects are compared in the following table:

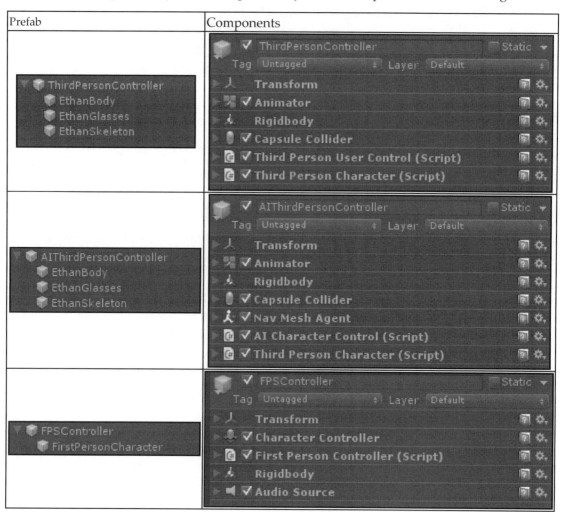

Prefab	Components

Let's discuss this in more detail.

ThirdPersonController

We've already used both of the third-person prefabs, `ThirdPersonController` and `AIThirdPersonController`, in `Chapter 2`, *Content, Objects, and Scale*, and `Chapter 4`, *Gaze-Based Control*, respectively.

The `ThirdPersonController` prefab has child objects that define the character's body, namely our friend Ethan. He is a rigged avatar (from the `.fbx` file), which means that humanoid animations can be applied to make him walk, run, jump, and so on.

The `ThirdPersonController` prefab uses a Rigidbody for physics and Capsule Collider for collision detection.

It has two scripts. A `ThirdPersonUserControl` script takes user input, such as thumbstick presses, and tells the character to move, jump, and so on. A `ThirdPersonCharacter` script implements physics movements and calls the animations that are needed for running, crouching, and so on.

AIThirdPersonController

The `AIThirdPersonController` prefab is identical to the `ThirdPersonController` prefab, but the former adds a `NavMeshAgent` and an `AICharacterControl` script, which constrains where and how the character can move around the scene. If you recall, in `Chapter 4`, *Gaze-Based Control*, we used the `AICharacterController` to make Ethan walk around the scene and avoid bumping into objects.

First-person FPSController

The FPSController prefab is a first-person controller that uses both a CC component and a Rigidbody. It has a child camera attached to it. When the character moves, the camera moves with it.

The core distinction between third-person controller prefabs and first-person controller prefabs is the **child object**. Third-person controller prefabs have a rigged humanoid child object, while first-person controller prefabs have a camera child object.

Its body mass is set to a low value (1) and IsKinematic is enabled. This means that it will have limited momentum and does not react to other rigid objects, but it can be driven by animations.

Its FirstPersonController script offers a plethora of parameters for running, jumping, audio footsteps, and more. The script also includes parameters and animations for a *head bob*, which bounces the camera in a natural way when the character is moving. If you use the FPSController script in your VR project, *be sure to disable any head bob features* or you might need to clean the puke off your keyboard!

RigidBodyFPSController

The RigidBodyFPSController prefab is a first-person controller with a Rigidbody but no CC component. Like FPSController, it has a child camera object. When the character moves, the camera moves with it.

A RigidBodyFPSController prefab's body mass is more substantial, set to 10, and is not kinematic. That is, it *can* get bounced around when it collides with other objects. It has a separate Capsule Collider component with the ZeroFriction physic material. The RigidBodyFirstPersonController script is different from the FPSController one, but the former has a lot of similar parameters.

Why am I going through all of this detail here?
If you've built any non-VR projects in Unity, then you've most likely used these prefabs. However, you might not have paid much attention to how they're assembled. Virtual reality is experienced from the first-person perspective. Our implementation toolbox is Unity. It is important to understand Unity's tools that manage and control this first-person experience.

Using glide locomotion

For our locomotion features in this chapter, let's take an *agile* approach to development. This means (in part) that we'll start by defining our new feature, or story, with a set of requirements. Then, we'll incrementally build and test this feature, one requirement at a time, by iterating and refining our work as we go along. Experimentation is not only allowed, it's encouraged.

 Agile software development is a broad term for methodologies that encourage small incremental and iterative development in a fashion that's easy to respond to changing and refined requirements. See the Agile Manifesto at http://agilemanifesto.org/.

The feature we want to implement is this: as a first-person character, when I start walking, I will move through the scene in the direction I am looking until I indicate to stop walking. Here are the requirements to achieve this feature:

- Move in the direction you're looking
- Keep your feet on the ground
- Don't pass through solid objects
- Don't fall off the edge of the world
- Step over small objects and handle uneven terrain
- Start and stop moving by clicking an input button

This sounds reasonable.

To begin, if you have a saved version of the scene from Chapter 4, *Gaze-Based Control*, you can start with that. Or, build a similar simple new scene containing a ground plane, some 3D objects as obstacles, and a copy of your MeMyselfEye prefab.

Move in the direction you're looking

We already have a MeMyselfEye object containing the camera rig. We're going to turn it into a first-person controller. Our first requirement is to move about the scene in the direction you're looking. Add a script named GlideLocomotion. Keeping it simple, let's start by performing the following steps:

1. Select the MeMyselfEye object in the **Hierarchy** panel
2. In the **Inspector** panel, select **Add Component | New Script** and name it GlideLocomotion

Then, open the script and code it, as follows:

```
using UnityEngine;

public class GlideLocomotion : MonoBehaviour
{
  public float velocity = 0.4f;

  void Update ()
  {
    Vector3 moveDirection = Camera.main.transform.forward;
    moveDirection *= velocity * Time.deltaTime;
    transform.position += moveDirection;
  }
}
```

The normal walking speed for humans is about 1.4 meters per second. In VR, that could make you feel sick. Let's travel a lot slower than that, at 0.4 m/s. During `Update()`, we check the current direction in which the player is looking (`camera.transform.forward`) and move the `MeMyselfEye` transform position in this direction at the current velocity.

Note the coding shortcuts for the self-modification of a variable (`*=` and `+=`). The last two lines of the preceding code could have been written out like this:

```
moveDirection = moveDirection * velocity * Time.deltaTime;
transform.position = transform.position  + moveDirection;
```

Here, I used the `*=` and `+=` operators instead. Save the script and the scene and try it in VR.

When you look forward, you move forward. Look left, move left. Look right, move right. It works!

Look up... *Whoa!! Did you expect that?! We're freakin' flying!* You can move up, down, and all around as if you're Superman or piloting a drone. Presently, `MeMyselfEye` has no mass and physics and does not respond to gravity. Nonetheless, it meets our requirement to move in the direction you're looking. So, let's continue.

Keep your feet on the ground

The next requirement wants you to keep your feet on the ground. We know that `GroundPlane` is flat and positioned at **Y** = 0. So, let's just add this simple constraint to the `GlideLocomotion` script, as follows:

```
void Update ()
```

```
    {
      Vector3 moveDirection = Camera.main.transform.forward;
      moveDirection *= velocity * Time.deltaTime;
      moveDirection.y = 0f;
      transform.position += moveDirection;
    }
```

Save the script and try it in VR.

Not bad. Now, we can move around the **Y** = 0 plane.

On the other hand, you're like a ghost, readily passing through the cube, sphere, and the other objects.

Don't pass through solid objects

The third requirement states *don't pass through solid objects*. Here's an idea. Give it a Rigidbody component, a collider, and let the physics engine take care of it. Follow these steps:

1. Select the `MeMyselfEye` object in the **Hierarchy** panel
2. In the **Inspector** panel, navigate to **Add Component** | **Physics** | **Rigidbody**
3. Then **Add Component** | **Physics** | **Capsule Collider**
4. Set the Capsule Collider **Height** to **2**
5. If your Character Controller's capsule collider (green mesh in the Scene window) extends through the ground plane, adjusts its **Center Y** to 1

Try it in VR.

Whoa!! What the...? It was going fine there for a second, but as soon as you knock into the cube, you go spinning out of control in wild directions, like a spacewalk gone bad in the movie *Gravity*. Well, that's a Rigidbody for you. Forces are being applied in all directions and axes. Let's add some constraints as follows.

In the **Inspector** panel's **Rigidbody** pane, check off the checkboxes for **Freeze Position: Y** and **Freeze Rotation: X** and **Z**.

Try it in VR.

Now that's pretty nice! You're able to move by looking in a direction, you're not flying (**Y** position constrained), and you don't pass through solid objects. Instead, you slide past them since only the **Y** rotation is allowed.

If your `KillTarget` script is still running (from `Chapter 2`, *Content, Objects, and Scale*), you should be able to stare at Ethan until he explodes. Do it, make Ethan explode... *Whoa!* We just got blown out of here by the explosion, spinning out of control in wild directions again. Maybe we're just not ready for this powerful physics engine yet. We can probably address this in the scripting, but for the time being, let's abandon the Rigidbody idea. We'll come back to it in the next chapter.

You may recall that CC includes a Capsule Collider and supports a movement that is constrained by collisions. We'll try that instead, as follows:

1. In the **Inspector** panel, click on the **Rigidbody** pane's *gear* icon and select **Remove Component**
2. Also, remove its **Capsule Collider** component
3. In the **Inspector** panel, navigate to **Add Component | Physics | Character Controller**
4. If your Character Controller's capsule collider (green mesh in the Scene window) extends through the ground plane, adjusts its **Center Y** to 1

Modify the `GlideLocomotion` script, as follows:

```
using UnityEngine;

public class GlideLocomotion : MonoBehaviour
{
  public float velocity = 0.4f;

  private CharacterController character;

  void Start ()
  {
    character = GetComponent<CharacterController>();
  }

  void Update ()
  {
    Vector3 moveDirection = Camera.main.transform.forward;
    moveDirection *= velocity * Time.deltaTime;
    moveDirection.y = 0.0f;
    character.Move(moveDirection);
  }
}
```

Instead of updating `transform.position` directly, we called the built-in `CharacterController.Move()` function and let it do it for us. It knows that the characters should behave with certain constraints.

Save the script and try it in VR.

This time, when we bump into objects (a cube or sphere), we kind of go over it and then remain in the air. The `Move()` function does not apply gravity to the scene for us. We need to add that to the script, which isn't so hard (see the Unity API docs at `http://docs.unity3d.com/ScriptReference/CharacterController.Move.html`).

However, there is a simpler way. The `CharacterController.SimpleMove()` function applies gravity to the move for us. Just replace the whole `Update()` function with the following one-liner:

```
void Update ()
{
    character.SimpleMove(Camera.main.transform.forward * velocity);
}
```

The `SimpleMove()` function takes care of gravity and also handles `Time.deltaTime`. So, all that we need to give it is the movement direction vector. Also, since it's introducing gravity, we don't need the **Y** = 0 constraint either. Much simpler.

Save the script and try it in VR.

Awesome! I think we've met all the requirements so far. *Just don't go walking off the edge...*

 The exercises in this section assume you're using VR in seated or standing mode, not room-scale. We're modifying the whole MyMyselfEye rig as we move the player. In room-scale, that's moving the play area bounds as well. Since we're attaching the collider to the MyMyselfEye position, if you physically step away from the center of the play area, the collider will not be aligned with your actual body position. Later on, we will address issues of locomotion with room-scale VR.

Don't fall off the edge of the world

Now that we have gravity, if we walk off the edge of the ground plane, you'll fall into oblivion. Fixing this isn't a first-person character thing. Just add some railings to the scene.

Use cubes, scaling them to the desired thickness and length and moving them into position. Go ahead and do it. I won't give you the step-by-step instructions for it. For example, I used these transforms:

- **Scale**: 0.1, 0.1, 10.0
- Railing 1: **Position**: -5, 1, 0
- Railing 2: **Position**: 5, 1, 0
- Railing 3: **Position**: 0, 1, -5; **Rotation**: 0, 90, 0
- Railing 4: **Position**: 0, 1, 5; **Rotation**: 0, 90, 0

Try it in VR. Try to walk through the railings. Whew! This is safer.

Stepping over small objects and handling uneven terrain

While we're at it, add a few things to walk on and over, such as a ramp and other obstacles. The result will look like this:

Try it in VR. Walk up the ramp and step off the cube. Hey, this is fun!

The CC component is taking care of the requirement to step over small objects and handle uneven terrain. You might want to tinker with its **Slope Limit** and **Step Offset** settings.

Caution: Glide locomotion can cause motion sickness, especially for players who are susceptible. Please use it with caution in your apps. This may become especially noticeable as you glide up the ramp and then jump off the block onto the ground plane. On the other hand, some people love rollercoaster VR! Also, giving the player control of the locomotion through a mechanic as simple as a button press can go a long way in helping reduce queasiness and motion sickness, which we'll add next.

Starting and stopping movement

The next requirement is *to start and stop moving by clicking an input button*. We'll look for a button press using the logical "Fire1" button. If you want to use a different button, or if you're targeting a platform that does not have a mapping to "Fire1" please refer to Chapter 5, *Handy Interactables*, under the topic *Basic button input*.

Modify the GlideLocomotion script as follows:

```
using UnityEngine;

public class GlideLocomotion : MonoBehaviour
{
  public float velocity = 0.7f;

  private CharacterController controller;
  private bool isWalking = false;

  void Start()
  {
    controller = GetComponent<CharacterController> ();
  }

  void Update () {
    if (Input.GetButtonDown("Fire1"))
        isWalking = true;
    else if (Input.GetButtonUp("Fire1"))
        isWalking = false;

    if (isWalking) {
      controller.SimpleMove (Camera.main.transform.forward * velocity);
    }
  }
}
```

On Daydream, you may call `GvrControllerInput.ClickButtonDown` and `ClickButtonUp` instead.

By adding a Boolean `isWalking` flag, we can switch the forward movement on and off, which can be signaled by a key press.

Adding comfort mode locomotion

We have mentioned the potential of motion sickness several times already in this chapter, and earlier in this book. In general, the more control you give the player in moving around within VR the better off she'll be and reduce the risk of feeling queasy. Offering a button to start/stop motion is one step, as we just saw. Another is what's commonly referred to as *comfort mode*.

It's been discovered that using glide locomotion around curves is worse than simply going in a straight line. So, one technique for getting around in a VR scene is only allowed forward motion, regardless of which direction the player is looking, and then use the thumbstick to change direction. Also, rather than allow the thumbstick to change the direction angle continuously, we limit it to fixed angle steps of 30 degrees, for example. We'll add this to our `GlideLocomotion` script as follows.

At the top of the class, add the following variables:

```
public float comfortAngle = 30f;
private bool hasRotated = true;
```

Then in `Update()`, add the following statements:

```
void Update()
{
  if (Input.GetButtonDown("Fire1"))
    isWalking = true;
  else if (Input.GetButtonUp("Fire1"))
    isWalking = false;

  if (isWalking)
    character.SimpleMove(transform.forward * velocity);

  float axis = Input.GetAxis("Horizontal");
  if (axis > 0.5f)
  {
    if (!hasRotated)
      transform.Rotate(0, comfortAngle, 0);
    hasRotated = true;
```

```
      }
      else if (axis < -0.5f)
      {
        if (!hasRotated)
          transform.Rotate(0, -comfortAngle, 0);
        hasRotated = true;
      }
      else
      {
        hasRotated = false;
      }
    }
```

Now, when the `"Fire1"` button is pressed and `isWalking` is true, we move the `MeMyselfEye` forward in the direction indicated in its transform, rather than the `Camera` look directions, changing the line to `character.SimpleMove(transform.forward * velocity)`.

When the user pushes the thumbstick to the right, that is, the logical `"Horizontal"` axis is positive, we will rotate the rig clockwise by 30 degrees (`comfortAngle`). When the thumbstick is pressed left, we rotate counter-clockwise. We check for greater than 0.5 rather than exactly 1.0 so the player does not need to jam the stick all the way to the edge.

We don't want to keep rotating, again and again, each update while the joystick is pressed, so we set a flag, `hasRotated`, and then ignore the axis until it comes to rest at the zero position. Then, we'll allow the player to press it again.

The result is a comfortable navigation mechanic where one button moves you forward and another lets you change direction in large increments.

For your reference, some button mappings used in this mechanic are as follows:

- In OpenVR on HTC VIVE, `"Fire1"` is the menu button on one controller, `"Horizontal"` is touching the touchpad on the other controller.
- In OpenVR on Oculus, `"Fire1"` is the right controller's **B** button, `"Horizontal"` is the left controller thumbstick.

- On Daydream, you should modify the code to use `GvrControllerInput`. To detect horizontal clicks on the touchpad, call `GvrControllerInput.TouchPosCentered`, which returns a `Vector2`, and check `x` for values between `-1` and `1`. For example, replace the call to GetAxis with the following:

```
Vector2 touchPos = GvrControllerInput.TouchPosCentered;
float axis = touchPos.x;
if (axis > 0.5f) ...
```

You're encouraged to extend the `ButtonTest()` function used in the beginning of Chapter 5, *Handy Interactables*, to determine which button mappings, axes, and SDK functions work best for your target VR device.

We just implemented glide locomotion, where you move forward smoothly in the direction you're looking, or with comfort mode, in the direction your body is facing, while your head can look around. Comfort mode reduces the chance of motion sickness by having you change the direction you're facing in jumps of 30-degree angles. But even that may not be comfortable enough, and some developers (and players) prefer no gliding at all, and instead let you just *teleport* from one location to another.

Other locomotion considerations

If you want to offer your players a VR ride, you can define a predefined *track* to glide along, like a guided tour of a building or art gallery. Tracks can be 3D, moving you up and down too, with gravity, such as VR roller coasters, or without gravity, such as a space tour. We do not recommend this mechanic except for the most hardcore thrill seekers as it has a good chance of causing motion sickness.

Another technique for comfort during locomotion is **Tunneling**. During the movement, the camera is cropped with a vignette and simple background, like a grid, is displayed in the player's peripheral vision, so the user only sees what is directly before them. Eliminating peripheral vision while moving can reduce the chance of motion sickness.

For vertical locomotion, apps have implemented a climbing mechanic, using your hands to reach, grab, and pull yourself up. Mountain climbing simulation games such as The Climb (http://www.theclimbgame.com/) takes this idea to the next level (literally!), providing a number of different reach mechanics and grip types to grab onto.

Other apps have also tried using your hands, not for climbing, but for walking. For example, reaching and pulling like a rope, or swinging your arms like a runner, or even a circular pulling motion like you're operating a wheelchair.

Of course, there are hardware devices, such as that implement locomotion mechanisms using your feet to walk and run. Examples include:

- VR treadmills such as Virtuix Omni (`http://www.virtuix.com/`) and VR Virtualizer (`https://www.cyberith.com/`), where you walk in place with your feet and legs to walk and run in VR.
- Exercise bikes such as VirZoom (`https://www.virzoom.com/`) where you can bike and even hang glide in VR.
- Body tracking sensors can be used not just for player locomotion but also motion capture for creating character animations. Devices include Optitrack (`http://optitrack.com/motion-capture-virtual-reality/`), Perception Neuron (`https://neuronmocap.com/`), ProVR (`http://www.vrs.org.uk/virtual-reality-gear/motion-tracking/priovr.html`), and others.

You probably need to write your app specifically for that device as there are no standards for these body tracking devices, but they're certainly a lot of fun.

Techniques for teleportation

Pointer teleportation is a mechanic where you point to a location you want to go to, and you jump there. No gliding. You just teleport to the new location. A laser beam or arc may be drawn, along with a teleport location receptacle to indicate where you may go.

As we've seen in previous chapters, we can make our own scripts. But since this is a core feature of VR applications, teleportation components are often included with device SDK toolkits. We'll write our own and consider some provided ones afterward.

To begin, if you have a saved version of the scene from `Chapter 4`, *Gaze-Based Control*, you can start with that. You may disable a few objects that we do not need, including `Ethan` and `WalkTarget`. Or, build a similar simple new scene containing a ground plane, some 3D objects as obstacles, and a copy of your `MeMyselfEye` prefab.

Looking to teleport

The mechanic we'll implement for our homegrown teleportation will work on any VR platform, using gaze-based pointing. Similar to how we controlled Ethan the zombie in `Chapter 4`, *Gaze-Based Control*, we'll cast a ray from the player's camera view to the ground plane to choose a move-to location.

In our script, we'll use a button press to initiate the teleport and release to jump there if you've selected a valid location. Alternatively, you could consider other input such as a forward push of the thumbstick using `Input.GetAxis`(*vertical*).

First, let's create a teleport marker (similar to the WalkTarget one), as follows:

1. Add an empty game object to the **Hierarchy** panel, and rename it `TeleportMarker`.
2. Reset its **Transform** values to position (0,0,0) (using the gear icon in the upper-right of the Transform pane).
3. Right-click on the mouse and navigate to **3D Object | Cylinder**. This will create a cylindrical object parented by `TeleportMarker`.
4. Reset its transform and change the **Scale** to (0.4, 0.05, 0.4). This will create a flat disk with a diameter of 0.4.
5. Disable or remove its **Capsule Collider**.

For now, we'll use the default material. Or, you could decorate your marker with another material. (For example, if you have Steam `InteractionSystem` installed, try the `TeleportPointVisible` material. If you have Daydream Elements installed, try the `TeleportGlow` material.)

Now, let's write the script:

1. Select the `MeMyselfEye` object in the **Hierarchy** panel
2. Disable or remove the `GlideLocomotion` component, if present
3. Select **Add Component | New Script** and name it `LookTeleport`

Write the script as follows:

```
using UnityEngine;

public class LookTeleport : MonoBehaviour
{
    public GameObject target;
    public GameObject ground;

    void Update()
    {
        Transform camera = Camera.main.transform;
        Ray ray;
        RaycastHit hit;

        if (Input.GetButtonDown("Fire1"))
```

```
      {
        // start searching
        target.SetActive(true);
      }
      else if (Input.GetButtonUp("Fire1"))
      {
        // done searching, teleport player
        target.SetActive(false);
        transform.position = target.transform.position;
      }
      else if (target.activeSelf)
      {
        ray = new Ray(camera.position, camera.rotation *
Vector3.forward);
        if (Physics.Raycast(ray, out hit) &&
            (hit.collider.gameObject == ground))
        {
          // move target to look-at position
          target.transform.position = hit.point;
        }
        else
        {
          // not looking a ground, reset target to player position
          target.transform.position = transform.position;
        }
      }
    }
  }
}
```

The script works as follows:

- When the player clicks, targeting begins, and the target marker is made visible (SetActive(true)).
- While targeting, we identify what the player is looking at (Raycast). And if it's the ground, we position the target there (hit.point). Otherwise, the target is reset to the player's position.
- When the player stops pressing the button, the target is hidden. And we position the player to the target's current position, thus completing the teleportation.

Notice that we are using the TeleportMarker target to store the state of our teleport mechanic while in targeting mode. When the target is active, we're targeting. When we exit targeting, we use the target's position as the new player position.

Save the script and in Unity:

1. Drag the `GroundPlane` object onto the Ground slot
2. Drag the `TeleportMarker` object onto the Target slot

Press **Play**. Pressing the input button will activate the target marker, which moves as you look. On releasing the button, you teleport to that position. You can cancel the teleport by looking at something other than the ground and releasing the button.

Teleporting between surfaces

In the previous script, we're using a plain Raycast to determine where to place the `TeleportMarker`. This really only works on Plane objects. For any other 3D object, the hit point might be any surface, not just the topside walkable one.

An alternative approach is to use NavMesh to identify surfaces you can teleport to within the scene. Back in `Chapter 4`, *Gaze-Based Control*, we generated a NavMesh for Ethan's `AIThirdPersonController` to control where he's allowed to roam. This time, we also use the NavMesh to determine where we (`MeMyselfEye`) can go. Feel free to go back and review our conversations about NavMesh.

The advantage of this approach is the available teleportation locations can be a subset of the ground plane. There can be multiple other object surfaces and even complex terrains. The teleportation locations will be limited to valid flat or slightly sloped surfaces.

In case you skipped that section, or if you've rearranged objects in your scene since then, we will regenerate the NavMesh now:

1. Select the **Navigation** panel. If it's not already a tab in your editor, open the Navigation window from the main menu by navigating to **Window | Navigation**.
2. Select its **Object** tab.
3. Select the **Ground Plane** in **Hierarchy**, then in the **Navigation** window's **Object** pane, check the **Navigation Static** checkbox. (Alternatively, you can use the object's **Inspector** window **Static** drop-down list.)
4. Repeat step 3 for each of the objects that should block your possible teleportation locations: the cubes, sphere, and so on.

For demonstration, we will now also add a second story platform:

1. In **Hierarchy**, create a new 3D **Cube** and name it Overlook
2. Set its **Scale** to (2.5, 0.1, 5) and its **Position** to (4, 2.5, 0.5)
3. In the **Navigation** window, select the **Object** tab and check **Navigation Static** for the overlook, then
4. Select the **Bake** tab and click on the **Bake** button at the bottom of the panel

Note that its height (**Y Scale**) of the platform is greater than **Agent Height** (2) in the **Navigation** Bake settings. This will ensure the player can go both beneath the platform and on top of it. In the **Scene** window, you can see the areas in blue defined by the NavMesh, shown next, including a nice lookout area on the second story platform:

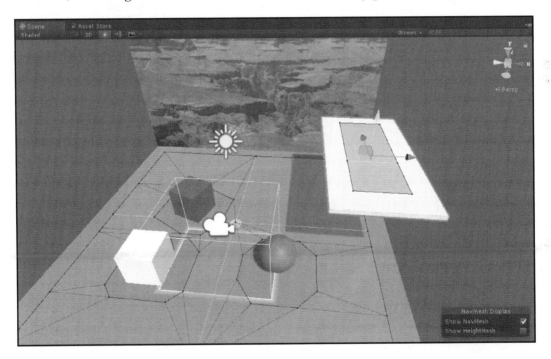

We can now modify the script to find our teleport target position on the NavMesh rather than the ground plane. Unfortunately, Unity does not provide a `Raycast` function for directly finding a hit point on the NavMesh. Instead, we find a hit point, as usual, using Physics colliders (which may be on the side or bottom of an object, not just the walkable surface), and then call `NavMesh.SamplePosition` to find the hit point position on the NavMesh. Modify the `LookTeleport` script as follows.

Add the following line at the top of your script to access the NavMesh API:

```
using UnityEngine.AI;
```

Now, modify `Update()` as follows:

```
if (Physics.Raycast(ray, out hit))
{
  NavMeshHit navHit;
  if (NavMesh.SamplePosition(hit.point, out navHit, 1.0f,
NavMesh.AllAreas))
    target.transform.position = navHit.position;
}
```

The call to `NavMesh.SamplePosition` takes the `hit.point` and finds the closest point on the NavMesh, within a given radius (we gave 1.0).

Press **Play**. Now, you can set the `TeleportMarker` not only on the walkable surface of the `GroundPlane` but also on top of the Overlook!

One more thing. Doing a `Physics.Raycast` can get quite expensive, especially in scenes with a lot of objects. You can limit the Raycast search by providing a layer mask. For example, create a layer named `Teleport` and set this layer for both `GroundPlane` and Overlook game objects. Then, modify the Raycast call as follows:

```
if (Physics.Raycast(ray, out hit, LayerMask.GetMask("Teleport")))
```

This will limit our Raycast to just the surfaces overlaid by the NavMesh, namely the ground plane and overlook.

The next scenario we'll consider is not permitting free roaming at all, but setting up a limited set of teleportation locations.

Teleport spawn points

It is very common in VR applications to limit teleportation to only specific predefined locations within the scene. In that case, you would not need any free-roaming glide locomotion or arbitrary teleportation targets. Instead, you can define the specific teleportation spawn points. Let's see how to do this.

First, let's create a `TeleportSpawn` prefab to mark our locations:

1. In Hierarchy, create a 3D **Sphere** and name it `TeleportSpawn`
2. Reset its transform (**gear icon** | **Reset**)
3. Set its **Scale** to `0.4, 0.4, 0.4`
4. Set its **Position** to something like (2, 0, 3)
5. Create a new layer named `TeleportSpawn` from **Inspector** | **Layers** | **Add Layer** and fill in the name in an empty slot
6. Select the `TeleportSpawn` object in Hierarchy again, and now set its layer (**Layers** | **TeleportSpawn**) to the one we just defined

Let's quickly make a material:

1. In your Materials folder, right-click to **Create** a new **Material** and name it `Teleport Material`
2. Set its **Rendering Mode** to **Transparent**
3. Set its **Albedo** color and give it a low alpha (such as 30) so it's translucent, such as our pale green (`70, 230, 70, 30`)
4. Drag the material onto the `TeleportSpawn` object

For this exercise, we'll replace the `LookTeleport` component on `MeMyselfEye` with a new `LookSpawnTeleport` one:

1. In Hierarchy, select `MeMyselfEye`
2. Disable the `LookTeleport` component, if present
3. Add **Component** | **New Script** and name it `LookSpawnTeleport`

Write the new script as follows:

```
using UnityEngine;

public class LookSpawnTeleport : MonoBehaviour
{
  private Color saveColor;
  private GameObject currentTarget;

    void Update()
    {
        Transform camera = Camera.main.transform;
        Ray ray;
        RaycastHit hit;
        GameObject hitTarget;
```

```
        ray = new Ray(camera.position, camera.rotation *
        Vector3.forward);
        if (Physics.Raycast(ray, out hit, 10f,
            LayerMask.GetMask("TeleportSpawn")))
        {
            hitTarget = hit.collider.gameObject;
            if (hitTarget != currentTarget)
            {
                Unhighlight();
                Highlight(hitTarget);
            }

            if (Input.GetButtonDown("Fire1"))
            {
                transform.position = hitTarget.transform.position;
            }
        }
        else if (currentTarget != null)
        {
            Unhighlight();
        }
    }
}
```

The `Update()` function does a Raycast to see if any of the spawn point objects is selected. If so, the object is highlighted (unhighlighting any previous ones). Then, if the `Fire1` button is pressed, it teleports the player to that location.

We add a couple of private helper functions, `Highlight()` and `Unhighlight()`. The first highlights an object by modifying its material color, making it more opaque (alpha 0.8). Unhighlight restores the original color when you look away:

```
private void Highlight(GameObject target)
{
    Material material = target.GetComponent<Renderer>().material;
    saveColor = material.color;
    Color hiColor = material.color;
    hiColor.a = 0.8f; // more opaque
    material.color = hiColor;
    currentTarget = target;
}

private void Unhighlight()
{
    if (currentTarget != null)
    {
      Material material =
```

```
currentTarget.GetComponent<Renderer>().material;
        material.color = saveColor;
        currentTarget = null;
    }
  }
```

OK, now let's place a few of the markers around the scene:

1. Drag the `TeleportSpawn` object from Hierarchy to your `Prefabs` folder in the **Project Assets**
2. Duplicate `TeleportSpawn` **three times**
3. **Position** one of them at (0, 0, −1.5) (the default `MeMyselfEye` position)
4. Move the others to suitable locations, such as (2, 0, 3), (−4, 0, 1), and if you have the Overlook, (3.5, 2.5, 0)

Alright! Press **Play**. When you look at a spawn point, it highlights. When you press the `Fire1` button, you teleport to the location.

It may be useful to add a reticle (small cursor) at the center of your camera view to help focus the player's attention on the teleport objects, as we did in `Chapter 6`, *World Space UI*, under the topic *The reticle cursor*.

Although the teleport works, it may be nice if it also sets your view direction. One way to do this is to carefully place the `TeleportSpawn` objects facing the direction we want the player to face, and setting the player's transform rotation, in addition to position.

To give a visual clue for the direction the spawn point is facing, we'll add a graphic. We have included an image file, `flip-flops.png`, with this book. Otherwise, use anything that indicates a forward direction. Perform the following steps:

1. Import the `flip-flops.png` texture by dragging it into your `Project Textures` folder (or navigating to **Import New Asset...**).
2. Create a new material in the Material folder and name it `FlipFlops`.
3. Drag the `flip-flops` texture onto the `FlipFlops` material's **Albedo** map and choose **Rendering Mode** as **Cutout**.
4. Select the `TeleportSpawn` object in **Hierarchy**.
5. Create a child **Quad** object (right-click **Create | 3D Object | Quad**).
6. Drag the `FlipFlops` material onto the `Quad`.
7. Set the Quad's **Transform Position** to (0, .01, 0) and its **Rotation** to (90, 0, 0) so that it lies flat on the ground plane.

8. Select the parent `TeleportSpawn` object and in Inspector, press **Apply** to save these changes to the prefab. Now all the spawns will have feet.
9. Note that for the one upon the Overlook, you can adjust its Quad so it's visible from below, such as **Position** (0, -0.2, 0) and **Rotation** (-90, 0, 180)

The modification to our script to apply the rotation is trivial:

```
if (Input.GetButtonDown("Fire1"))
{
    transform.position = hitTarget.transform.position;
    transform.rotation = hitTarget.transform.rotation;
}
```

There it is, a gaze-based teleportation system with predefined spawn points, as shown here in the **Scene** window:

Other teleport considerations

There's a lot more that can be said and done with teleportation. You may prefer to select the location using hand controllers rather than gaze. It is common to show the teleport pointer using an arced laser beam (using a Bezier curve). The teleport spawn point is often rendered using a glow or fiery effect. Many of these features have already been built and provided using higher-level VR toolkits (see next topic).

Blink teleport is a technique that does a fade-out fade-in between the change in player position. It is said to provide an additional degree of comfort. We won't show the code here, but there are several techniques for implementing fades for VR, such as creating a screen-space canvas that covers the entire camera with a black panel, and lerping its alpha channel as it fades (see `https://docs.unity3d.com/ScriptReference/Mathf.Lerp.html`). Some have even found fading with a literal blink effect is quite natural, where you rapidly fade out from top to bottom, and fade in bottom to top, like an eyelid closing and opening.

Another technique is to provide a third-person view of the scene from above, sometimes called a **mini-map**, **god view**, or **dollhouse view**. From this perspective, the player could point to a new location to teleport. This mini version of the scene could be an object the player uses as a tool in the main scene, or you transition to this view mode during the teleportation selection process.

You can also teleport to a different scene. Combined with the blink fade in/out, you call `SceneManager.LoadScene("OtherSceneName")` rather than simply changing the transform position. Note, you must add the other scene to the **Build Settings Scenes to Build** list (see `https://docs.unity3d.com/ScriptReference/SceneManagement.SceneManager.LoadScene.html`).

Clever use of teleportation and the player's direction can lead to efficient use of limited play space and give the perception of the VR space being much larger than actually in real life. For example, in room-scale VR, if you have the player walk toward the edge of the play space and enter an elevator (teleport), she could be facing the back of the elevator going in and must turn around when the doors open on the new level and can now physically walk forward. In fact, infinite corridors and connected rooms could be implemented this way while maintaining player immersion.

Teleportation toolkits

We have explored several different locomotion and teleportation mechanics. All of them use your gaze direction for selection. This is sometimes the best choice. Sometimes it's not. It certainly is the lowest common denominator between various VR devices, from high-end HTC VIVE and Oculus Rift to the low-end Google Cardboard, gaze-based selection with a simple click will always be available.

It is likely you will prefer to use the hand controller for selection. High-end systems include two positionally tracked controllers, one for each hand. Lower-end devices, such as Google Daydream, include a single 3DOF "laser pointer" controller. Another reason we avoided implementing with controllers so far is the coding varies greatly from one device to the next. Also, the device-specific toolkits often come with components and prefabs that implement this mechanic, optimized for their particular platform, including high-performance shaders for rendering arced laser beams and teleportation markers.

In this section, we will show how to implement teleportation using these higher-level components, using SteamVR Interaction System and Google Daydream Elements. If you're not using one of these, please see the toolkits project with your target device, or consider a generalized toolkit such as the open source VRTK (`https://github.com/thestonefox/VRTK`).

Teleporting with SteamVR Interaction System

The SteamVR Interaction System we first introduced in Chapter 5, *Handy Interactables* includes easy to use teleport components. If you are using SteamVR SDK, it can be found in the `Assets/SteamVR/InteractionSystem/Teleport/` folder. The teleport tools include a lot of extras we didn't get a chance to implement ourselves, including materials, models, prefabs, scripts, shaders, sounds, textures, haptics, oh my!

Specifically, the teleport toolkit includes:

- `Teleporting` prefab: Teleportation controller, add one per scene
- `TeleportPoint` prefab: Locations you want to teleport to, add one for each location
- `TeleportArea` component: Add to a game object, such as a Plane, to allow teleporting anywhere on that area

Interaction System includes its own `Player` camera rig which replaces the default `[CameraRig]` we have been using, as follows:

1. Locate the `Player` prefab in `SteamVR/InteractionSystem/Core/Prefabs`
2. Drag it as a child of `MeMyselfEye` in your scene **Hierarchy**
3. Delete or disable the `[CameraRig]` object

4. Drag a copy of `Teleporting` prefab from Project `Assets/SteamVR/InteractionSystem/Teleport/Prefabs` as a child of `MeMyselfEye` (this controller can actually go anywhere in the scene)
5. Select the **Player** in **Hierarchy**, and drag its parent `MeMyselfEye` onto its **Tracking Origin Transform** slot

This last step is important. The toolkit's teleportation components change the position of the `Player` object by default. We want to teleport the Player parent, `MeMyselfEye`, when we teleport. This might also be used if in your game, for example, the player is sitting in the cockpit of vehicle and you intend to teleport the whole vehicle, not just the Player itself.

If you followed the projects earlier in this chapter, disable the things we won't be using here:

1. On `MyMyselfEye`, disable or remove the **Look Teleport** and **Look Spawn Teleport** components
2. Disable or delete each of the `TeleportSpawn` objects

Now, for each teleport location:

1. Drag a copy of the `TeleportPoint` prefab from Project `Assets/SteamVR/InteractionSystem/Teleport/Prefabs` into the Hierarchy
2. Place one where you want in the scene. As previously, we used (0, 0, -1.5), (2, 0, 3), (-4, 0, 1), and on the Overlook (3.5, 2.5, 0)

That's it! Press **Play**. The teleport points do not show until you press the button on your controller, then they glow, a dashed laser arc lets you choose one, and you go there. In the Game window shown here, I am teleporting to the Overlook location:

Please review the many options on the Teleport component. You can modify or replace materials used for highlighting teleport points, sounds, and other effects. The Teleport Arc component has options for rendering the laser arc, and the `TeleportPoints` themselves can each be modified separately.

Teleporting with Daydream Elements

The Google Daydream Elements package we first introduced in Chapter 5, *Handy Interactables* includes some teleport components. If you are targeting Google Daydream, you can install the separate Daydream Elements download from GitHub (`https://github.com/googlevr/daydream-elements/releases`). And documentation can be found on the Elements site (`https://developers.google.com/vr/elements/teleportation`).

Once imported into your project, it can be found in the `Assets/DaydreamElements/Elements/Teleport/` folder. There is a demo scene, **Teleport**, and associated materials, models, prefabs, scripts, shaders, and textures.

Out of the box, the tools are pretty generic and very customizable. The primary prefab is `TeleportController`, which does all the work. The user input used to trigger teleport behavior can be configured in the Unity Editor by filling the component slots, as shown here:

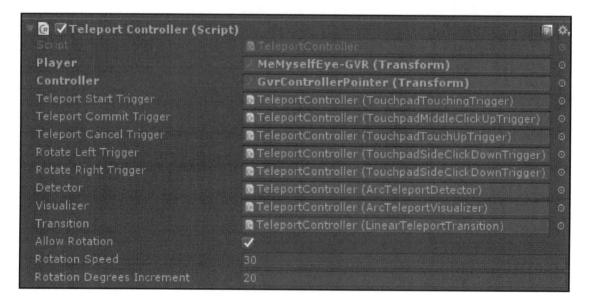

You can extend the teleporter by changing its *detector*, *visualizer*, and *transition* classes.

- **Detector**: Such as the `ArcTeleportDetector` does a curved arc Raycast to find objects in the scene and limits the hit to horizontal surfaces with adequate space to "fit" the player, so you do not teleport into walls.
- **Visualizer**: Such as the `ArcTeleportVisualizer`, renders the arc when teleport is triggered.
- **Transition**: Such as `LinearTeleportTransition`, animates the player to the new location. This could be modified to implement a blink effect, for example.

To add it to your scene:

1. Drag the `TeleportController` prefab into your **Hierarchy** as child of **Player** (for us that `MeMyselfEye` | **GVRCameraRig** | **Player**)
2. Reset its **Transform**, if necessary
3. Drag the `MeMyselfEye` object onto the `TeleportController` component's **Player** transform slot
4. Drag `GvrControllerPointer` (or whichever controller game object you're using) onto the **Controller** transform slot

Press **Play** and you can teleport all around your scene. There is no need to place specific teleport targets.

By default, the `TeleportController` will work by letting you land on any object in the scene that has a collider. You can limit the objects considered by the detector's Raycast by specifying the layer(s). Also, if you want arbitrarily shaped target areas that are not necessarily game objects in your scene, you can add sets of objects with just colliders, no renderers. This is how the teleport areas on the islands are implemented in the Daydream Elements teleport demo.

Resetting center and position

Sometimes in VR, the view presented in the headset is not quite in sync with your body's orientation. Device SDKs provide functions to reset the orientation of the headset with respect to the real-world space. This is often referred to as the **recentering** of the view.

Unity provides an API call that maps to the underlying device SDK to recenter the device, `UnityEngine.VR.InputTracking.Recenter()`. This function will center tracking to the current position and orientation of the HMD. It only works with seated and standing experiences. Room scale experiences are not affected.

At the time of this writing, Recenter does not work in SteamVR, even for seated configuration. The solution is to call the following code instead:

```
Valve.VR.OpenVR.System.ResetSeatedZeroPose();
Valve.VR.OpenVR.Compositor.SetTrackingSpace(Valve.VR.ETrackingUniverseOrigi
n.TrackingUniverseSeated);
```

The Daydream controller has reset built into the underlying system (press and hold the system button). This is because unwanted drift is so common on mobile VR devices. Also, for Cardboard (and Daydream users without a controller), there is a standard floor canvas menu you should include in your player rig (as we did in Chapter 3, *VR Build and Run*), that includes a reset and recenter buttons.

On other systems, you can choose a button that triggers a call to Recenter as needed.

Supporting room scale teleportation

As mentioned, the Unity Recenter function does not have any affect on room scale setups. We assume that room scale players are standing and mobilized, so they can just turn themselves to face "forward" within the VR scene.

When teleporting, however, we are moving the player to a new location, and possibly to an entirely different scene. When we reposition MyMyselfEye or any parent of the positionally tracked camera, the player is not necessary located at origin of that rig. If the player teleports to a new location, his whole play space should be ported and the player should end up standing on the virtual location he specifically chose.

The following function will compensate the teleport transform to the player's relative pose within the playspace. As written, it assumes it is a component on the MeMyselfEye player root object:

```
private void TeleportRoomscale( Vector3 targetPosition )
{
    Transform camera = Camera.main.transform;
    float cameraAngle = camera.eulerAngles.y;
    transform.Rotate( 0f, -cameraAngle, 0f);
    Vector3 offsetPos = camera.position - transform.position;
    transform.position = targetPosition.position - offsetPos;
}
```

To use it in our previous teleport script examples, replace the `transform.position = target.transform.position;` line with a call to `TeleportRoomscale( target.transform.position )` instead.

Managing VR motion sickness

VR motion sickness, or simulator sickness, is a real symptom and a concern for virtual reality. Researchers, psychologists, and technologists with a wide array of specializations and PhDs are studying the problem to better understand the underlying causes and find solutions.

A cause of VR motion sickness is a lag in screen updates, or latency when you're moving your head. Your brain expects the world around you to change exactly in sync. Any perceptible delay can make you feel uncomfortable, to say the least.

Latency can be reduced by faster rendering of each frame, keeping to the recommended frames per second. Device manufacturers see this as their problem to solve, in both hardware and device driver software. GPU and chip manufacturers see it as processor performance and throughput problem. We will undoubtedly see leaps and bounds of improvements over the coming years.

At the same time, as VR developers, we need to be aware of latency and other causes of VR motion sickness. Developers need to look at it like it's our problem too because ultimately, it comes down to performance and ergonomics. With an ongoing dichotomy of mobile VR versus desktop VR, there will always be upper bounds on the performance of devices that our players will be using.

But it's not just technology. I can get nauseous riding a real-world roller coaster. So, why wouldn't a VR one have a similar effect? Things to consider that help improve your players' comfort and safety include game mechanics and user experience design such as the following:

- **Don't move fast**: When moving or animating a first-person character, don't move too fast. High-speed first-person shooter games that work on gaming consoles and desktop PCs may not work out so well in VR.
- **Look forward**: When moving through a scene, if you're looking to the side rather than straight ahead, you're more likely to feel nauseous.

- **Don't turn your head too fast**: Discourage users from turning their head quickly with the VR headset on. The latency in updating the HMD screen is aggravated by larger changes in the viewport in small time slices.
- **Offer comfort mode**: When a scene requires you to quickly turn yourself a lot of times, provide a ratcheted rotation mechanism, also known as comfort mode, which lets you change the direction in which you look in larger increments.
- **Use fade or blink** cuts during teleportation and scene changes. When fading, go to a dark color, as white can be startling.
- **Use tunneling** or other techniques during locomotion. Reduce what is visible in the peripheral vision by masking the camera except what is just in front of you.
- **Use a third-person camera**: If you have high-speed action but you don't necessarily intend to give the user a thrill ride, use a third-person camera view.
- **Stay grounded**: Provide visual cues that help the user stay grounded, such as horizon lines, nearby objects in your field of view, and relative fixed-position objects, such as dashboards and body parts.
- **Provide an option to recenter the view**: Mobile VR devices, in particular, are subject to drift and the need to be recentered on occasion. With wired VR devices, it helps you avoid getting tangled in HMD wires. As a safety issue, recentering your view relative to the real world may help you avoid hitting furniture and walls in the physical space.
- **Don't use cut scenes**: In traditional games (and movies), a technique that can be used to transition between levels is to show a 2D cutscene movie. This does not work in VR if the head motion detection is disabled. It breaks the immersion and can cause nausea. An alternative is to simply fade to black and then open the new scene.
- **Optimize rendering performance**: It behooves all VR developers to understand the underlying causes of latency-specifically rendering performance-and what you can do to optimize it, such as lowering the poly count and choosing lighting models carefully. Learn to use performance monitoring tools in order to keep the frames per second within the expected and acceptable limits.
- **Encourage users to take breaks**: Alternatively, you can maybe just provide a puke-bag with your game! Or not.

Summary

In this chapter, we explored many different ways of moving around within your virtual environments. We started by examining Unity's components that support conventional third-person and first-person characters and quickly realized most of those capabilities are not too useful in VR. For instance, we don't want the app to bob our head up and down as we walk, and we don't necessarily want to go jumping off buildings either. Moving around is important, but player comfort is more so. You don't want to induce motion sickness.

Locomotion is moving smoothly and linearly across the scene, akin to walking. Using gaze-based mechanics, we implemented moving in the direction you're looking and used input buttons to start and stop. Then, we separated the locomotion from head direction, always moving "forward" and using a separate input (thumbpad) to change the angle our body is facing. With this *comfort mode*, you can locomote and still look around.

Jumping to a new location is called teleportation. We started again with a gaze-based mechanic, letting you select a teleport location where you're looking. We implemented a couple of ways of constraining where you are allowed to teleport, using NavMesh and using teleport spawn points. Then, we looked at some teleportation toolkits, from SteamVR and Google Daydream, which provide a rich set of capabilities, as well as a juicy user experience that is not trivial to implement from scratch. If you're targeting a different platform, such as Oculus, there are similar tools.

In the next chapter, we'll explore the Unity physics engine more and implement some interactive games.

Playing with Physics and Fire

8

In this chapter, we will use physics and other Unity features to build variations of an interactive ball game. Along the way, we explore managing objects, Rigidbody physics, and adding more interactivity to the virtual experience. You will see how properties and materials based on physics can be added to objects, as well as more on C# scripting, particle effects, and music.

In this chapter, you will learn about the following topics:

- The Unity physics engine, the Unity Rigidbody component, and Physic Materials
- Using velocity and gravity
- Managing object lifetime and object pooling
- Interacting with objects in VR using your head and hands
- Building a fireball using particle effects
- Synchronizing with music

 Note that the projects in this chapter are separate and are not directly required by the other chapters in this book. If you decided to skip any of it or not save your work, that's OK.

Unity physics

In Unity, the behavior of an object that is based on physics is defined separately from its mesh (shape), materials (UV texture), and the renderer properties. The items that play into physics include the following:

- **Rigidbody**: Enables the object to act under the control of the physics engine, receive forces and torque to move in a realistic way
- **Collider**: Defines a simplified, approximated shape of the object used for calculating collisions with other objects

- **Physic Material**: Defines friction and bounce effects of colliding objects
- **Physics Manager**: Applies global settings for 3D physics for your project

Basically, physics (in this context) is defined by the positional and rotational forces that affect the transform of an object, such as gravity, friction, momentum, and collisions with other objects. It is not necessarily a perfect simulation of physics in the real world because it's optimized for performance and separation of concerns to facilitate animation. Besides, virtual worlds might just need their own laws of physics that aren't found in our God-given universe!

Unity integrates the **NVIDIA PhysX** engine, a real-time physics calculation middleware, which implements classical Newtonian mechanics for games and 3D applications. This multiplatform software is optimized to utilize fast hardware processors when present. It is accessible via the Unity scripting API.

A key to physics is the Rigidbody component that you add to objects. Rigidbodies have parameters for gravity, mass, and drag, among others. Rigidbodies can automatically react to gravity and collisions with other objects. No extra scripting is needed for this. During gameplay, the engine calculates each rigid object's momentum and updates its transform position and rotation.

Details on Rigidbodies can be found at
http://docs.unity3d.com/ScriptReference/Rigidbody.html.

Unity projects have a global gravity setting, found in the project's Physics Manager by navigating to **Edit | Project Settings | Physics**. As you might expect, the default gravity setting is a **Vector3** with values (0, -9.81, 0) that apply a downward force to all Rigidbodies. Gravity is in meters per second squared.

Rigidbodies can automatically react to gravity and collisions with other objects. Extra scripting is not needed for this.

In order to detect a collision, both the colliding objects must have a `Collider` component. There are built-in colliders with basic geometric shapes such as a cube, sphere, cylinder, and a capsule. A mesh collider can assume an arbitrary shape. If you can, it's best to use one or more basic collider shapes that approximately fit the actual object, rather than a mesh collider to reduce the expense of calculating the actual collisions during gameplay. Unity requires that if your object will be used in physics and has a Rigidbody, then its mesh collider must be marked as convex and be limited to 255 triangles.

When rigid objects collide, the forces pertinent to each object in the collision are applied to the others. The values of the resulting forces are calculated based on the objects' current velocity and body mass. Other factors are also taken into consideration, such as gravity and drag (that is, resistance). Furthermore, you have options to add constraints to freeze the position or rotation of a given object in any of its x, y, and z axes.

The calculations can be further affected when a Physic Material is assigned to the object's collider, which adjusts the friction and the bounciness effects of the colliding objects. These properties will be applied only to the object that owns the Physic Material. (Note that it's really spelled *Physic Material* rather than *Physics Material* for historical reasons.)

So, let's say that Object A (Ball) hits Object B (Brick). If Object A has bounciness and Object B does not, Object A will have an impulse applied in the collision, but Object B will not. However, you have options to determine how their friction and bounciness combine, as we'll see next. It's not necessarily an accurate simulation of real-world physics. It's a game engine, not a computer-aided engineering modeler.

From a scripting point of view, Unity will trigger events when objects collide (`OnTriggerEnter`), each frame while objects are colliding (`OnTriggerStay`), and when they've stopped colliding (`OnTriggerExit`).

If this sounds daunting, read on. The rest of this chapter breaks it down into understandable bits and pieces.

Bouncy balls

The feature we'll implement here is, when a ball drops from mid-air and hits the ground, it bounces back up and down, and up again, diminished over time.

We are going to start simply with a new scene that consists of a ground plane and a sphere. Then, we'll add physics to it, a bit at a time, as follows:

1. Create a new scene by navigating to **File | New Scene.**
2. Then, navigate to **File | Save Scene As...** and name it BallsFromHeaven.
3. Create a new plane by navigating to **GameObject | 3D Object | Plane** and reset its transform using the Transform component's *gear* icon | **Reset.**
4. Create a new sphere by navigating to **GameObject | 3D Object | Sphere** and rename it BouncyBall.
5. Set its **Scale** to (0.5, 0.5, 0.5) and **Position** to (0, 5,0) so that it's above the center of the plane.
6. Drag the **Red** material from **Project Assets** (created in Chapter 2, *Content, Objects and Scale*) onto it so that it looks like a bouncy ball.

The new Unity scene defaults come with **Directional Light** and **Main Camera**. It's OK to use this **Main Camera** for the time being.

Click on the *Play* button. Nothing happens. The ball just sits in mid-air and doesn't move.

Now, let's give it a Rigidbody, as follows:

1. With BouncyBall selected, in **Inspector**, navigate to **Add Component | Physics | Rigidbody**.
2. Click on the *Play* button. It drops like a lead balloon.

Let's make it bounce, as follows:

1. In the **Project** panel, select the top-level **Assets** folder, navigate to **Create | Folder**, and rename it to Physics
2. With the Physics folder selected, create a material by navigating to **Assets | Create | Physic Material** (or right-click within the folder)
3. Name it Bouncy
4. Set its **Bounciness** value to 1
5. With the BouncyBall sphere selected in **Hierarchy**, drag the Bouncy asset from **Project** onto the sphere's **Collider** material field in **Inspector**

Click on the *Play* button. It bounces, but it does not go very high. We used the maximum value for **Bounciness** as 1.0. What's slowing it down? It's not the **Friction** settings. Rather, the **Bounce Combine** is set to **Average**, which determines how much of the bounciness of the ball (1) is mixed with that of the plane (0). So, it diminishes rapidly over time. We want the ball to retain all its bounciness. We will accomplish this, as follows:

1. Change the Bouncy object's **Bounce Combine** to **Maximum**.
2. Click on the *Play* button.

Much better. Actually, too much better. The ball keeps bouncing back up to its original height, ignoring gravity. Now, change the **Bounciness** to 0.8. The bounces diminish, and the ball will eventually come to a stop.

Let's check it out in VR, as follows:

1. Delete the default **Main Camera** from the **Hierarchy** root.
2. Drag the MeMyselfEye prefab from **Project Assets** into the scene. Set its **Position** to (0, 0, -4).

Run it in VR. Pretty neat! Even the simplest things look impressive in VR.

 Unity's Standard Assets package includes a handful of example physic materials, including Bouncy, Ice, Meta, Rubber, and Wood.

OK, let's have some fun. Make it rain bouncy balls! To do this, we'll make the ball a prefab and write a script that instantiates new balls, dropping them from random positions, as follows:

1. Drag the BouncyBall object from **Hierarchy** into the Project Assets/Prefabs folder, making it a prefab.
2. Delete the BouncyBall object from the **Hierarchy**, since we'll be instantiating it with a script.
3. Create an empty game controller object to attach the script to by navigating to **GameObject | Create Empty**. Rename it GameController.
4. In **Inspector**, navigate to **Add Component | New Script**, name it BallsFromHeaven, and open the script for editing.

Edit the script so that it looks like this:

```
using UnityEngine;

public class BallsFromHeaven : MonoBehaviour
{
  public GameObject ballPrefab;
  public float startHeight = 10f;
  public float interval = 0.5f;

  private float nextBallTime = 0f;

  void Update ()
  {
    if (Time.time > nextBallTime)
    {
      nextBallTime = Time.time + interval;
      Vector3 position = new Vector3( Random.Range (-4f, 4f),
        startHeight, Random.Range (-4f, 4f) );
      Instantiate( ballPrefab, position, Quaternion.identity );
    }
  }
}
```

The script drops a new ball from `startHeight` at the rate of every `interval` seconds (an interval of 0.5 means that a new ball is dropped every half second). The new ball position is at a random **X-Z** coordinate between `-4` and `4`. The `Instantiate()` function adds a new ball into the scene **Hierarchy**.

Save the script. We now need to populate the **Ball** field with the `BouncyBall` prefab, as follows:

1. With `GameController` selected in **Hierarchy**, drag the `BouncyBall` prefab from the `Project Assets/Prefabs` folder onto the **Ball Prefab** slot in the **Balls From Heaven (Script)** panel in **Inspector**.
2. Be sure to use the `BouncyBall` prefab from **Project Assets** so that can be instantiated.
3. Save the scene. Run it in VR. Fun!

This is what I get:

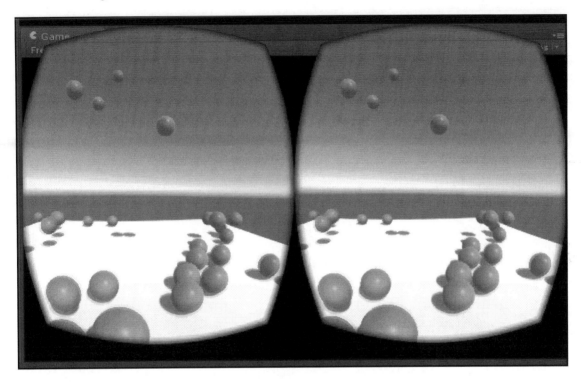

In summary, we created a sphere with a Rigidbody and added a Physic Material with a **Bounciness** property of 0.8 and **Bounce Combine** to **Maximum**. Then, we saved the BouncyBall as a prefab and wrote a script to instantiate new balls that drop from above.

Managing game objects

Whenever you have a script that instantiates objects, you must be aware of the life cycle of the object and possibly arrange to destroy it when it is no longer needed. You can destroy game objects, for example, after it is no longer visible in the scene, or after a specific life duration, or limit the scene to a maximum number of balls.

Destroying fallen objects

In our scene, we have a limited size ground plane and as balls hit one another, some will fall off the plane into oblivion. At that point, we can remove the fallen ball from the scene. Watch the **Hierarchy** panel as new balls are instantiated. Note that some balls end up bouncing off the plane platform but remain in the **Hierarchy** panel. We need to clean this up by adding a script that destroys the balls that are out of play, as follows:

1. Select the `BouncyBall` prefab in `Project Assets/Prefabs`
2. Navigate to **Add Component** | **New Script** and name it `DestroyBall`

Here's a `DestroyBall.cs` script, which will destroy the object if its **Y** position is well below the ground plane (**Y** = 0):

```
using UnityEngine;
using System.Collections;

public class DestroyBall : MonoBehaviour
{
  void Update ()
  {
    if (transform.position.y < -5f)
    {
      Destroy (gameObject);
    }
  }
}
```

Setting a limited lifetime

Another strategy for managing object life cycle is to limit their duration. This is especially effective for things like projectiles (bullets, arrows, bouncyballs) or other objects that the player cares about most when its instantiated and then isn't paying attention to as gameplay moves on.

To implement, you could put a timer on the object prefab itself to destroy itself when time runs out.

Modify the `DestroyBall.cs` script to destroy the object after `delay` seconds:

```
public float timer = 15f;

void Start ()
{
```

```
    Destroy (gameObject, timer);
  }
```

When you play, notice that the ground plane remains substantially less crowded than before. Each BouncyBall will be destroyed after 15 seconds or when it has fallen off the plane, whichever comes first.

Implementing an object pool

If your `GameController` Interval is 0.5 seconds and the destroy timer is 15, then (do the math) there will be at most 30 balls in play at a time. Or less, if some have fallen over the edge. In that case, we do not need to make our app continuously allocate new memory for a new instance of BouncyBall, only to delete that object up to 15 seconds later. Too much instantiation and destroying of objects results in fragmented memory. Unity will periodically go through and clean this up, a computationally expensive process called **garbage collection** (**GC**) that is best to be avoided whenever possible.

Object pooling is when you create a list of reusable objects to be used in your game, rather than continuously instantiating new ones. You will activate/deactivate the objects instead of instantiate/destroy.

To implement this, we will write a generic object pooler and add it to the `GameController` in the scene.

For this, we are also introducing you to the concept of lists in C#. As the name indicates, a list is an ordered collection of objects, like an array. Lists can be searched, sorted, and otherwise manipulated (see the documentation here: `https://msdn.microsoft.com/en-us/library/6sh2ey19.aspx`). We will use them simply to hold our pre-instantiated objects. Let's name the script `ObjectPooler`:

1. Select the `GameController` in Hierarchy
2. Navigate to **Add Component** | **New Script** and name it `ObjectPooler`

Open for editing. Let's start by declaring several variables at the top:

```
using System.Collections.Generic;
using UnityEngine;

public class ObjectPooler : MonoBehaviour
{
    public GameObject prefab;
    public int pooledAmount = 20;
```

```
        private List<GameObject> pooledObjects;

  }
```

The public `prefab` will get the prefab object we want to instantiate, namely `BouncyBall`. And `pooledAmount` says how many objects to initially instantiate. The actual list is held in `pooledObjects`.

Now, when the scene starts, we initialize the list as follows:

```
void Start () {
    pooledObjects = new List<GameObject>();
    for (int i = 0; i < pooledAmount; i++)
    {
        GameObject obj = (GameObject)Instantiate(prefab);
        obj.SetActive(false);
        pooledObjects.Add(obj);
    }
}
```

We allocate a new list and populate it in the `for` loop, by instantiating our prefab, initially making it inactive, and adding it to the list.

Now when we want a new object, we'll call `GetPooledObject`, which looks for one in the list that is presently not active. If all of them are active and none is available for reuse, we return `null`:

```
public GameObject GetPooledObject()
{
    for (int i = 0; i < pooledObjects.Count; i++)
    {
        if (!pooledObjects[i].activeInHierarchy)
        {
            return pooledObjects[i];
        }
    }

    return null;
}
```

That's it.

We can also enhance the script to optionally grow the list so it never returns null. Add the option at the top:

```
public bool willGrow = true;
```

And add the following statements to `GetPooledObject` after the `for` loop:

```
...
if (willGrow)
{
    GameObject obj = (GameObject)Instantiate(prefab);
    pooledObjects.Add(obj);
    return obj;
}

return null;
}
```

Save the script, attach it to `GameController`, and drag the `BouncyBall` prefab onto the **Prefab** slot for the component.

Now we need to modify our `BallsFromHeaven` script to call `GetPooledObject` from `ObjectPooler` instead of `Instantiate`. The updated `BallsFromHeaven` script is as follows:

```
using UnityEngine;

[RequireComponent(typeof(ObjectPooler))]
public class BallsFromHeaven : MonoBehaviour
{
    public float startHeight = 10f;
    public float interval = 0.5f;

    private float nextBallTime = 0f;
    private ObjectPooler pool;

    void Start()
    {
        pool = GetComponent<ObjectPooler>();
        if (pool == null)
        {
            Debug.LogError("BallsFromHeaven requires ObjectPooler
component");
        }
    }

    void Update()
    {
        if (Time.time > nextBallTime)
        {
            nextBallTime = Time.time + interval;
            Vector3 position = new Vector3(Random.Range(-4f, 4f),
```

```
startHeight, Random.Range(-4f, 4f));
            GameObject ball = pool.GetPooledObject();
            ball.transform.position = position;
            ball.transform.rotation = Quaternion.identity;
            ball.GetComponent<RigidBody>().velocity = Vector3.zero;
            ball.SetActive(true);
        }
    }
}
```

Note that we added a directive, [RequireComponent(typeof(ObjectPooler))], to ensure the object has an ObjectPooler component (and we also double-check in the Start function).

It's important to note that since we're not instantiating new objects but reusing them, you may need to reset any object properties to their starting values. In this case, we reset not just the transform but the RigidBody's velocity to zero.

The last part is we modify DestroyBall to just disable (deactivate) the object rather than literally destroying it. Initially, handle the *fallen off the ground plane* case as follows:

```
using UnityEngine;

public class DestroyBall : MonoBehaviour {

    void Update () {
        if (transform.position.y < -5f)
        {
            DisableMe();
        }
    }

    private void DisableMe()
    {
        gameObject.SetActive(false);
    }
}
```

Instead of calling Destroy, we changed Update to call a new function, DisableMe, which simply deactivates the object, returning it to the pool of available objects.

For the timed destroy, there's a number of different ways to implement this. Earlier, we called Destroy(gameObject, timer) from Start(). We can do something similar, using OnEnable instead of Start, since that's when this instance starts. And it calls Invoke(), instead of destroy directly:

```
void OnEnable()
{
    Invoke("DisableMe", timer);
}

void OnDisable()
{
    CancelInvoke();
}
```

We also provide an `OnDisable` to cancel the `Invoke`, since the object could be disabled should the ball fall over the edge before the timer is done and potentially re-enabled, we should make sure it's not being invoked twice at the same time.

Now when you press **Play**, you can see in Inspector that new BouncyBalls are instantiated at the start to initialize the list, and then as it plays the objects are disabled and reactivated as they are returned to the pool and reused, as shown here (deactivated **BouncyBall(Clone)** objects are dimmer than the activated ones):

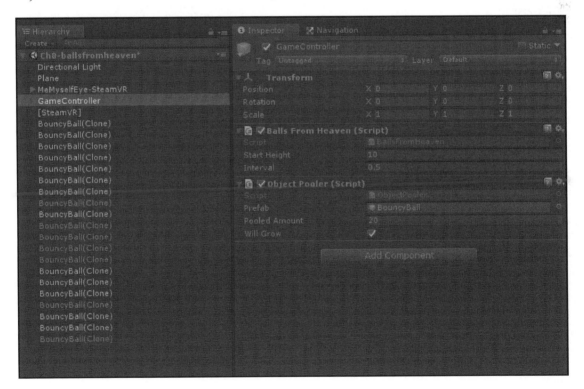

Headshot game

Wouldn't it be fun to actually play with these bouncy balls? Let's make a game where you aim the ball at a target using headshots. For this game, balls drop one at a time from above and bounce off your forehead (face), aiming for a target.

The feature we'll implement here is, when a ball drops from above your head, you bounce it off your face and aim for a target.

To implement this, create a cube as a child of the camera object. This provides a collider parented by the VR camera, so our head pose will move the face of the cube. I decided a cube-shaped collider will be better for this game than a sphere or capsule because it provides a flat face that will make the bounce direction more predictable. Balls will drop out of the sky. For a target, we'll use a flattened cylinder. We'll add audio cues to indicate when a new ball has been released and when a ball hits the target.

Create a new scene or, more simple, start here by doing a Save As, and implement the head as follows:

1. Navigate to **File** | **Save Scene As** and name it `BallGame`
2. Delete the `BallsFromHeaven` script component attached to `GameController` using the *gear* icon **Remove Component**. We won't need it
3. In **Hierarchy**, unfold `MeMyselfEye`, drilling down to the `Camera` object and selecting it (for OpenVR that might be `[CameraRig]/Camera (head)`; for Daydream, it may be `Player/Main Camera/`)
4. Create a new **3D Object** | **Cube**
5. With `GameController` selected, navigate to **Add Component** | **Audio** | **Audio Source**
6. Click on the small *circle-shaped* icon on the far right of the **AudioClip** field of **Audio Source** to open the **Select AudioClip** dialog box and choose the clip named `Jump`
7. With `GameController` selected, navigate to **Add Component** | **New Script**, name it `BallGame`, and open it for editing

You can decide to disable the cube's **Mesh Renderer**, but I think it's cool to watch it in the Scene window as you play. Since the camera is inside the cube, the player will not see it (since only the outward facing surfaces are rendered in the game view).

We'll play the `Jump` sound clip (provided with the `Characters` package of Unity's **Standard Assets**) to indicate when a new ball is dropped. You might try another, perhaps more interesting, effect.

Here's the `BallGame.cs` script. It looks a lot like the `BallsFromHeaven` one with just a few differences:

```
using UnityEngine;

public class BallGame : MonoBehaviour
{
    public Transform dropPoint;
    public float startHeight = 10f;
    public float interval = 3f;

    private float nextBallTime = 0f;
    private ObjectPooler pool;
    private GameObject activeBall;
    private AudioSource soundEffect;

    void Start()
    {
        if (dropPoint == null)
        {
            dropPoint = Camera.main.transform;
        }
        soundEffect = GetComponent<AudioSource>();
        pool = GetComponent<ObjectPooler>();
    }

    void Update()
    {
        if (Time.time > nextBallTime)
        {
            nextBallTime = Time.time + interval;
            soundEffect.Play();
            Vector3 position = new Vector3(
                dropPoint.position.x,
                startHeight,
                dropPoint.position.z);

            activeBall = pool.GetPooledObject();
            activeBall.transform.position = position;
```

```
            activeBall.transform.rotation = Quaternion.identity;
            activeBall.GetComponent<RigidBody>().velocity = Vector3.zero;
            activeBall.SetActive(true);
        }
    }
}
```

We instantiate a new ball every 3 seconds (`interval`) from a `startHeight` position above the current head position.

The drop point defaults to directly above the player's head position, as defined by the VR camera. That may feel uncomfortable on your neck, so let's extend it in front a little, 0.2 units:

1. As a child of `MeMyselfEye` (or as a child of your head or main camera object), create an empty game object and name it `Drop Point`
2. Set its Position to (0, 0, 0.2)
3. Drag this `Drop Point` onto the `GameController`'s Ball Game Drop Point slot

On positionally tracked VR rigs, if your drop point is relative to the camera, it will follow the player around. If it's relative to `MeMyselfEye`, it will be relative to your play space while the player can move around.

Try it in VR.

When you hear the ball, look up and aim the angle of your face to direct the bounce of the ball. *COOOL!*

Now, we need the target. Perform the following steps:

1. Create a flat cylinder for the target, navigate to **Game Object | 3D Object | Cylinder**, and name it `Target`.
2. Set its **Scale** to (3, 0.1, 3) and **Position** to (1, 0.2, 2.5) so that it's out in front of you on the ground.
3. Drag the `Blue` material from the `Project Assets/Materials` folder onto it, or make a new one.
4. Note that its default Capsule Collider is domed, and it really won't do. On the Capsule Collider, select its *gear* icon | **Remove Component**.

5. Then, navigate to **Add Component** | **Physics** | **Mesh Collider**.
6. In the new **Mesh Collider**, enable the **Convex** checkbox and the **Is Trigger** checkbox too.
7. Add an audio source by navigating to **Add Component** | **Audio** | **Audio Source**.
8. With the `Target` selected, click on the small *circle* icon on the far right of the **AudioClip** field to open the **Select AudioClip** dialog box, and choose the clip named `Land` (found in Standard Assets).
9. Uncheck the **Play On Awake** checkbox.
10. And a new script, navigate to **Add Component** | **New Script**, name it `TriggerSound`, and open it in MonoDevelop.

Since we enabled Is Trigger, when something hits the collider, the `OnTriggerEnter` and other event handlers will get a call when present on the target object. The following `TriggerSound.cs` script will play a sound clip when you hit the target with a ball:

```
using UnityEngine;
using System.Collections;

public class TriggerSound : MonoBehaviour {
  public AudioSource hitSound;

  void Start() {
    hitSound = GetComponent<AudioSource> ();
  }

  void OnTriggerEnter(Collider other) {
    hitSound.Play ();
  }
}
```

The ball enters the target's collider and the physics engine invokes a trigger enter event. The script uses the `OnTriggerEnter()` handler to play the audio clip.

For a full list of the collider properties and trigger events, including `OnTrggerEnter` and `OnTriggerExit`, see the documentation at `https:/ /docs.unity3d.com/ScriptReference/Collider.html`.

Try it in VR. It's a VR game! The following image shows the scene with the first person's colliders and a ball bouncing off the cube collider towards the target:

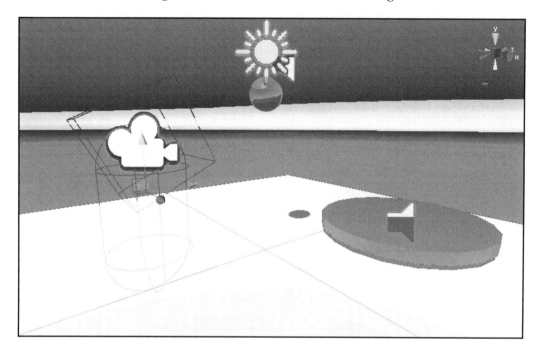

 Extra challenge: Keep score. Provide an aiming reticle. Add a backboard. Add other features to make the game more challenging. For instance, you can vary the fire interval or increase the initial ball velocity.

Up to this point, we assigned **Bounciness** through a Physic Material attached to a sphere object. When the ball collides with another object, the Unity physics engine considers this bounciness to determine the ball's new velocity and direction. In the following section, we'll look at how one can transfer a bounce force from one object to another.

Paddle ball game

Next, we'll add hand controlled paddles to hit the ball. To keep things somewhat generic, our game paddles will be simple objects parented by the hand controllers in your camera rig. We'll move the target to be on a wall instead of the floor, and serve the balls a little further out in front of you so they're reachable

To set up the scene, you can Save As a new name and we'll work from here. I'll name my `PaddleBallGame`.

1. Select **File** | **Save Scene As** and name it `PaddleBallGame`
2. Disable the head **Cube** we previously added as a child of the camera, if present

First, let's create a paddle. We'll construct a very simple model using cylinders. You can find better ones, shaped and textured, online.

1. In the **Hierarchy** root, **Create** | **Create Empty**, name it `Paddle`, and reset its **Transform**
2. Add a child cylinder object (**Create** | **3D Object** | **Cylinder**) and name it `Handle`
3. Set the Handle's **Scale** to ($0.02, 0.1, 0.02$)
4. Add another **Cylinder** as a sibling of Handle and name it `Pad`
5. Set the pad's **Scale** to ($0.2, 0.005, 0.2$), **Rotation** ($90, 0, 0$), and **Position** ($0, 0.2, 0$)
6. In your Project Materials folder, create a new material (**Create** | **Material**) and name it `Paddle Material`
7. Give the material **Albedo** a wooden color, such as ($107, 79, 54, 255$), then drag the material onto the **Handle** and **Pad** objects

Now, modify the colliders:

1. Select the **Handle**, and delete its **Capsule Collider**
2. Select the **Pad**, and delete its **Capsule Collider**
3. With Pad selected, add a Mesh Collider (**Add Component** | **Physics** | **Mesh Collider**)
4. Check the **Convex** checkbox

Save the paddle as a prefab:

1. Drag the **Paddle** into your Project Prefabs folder
2. Delete the **Paddle** from your Hierarchy

We want to parent the Paddle to your hands. This is platform-specific. If you are using OpenVR, for example, that may be `MeMyselfEye` / `[CameraRig]` / `Controller` *(right)*. On Daydream, that might be `MeMyselfEye` / `Player` / `GvrControllerPointer`.

1. In **Hierarchy**, select the hand controller within `MeMyselfEye` (such as Controller (right). or `GvrControllerPointer`)
2. Create **Empty** child game object and name it `Hand` (reset its **Transform** if needed)
3. Create another **Empty** child beneath **Hand** and name it `Attach Point` (and reset its Transform if needed)
4. Drag the **Paddle** prefab from Project into **Hierarchy** as a child of **Attach Point**

Now, we can adjust the paddle's relative position and rotation so its grip feels natural within your hand. The following values seem to work for me:

- In OpenVR, use the attach point **Rotation** (20, 90, 90)
- In Daydream, use **Position** (0, 0, 0, 05) and **Rotation** (0, 90, 90)

On Daydream, the `GvrControllerPointer` includes a `GvrArmModel` component that can be configured for simulating arm, elbow, and wrist movement with the simple 3DOF controller. Setting this up yourself can be confusing. Fortunately, a bunch of examples are provided in the **ArmModelDemo** scene the Daydream Elements package (in the `DaydreamElements/Elements/ArmModels/Demo/` folder) including prefabs with some preconfigured arm models. Let's add one. If you are on Daydream:

1. Find the `Elements/ArmModels/Prefabs` folder in Project Assets
2. Drag the `SwingArm` prefab into `MeMyselfEye` / `Player` as a sibling of `GvrControllerPointer`
3. Move `GvrControllerPointer` as a child of **SwingArm**

This will give more arm extension for using the paddle. You can further adjust the settings as needed, including try moving the SwingArm transform **Position** further in front (0, 0, 0.3).

Lastly, you might want to extend the ball drop location a little further out in front of you so it's more readily within hand reach. In the earlier version of the project, we defined a **Drop Point**; modify its position as desired (for example, z = 0.6).

The paddle in play using HTC Vive is shown here:

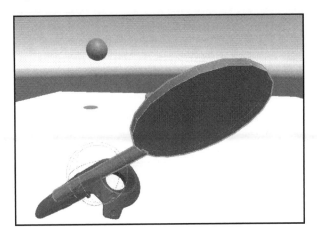

Deflector versus paddle

As implemented, our paddle acts more like a deflector shield than a paddle. The ball will bounce off the paddle's Pad in a direction based on the Pad's surface normal orientation. But if you whack the ball, that doesn't transfer any physics. We can change this by adding a RigidBody to the Pad, as follows:

1. Select the **Pad** of your **Paddle**
2. **Add Component** | **Physics** | **RigidBody**
3. Uncheck **Use Gravity** checkbox
4. Check the **Is Kinematic** checkbox
5. Click the **Apply** button at top of Inspector to save your changes in the prefab

By making it kinematic, our Pad will apply physics to objects colliding with it, but will not react to collisions itself. This is good, otherwise, the paddle would shatter when hit by a ball.

One important lesson in this project is the use of attach points for defining relative positions for specific behaviors. We used a Drop Point to mark the X, Z position where balls are dropped from. We used an Attach Point to mark the relative position and rotation of the paddle in your hand. We could have added a Grip Point to the paddle itself to specify its relative origin. And so on.

Shooter ball game

For the next iteration of this project, we'll shoot balls at the player and you have to hit them at a target on a wall. There's not a lot of innovation in this version, but it shows how you can take an existing mechanic and turn it on its side (both literally and figuratively).

To begin, lets make a wall and put the target on it:

1. In the **Hierarchy** root, create an **Empty** game object named `TargetWall` and
2. **Position** it at (0, 0, 5)
3. Create a child **Cube** and name it `Wall`
4. Set the Wall **Scale** to (10, 5, 0.1) and **Position** (0, 2.5, 0)
5. Create a new Material named `Wall Material`
6. Set its **Rendering Mode** to **Transparent**, and its **Albedo** color to (85, 60, 20, 75) so it's a translucent glassy color
7. Move the **Target** to a child of `TargetWall`
8. Modify the Target **Transform Scale** to (1.5, 0.1, 1.5), **Rotation** (90, 0, 0), and **Position** (0, 2.5, -0.25) so it's smaller and just in front of the wall itself

Next, instead of serving balls by dropping them out of the sky and relying on gravity, we'll shoot balls at you from a source on the wall:

1. Create a **Sphere** game object as a child of `TargetWall`, named `Shooter`
2. Set its **Scale** to (0.5, 0.5, 0.5) and **Position** (4, 2.5, -0.25)
3. Disable or remove its **Sphere Collider** component
4. Create a new Material named `Shooter Material`, with **Albedo** color (45, 22, 12, 255)

We'll add a gun barrel to the shooter:

1. Create another **Sphere** object as a child of Shooter, named `Barrel`
2. Set its **Scale** (0.1, 0.1, 0.1), **Rotation** (90, 0, 0), and **Position** (0, 0, -0.25)

Duplicate the Shooter and set the second one's **Position** to (-4, 2.5, -0.25) so there's one on either side of the Target. Here is a capture of the Scene view of the `TargetWall` with its sexy shooters:

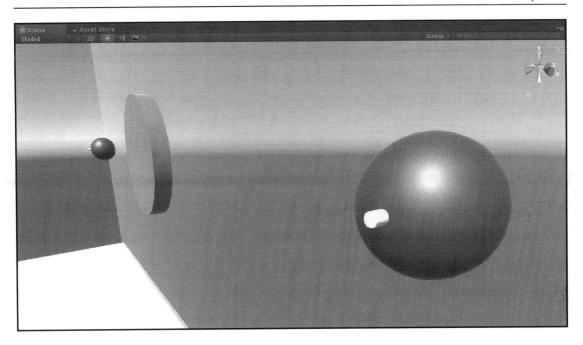

The game controller script is similar to the BallGame one we have, but sufficiently different we should create a new one:

1. In **Hierarchy**, select GameController and disable or remove the BallGame component
2. Create a new C# script named ShooterBallGame and open it for editing

Write the ShooterBallGame script as follows. We give it two shooters and the script alternates between them to shoot balls in the direction of a shootAt location. We play a sound effect each time a ball is shot. First, let's define the public and private variable we will need:

```
using UnityEngine;

[RequireComponent(typeof(ObjectPooler))]
public class ShooterBallGame : MonoBehaviour
{
    public Transform shootAt;
    public Transform shooter0;
    public Transform shooter1;
    public float speed = 5.0f;
    public float interval = 3f;

    private float nextBallTime = 0f;
```

```
    private ObjectPooler pool;
    private GameObject activeBall;
    private int shooterId = 0;
    private Transform shooter;

    private AudioSource soundEffect;
}
```

The Start function initializes the variable we get at runtime:

```
void Start()
{
    if (shootAt == null)
    {
        shootAt = Camera.main.transform;
    }
    soundEffect = GetComponent<AudioSource>();
    pool = GetComponent<ObjectPooler>();
    if (pool == null)
    {
        Debug.LogError("BallGame requires ObjectPooler component");
    }
}
```

And the Update function shoots the balls at specified intervals, alternating between the two shooter locations:

```
void Update()
{
    if (Time.time > nextBallTime)
    {
        if (shooterId == 0)
        {
            shooterId = 1;
            shooter = shooter1;
        }
        else
        {
            shooterId = 0;
            shooter = shooter0;
        }

        nextBallTime = Time.time + interval;
        ShootBall();
    }
}
```

Finally, here's the `ShootBall()` code we extracted into its own function:

```
private void ShootBall()
{
    soundEffect.Play();
    activeBall = pool.GetPooledObject();
    activeBall.transform.position = shooter.position;
    activeBall.transform.rotation = Quaternion.identity;
    shooter.transform.LookAt(shootAt);
    activeBall.GetComponent<Rigidbody>().velocity = shooter.forward *
speed;
    activeBall.GetComponent<Rigidbody>().angularVelocity =
Vector3.zero;
    activeBall.SetActive(true);
}
```

`ShootBall` grabs a new ball from the object pool and initializes its position based on the shooter position. It then rotates the shooter to be pointing at the `shootAt` position (using `transform.LookAt`) and uses its forward vector to define the ball's RigidBody velocity vector.

Back in Unity, we need to populate the public variable slots:

1. Drag the `Shooter` object (child of `TargetWall`) on to the **Shooter 0** slot
2. Drag the other `Shooter` object on to the **Shooter 1** slot

Leave the **Shoot At** slot empty for now, so it will default to the player's live head position.

Press **Play**. *Not bad*. The balls are too big and heavy. Let's create a new ball prefabs with different properties:

1. Drag the `BouncyBall` prefab from `Project` folder into the **Hierarchy**
2. Rename it `ShooterBall`
3. Set its **Scale** to (0.25, 0.25, 0.25)
4. Uncheck the **Use Gravity** checkbox (alternatively, you could play with its RigidBody **Mass** property)
5. Drag the **ShooterBall** from **Hierarchy** into your `Prefabs` folder, creating a new prefab for it
6. Delete the **ShooterBall** from the **Hierarchy**
7. Select `GameController` in Hierarchy, and drag the **ShooterBall** onto its **Object Pooler Prefab** slot

Now, the object pool will instantiate a collection of the new prefab objects.

Press **Play**. *Oh yeah!* The game is now much more challenging. Also, try modifying the **Interval** and **Speed** settings.

It may be awkward that the ball is always shooting towards your head, especially on Daydream where you have limited hand control. You can adjust the scene, for example, positioning the **ShootAt** empty game object, a child of `MeMyselfEye`, at **Position** (0, 0.9, 0.6), and setting it into the `GameController`'s **ShootAt** slot.

Some obvious gameplay improvement ideas should come to mind. You could make a moving target, perhaps in a predictable oscillating motion, or completely random. You could introduce some random variation in the ball velocity direction and speed or the intervals between shots. You could keep score, using `OnTriggerEnter` on the Target. You could disqualify bank shots that bounce first on the floor (using `OnTriggerEnter` on the ground plane).

Juicing the scene

Having the basic mechanics implemented, we can now *juice it!* One of my favorite VR games is the popular Audio Shield (`http://audio-shield.com/`). We're almost there building our own, we just need to add fireballs, a compelling environment scene, and synchronizing the fireball shots with music!

 The term *juice it* for game design was popularized by Jonasson and Purho in their presentation talk from 2012, *Juice it or lose it - a talk by Martin Jonasson & Petri Purho* (`https://www.youtube.com/watch?v=Fy0aCDmgnxg`). *A juicy game feels alive and responds to everything you do, tons of cascading action and response for minimal user input.*

Great balls of fire

In the previous section, we disabled **Use Gravity** on the shooting balls. We did this in anticipation of changing the balls from being bouncy balls to balls of fire. Let's make that magic happen now. We will use the Particle System to render it instead of mesh geometry.

There are a lot of ways to get particle effects into your Unity project. If you recall, in `Chapter 4`, *Gaze-Based Control*, we added a water hose, spark emitter, and explosion effects from the `Unity Standard Assets` package. Here, we'll build our own, but use one of the materials, `ParticleFireCloud`, provided with the package. In the Unity Asset Store, you can find many offerings of particle effects and system enhancements too.

First, make a new prefab derived from ShooterBall, named `FireBall`, as follows:

1. Drag a copy of `ShooterBall` prefab from the `Project` folder into **Hierarchy**
2. Rename it FireBall
3. Drag **FireBall** into the `Project` *Prefabs* folder to create a new prefab
4. Select the `GameController` from **Hierarchy**
5. Drag the `FireBall` prefab from `Project` *Prefabs* folder onto the **Object Pooler Prefab** slot

OK, now we can add the particle system:

1. Select the **FireBall** from **Hierarchy**
2. Disable its **Mesh Renderer**, as we will render it with particles instead
3. Right-click **FireBall** and select **Create | Effects | Particle System**
4. Rename it Fireball Particle System

There are a lot of details in working with particles, many options, and configuration parameters. As we step through this quick implementation of fireballs, observe the effects of each change as we make them one at a time. Note that you can preview the particle effects in the **Scene** window. Feel free to experiment on your own.

1. First, at the bottom of the Particle System **Inspector**, find the **Renderer** panel. In its **Material** slot, click the **doughnut icon** and choose the **ParticleFireCloud** material (located in `Standard Assets/Particle Systems/Materials`. If not present, you may need to import it using **Assets | Import Package | ParticleSystems**).
2. Near the top of the Particle System inspector, find the **Shape** panel. Select **Shape: Sphere**, and set its **Radius** to `0.1`.
3. Find the **Emission** panel, and set **Rate of Time** to `15`.
4. At the top of the inspector, set **Duration**: `2.00`.
5. **Start Lifetime**: `1`.
6. **Start Speed**: `0`.
7. **Start Size**: `0.5`.

8. For **Start Rotation**, click the **selector icon** on the right and choose **Random Between Two Curves**. Then click the slot and scroll to the **Curve Editor** at the bottom of the Inspector. If you're not familiar, the editor can take some getting used to. Choose a full range of values from 180 (at top of graph) to −180 (bottom of graph), as shown:

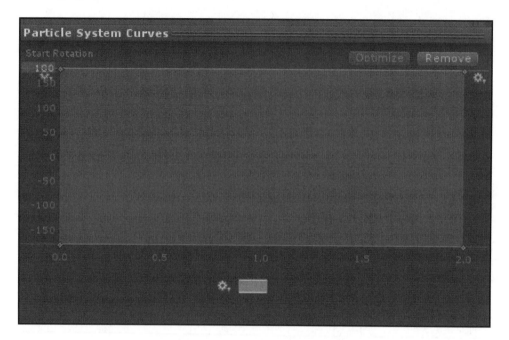

9. Enable **Color Over Lifetime** and click the slot to open its **Gradient Editor**. We want to adjust the **Alpha** curve so it starts at **Alpha** 0 at **Location** 0%, then becomes **Alpha** 255 at 10%, then fades out over time back to **Alpha** 0 at 100%. The editor is shown here:

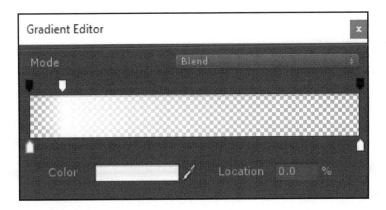

10. Set the **Start Color**, as **Gradient** (right-side selector) and then pick a range of colors such as yellow to red, as shown here:

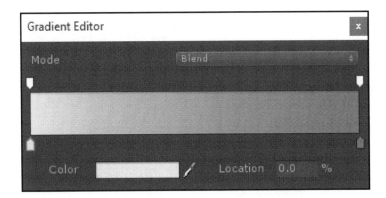

11. Next, set the **Velocity Over Lifetime**, using **Random Between Two Curves**. For each **X, Y, Z**, use the **Curve Editor** to set max and min values of 0.05 and −0.05 respectively. (You can modify the vertical axis of the graph by clicking the axis label and typing a number; you can copy curves, for example, by right-clicking the Z slot, choosing **Copy**, then right-clicking the Y slot and choosing **Paste.**)

At this point, we should adjust the fireball so it's about the same size as our original BouncyBall. To check:

1. Re-enable the FireBall's **Mesh Renderer**. Adjust the particle system by changing the Renderer's **Max Particle Size** to 0.1, or using the **Transform Scale**

2. Save your work by selecting **Apply** at the top of Inspector, to update your prefab

Now when you press **Play**, the Shooters will fire FireBalls. *Oh wow!*

If you'd like to add some sparkle effect to the fireball, we can do that with the **Trail** panel:

1. Enable the **Trail** panel
2. A warning may pop up tell you to add a trails material to the **Renderer**
3. In the **Renderer** panel, select the **doughnut icon** on the **Trail Material** slot, and choose **ParticleFireCloud** as we use for the main fireball

Speaking of trails, if you'd like to also implement trail effects on the fireball, there are several ways to do this too. A quick solution is to duplicate our fireball particle system and modify it to use a Cone shape instead of Sphere, as follows:

1. Select the **Fireball Particle System** in **Hierarchy.**
2. Right-click to **Duplicate**, move the duplicate as a child of Fireball Particle System and name it Trail Particle System.
3. Change its **Shape** to **Cone.**
4. Change its **Velocity Over Lifetime**. The **Z** curve needs a higher value range, such as 0.75 to 0.25.
5. The **X** and **Y** velocity curves should be smaller for some variation, such as 0.2 to -0.2.
6. Set the **Size Over Lifetime** range to 1.0 to 0.5.
7. In its Transform, set **Position** to ($0, 0, 0.5$) to give it an extra tail.

Here is a screenshot of the gameplay window paddling an incoming fireball!

Special thanks to Tyler Wissler for his instructional video *How To: Basic Fireballs in Unity* (June 2014), which was very helpful is developing this topic (`https://www.youtube.com/watch?v=OWShSR6Tr50`).

Skull environment

To spice up our game, even more, we should find an exciting environment and scene. Searching the Asset Store, I found the *Skull Platform* free asset (`https://assetstore.unity.com/packages/3d/props/skull-platform-105664`). You can use it too, or find something different.

Assuming you've found and installed the Skull Platform asset, we'll add it to our scene. First, let's render our target as a skull:

1. Drag **Platform_Skull_o1** as a child of **Target** (under `TargetWall`).
2. Set its **Transform Rotation** (`0, 0, 180`) and **Scale** (`0.3, 0.3, 0.3`).
3. Select the **Target** and disable its **Mesh Renderer**.
4. Also, create a new Spotlight (**Create** | **Light** | **Spotlight**) to shine on the skull. As a child of Target, I used the following settings: **Position** (`-1, -30, -0.6`), **Rotation** (`-60, 60, 0`), **Range**: 10, **Spot Angle**: 30, **Color**: `#FFE5D4FF`, **Intensity**: 3.

Next, let's add the big platform as a backdrop behind the wall. The quickest way is to merge in the Demoscene they provide:

1. Create an **Empty** game object in the **Hierarchy** root, name it SkullPlatform, reset its transform.
2. Drag a copy of the Skull Platform's demo scene named **Platform** (`Assets/Skull Platform/Demo/` folder) into the **Hierarchy**.
3. Select the Demo's **Scene**, **Lighting**, and **Particles** objects and drag them as children of **SkullPlatform.**
4. Now that we have the assets we want, right-click the **Platform** scene in Hierarchy and choose **Remove Scene**. When prompted, choose **Don't Save**.
5. Set the SkullPlatform **Position** to (`0, -1.5, 0`) so it's just below the ground plane.
6. Select the **GroundPlane** and disable its **Mesh Renderer**.

Now, we'll set up the scene environment lighting:

1. Delete the **Directional Light** from the scene Hierarchy.
2. Open the **Lighting** window. If it's not already a tab in your editor, use **Window |
   Lighting | Settings** and dock it next to the Inspector.
3. Set its **Skybox Material** to **Sky** (provided in the Skull Platform package).
4. In the **Environmental Lighting** section, set **Source: Color** to #141415.
5. Check the **Fog** checkbox (in **Other Settings**), **Color** to #8194A1FF, **Mode:
   Exponential**, and **Density** to 0.03.

Here is a screen capture of the scene with the skull platform environment and lighting.
Sweet!

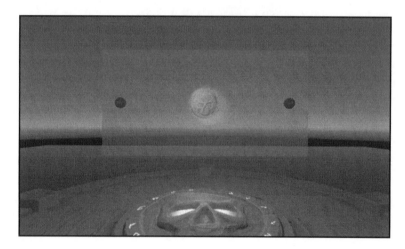

Audio synchronization

We're almost there building our own version of Audio Shield, we just need to
add synchronizing the fireball shots with music!

Unity provides an API for sampling audio source data, including
`AudioSource.GetSpectrumData` and `GetOutputData`. Extracting actual beats in the
music from this data is not trivial and requires a lot of math and some understanding of
how music encoding works.

Fortunately, we found an open source script that does this for us, called Unity-Beat-Detection (`https://github.com/allanpichardo/Unity-Beat-Detection`). It conveniently provides Unity Events for `onBeat`, which we'll use. (It also provides `onSpectrum` events, with music frequency bands per frame, which you could use too, for example, to change the color of the fireball or other things based on frequency bands.)

1. Download the `AudioProcessor.cs` script from GitHub (we've provided a copy with the files for this book for your convenience)
2. Drag the file into your `Scripts` folder (or use **Assets | Import New Asset**)

For your music, find any MP3 or WAV file that has a nice beat, and import it into your project. We looked on SoundCloud NoCopyrightSounds track (`https://soundcloud.com/nocopyrightsounds/tracks`) to find one named *Third Prototype - Dancefloor* (`http://ncs.io/DancefloorNS`).

1. In the Project window, create a folder named Audio
2. Drag your music file into the Audio folder (or use **Assets | Import New Asset**)

To implement this feature, we'll make a **MusicController** and then modify the `ShooterBallGame` script to use its beats to fireballs. In Unity, do the following:

1. In **Hierarchy**, create an **Empty** game object and name it MusicController
2. Add the **AudioProcessor** script as a component
3. Note that it automatically adds an **Audio Source** component too
4. Drag your imported music file onto **AudioClip** slot
5. Drag **MusicController** itself onto **Audio Source** slot

 Note the **G Threshold** parameter on **Audio Process**. You can use this to adjust the sensitivity of the beat recognition algorithm.

Now, update the `ShooterBallGame` script on `GameController` as follows:

```
void Start()
{
    if (shootAt == null)
        shootAt = Camera.main.transform;
    pool = GetComponent<ObjectPooler>();

    AudioProcessor processor = FindObjectOfType<AudioProcessor>();
    processor.onBeat.AddListener(onBeatDetected);
}
```

```
void onBeatDetected()
{
    if (Random.value > 0.5f)
    {
        shooterId = 1;
        shooter = shooter1;
    } else
    {
        shooterId = 0;
        shooter = shooter0;
    }
    ShootBall();
}
```

It's very similar to the previous version, but instead of calling `ShootBall` from `Update`, based on the time interval, we call it from `onBeatDetected`. In `Start`, we add `onBeatDetected` as an `onBeat` event listener.

Also, we've decided to randomly decide which shooter to use rather than just alternating back and forth.

Press **Play** and go at it! *Whoohoo,* we have our own version of Audio Shield! A screenshot of active gameplay is shown here:

Summary

In this chapter, we built a game that uses Unity's Physics Engine and a number of other features. First, we explained in layman's terms the relationship between Rigidbody, Colliders, and Physic Materials, and explored how the physics engine uses these to determine the velocity and collision of objects in the scene.

Then, we considered the life cycle of game objects and implemented an object pooler that helps avoid memory fragmentation and garbage collection, which can lead to performance problems and VR discomfort.

Using what we learned, we implemented several variations of a ball game, first aiming for a target with your head, then using hand paddles. We modified the game so that, instead of serving balls from above-using gravity, we shoot them from in front and apply a velocity vector. Lastly, we juiced up our game, changing the bouncy balls into fireballs, adding a cool level environment, and synchronizing the fireballs to music beats. In the end, we have a good start to making our own version of the Audio Shield VR game.

Animation and VR Storytelling

9

The stories we tell, and how we tell them, say a lot about who we are and what we will become. Storytelling between humans is as primal as any human activity, the basis of interpersonal communications, mythology, historical record, entertainment, and all of the arts. VR is emerging as one of the newest, and potentially most profound, storytelling media formats.

For this project, we are going to create a little VR experience, a simplistic story about a bird who gains its wings and learns to fly.

In this chapter, we are going to learn about the following topics:

- Importing and using external models and animations
- Using Unity Timelines to activate and animate objects
- Using the Animation editor window for editing property keyframes
- Controlling Animation Clips with an Animation Controller
- Making the story interactive

Composing our story

You start in a dark scene and notice a small sapling in the ground in front of you. It starts to grow into a tree. As dawn breaks, a bird's nest appears, and we notice it has an egg in it. The egg begins to shake, and then hatches. A baby bird emerges, hops around, grows, and tests its wings. Finally, in daylight, it flies away to freedom.

Our story is about birth, growth, spreading your wings (literally and figuratively), and moving on. We will start with a music soundtrack and animate our graphics based on its parts.

We are using free, off-the-shelf assets. Of course, you can use your own music and graphics, but we'll assume you're following along using the ones we have selected, which are all available online for free (links are given). As an instructive project, it's minimalistic and not embellished with effects that one might expect of a polished product. But you'd be very proud of your 9-year old cousin or nephew if they made it!

The soundtrack we will use is a rendition of The Beatles and Paul McCartney song, "Blackbird". (A download link is in the next section, and a copy is included with the files for this chapter for convenience.) Based on our mp3 recording of the song, we sketched out a rough timeline plan of our VR experience on a chart, shown here:

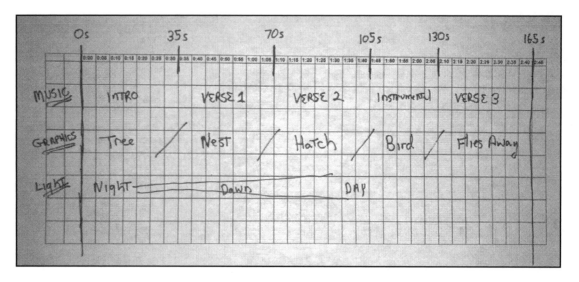

 As indicated, the entire song is 165 seconds (2:45). It starts with a 35-second instrumental intro, then verse one and verse two (also 35 seconds), a 25-second instrumental, and then verse three is 35 seconds. We'll use this to divide our story into five segments.

Plenty of other features ought to be planned out as well. The scene lighting, for example, will start in the dark of night and gradually lighten the sky into dawn and then daytime.

Gathering the assets

As mentioned, we're going to build our story from a variety of sources of free and simplistic assets. I recommend you download and install each of them now (or your own substitutions) so they're accessible as we work:

- Music: The Beatles and Paul McCartney song, "Blackbird" performed by guitarist Salvatore Manalo. Mp3 download: `http://mp3freeget4.online/play/the-beatles-paul-mccartney-blackbird-cover/chSrubUUdwc.html`
- Scene and tree: Nature Starter Kit, `https://assetstore.unity.com/packages/3d/environments/nature-starter-kit-1-49962`
- Nest and egg: Use the `NestAndEgg` prefab file provided with this book (source: tutorial using Cinema 4D: `https://www.youtube.com/watch?v=jzoNZslTQfI`, `.c4d` file download, `https://yadi.sk/d/ZQep-K-AMKAc8`)
- Living Birds: `https://assetstore.unity.com/packages/3d/characters/animals/living-birds-15649`
- Wispy Skybox: `https://assetstore.unity.com/packages/2d/textures-materials/sky/wispy-skybox-21737`

Note that the nest and egg object we are using is modified from the one found online. That was in `.c4d` format, and we have converted it to `.fbx`, packaged them into a prefab, and made a few other changes.

Creating the initial scene

We're going to make a simple, minimalist scene using a plane for the ground and some rocks from the Nature Starter Kit, a bird's nest with an egg, and a bird:

1. Create a new scene (**File | New Scene**) and name it "Blackbird" (**File | Save Scene As**)
2. Create a 3D **Plane** named `GroundPlane`, reset its **Transform**, then **Scale** it to (`10, 10, 10`)
3. Create a new **Material** named `GroundMaterial`, set its **Albedo** color to an earthy brown (such as `#251906ff`), and drag the material onto the plane
4. Set the **Main Camera Position** to (`0, 2, -3`)

You can replace `Main Camera` with the `MeMyselfEye` camera rig we've been using throughout the book, but it is not necessary in this project as we will not be using device-specific input or other features. The `Main Camera` will provide a sufficient VR camera based on the SDK you've selected in **Player Settings**.

 We are using a simple ground plane, as it gives the aesthetic we want. But this could be a good opportunity for you to explore the Unity Terrain system. This is another rich and very powerful topic, where you can "paint" complex landscapes with trees and grasses. See the manual at https://docs.unity3d.com/Manual/script-Terrain.html.

Now, add a tree and some rocks:

1. From the `Assets/NatureStarterKit/Models/` folder, drag the **Tree** into the scene. Reset its **Transform**, so it's at the origin.
2. Add a few rocks near the tree, move them so they're partially buried below the ground. You might put these under an **Empty** game object named `Environment`.
3. Add a Wind Zone (**Create** | **3D Object** | **WindZone**), so the Tree object responds to wind and rustles its leaves.

The rocks in my scene are placed as follows (all at **Scale** `100`):

Prefab	Position
rock03	(2.9, -0.6, -0.26)
rock03	(2.6, -0.7, -3.6)
rock04	(2.1, -0.65, -3.1)
rock01	(-6, -3.4, -0.6)
rock04	(-5, -0.7, 3.8)

Next, we'll add the nest:

1. Drag a copy of the **NestAndEgg** model into the scene.
2. **Scale** and **Position** it on the ground so it's in easy view, near the tree, and not too small. We chose **Position** (`0.5, 0.36, -1.2`) and **Scale** (`0.2, 0.2, 0.2`).

And add a bird. The Living Birds package doesn't have a blackbird, but it does have a bluejay, which is close enough:

1. From the **Project** `Assets/living birds/resources/` folder, drag the `lb_blueJayHQ` prefab into the **Hierarchy**. For convenience, rename it `Bluejay`.

2. **Scale** and **Position** it so it appears full grown and perched on the edge of the nest. We chose **Scale** (`8, 8, 8`), **Position** (`0.75, 0.4, -1.25`), and **Rotation** (`0, 0, 0`).

The bird is inserted into the scene in a T pose. It has animations attached, which we'll control later in this project. Like most character animations, it runs an `Idle` animation initially. (Note, don't rotate the bird object, it messes up the flying animations.)

Remember to press **Play** and check how it looks in VR. It's always much different within VR than the view you see on the flat screen. Our scene and hierarchy is shown in the following screen capture. You many also want to adjust the Main Camera position now:

Timelines and Audio tracks

Earlier, we planned out our movie using a graph paper timeline. Unity provides the tools to implement that almost directly. This Timeline feature was introduced with Unity 2017.

Timelines consist of one or more tracks that play over time. It's like an Animation (which controls the properties of a single game object), but Timelines work with many different objects and different types of tracks. As we'll see and explain later, Timelines can have Audio Tracks, Activation Tracks, Animation Tracks, and Control Tracks.

Timelines are a type of Unity *Playable*. Playables are runtime objects that "play" over time, updating each frame based on its prescribed behavior. Animations are playables too. For more details, see `https://docs.unity3d.com/ScriptReference/Playables.Playable.html`.

Presently we'll add a Timeline to the project and add an Audio Track. To create the Timeline object and open it in the Timeline Editor window, do the following steps:

1. In **Hierarchy**, create an **Empty** game object and name it `BlackbirdDirector`.
2. Open the **Timeline Editor (Window | Timeline)**.
3. In the window you will see a message "*To begin a new timeline with BlackbirdTimeline, create a Director component and a Timeline asset*" with a **Create** button.
4. Press the **Create** button.
5. You are then prompted to save a new Playable asset in your **Project** *Assets* folder. Name it `BlackbirdTimeline`. Press **Save**.

At this point, you may have noticed a few important things just happened:

- The `BlackbirdTimeline` asset was created in the `Asset` folder you specified
- A `Playable Director` component was added to the `BlackbirdDirector` game object, associating it with that `BlackbirdTimeline`
- The `Timeline Editor` window is opened for the `BlackbirdTimeline`

The next screenshot shows the `BlackbirdDirector` inspector with its `Playable Director` component. A Playable Director component controls when and how a Timeline instance plays, including whether to **Play On Awake**, and **Wrap Mode** (what to do when the Timeline is done playing: **Hold**, **Loop**, or **None**):

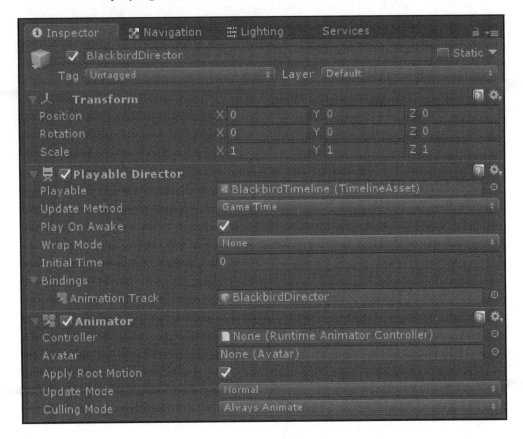

Here is the **Timeline Editor** window for the `BlackbirdTimeline`:

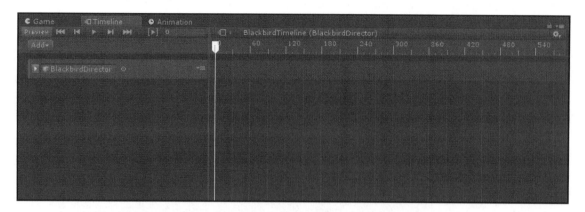

Let's now add an **Audio Track** to the timeline, with our Beatles song:

1. Locate the mp3 file in your **Project Assets**, and drag it directly onto the **Timeline Editor**
2. Press **Play** to play your scene as normal and now the music should start playing as well

Here is the **Timeline Editor** now containing the **Audio Track**:

The white vertical cursor, or *Playhead*, indicates the current time frame. The default scale is **Frames**, but in the previous screenshot we have already changed it to **Seconds** (using the gear-icon in the upper right). You can see this clip is set start at 0 and continues to about 165 seconds.

 You can scale the view using the scroll wheel on your mouse. View all by pressing "A" on the keyboard. When the Timeline contains multiple tracks, you can focus on a specific clip by pressing "F" on the keyboard.

You may notice in the upper left of the Timeline Editor are preview controls. These let you play a preview of the Timeline itself, rather than the whole scene using the usual Editor Play button.

 Unfortunately, at the time of this writing, the Timeline preview play mode does not play audio clips. You need to use the Editor Play mode for audio.

 In this scene, we decided to make the music to be ambient audio. The audio will play in 2D mode if no audio source is selected. If you want to play it as spatial audio, emanating from a specific location in the scene, you should create an audio source and put that in the timeline track instead.

Using a Timeline to activate objects

We just added an **Audio Track** to the Timeline. Another type of Timeline track is an **Activation Track**. Associated with a specific game object, an **Activation Track** with enable or disable that game object at the specified times.

According to our plan, when the timeline starts, the bird's nest will be hidden (NestAndEgg object). At the 35-second mark, it becomes enabled. Also, when the nest is first enabled, it should have the WholeEgg. Then at the 80-second mark, it is hidden and the HatchedEgg is enabled instead.

The `NestAndEgg` game object hierarchy, as shown here, contains the `Nest` itself, a `WholeEgg` object, and a `HatchedEgg` (which has the two eggshell halves):

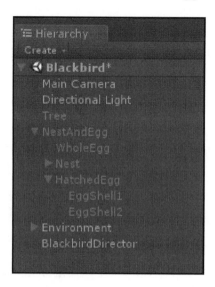

Let's add the activation sequence to the Timeline now:

1. With `BlackbirdDirector` selected in **Hierarchy**, drag the `NestAndEgg` object from **Hierarchy** into the **Timeline Editor** window.
2. A menu pops up, asking what type of track to add; choose **Activation Track.**
3. A small rectangular track marker is added to the track. Click and drag it into place.
4. Position and size the track to start at `35:00` and end at `165:00`.

Now for the eggs. Although the egg models are children of NestAndEgg, they can be activated separately from the parent (of course, only when the parent itself is already enabled):

1. Drag the `WholeEgg` object from **Hierarchy** onto the **Timeline** as an **Activation Track**
2. Position it to start at `35:00` and end at `60:00`
3. Drag the `HatchedEgg` object from **Hierarchy** onto the **Timeline** as an **Activation Track**
4. Position it to start at `60:00` and end at `165:00`

Similarly, activate the bird when the egg hatches, at the 60-second mark:

1. Drag the `Bluejay` object from **Hierarchy** onto the **Timeline** as an **Activation Track**
2. Position it to start at `35:00` and end at `60:00`
3. Drag the `HatchedEgg` object from **Hierarchy** onto the **Timeline** as an **Activation Track**
4. Position it to start at `60:00` and end at `165:00`

The **Timeline** with **Activate Tracks** now looks like the following. You can see, on the left, each track has an object slot containing the game object being controlled by the track.

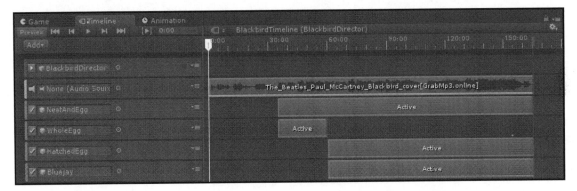

Using **Preview Play** (control icons in the upper left of the **Timeline Editor**) you can play and review these tracks. You can scrub through the time frames by dragging the white Playhead cursor. You will see the nest, eggs, and bird activate and deactivate as specified.

Recording an Animation Track

As you would expect, in addition to audio and activation tracks, Timelines can include animation tracks. Unity's animation features have evolved over the years and Timeline greatly simplifies basic animation capabilities within Unity. You can create and edit animations directly within Timeline without having to create separate Animation Clips and Animator Controllers. These we will get to later in this chapter. For now, we will start simple, animating just a few Transform parameters on the tree and the nest.

A growing tree

We want to add an animation of the tree growing from small (scale 0.1) to full size, from 0 to 30 seconds in the Timeline. We do this by adding an Animation Track for the Tree, and then recording the parameter values at each keyframe time:

1. Ensure `BlackbirdDirector` is selected in **Hierarchy** and the **Timeline Editor** window is open
2. Drag the `Tree` from **Hierarchy** into the **Timeline** window
3. Select **Animation Track** as the type of Track we are adding

Now, we can begin recording the keyframes:

1. Ensure the **Playhead** cursor is set to 0:00
2. Press the red **Record** button on the Tree track in Timeline to begin recording
3. Select the `Tree` in **Hierarchy**
4. Set its **Scale** to (0.1, 0.1, 0.1)
5. Slide the Playhead to the 30-second mark
6. With Tree still selected in Hierarchy, set its **Scale** to (1, 1, 1)
7. Press the blinking red **Record** button again to stop recording
8. Click the small graph icon to reveal the animation curve, as shown here:

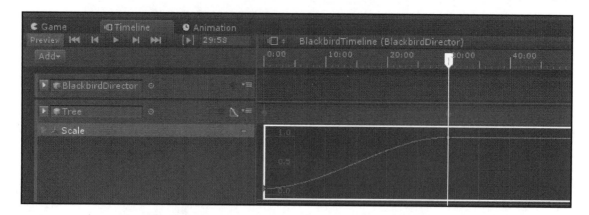

You can see, our Timeline now has an **Animation Track** that references the `Tree` game object. It has two keyframes, starting at o and ending at 30 seconds. Unity fits a gentle curve to ease in and ease out the transition between the polemic key values.

When you grab and slide the **Playhead** cursor across the timeline curve, you can see the tree change size in your **Scene** window. If you press the **Preview Play** icon, you can play the animation.

A growing bird

Repeat the previous exercise, this time growing the Bluejay. Scale it from a baby bird (**Scale** = 1) to full size (**Scale** = 8), for 10 seconds between the 60 and 70-second marks.

Using the Animation editor

Next, we'll create another animation track, to animate the nest so it starts positioned in the grown tree and then drifts slowly to the ground, wafting like a falling leaf. We want it to exhibit a gentle rocking motion. This is a little more complicated than the simple two-keyframe animation we just did, so we'll do our work in a separate Animation Window instead of the narrow track band on the Timeline Editor. It will animate from 0:35 to 0:45.

Animations are based on Keyframes. To animate a property, you create a Keyframe and define the property values for that frame in time. In the previous example, we had just two Keyframes, for the start and end Scale values. Unity fills in-between values with a nice curve. You can insert additional Keyframes, and edit the curve shape.

A wafting nest

Let's assume your scene already has the nest positioned on the ground, where we want it to end up with the following steps:

1. Drag the `NestAndEgg` object from **Hierarchy** into the **Timeline** window.
2. Select **Animation Track** as the type of track.
3. Set the **Playhead** cursor to 35:00.
4. Note that the **Record** icon will be disabled when the object is inactive. The **Playhead** must be within the object's **Activation track**'s **Active** range.
5. Press the **Record** icon for the NestAndEgg **Animation Track** to begin recording.
6. Select the `NestAndEgg` object in **Hierarchy.**
7. Copy the current **Transform** values to the clipboard (in **Inspector**, select the **gear-icon** on the Transform component, and **Copy Component**).
8. In the **Scene** window, ensure the **Move gizmo** is presently selected.

9. Reposition the nest up in the Tree. **Position Y** = 5 works for me.

10. Slide the **Playhead** to 45:00.

11. In the NestAndEgg **Inspector**, click the Transform's **gear icon** and **Paste Component Values.**

12. Press the blinking red **Record** button again to stop recording.

Having defined an initial Animation recording, we can now work on it in an Animation editor window:

1. On the track, click the little **menu icon** in its upper right

2. Select **Edit in Animation Window**, as shown here:

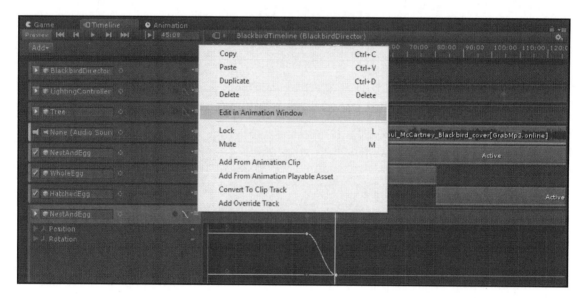

The **Animation Window** has two view modes: **Dopesheet** and **Curves**. The **Dopesheet** view lets you focus on the Keyframes for each property. The **Curves** view lets you focus on the transitions between Keyframes.

The goal is to animate a subtle floating action, where the Nest rocks from side to side (X and Z axes) and rotates lightly on each of the axes. To do this, first we'll "anchor" the Nest at the beginning, middle and end of the fall. (We already have the begin and end positions.) Then, we'll add a couple more keyframes with arbitrary values to implement the gentle motion.

Using the **Dopesheet** view, we're first going to ensure we have keyframes at the start and end times, and one in between. Add keyframes at 35, 40, and 45 seconds as follows:

1. If not present, add **Rotation** properties too (**Add Property | Transform | Rotation | "+"**)
2. Position the **Playhead** at the start of our animation (35:00)
3. Click the **Add Keyframe icon** in control bar atop the properties list (highlighted in the screen capture below)
4. Move the **Playhead** about halfway, to the 40 second mark
5. Click **Add Keyframe icon**
6. And again, make sure there's Keyframe markers at the end (45:00)

You can use hotkeys to move between Keyframes. Press "Alt+." (Alt+period) for next Keyframe. Press "Alt+," (Alt+comma) for previous Keyframe, and "Shift+," (Shift+comma) for first Keyframe.

Now, we'll add a Keyframe at 37.5:

1. Move the **Playhead** to **37.5**
2. Click the **Add Keyframe icon**
3. Click the red **Record** icon in the upper left to capture new values
4. Select the NestAndEgg object in **Hierarchy**
5. In the **Scene** view, using the **Move Tool** gizmo, move the nest a little bit along the X and Z axes (about 0.4 units)
6. Using the **Rotate Tool**, rotate the nest gently on any combination of axes (up to 10 degrees)
7. Move the **Playhead** to 42.5 and repeat steps 2-6

The resulting **Animation Window** in **Dopesheet** view, with its **Position** and **Rotation** property values, is shown here at Keyframe 37.5. The **Add Keyframe icon** is identified for the reader:

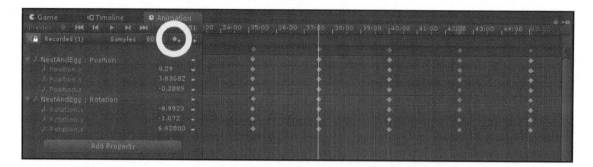

The **Curves** view lets you focus on the transitions between Keyframes, and provides the ability to adjust the values and shape the curve splines. My current Curves view is shown here:

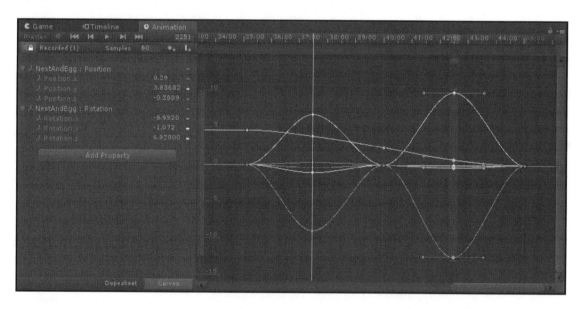

 The length of the scrollbars in the Animation Window indicate the current zoom view. The oval ends of each scrollbar are grab-able controls that let you directly adjust the zoom as well as position of the view.

Go back to the TImeline Editor window. You can slide the **Playhead** cursor to see animations in your **Scene** window, or press the **Preview Play** icon to play them.

Animating other properties

In our story, we want the lighting to start at night and progress through dawn to daylight. We'll do it by manipulating the Directional Light, Skybox Material, and a Spot Light.

Animating lights

For dramatic effect, let's make the scene slowly fade from night to daytime. We will turn off the Directional Light at the start and slowly increase its Intensity:

1. Select `BlackbirdController` in **Hierarchy** and open the **Timeline Editor** window
2. Drag the `Directional Light` object from **Hierarchy** onto the **Timeline**
3. Press its **Record** button
4. Ensure the **Playhead** is at `0:00`
5. Select the `Directional Light` in **Hierarchy** and change its **Intensity** parameter to `0`
6. Move the **Playhead** to the `40:00` second mark
7. Set the **Intensity** to `1`

The Directional Light's Animation Track with the Intensity parameter curve is shown here:

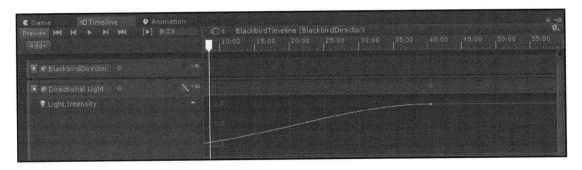

Other parameters of the light could also be animated, including its Color and the Transform Rotation angles. Just imagine the possibilities!

Let's also add a Point Light. For dramatic effect, position it at the same location as the Nest resting position. This will illuminate the baby tree at first, and focus the user's attention on the egg in the nest once the nest settles onto the ground:

1. **Create | Light | Point Light**
2. In **Scene** view, use the **Move Tool** gizmo to position it inside the Nest at the Nest's ground position
3. Select `BlackbirdDirector` and open the **Timeline Editor**
4. Drag the `Point Light` onto the **Timeline Editor**
5. Choose **Activation Track**
6. Enable the light from `0s` to about `95s`, sometime after the egg hatches

Things are looking pretty good!

Our Timeline is starting to get a little crowded. Let's move the lights into a **Track Group**:

1. In **Timeline**, choose **Add | Track Group**
2. Click its label and name it "Lights"
3. Drag each of the light tracks into the group

Use Group Tracks to organize your Timeline in a nested tree structure

Animating a scripted component property

As we're seeing, you can animate just about any GameObject property that you can modify in the Inspector. This includes your own C# script component's serialized properties.

We want to fade the environmental lighting from night to day. There are several ways to achieve this. We've decided to do it by modifying the Skybox Material's Exposure value (o is off, 1 is all the way on). But Timeline can only animate GameObject properties, and this is not one. So what we'll do is create an empty LightingController GameObject and write a script that controls the Skybox Material.

Let's add our own Skybox Material to the scene. You can use any skybox texture you like. We will grab one from the WispySkybox package, `WispyCubemap2`, that we imported earlier:

1. Create a new **Material (Assets | Create | Material)**, name it `BlackbirdSkyMaterial`
2. In **Inspector**, for its **Shader**, select **Skybox/Cubemap**
3. Click **Select** in its **Cubemap** texture chip, and select `WispyCubemap2`
4. Open the **Lighting** window (if not already in the Editor, choose **Window | Lighting | Settings**)
5. Drag the `BlackbirdSkyMaterial` from **Project Assets** onto the **Skybox Material** slot
6. Uncheck the **Mixed Lighting Baked Global Illumination** checkbox

We don't want to bake any of the environment lighting since we're going to modify its settings at runtime.

Selecting the `BlackbirdSkyMaterial` again, see what happens when you slide the **Exposure** value between `1` and `0`. It fades the brightness of the skybox. We will animate this value to modify the ambient light in our scene. But Animations can only modify GameObject parameters, so we'll write a script:

1. Create a new C# script and name it `SkyboxMaterialExposureControl`.
2. Open the script and write it as follows:

```csharp
public class SkyboxMaterialExposureControl : MonoBehaviour
{
    public Material skyboxMaterial;
    public float exp = 1.0f;

    private void Update()
    {
        SetExposure(exp);
    }

    public void SetExposure(float value)
    {
        skyboxMaterial.SetFloat("_Exposure", value);
    }
}
```

Save the file. In Unity, lets make a LightingController object that uses the script as follows:

1. Create a **Empty** object in **Hierarchy**, named "LightingController"
2. Add the `SkyboxMaterialExposureControl` to this object
3. Drag the `BlackbirdSkyMaterial` onto its **Skybox Material** slot

Now, let's animate this parameter:

1. Select `BlackbirdController` in **Hierarchy** and open the **Timeline Editor** window
2. Drag the `LightingController` object from **Hierarchy** onto the **Timeline**
3. Press its **Record** button
4. Ensure the **Playhead** is at `0:00`
5. Select the `LightingController` in **Hierarchy**, and change its **Exp** parameter to `0`
6. Move the **Playhead** to the `100:00` second mark
7. Set the **Exp** to `1`

The Timeline Editor window with a **SkyboxMaterialExposureControl** track is shown here:

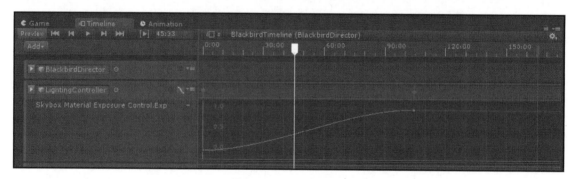

Press **Play**, and the scene lighting will fade from night to day as the skybox material's Exposure animates from 0 to 1. (Note it's not available in the Timeline preview Play, just the Editor Play). Here is a screenshot of the scene playing at about 45 seconds:

Controlling particle systems

You could continue to improve the scene with other effects. We'd like to include falling leaves, which can be implemented using particle systems and played using a **Control Track**.

Unfortunately, we cannot recommend a specific free "falling leaves" asset as all the ones we found in the Asset Store are paid ones. There's an out-of-date free Sky FX package (`https://assetstore.unity.com/packages/vfx/particles/environment/sky-fx-pack-19242`), from which we borrowed the textures and made our own particle system prefab, included with this book.

Assuming you have a FallingLeaves particle system, we can add it to the project now:

1. Drag a copy of the `FallingLeaves` prefab into the scene.
2. In the **Timeline Editor** window (with `BlackbirdDirector` selected), click **Add** and choose **Control Track.**
3. In the Control Track's menu icon, choose **Add Control Playable Asset Clip.**
4. This creates a small rectangle for the clip on the track. Select it.
5. In **Inspector**, drag the `FallingLeaves` game object from **Hierarchy** onto the **Source Game Object** slot.
6. Going back to the Timeline window, grab and slide the rectangle to the 120-second position, then stretch its right edge to the end of the timeline (165s).

The playable asset's **Inspector** is shown here:

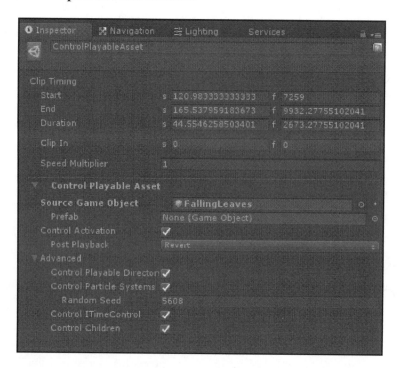

And the Timeline with this **Control Track** is as follows:

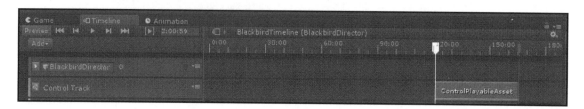

Likewise, if you have multiple Timelines in a scene, you can control them from another Timeline using a Control Track (via game objects with `PlayableDirector` components). In our app, we're using a single Timeline, with **Play On Awake**, so it starts at the beginning of the app and plays through. However, with multiple Timelines in a scene, you can play them on demand.

You can write your own custom Timeline track classes too. For example, using a Control Track for playing Particle Systems is limited. Here (`https://github.com/keijiro/TimelineParticleControl`) is a custom track class, `ParticleSystemControlTrack`, that offers control of emission rate, velocity, and other functionality. And if you look into their `.cs` code, it provides a good example of how to write a custom track class.

Separate Animation Clips are another Playable asset you can add and sequence in Timeline tracks. We look at that next.

Using Animation clips

For the next animation example, we'll get the egg to rattle and shake before it hatches. We will create a simple animation and make it loop for its duration. To illustrate, we'll make an Animation Clip of the WholeEgg rattling and then add it to the Timeline on an Animation Clip Track.

Shaking an egg

To create a new Animation Clip on the WholeEgg object, follow these steps:

1. In Hierarchy, select the WholeEgg object (child of NestAndEgg)
2. Open the Animation Window (**Window** | **Animation**)
3. You should see a message, **To begin animating WhileEgg, create an Animation Clip** and a Create button
4. Press **Create**
5. When prompted for a file name, save it to `EggShaker.anim`

We've seen the Animation Window earlier in this chapter. We're going to make a very short, 2-second animation that rotates the egg on the X axis and Z axis by manipulating the animation curves:

1. Show the Curves view using the Curves button on the bottom of the window.
2. Press Add Property and **WholeEgg** | **Transform** | **Rotation** | **+** to add the Rotation properties.
3. Select the **WholeEgg: Rotation** property group on the left.

4. Press *A* on the keyboard to zoom all; you should see three flat lines, one for each X, Y, Z rotation axes.
5. Click the Add Keyframe icon in the upper right of the control bar.
6. There may already be a Keyframe at one second (1:00) by default. If not, move the Playhead and click Add Keyframe.
7. Scroll out (middle scroll wheel on mouse, or using the horizontal scrollbar oval-end handles) so you can see the 2:00-second marker.
8. Move the Playhead to 2 seconds and Add Keyframe.
9. Move the Playhead back to the 1 second mark.

Now, we'll edit the animation spline curves. If you're familiar with spline editing, there is a line at each node representing the tangent of the curve at that point, and handles at the ends of the line for editing the curve. (You also modify the operation of this gizmo by right-clicking the node.)

1. Click the 1:00s node for the Rotation.X property, then grab one of the handles to make a smooth S-curve. Not too steep, something between 30 and 45 degrees
2. Repeat this for the Y and Z axes, with some variation, as shown here:

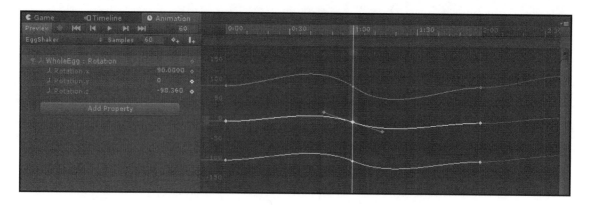

For one or two of the axes, add an extra Keyframe to make the curves look a little more random. My final curves are shown here.

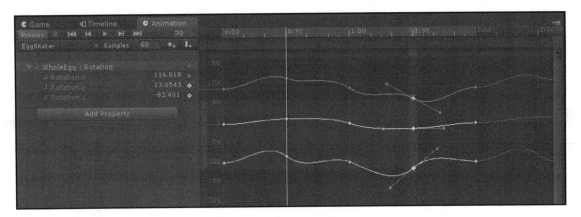

With that done (the curves can be edited and refined later), select **BlackbirdDirector,** open the Timeline window, and perform the following steps:

1. Select **Add** and choose **Animation Track**
2. Drag the WholeEgg object from **Hierarchy** onto the **Timeline**
3. Choose **Animation Track**

This time, instead of recording we'll use the one we just created, and make it animate back and forth as follows:

1. Using the menu-icon on the track, choose **Add From Animation Clip.**
2. A small rectangle is added to the track. Slide it to about 50 seconds, when the nest is on the ground but the chick has not yet hatched.
3. In **Inspector**, we now have more clip options. Under **Animation Extrapolation,** choose **Post-Extrapolate: Ping Pong.**

Animation Clips with Timeline can be quite flexible. You can add multiple Animation Clips to an Animation Track, and blend between them by sliding them into one another. If you need even more control, you'd use an Animator Controller instead.

Using Animator Controllers

While recording animations as Timeline tracks is very convenient, it does have limitations. Those animations "live" in the Timeline. But, sometimes you want to treat animations as assets in their own right. For example, you would use Animation Clips if you want an animation to loop repeatedly, or transition between animations, or blend their actions, or apply the same set of animation curves to other objects.

We will take a look at a couple of existing examples of Animators and then use the existing birds one to make our Bluejay fly.

Definitions for Animation and Animator

Animators have been the standard way of managing *Animation Clips* in Unity, before Timeline. It uses an **Animator Component**, an **Animator Controller**, and an **Animation Clip**. Fortunately, if you create a new Animation Clip on an object, Unity creates each of these items for you. But it's important to understand how they fit together.

Briefly, from the Unity manual (`https://docs.unity3d.com/Manual/animeditor-CreatingANewAnimationClip.html`):

> *"To animate GameObjects in Unity, the object or objects need an **Animator Component** attached. This Animator Component must reference an **Animator Controller**, which in turn contains references to one or more **Animation Clips**."*

These objects originate from the Mecanim animation system folded into Unity a few versions back (you may still see references to Mecanim in the Unity Manual and web searches). This animation system is especially tailored for humanoid character animations (see `https://docs.unity3d.com/Manual/AnimationOverview.html`). The terminology can seem redundant and confusing. The following definitions may help (or not!). Pay especially close attention to the use of "animator" versus "animation":

- *Animation Clips*: Describes how an object's properties change over time.
- *Animator Controller*: Organizes clips in a state machine flowchart, keeps track which clip should currently be playing when animations should change or blend together. References the clips it uses.

- *Animator component*: Brings together Animation Clips, the Animation Controller, and the Avatar if used.
- Do not use *legacy Animation components:* Animation component is legacy but the Animation window is not!
- *Animation window*: Used to create/edit individual Animation Clips, and can animate any property you can edit in the inspector. Shows a **timeline** but is not the same as the Timeline window. Offers Dopesheet versus Curves view.
- *Animator window*: Organizes existing animation clip assets into a flowchart-like state machine graph.

 Actually, Timeline animation recordings also use Animation Clips, you just don't need to explicitly create them. Each recorded Animation Track in a Timeline has a corresponding animation playable file (named "Recorded (n)") in your Assets folder.

ThirdPersonController Animator

The `ThirdPersonController` character prefab we used for Ethan in previous chapters uses an animator controller to manage humanoid animation clips on the rigged model. For curiosity, let's examine it now (although we will not use it in this scene):

1. Temporarily drag a copy of the `ThirdPersonController` prefab from your **Project** `Assets/Standard Assets/ Characters/ThirdPersonCharacter/Prefabs/` folder into the scene.
2. Notice in **Inspector**, it has an **Animator** component and the **Controller** slot references `ThirPersonAnimatorController`. Click on that.
3. This will highlight the controller asset (in `Assets/.../ThirdPersonCharacter/Animator`).
4. Double-click `ThirdPersonAnimatorController` to open it in an **Animator** window.

The Animator graph for Ethan is shown next. You can see that when the character is activated (Entry), it initializes to the Grounded state. The oval boxes are **States**; the lines between them are **Transitions**. On the left is the list of state **Properties** that the Animator can use. When Crouch is true, for example, the animation transitions to Crouching, plays that, then transitions back (and clears the Crouch state flag):

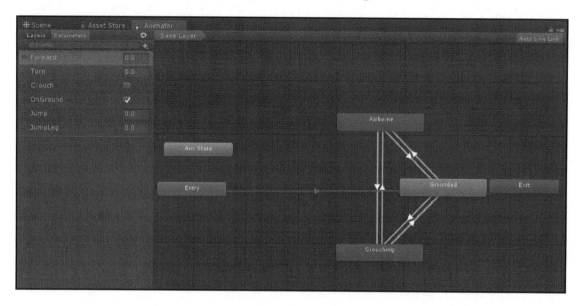

If you open the Grounded state (double-click), you can see a **Blend Tree** with an impressive collection of **Animation Clips** for standing idle, walking, turning, and so on. These will be activated and combined (blended) based on user input.

Next, let's look at another example, the BirdAnimatorController used by our Bluejay.

You can now delete the ThirdPersonController object from the scene.

Living Birds Animator

The Living Birds package comes with a lot of animation clips. You can actually open the FBX models in Blender or another animation application and examine how the models and animations are defined. These have been combined into a BirdAnimationController. Examine the Animator using the following steps:

1. Select the Bluejay in **Hierarchy.**

2. Notice in **Inspector**, it has an **Animator** component, and the **Controller** slot references `BirdAnimatorController`. Click on that.

3. In **Project Assets**, double-click the `ThirdPersonAnimatorController` to open it in an **Animator** window.

The Animator graph is shown here:

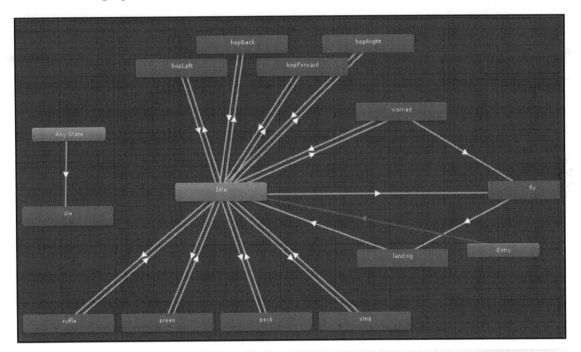

You can see that almost all the animations readily transition to and from the Idle one, whether Preen, Peck, Sing, or HopLeft, HopRight, HopForward, and so on. Also, note the Idle -> Fly -> Landing -> Idle loop, as we're going to use that.

The Bluejay also has a C# script, `lb_Bird`, which invokes the Animator behaviors. It's not the cleanest code, but it is useful. The most pertinent functions are `OnGroundBehaviors` and `FlyToTarget`:

- `OnGroundBehaviors` randomly chooses and plays one of the idle animations every 3 seconds
- `FlyToTarget`, will cause the bird to fly to a given position, including takeoff and landing and random fluttering around; it looks reasonably natural

So in our project, rather than recording the Keyframe position details of the bird's animation path like we did the falling nest, we'll define specific targets and let the `lb_Bird` script actually control the bird transforms. This is a lot like using a **Navmesh** to direct Ethan's movement as we did in Chapter 4, *Gaze-Based Control*. We will use Timeline to select one target position to the next, over time.

Learning to fly

First, let's create a `BirdController` and specify a list of locations where the bird should fly between. Then, we'll add this to the Timeline:

1. In **Hierarchy**, create an **Empty** game object named `BirdController` and reset its **Transform.**
2. Create a child **Empty** object, named `Location1`. Move it to be just atop the rock closest to the Nest .
3. Create another **Empty**, named `Location2`, positioned back near the Nest but not in it this time.
4. Continue creating location markers. The values I used, based on my scene and rock locations, are shown in the following table.
5. The last location should be far away. The bird will head there at the end of the video.

Name	Position	Description
Location0	(0.75, 0.4, -1.25)	Start position of the Bluejay
Location1	(3, 0.8, 0)	Atop nearest rock
Location2	(1.2, 0.2, -1.7)	Ground near Nest but not in it
Location3	(2.5, 0.8, -3.4)	Atop next nearest rock
Location4	(-5.85, 0.8, -0.3)	Next rock
Location5	(-5, 0.33, 3.5)	Last rock
Location6	(45, 11, 45)	In the distance

Create a new C# script on the `BirdController`, named `BirdController`, and write it as follows:

```
using System.Collections;
using System.Collections.Generic;
using UnityEngine;
```

```
public class BirdController : MonoBehaviour
{
    public GameObject bird;
    public List<GameObject> targets = new List<GameObject>();
    public int animIndex;

    public bool collideWithObjects = false;
    public float birdScale = 1.0f;

    private int prevIndex;

    void Start()
    {
        prevIndex = 0;
    }

    void Update()
    {
        if (animIndex != prevIndex &&
            index > 0 &&
            index < targets.Count)
        {
            prevIndex = animIndex;
            bird.gameObject.SendMessage("FlyToTarget",
    targets[index].transform.position);
        }
    }
}
}
```

There are a number of things going on here. We'll explain.

BirdController has a reference to the bird, and a list of location targets. We'll populate this list in the Unity Editor. Each location is identified by an index value between 0 and the size of the list. An integer, animIndex, will be the parameter controlled by the Timeline, telling the controller which location the bird should fly to.

On each Update, we check whether the animIndex has changed. If so, and it's within the range for our list, it calls FlyToTarget on the bird. (We use SendMessage, not a best practice way of triggering functions in another object, but it's the least disruptive given the existing scripts provided with the Living Birds package.)

The extra two variables, collideWithObjects and birdScale, are not used but are required by the lb_Bird.cs script on the Bluejay.

Save the script. Now, in Unity:

1. Drag the `BirdController` script onto the `BirdController` object as a component
2. Drag `Bluejay` onto the **Bird** slot
3. Unfold the **Targets** list and set **Size** to 7
4. Drag `Location0` onto **Element 0**, `Location1` onto **Element 1**, and so on

The Hierarchy with the BirdController component is shown here:

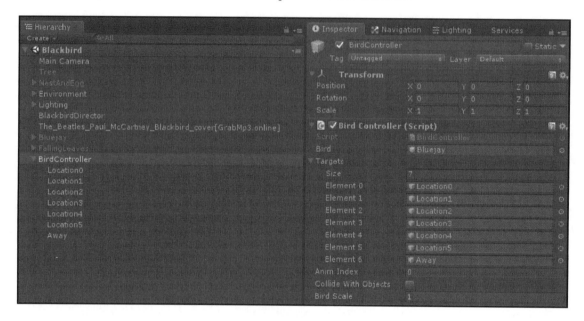

Hacking the birds

Unfortunately, like a lot of code you'll find on the internet, the Living Birds code works for its own purposes but not necessarily ours. In this case, the package is designed for generating a flock of various birds that fly and land randomly, avoid collisions and can even be killed. We have just one bird and want more control over the landing locations, so we'll make a change to use our `BirdController` rather than the `lb_BirdController` in the package.

Open the `lb_Bird.cs` file (attached to `Bluejay`) and modify it as follows:

Replace the definition of `controller` to be our `BirdController`:

```
// lb_BirdController controller; // removed
public BirdController controller; // added
```

Comment out or remove the `SetController` function:

```
// remove this
// void SetController(lb_BirdController cont){
//     controller = cont;
// }
```

Save it. In Unity, drag the `BirdController` object onto the **Bluejay**'s **LB_Bird Controller** slot.

Fly away!

Now, we'll add the BirdController as an Animation Track in our Timeline. The AnimIndex parameter is an integer value that will step up in value along the timeline. We want Bluejay to start learning to fly around 80 seconds, and jump from location to location about 10 seconds apart (80, 90, 100, 110, 120, and away at 130).

1. Open the **Timeline Editor** window for the `BlackbirdDirector`.
2. Drag the `BirdController` object from **Hierarchy** onto the **Timeline**, adding a new **Animation Track.**
3. Press its red **Record** button.
4. Select the `BirdController` in **Hierarchy.**
5. Move the **Playhead** to 80, and in **Inspector**, set **Anim Index** to 1.
6. Move the **Playhead** to 90 and set **Anim Index** to 2.
7. Continue for the other indexes 3 through 6.
8. Press the red **Record** button again to stop recording.
9. Preview the curve. If it doesn't start at 0 (prior to 80s), use **Edit in Animation Window** and add another Keyframe with value 0.

The **Animation Track** curve for the **Anim Index** parameter is shown here, simply incrementing by one at each keyframe:

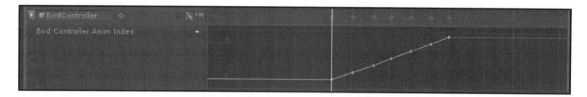

Play it through. Wow! The bird flies from rock to rock, and eventually flies away!

You can adjust the bird's path and timing between landings by moving the location objects and the animation curve keyframes, respectively. You could also try animating the BirdController's **Bird Scale** parameter to make the bird increasingly more bold and strong as it learns to fly. A screen capture is given here with the bird flying and leaves falling:

We have a completed story. To wrap this up, let's add a little bit of interactivity, so the player can control when the story begins playing.

Making the story interactive

So far, we used the Timeline to drive our entire VR story experience from start to finish. But in fact, Timelines are a playable asset like others in Unity. For example, if you select the BlackbirdDirector object and look in Inspector at its Playable Director, you'll see it has a Play On Awake checkbox, and it's presently checked. What we're going to do now is not play on awake, but rather start playing on a user event, namely looking directly at the small tree for a few seconds. And when the story ends, it resets itself.

Look to play

First, we'll add a LookAtTarget encasing the small tree and then use that to trigger playing the timeline:

1. Select the `BlackbirdDirector` and uncheck the **Play On Awake** checkbox
2. For reference, set the Tree game object Scale to its starting keyframe Scale (`0.1, 0.1, 0.1`)
3. In **Hierarchy**, create a cube (**Create | 3D Object | Cube**) and name it `LookAtTarget`
4. Scale and place it to encase the small tree, **Scale** (`0.4, 0.5, 0.4`), **Position** (`0, 0.3, 0`)
5. Disable its **Mesh Renderer**, but keep its **Box Collider**
6. Create a new C# script on the cube, named `LookAtToStart`, and write it as follows:

```
using System.Collections;
using System.Collections.Generic;
using UnityEngine;
using UnityEngine.Playables;

public class LookAtToStart : MonoBehaviour
{
    public PlayableDirector timeline;
    public float timeToSelect = 2f;
    private float countDown;

    void Start()
    {
        countDown = timeToSelect;
    }
```

```
    void Update()
    {
        // Do nothing if already playing
        if (timeline.state == PlayState.Playing)
            return;

        // Is user looking here?
        Transform camera = Camera.main.transform;
        Ray ray = new Ray(camera.position, camera.rotation *
Vector3.forward);
        RaycastHit hit;
        if (Physics.Raycast(ray, out hit) &&
            (hit.collider.gameObject == gameObject))
        {
            if (countDown > 0f)
            {
                countDown -= Time.deltaTime;
            }
            else
            {
                // go!
                timeline.Play();
            }
        }
        else
        {
            // reset timer
            countDown = timeToSelect;
        }
    }
}
```

The script is similar to ones we wrote in Chapter 4. We use the main camera and determine the direction it is looking. Using the physics engine, we call `Physics.Raycast` to cast a ray in the view direction and determine if it hit this object. If so, we start or continue a countdown timer and then play the timeline. Meanwhile, if you look away, we reset the timer.

Try it now. The Timeline will not start playing until you look at the cube for a few seconds.

Resetting the initial scene setup

You probably noticed, unfortunately, that the default start scene is not necessary the same
state we have for the beginning of the timeline. You could fix this by manually ensuring
that every object in the scene Hierarchy has the same initial state as the start of the timeline.
Instead, we'll add a little hack that plays the timeline for a brief 0.1 seconds to reset the
objects.

We will implement this using a coroutine. Modify the `LookAtToStart` script as follows.
Add a new variable, `resetSetup`, and initialize it to true:

```
private bool resetSetup;

void Start()
{
    countDown = timeToSelect;
    resetSetup = true;
}
```

Add a `PlayToSetup` function that will be run as a coroutine. Coroutines are a way to run a
function, let Unity do other stuff momentarily, and then resume where you left off (via the
`yield` statement). Here, we start playing the timeline, go away for 0.1 seconds, and then
tell it to stop playing:

```
IEnumerator PlayToSetup()
{
    timeline.Play();
    yield return new WaitForSeconds(0.1f);
    timeline.Stop();
}
```

Call the coroutine from `Update` when we want to reset the setup:

```
void Update()
{
    if (timeline.state == PlayState.Playing)
    {
        return;
    }
    if (resetSetup)
    {
        StartCoroutine("PlayToSetup");
        resetSetup = false;
    }
}
```

We also want the scene to reset after the timeline plays all the way through, so we set `resetSetup` as soon as the timeline starts playing. It'll be recognized once `timeline.state` is no longer playing:

```
...
    // go!
    timeline.Play();
    resetSetup = true;
}
```

Press Play. Look at the tree. Enjoy the experience. When it ends, you're reset to the beginning and can look at the tree again to replay.

More interactivity ideas

We're going to stop developing now. Some suggestions on how to improve the interactivity and user experience include:

- Add a particle effect around the tree to indicate that it's a trigger
- Highlight the tree as feedback when you're looking at it
- Display a countdown cursor to indicate the timer has started and when the story will begin playing

Here are other suggestions for interactable objects you could add to the story:

- Look at the egg in the nest causes it to hatch sooner than its default timing
- When you look at the bird while it's idle, it will turn to look back at you
- If you poke the bird with your hand controller, it jumps out of the way
- You can pick up a rock and throw it to kill the bird (nooo, just kidding!)

Summary

In this chapter, we built an animated VR story. We began by deciding what we want to do, planning out the timeline, music track, graphic assets, animation sequences, and lighting. We imported our assets and placed them in the scene, then created a Timeline and roughed out when specific objects are enabled and disabled using an Activation Track. Next, we animated several objects, including growing the tree, floating the nest, and rumbling the egg. We also animated the lighting, learning how to animate game object parameters other than Transforms.

We also used Animation Clips and an Animator Controller, using animations imported from a third-party package. We reviewed a script that calls into the Animator and wrote a controller on top of that, to fly the bird from location to location. Lastly, we added interactions to the story, using gaze-based control to start and replay the experience.

10
What AR is and How to Get Set up

This chapter begins with some introductory information and theory regarding **Augmented Reality (AR)**. Unfortunately, we can't just jump right into programming without first properly tackling the fundamentals. Without knowing the fundamentals and theory behind how AR projects work, we would not be able to fully understand how the technology works or how to take advantage of some of the more abstract features of the technology. This doesn't mean that you wouldn't be able to use the technology, just that there are many underlying features that would be difficult to grasp at more advanced levels.

At least two projects will require the use of Xcode and will require a macOS and iOS device to compile and run properly. If you do not have, at the bare minimum, a 2011 model or later macOS, you should skip implementing the examples in the chapters and sections that deal with ARKit entirely, as you will not be able to follow along with the book. Feel free to read the sections, though, as there is always something to learn, even if you can't follow the examples.

The version of Unity3D we will be using for this book is Unity 2017.2.0f3 (64-bit) for both Windows 10 and macOS. We will be using Windows 10 version 1703 build number 15063.726 to build for Android, and macOS High Sierra (version 10.13) for building for iOS, as these are the latest versions of both operating systems at the time of writing this book.

The core information we will go over is as follows:

- Which AR toolkits are available for usage
- How to get started with each toolkit
- What the pros and cons of each toolkit are
- Reasons for developing AR applications and games

Available AR packages

Unity3D has several options readily available via plugins for creating AR applications and games:

- Vuforia AR Starter Kit
- ARCore (Tango)
- ARToolKit
- ARKit

It should be noted that Vuforia Starter Kit has been fully integrated into Unity3D and is quite easy to jump right into creating projects with. ARKit and ARCore, however, are slightly different. Because they are still in the experimental and early developmental phases, Apple and Google have not released full and proper SDKs for Unity Technologies to incorporate into the engine.

There is a plugin that exists for both of them that you will have to compile to get it to work with your project for Apple and Android devices, and we will go into how to compile and integrate into Unity3D to get it to work appropriately later in this chapter. For now, it is good to know that there is a little bit more setup involved with getting AR to work with iOS and Android.

With the introduction out of the way, we can finally begin to really talk about AR, what it is exactly, and how to set up Unity3D to take advantage of the SDKs available to create your own AR games and applications. Without further ado, let's define what AR actually is.

Defining AR

AR is augmented reality. Augmented reality is taking some form of reality and changing it in a specific way to enhance the experience. What augmented reality typically refers to is as follows:

1. Sound:

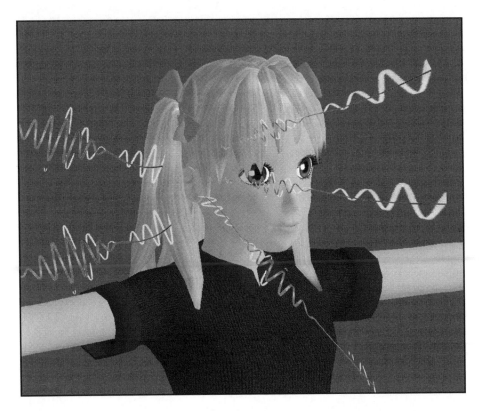

Sound perception

2. Video:

The text in this image is not important. We are just showcasing the video perception overlay

3. Graphics:

The text in this image is not important. We are just showcasing the Graphic perception overlay

4. Haptics:

Haptic perception

5. GPS data:

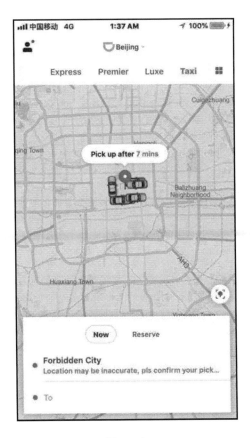

GPS perception

This means that we could boost the visual graphics of an object and view it in a different perspective than what we are accustomed to, or we could add something that isn't there. The video is a little bit different, as it requires the software to interface with specialized hardware, such as glasses, cell phones, HUDs, and other devices.

We could boost the auditory aspect of the world around us. We could take words we see in one language and have it say those words in another, or we could pick up those faint sounds that we always hear and tune out, then amplify them and really bring them to the forefront.

Haptic perception is a little more difficult, but it could be achieved with sensors that emulate touch. We could make something vibrate softly or harshly to simulate various effects, or we could make the game or application entirely touch- or motion-sensor-based. There are many other things we could use for haptic perception in applications or games. It is a field that is constantly being researched and expanded upon.

For GPS data, we can use the user's location to know where the user is in the app or game world. Another use for GPS data would be to know if something of interest to the user should be shown to them.

Because Unity3D loves to take care of most of the finer details of implementation for us, we don't have to worry too much about incorporating DLLs (dynamic-link libraries) or writing the wrapper classes to work with the majority of the popular AR and VR devices. There are exceptions to this rule, depending on the platform and whether the engine has been updated to specifically work with those devices.

Android and iOS are the most popular devices for applications and games to have AR incorporated into them, however, the various tech giants have been working hard to add more and more devices into the mix, with varying amounts of success.

An incomplete list of AR devices

Let's take a quick look at some AR-capable devices. This should give us a slightly better idea of the different types of devices we can use and deploy to:

- The **Meta 2** is a head-mounted display headset that uses a sensory array for hand interactions and positional tracking, it has a visual field view of 90 degrees, and a resolution of 2560 x 1440:

Meta 2

- AR displays can be rendered on devices resembling eyeglasses, such as the **Google Glass**:

Google Glass

- Another such device is the HoloLens:

HoloLens

- There is something called a **head-up display**, which is commonly referred to as a **HUD**. It is an alternate implementation of AR displays:

HUD

- There are many new devices being researched and created all the time. Augmented reality is still in its infancy.

All throughout this book, we will create applications and games that are inspired by the definition of AR. Since there are four main aspects of AR, we will use those four aspects and create a specific application or game for that chapter. Since we have a finite number of sensors that are available for Android and iOS devices, some sensors will be utilized in multiple projects.

Advantages and disadvantages of the different AR toolkits available

In this section, we will discuss the advantages and disadvantages of ARCore, Vuforia, ARToolKit, and ARKit.

ARCore

ARCore is a platform for building augmented reality apps for Android devices. ARCore uses three key technologies to integrate virtual content with the world through the camera. It uses motion tracking, environmental understanding, and light estimation. ARCore works by tracking the position of the device as it moves and builds its own understanding of the real world. It is able to identify interesting points and readings from the phone's sensors and has the ability to determine both the position and the orientation of the phone as it moves. ARCore only has a few supported devices at the present time, which are as follows:

- Google Pixel
- Pixel XL
- Pixel 2
- Pixel 2 XL
- Samsung Galaxy S8

If you don't own one of these devices, you are stuck using the Android Emulator for testing purposes. This is a very obvious downside, since not everyone owns one of these specific phones; additionally, the Android Emulator is an experimental piece of software and is subject to change often. The upside is that ARCore works with Unity3D and Unreal Engine as well as native to Android devices using the Java programming language.

ARKit

ARKit, which was introduced in iOS 11, is a framework for easily creating augmented reality projects for the iPhone and iPad. ARKit's features include:

- TrueDepth Camera
- Visual Inertial Odometry
- Scene Understanding
- Lighting Estimation
- Rendering Optimizations

The downsides to ARKit are that it is experimental software and subject to change often and that it requires the use of the Apple iPhone X to take full advantage of the TrueDepth Camera. You cannot compile this on Windows for Mac, so it is a requirement to have a macOS to even test the code properly. The pros, however, are that ARKit works with Unity3D and Unreal Engine and can utilize the A9, A10, and A11 Apple processors. In other words, it works with the iPhone 6S and beyond.

Vuforia

Vuforia is one of the most popular platforms to help you work with augmented reality development. It supports the following:

- Android
- iOS
- UWP
- Unity3D Editor

Vuforia is able to do many different things, such as recognition of different types of visual objects (such as boxes, cylinders, and planes), text and environment recognition, and VuMark, which is a combination of picture and QR code. Also, using the Vuforia Object Scanner, you can scan and create object targets. The recognition process can be implemented using the database (local or cloud storage). The Unity plugin is simple to integrate and very powerful. All plugins and functionalities of the platform are free to use but include the Vuforia watermarks.

The limitations just relate to the number of VuMarks and the amount of Cloud recognition:

- Paid plan without watermarks
- 1,000 Cloud recognitions
- 100,000 targets
- Costs $99 per month

The obvious downside is that this is not 100% free software, although they do have a developer tier with 1,000 cloud recognitions and 1,000 targets for free per month.

ARToolKit

ARToolKit is an open source tracking library for AR projects. It is supported on Android, iOS, Linux, and macOS. ARToolKit has the functionality to utilize the following:

- Single or stereo camera for position/orientation tracking
- Tracking of simple black squares
- Tracking of planar images
- Camera calibration
- Optical stereo calibration
- Optical head-mounted display support

It is fast enough for real-time AR applications. It is also free and open source software, with plugins for Unity and OpenSceneGraph. The downside to this software is that it has a huge variety of functions, so it is difficult to integrate the library, and it takes more time to explore all the available options and settings.

Building our first AR applications

This section will define all the main points of each of the different SDKs available to us, and we will build our first program with them. This will be in a step-by-step and very in-depth tutorial design sort of way, since this is a lot of information to package and condense into a small section without needing to reiterate the information in later chapters.

Setting up Vuforia

It is now time to set up a Unity3D project for each of the different SDKs that will serve as the basis for later chapters when we use each of them to build an application or a game. Let's start with Vuforia, since it is the simplest one to set up:

1. We now need to register with Vuforia. Navigate to `https://developer.vuforia.com/vui/user/register` in order to go to the registration landing page. If you live in a country in which Google is blocked, you should use a VPN, because the registration page uses the Google-powered reCAPTCHA and you can't continue without it:

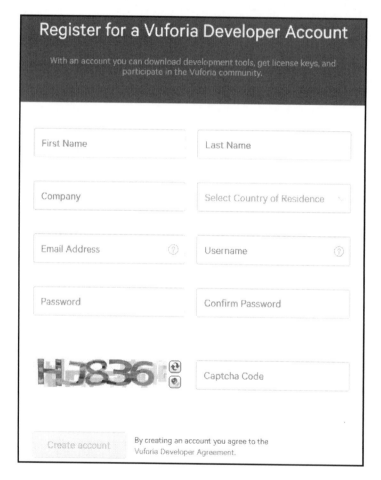

Registering on Vuforia

2. Once you can log in, navigate to the **Develop** tab; alternatively, follow this link: `https://developer.vuforia.com/targetmanager/licenseManager/ licenseListing`.

3. You will see two main items, **License Manager** and **Target Manager**. The License Manager will allow you to create a free Development Key or purchase a Development Key. We want to create a free one. Click on **Get Development Key**. Enter a name for the app, which you can change at any time. I shall call mine `VuforiaIntro`:

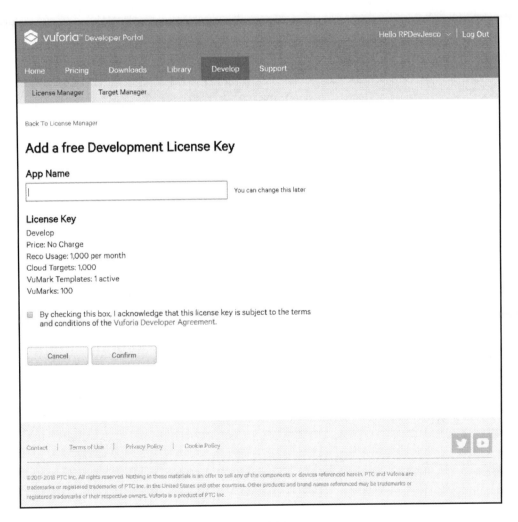

Adding a Vuforia key

4. Now, we have our key with Vuforia. In order to see the license key, we need to click on the name of our app:

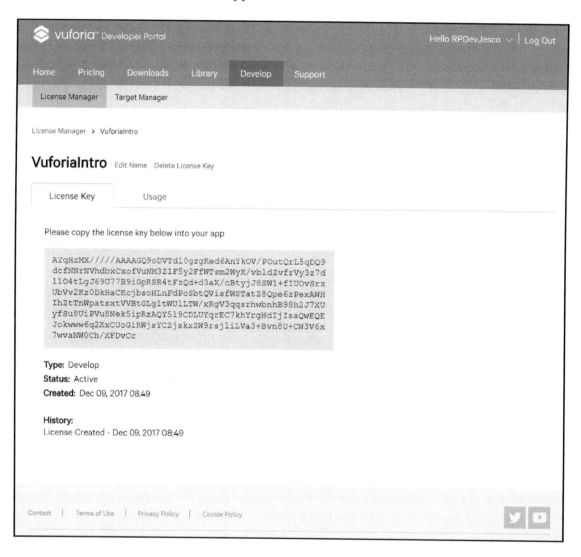

Vuforia key info

5. This next page gives us two very important pieces of information: **License Key** and **Usage** details. The **Usage** details tell us how many Cloud recognitions, Cloud databases, Recognitions used, Cloud targets used, VuMarks generated, VuMark databases, VuMark templates, and VuMarks we have used or currently have remaining:

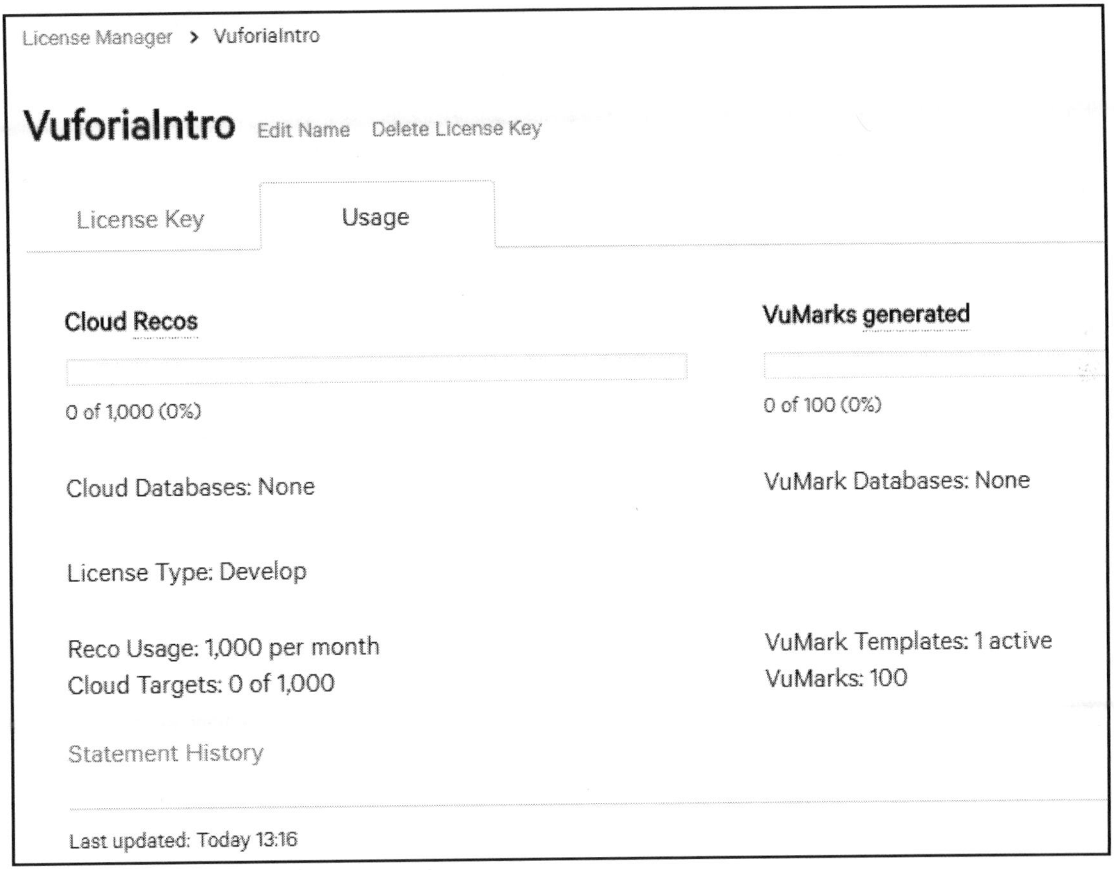

License Manager > VuforiaIntro

VuforiaIntro Edit Name   Delete License Key

License Key	Usage

Cloud Recos

0 of 1,000 (0%)

Cloud Databases: None

License Type: Develop

Reco Usage: 1,000 per month
Cloud Targets: 0 of 1,000

Statement History

VuMarks generated

0 of 100 (0%)

VuMark Databases: None

VuMark Templates: 1 active
VuMarks: 100

Last updated: Today 13:16

6. The **License Key** details tell us our key (which is easy to copy to the clipboard), the type of key it is, the status of the key, the date it was created, and the history of the key.

Now, we are ready to set up Vuforia and get the demo project working appropriately.

As stated previously, Vuforia is fully integrated into Unity3D as of 2017.2, and is a dream to work with once you learn the basics of the SDK. Vuforia is made to strictly deal with the graphics portion of AR. It can recognize images and objects, and it has the ability to interact with the real world because it uses computer vision. Since Vuforia is built into Unity3D, we will do the installation of Unity with Vuforia all in one go.

If you don't have Unity3D installed on your computer now, let's go ahead and do that:

1. Navigate to `http://www.Unity3D.com` and download the latest Personal edition (or one of the others, if you are a high roller) installer for Unity:

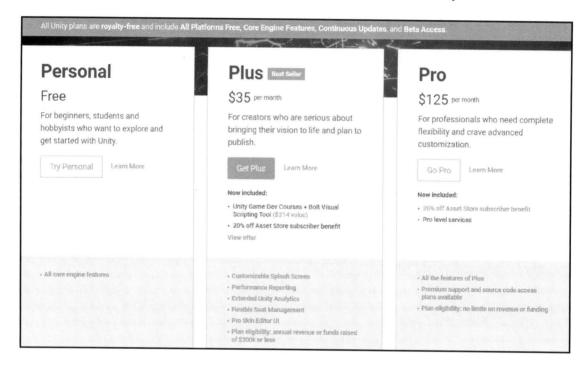

2. When you get to the components section of the installer, make sure to select all the platforms you want to support. I typically select **Android Build Support, Linux Build Support, SamsungTV Build Support, Tizen Build Support, WebGL Build Support**, and **UWP (Universal Windows Platform) Build Support**. There is one additional one you need to make sure you select, and that is **Vuforia Augmented Reality Support**:

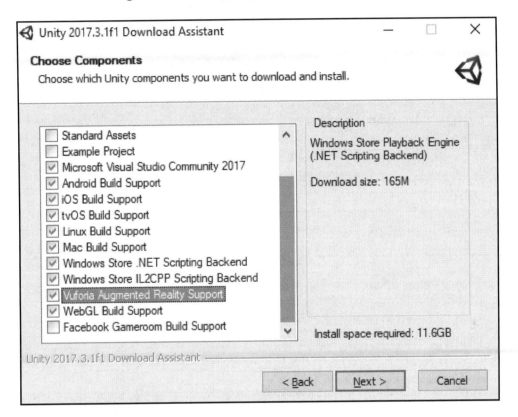

Vuforia Unity installation

Now that Unity3D has been installed, let's create a brand new Unity project:

1. Vuforia recommends that you use a 3D project setup for their AR apps, so, with that in mind, I will keep it as a 3D project with Enable Unity Analytics disabled, and the name of the project shall be `VuforiaIntro`:

2. Once the project has loaded, we can take a look at some of the additional editor items we have access to now. In the toolbar at the top of the Unity Editor, we will see **File**, **Edit**, **Assets**, **GameObject**, **Component**, **Window**, and **Help**:

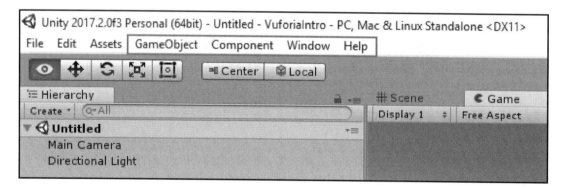

3. **GameObject**, **Component**, **Window**, and **Help** have additional items added to them. Looking at **GameObject**, we can see that the additional item is **Vuforia**. Inside the **Vuforia** item, we have **AR Camera**, **Image**, **Multi Image**, **Cylindrical Image**, **Cloud Image**, **Camera Image**, **VuMark**, and **3D Scan**:

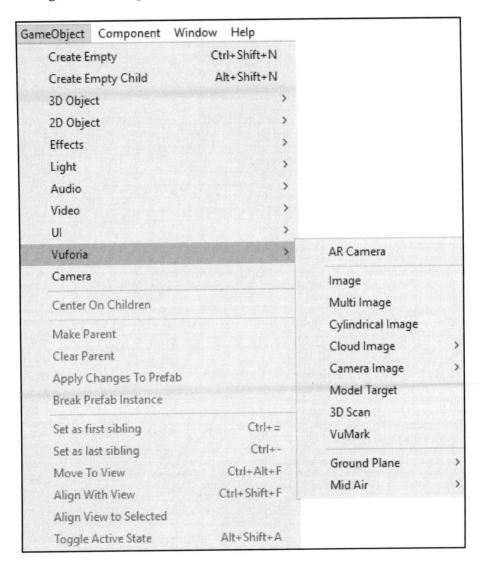

4. **Cloud Image** has some additional items, so let's take a look at that. We have **Cloud Provider** and **Cloud Image Target** available to us:

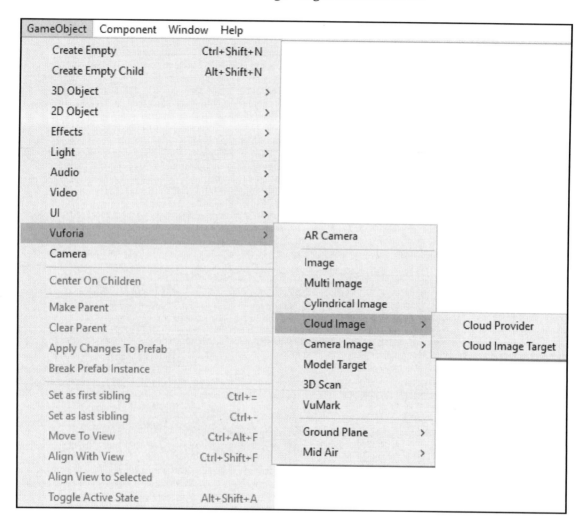

5. **Camera Image** also has some additional items, so we should also be familiar with those options. The options available are **Camera Image Builder** and **Camera Image Target**:

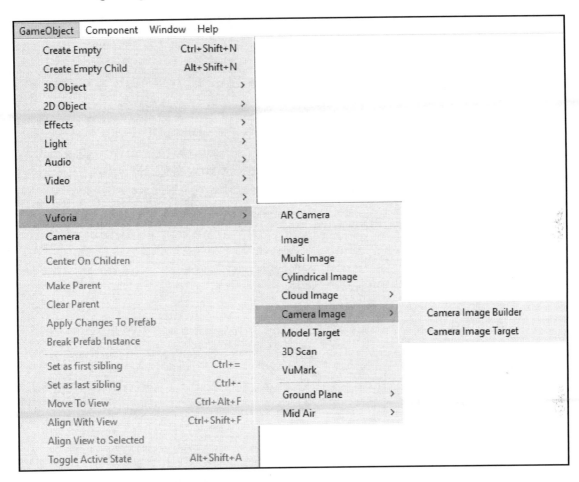

Before we go any further, we should know exactly what these options do and how they look when added to the project prior to the license being applied.

AR Camera replaces the standard camera, as it has the base camera component and **Audio Listener** components. We also see that it has two scripts attached, **Vuforia Behavior** and **Default Initialization Error Handler**:

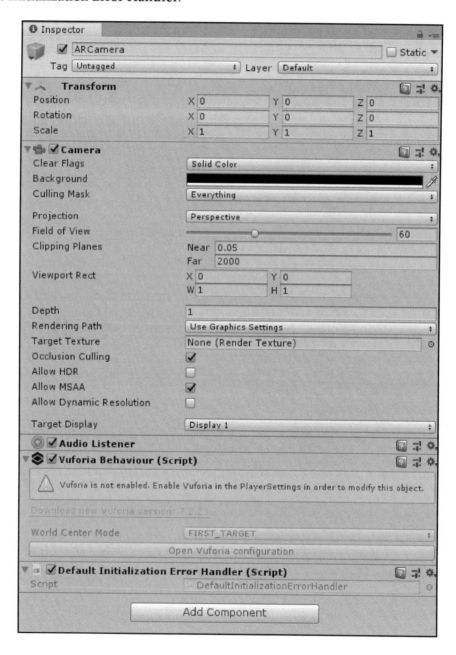

- **Image** is what allows you to add a trackable object into your AR project and serves as the basis for allowing you to have a mount point for bringing models into the camera feed.
- **Multi Image** allows you to add multiple trackable objects into your AR project and serves as the anchor for bringing models into the camera feed in real time.
- **Cylindrical Image** is an anchor for images wrapped onto objects that are cylindrical in shape.
- **VuMark** is a custom barcode made by the Vuforia team. It allows you to encode data into it as well as act as an AR target like the Image, Multi Image, and Cylindrical Image.
- **Cloud Provider** is a direct link to your cloud database for specialized AR-designed branding. It is supposed to be used for publications (catalogs, magazines, newspapers, and so on), retailers (product visualization and in-store traffic generation), advertisers (multi-branded content, coupons, and promotions), and product recognition (wine labels/ bottles, cereal boxes, and so on).
- **Cloud Image Target** is what allows you to add a trackable object into the AR project and serves as the anchor for the app to send the recognized data to the cloud database to retrieve the information and display it as you wish.
- **Camera Image Builder** is what allows you to define a target image to be stored in a database for retrieval and usage in an AR application.
- **Camera Image Target** serves as the anchor for which to use the self-defined target image to display what you want on screen when recognized.

The next set of items to talk about is in the **Component** toolbar. The special components lie within the **AR**, **Scripts**, and **XR** portions of the **Component** window, as marked in the following screenshot for reference. In order to use them, you have to have a **GameObject** in the scene and add the component from the toolbar to it. We have **World Anchor**, **Tracked Pose Driver**, **Spatial Mapping Collider**, and **Spatial Mapping Renderer** available.

We should do a deep dive in so that we can know exactly what these items do:

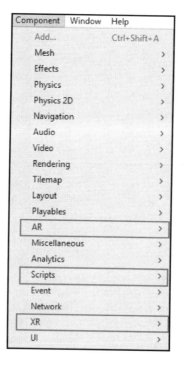

- **World Anchor** is a component that represents a link between an exact point in the physical world and the parent GameObject of the World Anchor. Once added, a GameObject with a World Anchor component remains locked in place to locations in the real world.
- **Tracked Pose Driver** is a component that applies the current Pose value of a tracked device to the transform of the Game Object.
- **Spatial Mapping Collider** allows for holographic content (or character) interaction, such as physics, with the spatial mapping mesh.
- **Spatial Mapping Renderer** is a component that gives a visual representation of Spatial Mapping surfaces. This is useful for visually debugging surfaces and adding visual effects to the environment.

It should be noted that there are items related to Vuforia in the **Scripts** section, however, we will not cover those here. But, just for the sake of making sure that the items are listed, they are as follows:

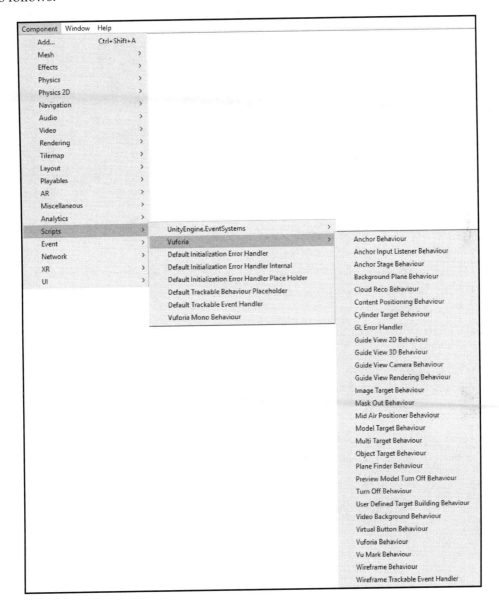

- Background Plane Behaviour
- Cloud Reco Behaviour
- Cylinder Target Behaviour
- GL Error Handler
- Image Target Behaviour
- Mask Out Behaviour
- Multi Target Behaviour
- Object Target Behaviour
- Prop Behaviour
- Reconstruction Behaviour
- Reconstruction From Target Behaviour
- Surface Behaviour
- Text Reco Behaviour
- Turn Off Behaviour
- Turn off Word Behaviour
- User Defined Target Building Behaviour
- Video Background Behaviour
- Virtual Button Behaviour
- Vuforia Behaviour
- Vuforia Deinit Behaviour
- Vu Mark Behaviour
- Wireframe Behaviour
- Wireframe Trackable Event Handler
- Word Behaviour

In the **Inspector** pane, we have Vuforia Configuration. The following is a screenshot of it; next, we will define what it does:

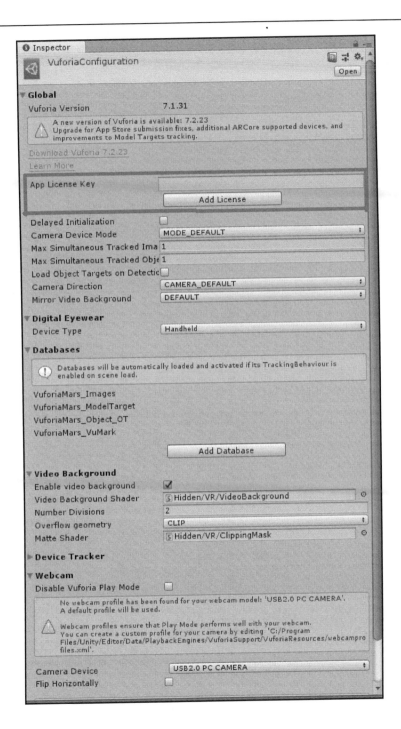

Vuforia Configuration allows you to enter your License Key. Clicking on **Add License** will load the Vuforia Developer landing page. It also allows you to specify what you want Vuforia to be configured to work for, such as a HUD, smartglasses, a webcam, or a smartphone.

Since we are here, let's go ahead and add our app key to Vuforia (see Vuforia Add License for its location):

1. You should create your own app key, since my app key will not be valid by the time of the release of this book. After copying and pasting your key into the license key box, just press the *Return/Enter* key and you are done:

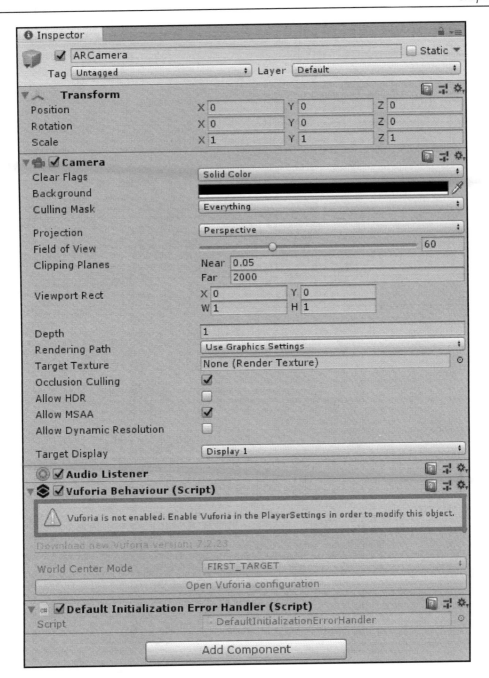

2. Since we are testing on PC and if you have a webcam that works for said PC, make sure that the **Camera Device** selects the proper webcam for usage:

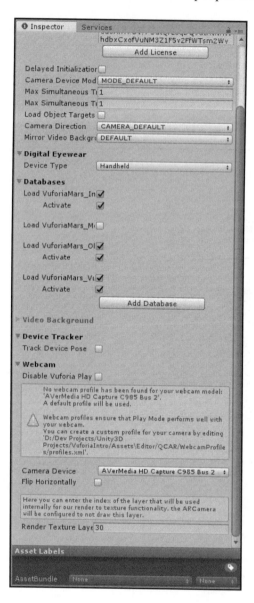

3. Next, we need to go into the Unity Player Settings and fix some options. Navigate to **File** and click on **Build Settings**. The **Build Settings** box should appear. Make sure you change the project type to build to **Android**, and then click on **Player Settings**:

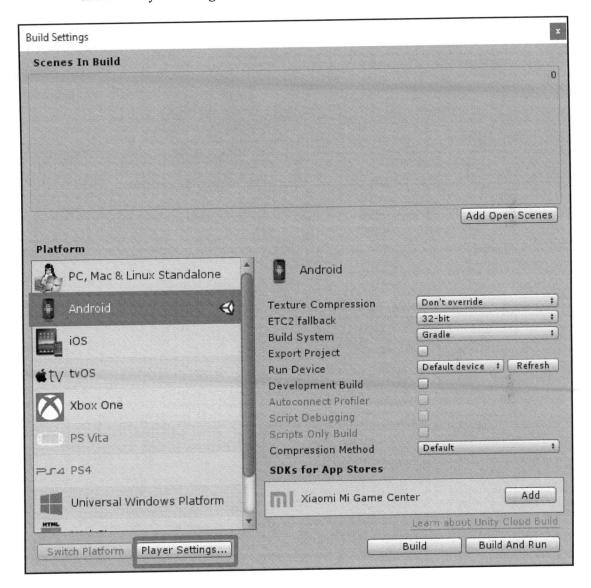

4. Vuforia does not support **FAT device filter** or **Android TV**, so we need to change those two options. **Device Filter**, which is located in **Other Settings**, needs to be changed to **ARMv7**, and **Android TV Compatibility** needs to be unchecked.

5. Now, we can finally build our "Hello World" AR application for testing to make sure Vuforia and Unity3D are working well together. If you haven't done so already, remove the regular camera component from the **Hierarchy** Pane and replace it with the **ARCamera**:

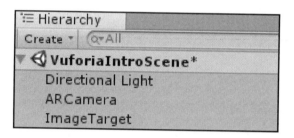

6. The next step is to add the Vuforia Image to the scene, which is also known as the **ImageTarget**:

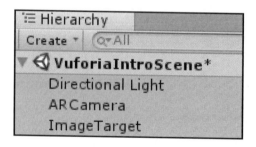

7. We now need to download and add a 3D model to the scene. So, let's go with the easy route and just add a sphere to the scene with the *x*, *y*, and *z* scale set to 0.3. Take extra special care to make sure that the sphere is a child of the **ImageTarget**. *This is very important*:

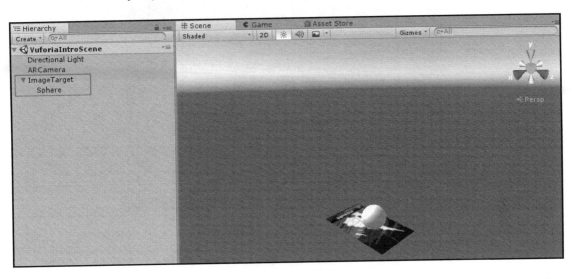

8. The next step is to navigate to **Editor | Vuforia | ForPrint | ImageTargets**, and print out on a piece of paper target_images_A4 or target_images_USLetter:

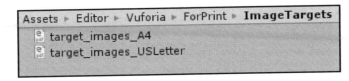

9. Once you have it printed, we can begin the final portion of the test, which is to run the program and hold the printout of the drone in front of the webcam:

The text in this screenshot is not important. It shows a sphere that appears on the camera feed when the image is recognized.

10. Vuforia has now been properly configured and tested appropriately, so we can move on to the next SDK to set up and configure.

Setting up ARToolKit

ARToolKit is a bit more difficult to set up and get started with.

 ARToolKit has been depreciated and is now part of the Daqri Vos API. which you can view
at https://developer.daqri.com/#!/content/develop
This section has been kept in for incase you want to utilize ARToolkit from the github link https://github.com/artoolkit/arunity5

There are two different ways you can get ARToolKit in a project and ready to develop with. The first option is the easiest, and that is through the Asset Store: https://assetstore.unity.com/packages/tools/artoolkit-6-unitypackage-94863. This is the latest version of ARToolKit in the Asset Store and it will be imported directly into Unity for you. The other option is to go to the main website of ARToolKit: https://github.com/artoolkit/artoolkit5. This allows you to get additional tools and the actual SDK, along with the Unity Package.

For installation into Unity3D, we will go with the second option, since it is less intuitive than the first option:

1. Navigate to the main website for ARToolKit and click on **DOWNLOAD SDK**. The macOS, Windows, iOS, Android, Linux, Windows 8.1, and Source Dependencies don't need to be downloaded, but they can be if you want to go deeper into how ARToolKit works under the hood or if you want to use it in a non-Unity capacity. Instead, head toward the bottom of the page and click on the **DOWNLOAD UNITY PACKAGE** button:

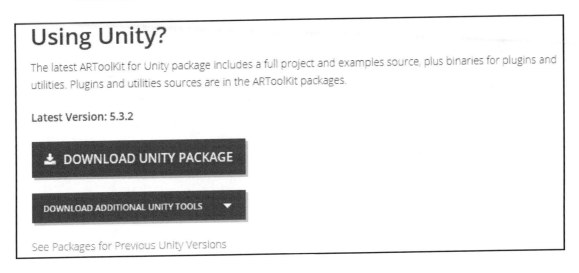

Unless you are doing something more involved, you don't need the additional Unity tools at the present time if you are on a macOS, but if you are on a PC, I suggest getting the Windows Tools, since ARToolKit needs them to debug on PC without using the Android Emulator or testing on Linux.

2. Now that the package has been downloaded, we need to open Unity3D and create a new project. I will call mine `ARToolKitIntro`. Keep the settings as default for simplicity's sake:

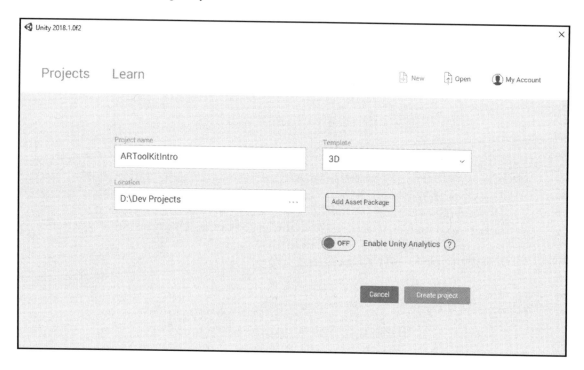

3. Now, we need to import the Unity Package into Unity. This is pretty straightforward. Right-click the `Assets` folder, highlight **Import Package**, and select **Custom Package**:

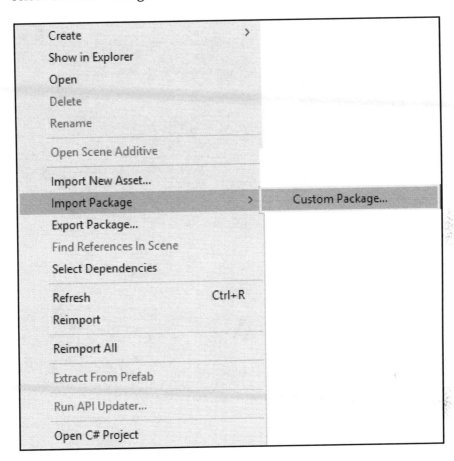

4. Navigate to the folder that houses the downloaded Unity Package, click on it, and select **Open**. You should see a dialog box with checkboxes inside. Click on **All** and then click on **Import**:

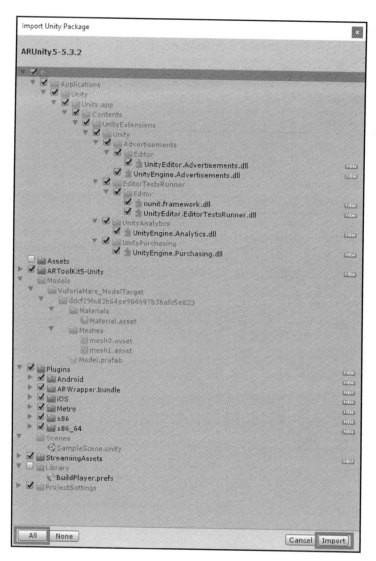

5. You will see three folders after the import is complete (ARToolKit5-Unity, Plugins, and StreamingAssets):

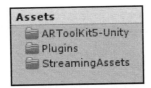

Inside the `ARToolKit5-Unity` folder, there are the `Example Scenes`, `Examples`, `Materials`, `Resources`, `Scripts`, `Changelog`, and `Readme` files and folders:

- Inside `Scripts`, we have an `Editor` folder with the features shown in the following screenshot:

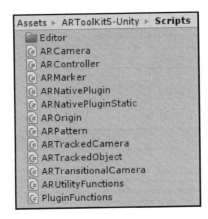

- Inside the `Editor` folder, we have the following:

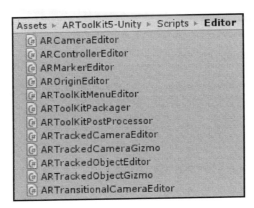

- Next up is the `Plugins` folder. It has folders listed as follows:

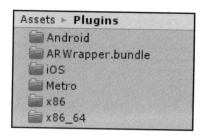

- If you look at the menu bar at the top of the Unity Editor, you will see an additional toolbar item: **ARToolKit**. The drop-down menu shows several options: **ARToolKit for Unity Version 5.3.2, Download Tools, Build, Support,** and **Source Code**:

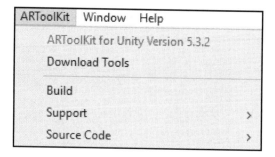

- **Support** has **Home Page, Documentation,** and **Community Forums**:

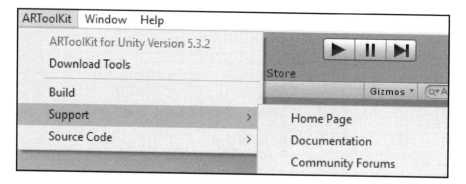

- **Source Code** has **View ARToolKit Source** and **View Unity Plugin Source**:

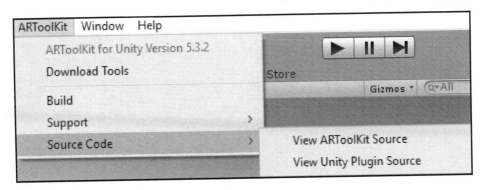

The basics are out of the way, so we can begin building our "Hello World" with ARToolKit:

1. The first thing we need to do is create an empty game object in the **Hierarchy** pane and rename it ARToolKit.
2. The next step is to add the ARController script to the game object and delete the Camera:

3. The ARController script handles the creation and management of AR tracking. It automatically adds a camera at runtime and is controlled by the user layers that we provide.

4. With this latest version of ARToolKit, the basic user layers are provided for you already: `AR background`, `AR background 2`, and `AR foreground` for **User Layer 8**, **User Layer 9**, and **User Layer 10**, respectively:

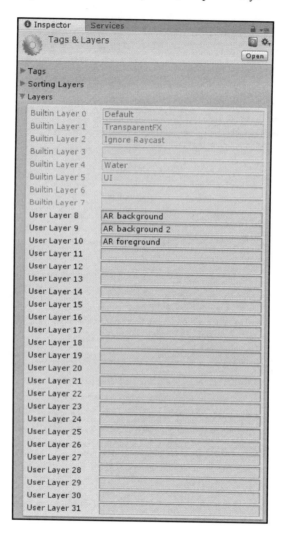

5. The **AR Controller** script has a **Video Options** drop-down menu:

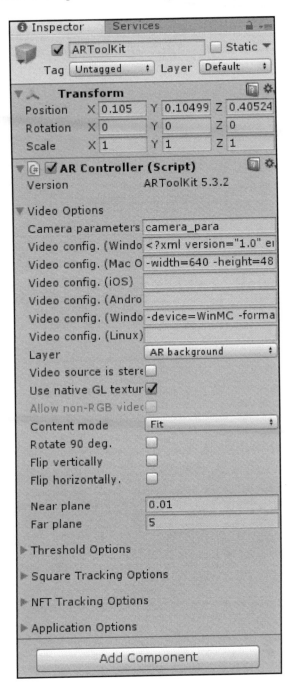

6. Since we have so many different options for video, we need to set it up properly:

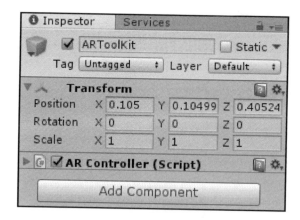

7. If you get errors in the console of the Unity Editor, then you don't have the latest version of ARToolKit with the version of Unity we are using in this book.

Since I am building for Windows, I will go to the first option of Video config and input the following:

```
<?xml version="1.0" encoding="utf-8"?>
<dsvl_input>
<camera show_format_dialog="false" frame_width="1280" frame_height="720"
frame_rate="29.97">
<pixel_format>
<RGB32 flip_v="true"/>
</pixel_format>
</camera>
</dsvl_input>
```

Now, since my computer does not presently have a webcam attached to it, I get an in-game error message, but the code compiles and runs as expected. If you have a webcam attached and it is recognized appropriately, you should have a direct feed from your webcam.

This concludes the Hello World for ARToolKit; we will be revisiting this one later on for more in-depth and fun usage of this SDK.

Setting up ARCore

ARCore and ARKit are fundamentally very similar, but you can't compile ARKit on a Windows environment, which is what I'm presently using. Not to worry; when we get to ARKit, I will be using a macOS to give you a proper view and feel of how things are when using it.

That being said, it is now time to take a deeper look at ARCore.

ARCore was made by Google and is currently in the early preview stages; it hasn't even reached release 1.0 yet, so there are bound to be many changes, some of which could be extremely damaging to existing apps or games.

There are two ways to get the SDK preview for Unity. The first is through a Unity Package file (`https://developers.google.com/ar/develop/unity/quickstart-android`) and the other is through GitHub (`https://github.com/google-ar/arcore-unity-sdk`). Now, since I have been having an issue with downloading from Amazon Web Services lately, I will use the second link:

Setting up your development environment

- Install the Android SDK version 7.0 (API Level 24) or higher.
    - To install the Android SDK, install Android Studio.
    - To update the Android SDK, use the Android SDK Manager tool in Android Studio.
- Install Unity 2017.3.0f2 or higher, with the **Android Build Support** component. For more info, see Downloading and Installing Unity.
- You will need to get the ARCore SDK for Unity. You can either:
    - Download the SDK for Unity and extract it.

    -or-

    - Clone the repository with the following command:

    ```
    $ git clone https://github.com/google-ar/arcore-unity-sdk.git
    ```

- You will need a supported Android device.

It is key to remember that, if you don't have a Samsung Galaxy 8 or a Google Pixel phone, you will not be able to run proper tests on your device. However, if you also install Android Studio, you do get access to the Android Emulator:

1. To begin, create a new project in Unity and call it ARCoreTutorial:

2. We need to change the **Build Settings** to **Android** before doing anything else:

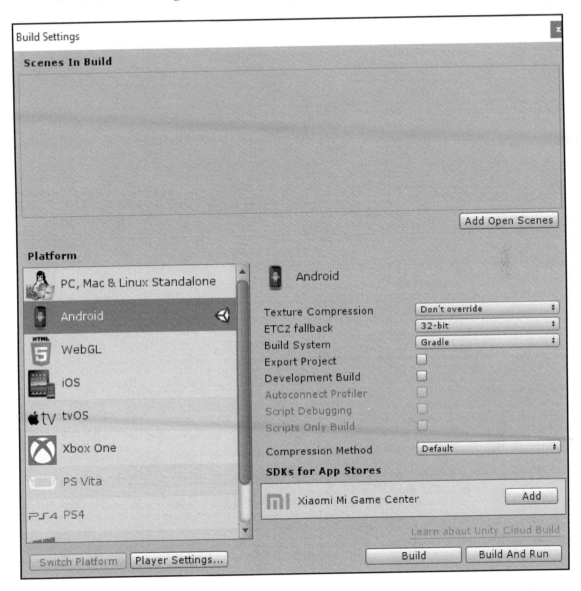

3. Next up, we need to change the **Player Settings**. The main settings we need to change are within the **Other Settings** tab, so let's take a look at what needs to be changed.

4. Other Settings: We want **Multithreaded Rendering** unchecked; **Minimum API Level** should be **Android 7.0 'Nougat' API level 24**; and **Target API Level** should be **Android 7.0 'Nougat' API level 24** or **Android 7.1 'Nougat' API level 25**:

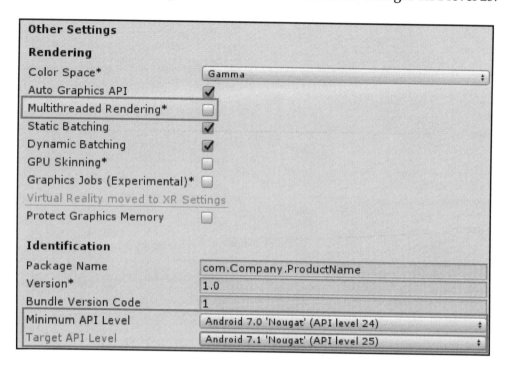

5. **XR Settings**: We want **ARCore Supported** to be checked:

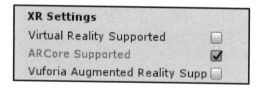

6. Next up, we want to unzip the SDK or import the package into Unity3D:

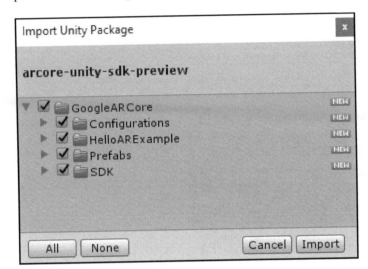

Right away, we should see a **DLLNotFoundException** for `tango_client_api2`. This is normal and is well-known by the community. It should not cause any errors at runtime, though; it should be fixed in a later release.

Setting up ARKit

ARKit requires the usage of macOS High Sierra, because of the XCode 9 and above requirement for compiling and making changes to the API itself. So, I would highly suggest having a macOS from late 2011 or newer. I am utilizing a Mac Mini 2011 model with 8 GB of RAM, although the standard 4 GB should be plenty. Unity3D does utilize OpenCL/OpenGL extensively, which requires a GFX card capable of utilizing Metal. 2011 and earlier macOSs do not have this ability natively; this could be circumvented by having an external GPU (Radeon RX 480 is currently the only GPU supported officially for this).

With that out of the way, we can begin with installing and configuring ARKit for Unity3D on our macOS.

There are a couple of ways you can install ARKit:

1. We can navigate to the plugin page on the Asset Store (`https://www.assetstore.unity3d.com/en/#!/content/92515`):

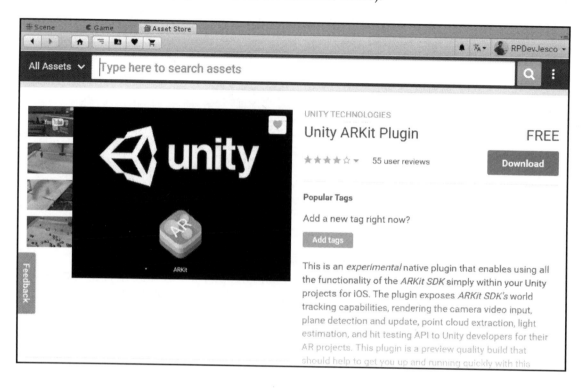

2. Or we can download the plugin directly from the Bitbucket repository (`https://bitbucket.org/Unity-Technologies/unity-arkit-plugin/overview`):

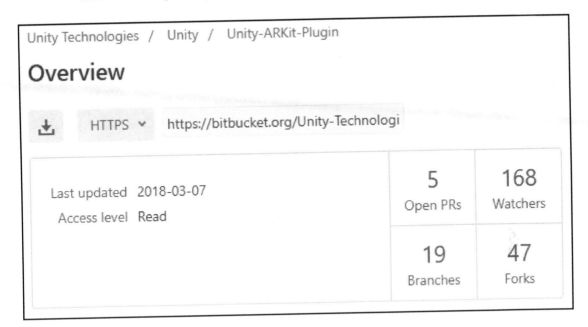

3. If we go the first route and install from the Asset Store, we don't have to worry about copying the files into our project ourselves, but either way it is simple enough to do, so take your pick on the method you want to go with and create a new project called `ARKitTutorial`:

Next up, we have quite a bit to unpack regarding what is actually in this package:

- `/Assets/Plugins/iOs/UnityARKit/NativeInterface/ARsessionNative.mm` – This is the Objective-C code that is the actual interfaces with the ARKit SDK.

- `/Assets/Plugins/iOS/UnityARKit/NativeInterface/UnityARSessionNativeInterface.cs` – This is the scripting API that glues the native code to ARKit.

- `/Assets/Plugins/iOS/UnityARKit/NativeInterface/AR*.cs` – These are the equivalents of the data structures exposed by ARKit.

- `/Assets/Plugins/iOS/UnityARKit/Utility/UnityARAnchorManager.cs` – This is a utility script that tracks the anchor updates from ARKit and can create the proper corresponding GameObjects in Unity for them.

- `/Assets/Plugins/iOS/UnityARKit/Editor/UnityARBuildPostprocessor.cs` – This is an editor script that runs at build time on iOS.

- `/Assets/Plugins/iOS/UnityARKit/UnityARCameraManager.cs` – This is the component that should be placed on a GameObject in the scene that references the camera that you want to control. It will position and rotate the camera as well as provide the correct projection matrix based on updates from ARKit. This component also initializes as ARKit Session.
- `/Assets/Plugins/iOS/UnityARKit/UnityARVideo.cs` – This is the component that should be placed on the camera and grabs the textures needed for rendering the video. It sets the material needed for blitting to the backbuffer and sets up the command buffer for blitting.
- `/Assets/Plugins/iOS/UnityARKit/UnityARUserAnchorComponent.cs` – This is the component that adds and removes Anchors from ARKit based on the life cycle of the GameObject it is added to.

Before we build our own "Hello World" example, we should build the `UnityARKitScene.unity` to iOS to get a taste of what ARKit is capable of, as it demonstrates all of the basic functionality of ARKit in that scene.

`UnityARKitScene` is included in the plugin as well as a couple of other example projects. We will compile the `UnityARKitScene` as our Hello World application.

However, before we do that, we need to talk about the file structure, because those who are not well-versed with compiling to iOS will have some serious issues compiling without further clarification. You may have noticed quite a few items that we have not mentioned that are in the plugin, so let's go ahead and discuss what all of them do before moving on.

`\UnityARKitPlugin` main directory files:

- `ARKitRemote` – Allows you to send remote commands from your device to the Unity3D editor
- `Examples` – This directory houses example scripts and scenes to showcase various things you can do with ARKit and this plugin
- `Plugins` – Houses the directories required to run ARKit
- `Resources` – Houses the resource files required for ARKit

`Plugins\iOS\UnityARKit\NativeInterface` cs files:

- `ARAnchor` – Anchors an object to a location in the world from the camera feed.
- `ARCamera` – Tracks the camera's position.
- `ARErrorCode` – Error codes.
- `ARFaceAnchor` – Face tracking anchor.

- `ARFrame` – Returns data about the camera, anchors, and light estimates.
- `ARHitTestResult` –Returns any collision results.
- `ARHitTestResultType` – Enumeration for the hit test types available.
- `ARLightEstimate` – Calculates how much luminosity is in the image or video.
- `ARPlaneAnchor` – Anchors a plane to a specific 4x4 matrix.
- `ARPlaneAnchorAlignment` – Aligns the anchor horizontally with respect to gravity.
- `ARPoint` – A point struct for x and y values as a double.
- `ARRect` – A struct that takes `ARPoint` as the origin and `ARSize` as the size.
- `ARSessionNative` – Native plugin used to specify framework dependencies and the platforms the plugin should work for.
- `ARSize` –A struct that takes a width and height value as a double.
- `ARTextureHandles` – A native Metal texture handler for the camera buffer which takes an `IntPtr` (`int pointer`) for both `textureY` and `textureCbCr` values.
- `ARTrackingQuality` – Enumeration for tracking qualities available.
- `ARTrackingState` –Enumeration for tracking states. **Limited**, **Normal**, and **NoAvailable** are the options.
- `ARTrackingStateReason` – Enumeration for the state reasons. Options are **Excessive Motion, Insufficient Features**, and **Initializing**.
- `ARUserAnchor` – Defines this anchor's transformation matrix for rotation, translation, and scale in world coordinates.
- `UnityARSessionNativeInterface` – Native plugin wrapper code.

`\Plugins\iOS\UnityARKit\Helpers` cs files:

- `AR3DOFCameraManager` – A helper class for 3D objects with the AR Camera
- `ARPlaneAnchorGameObject` – A class that attaches a GameObject with the `ARPlaneAnchor`
- `DontDestroyOnLoad` – Makes sure the GameObject doesn't get destroyed on load
- `PointCloudParticleExample` – Creates a point cloud particle system
- `UnityARAmbient` – A helper function for ambient lighting
- `UnityARAnchorManager` – A manager for `ARPlaneAnchorGameObjects`
- `UnityARCameraManager` – A helper class for the `ARCamera`

- `UnityARCameraNearFar` – Sets the Near Far distance of the camera appropriately
- `UnityARGeneratePlane` – Creates an `ARPlaneAnchorGameObject`
- `UnityARHitTestExample` – Tests collisions with various amounts of planes, from few to infinite
- `UnityARKitControl` – A helper class designed for creating a test `ARSession`
- `UnityARKitLightManager` – A helper class for managing the various lighting possibilities
- `UnityARMatrixOps` – A class for converting a 4x4 matrix to Euclidean space for quaternion rotation
- `UnityARUserAnchorComponent` – A helper class for creating Anchor added and removed events
- `UnityARUtility` – A helper class to do coordinate conversions from ARKit to Unity
- `UnityARVideo` – A helper function to render the video texture to the scene
- `UnityPointCloudExamples` – A helper function to draw a point cloud using particle effects

`\Plugins\iOS\UnityARKit\Shaders` shader files:

- `YUVShader` – A gamma Unlit Shader for rendering Textures
- `YUVShaderLinear` – A linear Unlit Shader for rendering Textures

`\UnityARKitPlugin\Resources` file:

- `UnityARKitPluginSettings.cs` – Is a scriptable object that toggles whether ARKit is required for the app and toggles Facetracking for the iPhone X.

`UnityARKitPlugin\ARKitRemote` files:

- `ARKitRemote.txt` – A text file that explains how to set up and use ARKitRemote
- `EditorTestScene.unity` – Test scene that should run when running ARKitRemote
- `UnityARKitRemote.unity` – Scene that should be compiled and installed on an applicable device
- `ARKitRemoteConnection.cs` – Used to send data from the device to the UnityEditor

- ConnectionMessageIds – GUIDs for the Editor Session Message
- ConnectToEditor.cs – Creates a network connection between the editor and the device
- EditorHitTest – Returns collision data from device to editor
- ObjectSerializationExtension.cs – An extension to convert an object to a byte array
- SerializableObjects.cs – Serializes Vector 4 data and a 4x4 matrix
- UnityRemoteVideo.cs – Connects to the editor and transfers a video feed from the device to the editor

UnityARKitPlugin\Examples files:

- AddRemoveAnchorExample – An example program to add and remove anchors
- Common – Has common materials, models, prefabs, shaders, and textures that are used in various projects
- FaceTracking – Face tracking example application
- FocusSquare – An example scene where it finds a specific anchor
- UnityARBallz – An example scene where you play a game with balls
- UnityARKitScene – A basic scene with minimal scripts attached to test if ARKit works appropriately
- UnityAROcclusion – An example project that showcases various lighting conditions
- UnityARShadows – An example project that handles low lighting conditions
- UnityParticlePainter – An example project that lets you paint with particles

Now that we have a fundamental understanding of everything inside this package, let's build our Hello World with ARKit.

Building Hello World in ARKit

The first thing we need to do after we open the UnityARKitScene is to set up the build settings:

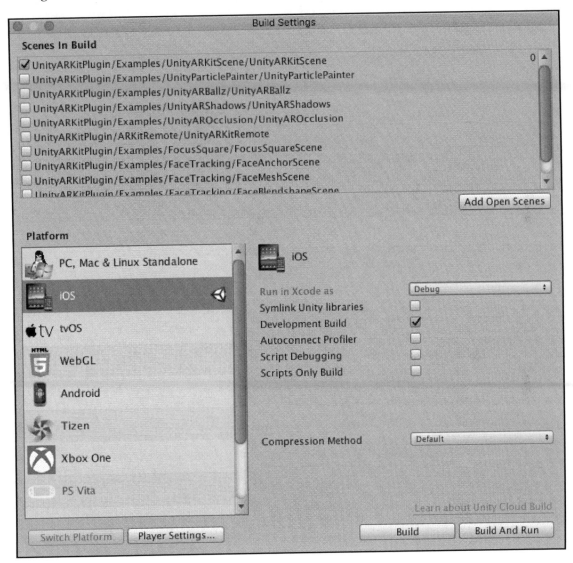

1. Click on **Build Settings** and select **Player Settings**.
2. We want to scroll down to **Identification**. The **Bundle Identifier** should be set to com.unity.ARKitHelloTutorial, **Version** to 0.1, **and Build** to 10.1. The **Automatically Sign** checkbox should be checked. Leave the **Automatic Signing Team ID** settings blank:

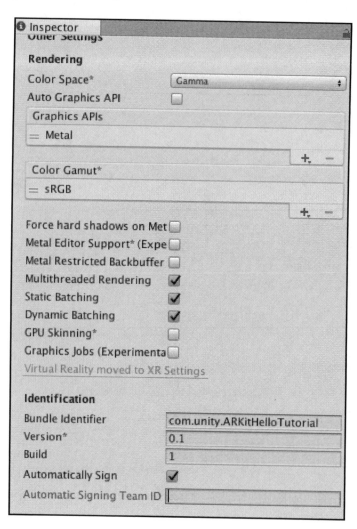

3. Build the `UnityARKitScene` for iOS only. Run Xcode in **Debug** mode.

4. Only the **Development Build** checkbox should be checked; everything else should be left as default.

5. Click **Build**. I will save the file as `iOSTest` in my data drive within a folder called `iOS`:

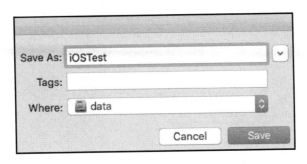

6. Building should not take very long at all, perhaps around two minutes for a first build.

7. The next thing we want to do is open the folder we saved the project in and open the `.xcodeproj` file in Xcode:

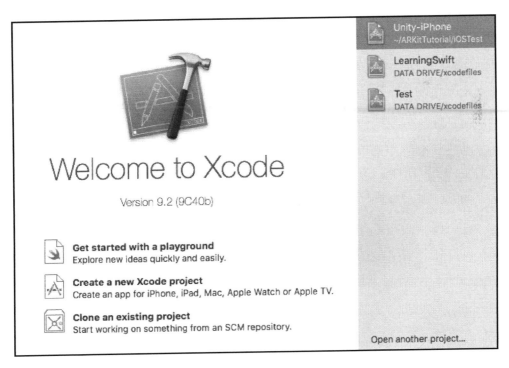

8. Let's take a look at the Base project you will see in Xcode:

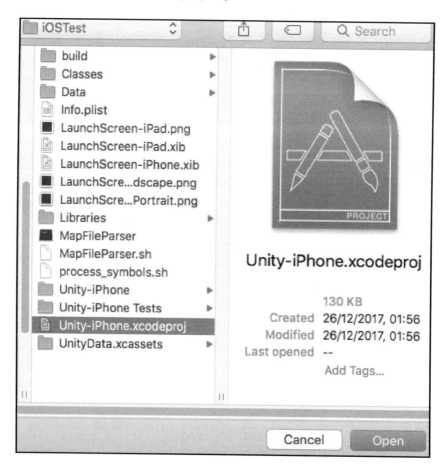

9. The first thing we want to check is the **Identity** tab to make sure that these settings are the same as in Unity3D:

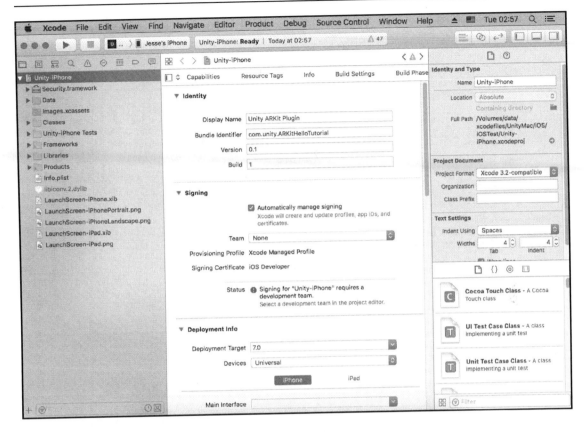

10. Now, we need to look at the **Signing** subsection:

11. We need to make sure to add our Personal Team name to it, which you can get by signing in to your Apple Developer account and clicking on the arrow for the team you want to use:

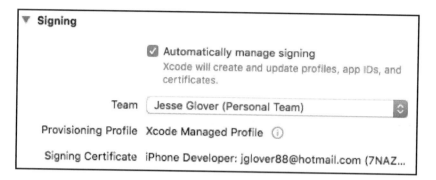

12. **Deployment Info** is next. The **Deployment Target** needs to be changed to 11.2. Devices should be set to **iPhone** only. The **Main Interface** is LaunchScreen-iPhone.xib:

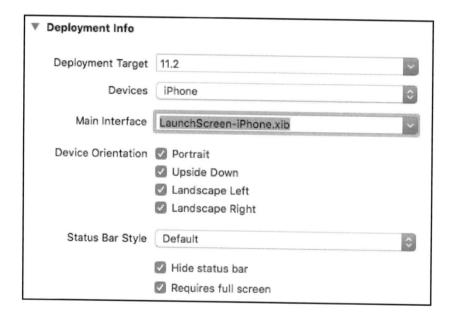

13. Click on **Build Settings** at the top, as there are a few settings we need to change here as well.

14. In **Architectures**, **ARCHS** for iPhone should be set to **Standard**. **SDKROOT** should be **Latest iOS (iOS 11.2)**. **SUPPORTED_PLATFORMS** should be **iOS**:

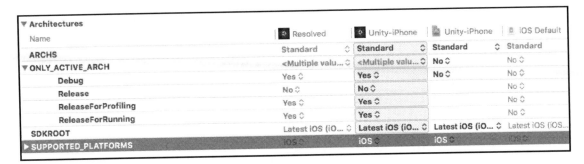

15. Next up, scroll down to look at signing, and the values should be already set to the correct ones:

16. Now, click on **Product** and **Build**:

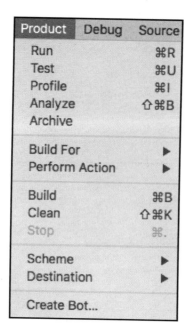

17. The build should have completed successfully with roughly 47 warnings, which is normal:

18. Now, we can build and test in the simulator. What we want to do is change from the iPhone to one of the simulators in the list, so click on the device list next to your iPhone or whatever device you have:

19. You will see a big list of devices you want to use. This will range from simulations of devices to the iOS device you have connected to your macOS:

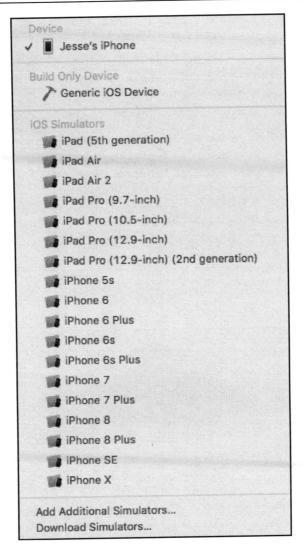

20. Click on the simulation you want to use, and then build and run the application.

Congratulations! We have completed this Hello World application.

Summary

We learned the basics of the four main AR SDKs made available to us from many companies. We installed and compiled a working example in each one of the SDKs with minimal effort, and we can now move on to utilizing these SDKs to their full potential, as they currently stand in their respective stages of development.

We can see that all four SDKs are simple enough to use and are relatively easy to install. In my opinion, the best SDK to use at the moment is Vuforia. It has the most robust API and is extremely well-documented for usage and further learning.

In the next chapter, we will focus on learning the history of GIS and how that history has shaped the way we use GIS in AR applications and games today.

GIS Fundamentals - The Power of Mapping

11

When it comes to **GIS**, which is the abbreviated form of **Geographic Information Systems**, and data and usage in AR programming, it comes in many flavors and usages. However, before we get into how to use GIS data in AR games and applications, we must first understand what GIS actually is. So, we will go over things like: when GIS was developed, who the father of GIS is, where GIS can be used, and how GIS works with game and application development. The reason this is important is that the history of GIS plays directly into how data is used today in AR applications and games; it also allows us to appreciate the hard work of those in the past who made it possible for us to take advantage of readily available data online. We will go over some examples of how we can use what we have learned from the history of GIS to create applications and games later on in this chapter. The following topics will be covered in this chapter:

- Understanding what GIS is
- History of GIS and data analysis
- GIS statistics
- Implications of GIS
- GIS and AR

To understand what GIS actually is, we must dive a little deeper to discover the underlying principles of GIS and how it started. The history of GIS and data analysis is fascinating and will expose many things that allow us to understand the underlying structure of how it is set up and used. GIS statistics will allow us to be able to know which mathematical methods are commonly used so that we can take advantage of them. The implications of GIS will show us many uses of GIS, not only in academia, but also in education and real-world usage.

GIS and AR will show us some much-needed examples of how AR applications and games have incorporated GIS into them. This will give us a clear idea on what we could develop in the future.

In this chapter, we will cover the following topics:

- GIS fundamentals – the power of mapping
- GIS and augmented reality

What is GIS?

The most common definition of GIS is geographic information systems. It is comprised of a full software and hardware system that can capture geographic data and information via cameras, store it via a database, manipulate it via software, analyze it via statistical and visualization tools, and manage and present spatial or geographic data. There are other well-known defination for GIS, such as geographic information science, although that has fallen out of general use as it refers to the academic discipline that studies geographic information systems. It is not commonly used for the definition of GIS, because it is a large domain within the much broader academic discipline of geoinformatics.

This essentially boils down to the ability to describe any information system that can combine, keep for future usage, manage, examine, distribute, and manifest geographic information. In essence, you can create tools that allow for users or other tools to create two-way flows of informational queries, examine spatial data, manipulate and inspect map data, and showcase the results of all of these operations in either visual or data form.

There are many tools and a plethora of different applications related to the engineering, arrangement, administration, logistics, insurance, transport, telecommunications, and business of GIS, and due to all this, GIS and location intelligence applications are the foundations for many location-enabled services such as Google Maps, Apple Maps, Bing Maps, Pokémon Go, and many more.

The history of GIS

The first known use of the term "geographic information system" was by Roger Tomlinson in 1968. It was used in his paper called *A Geographic Information System for Regional Planning*, and because of this, he is commonly known as the "father of GIS".

The first known application for spatial analysis was in 1832 by a French geographer named Charles Picquet. He represented the 48 districts of Paris by halftone color gradients following the number of deaths incurred by the outbreak of cholera per 1,000 inhabitants.

John Snow was determined to find the source of a cholera outbreak in 1854. He attempted to find the source of the cholera outbreak in London's Broad Street region by marking points on a map to depict where the cholera victims lived, and by connecting the cluster he found, he was able to link the source of the outbreak to a water source that was nearby. This was one of the first known effective employments of geographic procedures in the study of disease transmission.

In his map, he used bars to represent deaths that occurred at specified households; however, in his first map, there were several minor errors. One of these errors was the location of the Broad Street pump:

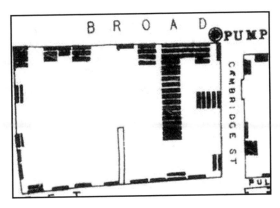

The text in this image is not important. It gives a gist of John Snow's first map

With the second map he published, he fixed his errors, which included the location of the pump:

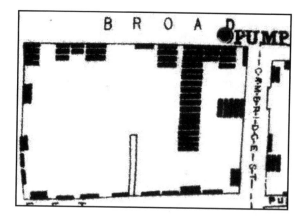

The text in this image is not important. It gives a gist of John Snow's second map

While essential components of geology existed beforehand in cartography, John Snow's guide was extremely remarkable. It was novel because of the way that he utilized cartographic techniques to portray as well as examine groups of geologically subordinate wonders. And because of this, John Snow is known to many as a pioneer in disease mapping, in which many of the concepts he established are still used today in conjunction with many other aspects of GIS by the **Centers for Disease Control and Prevention (CDC)**.

By the early 20th century, we saw the advancement of photozincography (also known as heliozincography). Photozincography gave the ability for maps to be split into layers. This meant that each layer could hold information only relevant to that specific layer, such as vegetation, trees, or waterways. It was mainly used for printing contours, since drawing these was a very labor-intensive task and thus made this technique extremely useful for cartographers. Having conduits, trees, or vegetation on independent layers implied that they could be chipped away at without alternate layers there to confound the artist, or to cause issues when, say, structures were obstructing something that should have been checked. This is also still used today; one such usage is when marking the location of electrical lines that are underground, or water pipes for houses:

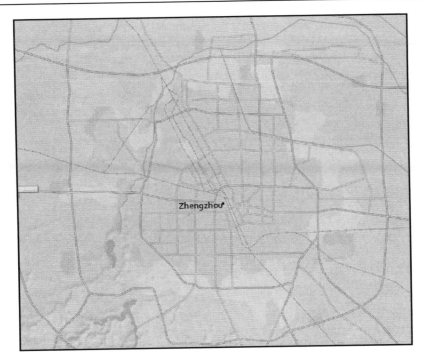

With photozincography, maps like this were initially drawn on glass plates but were later changed over to plastic film as there were numerous points of interest regarding plastic over glass. Plastic was lighter, required less space for capacity, was less fragile, and more. At the point when the greater part of the layers were done, they were joined into a solitary picture utilizing an extensive procedure camera. When color printing became available, the layers' conception was withal utilized for engendering separate plates for engendering each color.

The utilization of layers later became one of the main features of contemporary GIS, and the photographic process described is not considered to be a component of GIS itself as the maps were and are just images without any databases linked to them. Advancement of PC equipment that was impelled by atomic weapons prompted broadly useful PC mapping applications in the mid-1960s. In 1960, the world's first obvious operational GIS by the Federal Department of Forestry and Rural Development in Ottawa, Ontario, Canada was created.

This first obvious operational GIS was created by none other than Dr. Roger Tomlinson. This GIS was known as the **Canada Geographic Information System (CGIS)**, and it was utilized to store, break down, and control the information gathered for the Canada Land Inventory. The Canada Land Inventory was an administration push to decide the land capacity for provincial Canada by mapping data regarding the dirt, horticulture, amusement, untamed life, waterfowl, ranger service, and land use at a size of 1 to 50,000. Due to the scale and the amount of information that needed to be stored, a rating classification factor was created to permit easier and more effective analysis.

While there were other computer mapping applications at the time, CGIS made massive improvements as it provided capabilities for overlay, measurement, scanning, and digitizing the map data. It was also able to support a national coordinate system that spanned the entire continent with coded lines as arcs. This meant that it had a true embedded topology and it stored the attributes and locational information in separate files. The utilization of overlays in advancing the spatial investigation of focalized geographic information is the motivation behind Tomlinson turning out to be known as the "father of GIS".

In 1964, Howard T. Fisher shaped the Laboratory for Computer Graphics and Spatial Analysis at the Harvard Graduate School of Design (LCGSA 1965 – 1991), where a large number of essential hypothetical ideas in spatial information to be handled were produced. By the 1970s, seminal software code and systems were distributed by the LCGSA. These systems were SYMAP, GRID, and ODYSSEY; not only did these systems serve as sources for subsequent commercial development, but they themselves were distributed to colleges, research centers, and business conglomerates worldwide.

MOSS and GRASS GIS were two public GIS systems that were in development by the late 1970s. Roughly a few years later, in the early 1980s, new commercial vendors for GIS software emerged. Those commercial vendors were the Environmental Systems Research Institute, CARIS, MapInfo Corporation, ERDAS, and M&S Computing, along with Bentley Systems Incorporated for CAD. These sellers were fruitful in having the capacity to fuse numerous new highlights and ways to deal with GIS programming, for example, consolidating the original ways to deal with the partition of spatial and characteristic data with second-age ways to deal with sorting out trait information into database structures and additionally fusing CGIS highlights.

The first well-known work area GIS item that was discharged for the DOS OS was known as the Mapping Display and Analysis System and was released to the public in 1986. In 1990, MIDAS was ported to the Microsoft Windows platform and was renamed to MapInfo for Windows during that process. This marked the process of moving GIS from the research sector over into the business sector.

One critical note to include is that CGIS kept going great into the 1990s and had fabricated a substantial advanced land asset database in Canada. CGIS was created as a centralized server-based framework for the government as a commonplace asset for arranging and administration programming. Along these lines, it had the capacity to do mainland wide investigation of complex datasets, however, CGIS was never made accessible in the business market sphere.

At the turn of the 20th century, users were beginning to explore GIS data over the internet. This called for data and transfer standardization. All of this was caused by the rapid growth in various systems and, as such, showcased the flaw that there were many different systems that used very few similar methods or data formats and needed to be consolidated.

As of late, there is an ever-growing number of open source GIS packages that run on a range of operating systems and software that are very easily customized to perform specific tasks. Research institutes and hobbyists are making mapping applications and geospatial data readily available via the internet.

GIS techniques and technologies

As stated in the previous section, GIS technologies heavily utilize digital information. There are quite a few different digital data formulation methods that are used. The most common method of data formulation, however, is digitization, for obvious reasons. Let's take a quick step back and define digitization. Digitization is where you have a physical copy of a map or survey data and transfer it into a digital medium by means of CAD or similar programs that have georeferencing capabilities. With the abundance of orthorectified imagery devices such as satellites, aircraft, Helikites, and UAVs, heads-up digitizing is becoming the go-to resource by which geographic data is extricated.

Heads-up digitizing is copying via tracing geographic data directly on top of aerial imagery. Heads-down digitizing is the process of tracing the geographic form onto a separate digitizing tablet and is the more traditional method.

GIS can reference any variable that can be located spatially and temporally. Areas or degrees in Earth spacetime might be recorded as dates and times of event with the x, y, and z facilitates speaking to longitude, scope, and height. These GIS directions may speak to other information for measured frameworks of temporospatial reference. These GIS coordinates may represent other data for quantified systems of temporospatial reference. Some examples of temporospatial references include the film frame number, stream gauge station, highway mile markers, surveyor benchmarks, building addresses, entrance gates, street intersections, water depth sounding, and POS or CAD origin or units.

Temporospatial data recorded units that are applied can vary widely; this includes using the exact same data, and because of this, all Earth-based spatial-temporal location references are relatable to one another. This makes it so that, ultimately, all of these references are able to represent a real physical location or extent in spacetime.

GIS data represents real objects with digital data determining the mix. That data includes objects such as roads, land use, elevation, trees, waterways, highways, and so much more. These real objects are generally divided into two distinct abstractions: discrete objects and continuous fields. Discrete objects are those such as houses, and continuous fields are things such as rainfall amount and evaluations. There are two broad methods that are used to store data in a GIS for both kinds of abstractions mapping references that have become a tradition: raster images and vectors. Points, lines, and polygons are typically used to map location attribute references.

There is a new hybrid method for storing data that is currently being used, which is able to combine three-dimensional points with RGB information at each point. This is able to return a 3D colorized image. GIS thematic maps are becoming much more realistically descriptive in what they are able to show or determine.

There are some very popular GIS file formats that are used by different software applications, such as the following:

- Shapefiles
- Geopackage
- World file
- AutoCAD DXF
- Cartesian coordinate system
- ADRG
- Binary files such as BSQ or BIP
- DRG
- ECRG
- GeoTiff
- JPEG2000
- RAW

Ways to capture GIS

Capturing GIS data consumes most available time for those that are practitioners of GIS. As such, there are a variety of methods used to enter data into a GIS where it is stored in a digital format. All existing data that has been printed on paper or PET film is able to be digitized or scanned to produce digital data. This would be a good time to define what a digitizer is and does.

A manual digitizer is a modified graphics tablet that uses a special magnetic pen, stylus, or puck that delivers information into a computer to create a digital map. These are rather expensive, however, they are very useful for GIS digitization (`http://www.digitizerzone.com/calcomp-db6.html`):

Digitizers can produce vector data as operator trace points, lines, and polygonal boundaries from a map. A scanner is able to scan the results into raster data, which needs to be further processed to produce vector data:

`https://largeformatscanners.com/large-format-technical-scanners.htm`

Using survey instruments and a technique called coordinate geometry, the data can be directly entered into a GIS. GPS (global positioning systems) positions can also be collected and imported into GIS software. The current popular approach to data collection allows for field computers to edit live data via wireless connections or offline editing sessions.

The higher availability of lower-cost mapping-grade GIS with the ability of to-the-decimeter accuracy in real time enhances the ability to use field computers to edit the live data as well as positions collected by laser rangefinders. The advantage of using this technique is that it eliminates most of the postprocessing, importation, and updating of the data in the office after fieldwork.

More and more new technologies are being developed that allow users to create maps and conduct analysis in the field directly, which makes projects and mapping more efficient and accurate. Remote sensor data is an important if not critical role in data collection, which consists of sensors attached to a platform. These sensors include cameras, digital scanners, and lidar, and the platforms usually consist of aircraft and satellites.

In the mid-1990s, England created a kite and balloon hybrid called HeliKites. They pioneered the use of compact digital cameras as geoinformation systems for aerial GIS data collection. Aircraft measurement software is accurate to 0.4 mm and is able to link the photographs with the measurements to the ground. The advantage of using HeliKites is that they can be used over towns, railways, and roads, where UAVs (unmanned aerial vehicles) are banned from usage. Miniature UAVs such as drones have recently been used for aerial data collection. Most digital data is collected from aerial photographs currently.

There are soft copy workstations that are used to digitize features from stereo pairs of digital photographs. The stereo pairs of digital photographs allow for data to be captured in both two and three dimensions. Elevation is measured using principles of photogrammetry. If analog aerial photos are used, they must be scanned before they can be entered into a soft copy workstation, however, if a high-quality digital camera is used, then this step can be skipped.

Remote sensing from satellites is another important source used for spatial data. Satellites use different sensor packages to measure the reflectance from parts of the electromagnetic spectrum and/or radio waves. Remote sensing from satellites collects raster data that is further processed with different frequency bands; this allows for better identification of objects and areas of interest.

No matter the source of captured data, it is important to consider if the data is captured with relative or absolute accuracy. Choosing between relative or absolute accuracy influences how the information is interpreted and the direct cost to capture the data.

After the data has been entered into a GIS, the data usually requires editing. The editing ensures that errors can be removed or designates which portions of the data need to be further processed. Scanned maps may have blemishes on the source map that may need to be removed from the raster image. Vector data has to be made topologically correct before usage with advanced analysis.

Converting from raster to vector

Data restored by GIS software can be converted into different formats. GIS can convert satellite image maps into vector structures. This is done by generating lines around cells within the same classifications. They can also determine cell spatial relationships, such as adjacency and inclusion.

Image processing can do much more advanced data processing. This technique was developed in the 1960s by NASA and was further enhanced by the private sector. They can do two-dimensional Fourier transforms, contrast enhancements, false color rendering, and a plethora of other techniques. Since digital data is stored and collected in different ways, the data sources tend to not be compatible with one another. To solve this compatibility problem, software built upon GIS technologies must be able to convert geographic data from one to the other. GIS is able to do this because they employ implicit assumptions behind different ontologies and classifications that require heavy analysis. Object ontologies have become much more prominent as a consequence of **object-oriented programming (OOP)**, which makes it more compatible with game development and sustained work by Barry Smith and his coworkers.

Projections and coordinate systems

The Earth can be represented by various models, and all of them provide a different coordinate set for every point on the surface of the Earth. The simplest model assumes that the Earth is a perfect sphere, although we know it isn't. And as more measurements of the Earth have been accumulated, consequently, the models of Earth have become extremely sophisticated and accurate. There are models that have different data that apply to different areas of the Earth, which provides increased accuracy. NAD83 is a US measurement, and WGS84 (World Geodetic System) is for worldwide measurements.

There are clear but very minor differences between NAD83 and WGS84, besides one being worldwide and the other being US-based. WGS84 uses the WGS84 ellipsoid and has an error margin of less than 2 cm from the center of mass, whereas the NAD83 uses the Geodetic Reference System (GRS80) ellipsoid with an offset of about two meters. NAD83 uses points over the Northern American plate that do not change, and WGS84 uses points with respect to the average of stations all over the world and are not fixed. NAD83 has not changed since its inception; WGS84 has been revised to use a deviation of 105 m to +85 by the new EGM96 geoid. WGS84 is used by the US DOD (Department of Defense), and NAD83 is used by many other agencies within governments.

Although WGS84 and NAD83 have different parameters, the results have negligible effects during surveys. For example, the semi-minor axis has a difference of 0.00010482 between WGS84 and NAD83, and the inverse of flattening has a difference of 0.000001462 between the two. To better showcase this, let's look at a comparison of the US map from the results of WGS84 and NAD83:

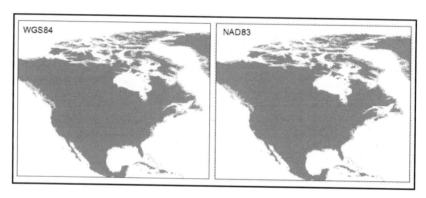

Spatial analysis with GIS

Spatial analysis allows us to better understand spatial relationships and patterns, which in turn allows us to better understand our world. Because of this, we are able to map where things are, how they relate to one another, what it all means for the environment, and actions to take to reverse any adverse effects we may cause. We are also able to find optimum routes, select sites for a plethora of different building projects, advanced predictive modeling, and so much more.

We can use the predictive modeling aspect to see how a forest fire would spread based on vegetation, dryness of the particular region, and wind. Not only that, but we could use it to find the optimal location for a store to be built that would likely attract the most customers.

Spatial analysis with GIS is a rapidly changing field. GIS packages are getting increasing amounts of analytical tools, which includes standard built-in libraries as well as optional toolsets and add-ons. Original software suppliers have provided these in many instances, however, third parties have been providing and developing these as well in increasing amounts. Many products offer SDKs (software development kits) that are compatible with specific programming languages, scripting capabilities, and the ability to develop custom analytical tools.

The website Geospatial Analysis (`http://www.spatialanalysisonline.com/`) and the associated book written by Michael J de Smith, Michael F Goodchild, and Paul A Longley are able to provide a fairly comprehensive guide on the subject matter. The massive increase in availability has created a new dimension to business and spatial intelligence to be able to make the geographic and social network data available to everyone. Geospatial intelligence, which is commonly referred to as GIS spatial analysis, has become a key element in security in the real world.

Data analysis with GIS

When trying to relate wetland maps to rainfall amounts recorded at different points, it can be difficult to do so, especially in places such as airports, schools, and television stations. A GIS can be used to visualize two-dimensional and three-dimensional characteristics of the Earth's surface. This also includes the atmosphere and subsurface from informational points as well. GIS can quickly generate map data from contour lines that have the ability to give the indications of differing amounts of precipitation. This type of map is called a rainfall contour map.

Many methods are able to estimate the characteristics of surfaces from limited point measurements and require a high level of sophistication to do so accurately. Two-dimensional contour maps that are created from the surface modeling precipitation points can be overlaid with any other map in GIS covering the same areas. This derived map is able to provide additional information; in this case, this would be the potential viability of water power as a renewable energy source. GIS can be used to compare many other renewable energy resource viability options for any geographic region.

Additionally, from a series of three-dimensional points, elevation contours can be generated from slope analysis, which would make it to easily define watershed locations by computing all the areas uphill from any point of interest. An expected line connecting the lowest points of successive cross-sections along the course of a valley or river can be computed from elevation data as well.

From all of this, we are able to ascertain that there are five main steps in the data analysis process:

1. Framing the question
2. Exploring and preparing the data
3. Choosing the methods of analysis and the tools
4. Performing the analysis
5. Examining and refining the results

Framing the question: It is a good idea to frame the question to make the subsequent steps easier to go through, for example, frame the question in a manner that helps determine which GIS tools and methods will be used for analysis.

Exploring the data: This step is known to be the most time-consuming, and you aren't guaranteed to have all the data needed for the analysis. It is a good idea to know the data format that will be used, how current that data is, the scale and detail of the data, the coordinate system used, whether the data uses any geometry work with the analysis, whether the data has the attributes needed, and whether the data has any access or usage constraints.

Preparing the data: During this step, the data format to use will be extremely important to know as it will determine which set of tools will need to be used. Make sure the data is organized, the data is readily extractable, and there are no errors that occur when using the data in the tools that will be used.

Choosing the methods of analysis and the tools to be used: The methods and tools should be readily and easily defined by the question framed. Generally, the question should have a direct one-to-one for the methods and tools, and having a simple diagram for the analysis is considered good practice. A simple example is provided in the following image:

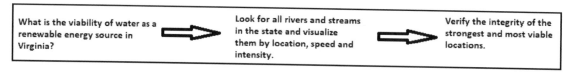

| What is the viability of water as a renewable energy source in Virginia? | | Look for all rivers and streams in the state and visualize them by location, speed and intensity. | | Verify the integrity of the strongest and most viable locations. |

Performing the analysis: Since diagramming is considered good practice, all that needs to be done here is to follow the tasks in sequence. The more complex the analysis, the more it may be necessary to create a model with ModelBuilder to automate the process, which will make it easier to change a parameter and run the model again for different scenarios.

Examining and refining the results: This step is just to look at the results and see if there are additional parameters missed in the original question and add some tweaks to better fit the original vision of the question.

For a more detailed look, along with some tutorials on the steps in the data analysis process, visit `http://www.bcps.org/offices/lis/researchcourse/data_process.html`.

GIS modeling

GIS is able to recognize the spatial relationships that exist within stored spatial data as well as analyze said data. This allows for complex spatial modeling to be performed, studying the relationship between the properties of geometric forms that remain invariant, including adjacency, containment, and proximity. We can use this information to more accurately model and analyze the data.

Geometric networks

All of this leads us to geometric networks. Geometric networks are linear networks of objects that can be used to represent interconnected features and perform spatial analysis on them. Geometric networks are composed of edges that are connected at junction points. This is extremely similar to graph theory, which is heavily used in mathematics and computer science:

As we can see from the screenshot, networks can have weight and flow assigned to the edges, which are used to represent various connected features more accurately. The general use case for geometric networks is to model road networks and public utilities such as electric and water networks. They are also used to plan for transportation networks, infrastructure modeling, and hydrological modeling.

Hydrological modeling

Hydrological models in GIS provide spatial elements and analysis with variables such as slope, aspect, and catchment area. This includes terrain analysis, as it is fundamental to hydrology since water always flows down a slope. Slope and aspect can be used to determine the direction of surface runoff and flow accumulation for streams, rivers, and lakes.

Areas of divergent flow also give a clearer indication of boundaries regarding catchment. As flow direction and accumulation matrixes are created, queries can be performed to show dispersal areas. This allows for more details to be added to the model. This would be things such as roughness, vegetation types, soil types, evapotranspiration rates, and surface flow. All of this means that hydrological modeling is perfect for usage with environmental contamination research.

Cartographic modeling

Dana Tomlin coined the term "cartographic modeling" in his PhD dissertation in 1983, and he later used it in the title of his book *Geographic Information Systems and Cartographic Modeling*, which was published in 1990.

Cartographic modeling is the process wherein thematic layers of the same area are produced, processed, and analyzed. It should be noted that Tomlin used raster layers, however, the overlay method can be used in most general situations. Operations on map layers are able to then be combined with the usage of algorithms to be incorporated into simulations or optimization models.

Map overlays

Map overlay is the combination of several spatial datasets to create a new vector output dataset. You can visualize this by stacking several maps of the same area. Another way to visualize this is to think of the Venn diagram overlay used in mathematics. There are three types of overlays – union, symmetric difference, and intersect overlay – that are used for different reasons, which will not discussed here as they fall outside the scope of this book:

1. Union overlay is to combine geographic features and attribute tables of both inputs and output it to a single output
2. Intersect overlay is to define the area where both inputs overlap and retain a set of attribute fields for each

3. Symmetric difference overlay is to define the output area that includes the total area of both inputs EXCEPT for the overlapping area

Data extraction in GIS is very similar to a vector overlay with the ability to be used in either vector or raster data analysis. Instead of combining properties and features of both datasets, extracting the data can involve using a clip or mask to extract certain features of one dataset that are relevant to the other dataset.

Raster data analysis uses local operation on multiple raster datasets or map algebra. Map algebra has a function that combines the values of each raster's matrix and can be coupled with another function that can weigh some inputs higher than others through an index model that reflects the influence of various factors from within a geographic phenomenon.

Statistics used with GIS

Statistics is heavily used in GIS, and there is a special branch of statistics that deals with field data specifically. This special branch of statistics uses spatial data with a continuous index. It is able to provide methods to model spatial correlation and predict values at arbitrary locations, which is also known as interpolation.

When geographic phenomena are measured, the observation methods can dictate the accuracy of any analysis. There are limits caused by the nature of some data, where there is a constant or dynamic degree of precision that is always lost in measurement. This loss of precision is determined by the scale and distribution of the data collection.

When determining the statistical relevance of any analysis, the average has to be determined so that the points outside of any measurement can be included to their predicted behavior. Applied statistics and data collection methods have a limitation to predicting the behavior of particles, points, and locations, which causes them to not be directly measurable.

Interpolation is where a surface is created by raster datasets through the input of data collection at a certain number of sample points. There are, however, several different forms of interpolation, and each of them treats data differently, which is dependent on the properties of the dataset. When interpolation methods are compared, several points need to be considered. The first is whether or not that data source will change and whether exact or approximate data collection will be used. The next is whether a method is subjective, which essentially means whether human interpretation or objective interpretation methods will be used. Next is the nature of transitions between the points: are they gradual or abrupt? Finally, checking to see whether a method is local or global.

A global method utilizes the entire dataset to form the model, and a local method uses an algorithm to repeat for a small section of terrain. Interpolation is utilized as the fundamental technique for estimation because of the spatial autocorrelation rule, which says that information gathered at any position will have comparability to or impact over those areas inside its prompt region.

The mathematical methods to produce interpolative data are as follows:

- Digital elevation models
- Triangulated irregular networks
- Edge finding algorithms
- Thiessen polygons
- Fourier analysis
- Weighted moving averages
- Inverse distance weighting
- Kriging
- Spline
- Trend surface analysis

Geocoding

Geocoding is interjecting the *x* and *y* arrange spatial areas. These can be from road addresses or some other spatially referenced information, for example, ZIP codes, divide, and address areas. A reference topic is required to geocode singular locations, for example, a street centerline document with address ranges.

The individual address areas have verifiably been added, or assessed, by inspecting the address that goes along a street section. These are generally given in a table or database. The product will then place a spot around where that address has a place along the section of centerline. Geocoding can likewise be connected against genuine bundle information.

Reverse geocoding

Reverse geocoding is the way toward restoring an expected road address number, as it identifies with a given facilitate. You can think about this like an invert telephone number look-into table. Also, similar to reverse phone look-into tables, switch geocoding does not return real road addresses, just the gauge of what ought to be there in light of a foreordained range. Combined with GIS, multi-criteria choice examination techniques bolster leaders in breaking down an arrangement of option spatial arrangements. MCDA utilizes choice tenets to total the criteria, which enables the elective answers to be positioned or organized. GIS MCDA may diminish expenses and time engaged with recognizing potential reclamation destinations.

Open Geospatial Consortium Standards

The **Open Geospatial Consortium (OGC)** is a non-profit association that was established in 1994 and has more than 384 organizations, colleges, government offices, and individuals taking part to grow freely accessible geoprocessing particulars.

OpenGIS Specifications have conventions and interfaces characterized to help arrangements that empower the web, remote, area administrations, tech engineers, and standard IT to make complex spatial data and administrations available and valuable for a heap of utilization composes.

Web Map Services and Web Feature Services are incorporated into the OGC conventions. Any product items that consent to OGC's OpenGIS particulars are known as Compliant Products, and when an item has been tried and affirmed by the OGC testing program, it is consequently enlisted as consistent on the open geospatial database.

The procedure by which to wind up "OGC guaranteed" has five stages:

- Go to the testing website and select the standard for the product desired
- Go to the OGC Online Certification system and provide the information about the product, testing account, and standard for certification desired

- OGC will review and contact regarding the licensing fee and a new or revised trademark license agreement
- Receive the certificate, and the OGC compliance logos are then open for usage
- Product will then appear as certified in the OGC implementing database

Full information can be found at the official website at `http://www.opengeospatial.org/compliance/getCertified`:

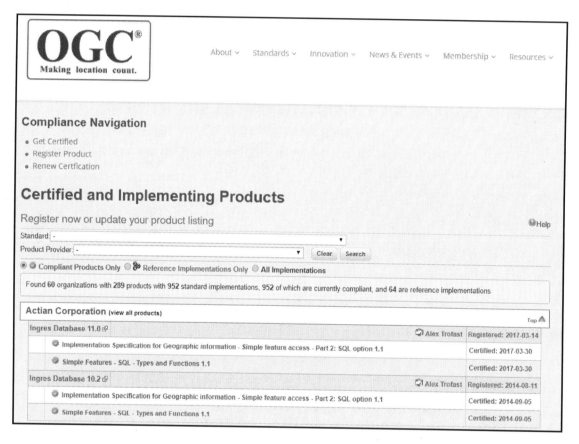

Note that consistence tests are not accessible for all determinations. Designers can enroll their items as actualizing draft or endorsed particulars, despite the fact that OGC maintains whatever authority is needed to audit and check every section.

Web mapping

As of late, numerous allowed to utilize and effectively available exclusive mapping programming, for example, Google Maps, Bing Maps, Apple Maps, and Baidu Maps, what's more, there are additionally some free and open source options like OpenStreetMap, GMap.NET, Wikimapia, RMaps, and uebermaps. These administrations give the free to a lot of GIS injected mapping information.

A significant number of them offer an API (application programming interface) that take into account clients to make custom applications or broaden the current application. These libraries or systems tend to offer road outline, satellite symbolism, flying symbolism, geocoding, georeferencing, geofencing, seeks and directing usefulness. Crowdsourcing geodata in ventures such as web mapping has been found to make a communitarian task to make free and editable maps of the world for all that need to utilize that particular application or informational index.

GIS and adding dimension of time

The state of the Earth, this is the subsurface, environment, and surface can be broken down by encouraging satellite information into GIS programming. GIS have enabled specialists to utilize the innovation to investigate the varieties of the Earth's procedures over days, months, years, and even decades. Vegetation wellbeing changes through the developing season can be reenacted to decide when a dry season would have the most serious effect in any given district. The outcomes can give a harsh measure of the soundness of the plants in a recreated district. Simply utilizing two factors and estimating them after some time enables analysts to decide separations in the decay of precipitation and the outcomes on the locale's vegetation.

The accessibility of advanced data with both local and worldwide scales empowers GIS innovation to make such examinations. Satellite sensors deliver pictures of a specific area of the Earth twice every day. MODIS (Moderate Resolution Imaging Spectroradiometer) and AVHRR (advanced very-high-resolution radiometer) are two of numerous sensor frameworks utilized for examination of the Earth's surface. These sensor frameworks can recognize the measures of vitality reflected from the Earth's surface crosswise over different groups of the recurrence range for territories up to one square kilometer.

Not exclusively is time being incorporated into ecological examinations with GIS, however, the capacity to track and model the advancement of people and creatures all through their everyday schedules is being investigated. This can be seen with the Google and Facebook area benefits that track a man for the duration of the day for a considerable length of time, months, or even a very long time after use. This composes information creation and control could never have been conceivable without GIS and the extraordinary type of insights utilized. Organizers can, likewise, test strategy choices by utilizing spatial choice emotional supportive network by utilizing models to extend the information encased inside a GIS forward in time.

Semantics

The World Wide Web Consortium's Semantic Web ended up being amazingly helpful for incorporating information issues in data frameworks through devices and advances that have been developing. These apparatuses and innovations have been proposed as methods for interoperability and information reuse among different GIS-based applications and take into consideration new examination mechanics.

A few arrangements of ideas and classes of this space to indicate formal and machine-clear particulars of their ideas and connections have been made. This takes into account GIS to center around the information rather than the language structure or structure of the information. Easier ontologies alongside semantic metadata measures have been recommended by the W3C Geo Incubator Group, particularly to speak to geospatial information on the web. One such case is GeoSPARQL, which is a Geographic Query dialect for **Resource Description Framework (RDF)** Data, in which there are different advancements that are based on RDF and give dialect to characterizing the real structure, for example, **Web Ontology Language (OWL)** and **Simple Knowledge Organization System (SKOS)**.

GeoSPARQL was produced by the **Open Geospatial Consortium (OGC)** and has been bolstered by numerous people in the field and not restricted to the Ordinance Survey, United States Geological Survey, Natural Resources Canada, Industrial Research Organization, and Austrialia's Commonwealth Scientific. GeoSPARQL gives OGC literals, for example, **Geography Markup Languague (GML)** and WTK (surely understood content) and simple highlights, for example, RCC8 (locale association analytics) and DE-9IM (Dimensionally Extended nine-crossing point demonstrate) give topological relationship and subjective thinking and, in addition, SPARQL expansion capacities and **Rule Interchange Format (RIF)** center derivation rules for questioning change and elucidation.

Later research comes about here and can be found at the International Conference on Geospatial Semantics web workshop and International Semantic Web Conference.

The implications of GIS in society

GIS is ending up, to a great degree, well-known with basic leadership as of late, and researchers have started to look profoundly into the social and political ramifications of GIS. Similarly, as with any frame and information accumulation and examination, GIS is defenseless to be abused to misshape reality for political and individualistic pick up. The generation, circulation, use, and portrayal of geographic data has been contended to be generally identified with the social setting, and furthermore holds the potential for expanded native doubt in the administration.

Different points that are investigated intensely are regarding potential copyright infringement, oversight, and protection. Many in the field are more hopeful, and they trust that the social approach that many will adopt is to strategize GIS appropriation as an instrument for open cooperation.

GIS in the real world

Not only can GIS be used in the academic sector, but it can also be used in the real world very effectively. We have seen the rise of GPS apps, which have largely replaced traditional maps, apps that know your exact location, apps that can find a lost device or child, and so much more. By taking all of the topographical and statistical data that can be obtained, almost every sector in modern life has been or can be utilized for GIS data.

We can really see this from historical events; let's use the bubonic plague as an example. Unlike those in the past, we are armed with hindsight that is 20/20; we know that it was rats that spread the disease. Let's say we had all of the data that showcased the movement and travel information of the rats, which we could then have used to study their patterns and have a much more accurate description of where the plague started and how it traveled.

It doesn't stop there since that is more on the academic approach as well. Let's say we want to track our own daily patterns within the last five years. We can use location data along with GIS to accurately depict our daily routine. We can move forward and also think about how we can use GIS to track our internet usage by creating a GIS specific for IP addresses that showcases how frequently and infrequently websites are accessed.

Then, there are video games; we can apply GIS to video games in a multitude of ways, from recreating terrain used in historic battle locations from all around the world, to create a completely alien world from mixing GIS data from various planets and moons. But we could also use GIS to augment the reality around us by injecting GIS data into the camera to transform or recognize similar data from which it reads in real time.

GIS in education

At the turn of the 20th century, GIS was starting to be recognized as a tool for use in the classroom. GIS used in education has the benefit of being focused on the development of spatial thinking. The downside is that there is little statistical data to show the scope of the usage of GIS around the world, although countries that specifically have a curriculum that mentions GIS have expanded faster.

GIS in local governments

GIS has proven to be an organization-wide enterprise and a highly enduring technology that continues to adapt to how the local government operates on many tasks. Many, if not all, governmental agencies have adopted GIS technology as a method to better manage and improve upon many of their organizations, such as:

- Public Safety operations such as Emergency Operations Centers, Fire Prevention, Police and Sheriff mobile technology and dispatch, and mapping weather risks
- Parks and Recreation departments and their functions in asset inventory, land conservation, land management, and cemetery management
- Public Works and Utilities, tracking water and storm water drainage, electrical assets, engineering projects, and public transportation assets and trends
- Fiber Network Management for interdepartmental network assets
- School analytical and demographic data, asset management, and improvement/expansion planning
- Public Administration for election data, property records, and zoning/management

The Open Data Initiative has pushed the local government to take advantage of the technology and also share their own data with their requirements to fit the Open Data and Open Government model of transparency. Because of Open Data, local government organizations can implement their online portals which allow citizens to view and utilize this information. This push for open data from within and outside of government organizations has been a huge driving force for local government GIS tech spending and database management.

GIS and augmented reality

As discussed in the previous section, the application of GIS with augmented reality is only really hampered by your imagination, especially when you consider that there are tons of data types that you can utilize from GIS data. So, in the next section, we will go over and think of ways we can apply GIS to augmented reality applications and games.

Applications of GIS

As Richie Carmichael of the Esri Applications Prototype Lab said to Keith Mann in an online article (http://www.esri.com/news/arcuser/0311/augmented-reality-and-gis. html):

> *"Imagine that you could point the camera on your phone at the ground and see the location and orientation of water pipes and electric cables buried under the ground because your AR app is cross-referencing the GIS system with your location and giving you a kind of x-ray vision so that you can visualize the infrastructure that is underneath you."*

This mindset has been reflected by many companies such as Google, Tencent, Microsoft, Facebook, Twitter, Apple, and many more. China's Tencent has done quite a few things with augmented reality and GIS. I think it is very worthwhile to go over some of the things China have done with AR and GIS.

China does not use Google's services whatsoever and had to create their own search engine, which is called Baidu. This also means that they had to make mapping software which fully utilizes GIS. They created Baidu Maps, which works just like Bing Maps and Google Maps, however, they have added a slight twist to it. You can add a separate package for it that allows it to be easily used or integrated into AR applications.

By wearing smartglasses, it will project the map in front of you with the number of steps you have walked, and a first-person overlay of where you need to go to get to your destination.

They have also heavily integrated their social media platforms, QQ, and Wechat, to work with their map software, which leads me to Wechat's share real-time location function. It displays where you are and the location of the person you are trying to meet in real time, and updates with every step you take.

Google, of course, has Google Maps, which obviously works very similarly to Baidu Maps and Bing Maps. This leaves Apple Maps, which was the first to heavily integrate AI for auditory augmentation into their map service. AutoCAD and Blender are two programs that have the ability to read and manipulate GIS data. They can import shapefiles and create a 3D representation of the terrain, or export this as a specified file format. In AutoCAD's case, it can export the data to XML, which can then be used to extract specific information that is wanted, such as population densities, or things along those lines.

AuGeo was made by Esri and it is a form of open source programming. This product enables you to control, download, and see information straightforwardly on a cell phone in a first-person view. AuGeo consolidates enlarged reality with GIS and shows highlighted information upon a live camera feed so that you can investigate your GIS information.

Augview, made by Augview Limited, is both a versatile GIS, enabling clients to see and alter their benefit information from the field, and an increased reality application, enabling clients to imagine underground protests they wouldn't normally observe. These are just a couple of players in the immense pool of organizations and applications that have been created to use, see, and/or control GIS information. Before we proceed, we should investigate a few applications that exploit GIS and augmented reality.

EyeMaps enables you to get data on a chosen dialect. Simply utilize camera mode to get thoughts about the world around you. It immediately gives you the names of mountains, urban communities, towns, exhibition halls, and much more. Take after connections to Wikipedia to get more data. Watch and offer your photographs on a 3D outline. This current application's primary highlights are making a 3D guide of your general surroundings while giving you data checks on it.

Vortex Planetarium is an excellent and simple application about everything in the sky. Huge amounts of information exist, including everything of the night sky substance, a large number of stars, groups of stars, messier articles, Caldwell items, and significantly more. This present application's fundamental highlights are exceedingly configurable substances. Set the straightforwardness of a group of stars workmanship or tap the number of stars you wish to find in the night sky.

Plane Finder lets you see all air activity around the globe continuously. Interim the application gives you profoundly redid substance to set everything for your requirements. With Augmented Reality, you can recognize planes overhead with your gadget camera. The application additionally permits to set warnings when a plane shows up in the sky above you. This present application's fundamental highlights are that it works by getting ongoing ADS-B signals. This innovation is speedier than a customary radar!

iOnRoad enables you to make a highly practical gadget from your cell phone. It offers help to you with GPS, activity checking, video, and picture catching, and considerably more. This present application's principal highlights are that it utilizes your gadget's local camera, GPS, and sensors to recognize vehicles before you, preparing drivers when they are in danger.

Dino around my work area AR amusement allows you to attempt to pet a virtual dinosaur. Inquisitive and adorable looking dinosaurs from ages past will meander around your work area. You may play with it by hand, or by tapping it in plain view of the screen. You may even sustain it. Be that as it may, whatever you do – remember, it has a voracious temper! This current application's principal highlights are that it enables you to play and find out about the ancient universe of dinosaurs.

The EmotionsAR application is for the individuals who saw vivified photographs in Harry Potter and constantly needed one for themselves. EmotionsAR furnishes you with a selective shot that enables you to make the photo come alive. What it would be? A short-energized photograph, or a long video story? That's for you to decide. This present application's principle highlights are that you can create your own particular photographs with AR video content!

Crayola Color Alive enables you to breathe life into your shading illustrations with vivid models that ascent up from the Crayola-lined pages. Spare your best characters to impart to your loved ones and utilize them whenever. This present application's principle highlights are that it has huge amounts of characters, enables you to print free pages, or obtained packs, at that point shading them and breathing life into them.

Gaming and GIS

Gaming and GIS is a very interesting topic, and there is a multitude of ways to incorporate this idea with AR since AR has different ways of being implemented. To really showcase a prime example of incorporating GIS into games and applying a form of augmented reality, we need to look no further than the most well-known MMO of all time, World of Warcraft.

To set the stage, we first need to explain some of the features of World of Warcraft and what data modders have to work with. World of Warcraft has many different professions that you can do, and all of them require that you collect the materials necessary to craft the items. There are different types of cloth, ore, flowers, archeology spot locations, cooking recipes, and many different crafting recipes that can be found all throughout the world. And this is ignoring armor, weapons, randomly spawning rare mobs, and world boss locations that can be found through the world.

In order to incorporate GIS into World of Warcraft, people mapped the terrain of the world map or pulled the data from the data files in the game, mapped locations of everything that spawns all throughout the world, and abstracted them into different layers that correlate with what they reference. Then, they overlay them over the world map and attach them to the mini map to show where they are while playing the game with the mod enabled.

As you can see, augmented reality doesn't just apply to the real world, but also the fantasy world as well. This makes AR very versatile, especially when you can find ways to incorporate GIS into it. Next up, let's take a look at some pure AR games that focus on the real world. The primary game we will look at is GeoGuessr. GeoGuessr began as a little web application that gives you the test of speculating the areas of a progression of irregular Street View pictures. After you've made your guess, it uncovers the genuine area and honors focus in view of how close you get.

The next game we will look at is Pursued. It is a sought-after shockingly fun Street View amusement game from Hungarian diversion designers Nemesys Games. The fundamental subject of the diversion is as per the following: "You've been taken all of a sudden. A companion is endeavoring to help you; however, you should make sense of where you are!" The point of the amusement is to guess the name of the city you take a gander at and type the name in the textbox as quickly as possible. In case you can't guess by the visual pieces of information in the Street View, you can move around by clicking in the Street View picture and utilize your '+' and '-' keys to zoom in and out.

Third on the rundown is Smarty Pins. Smarty Pins is a game created by Google Engineers. The point is to discover the response to an inquiry and stick point this area on the guide. For instance, you would get the inquiry "Where is the most seasoned British college?" and you would need to put a stick on Oxford. The main inquiries are normally situated in a player's nearby nation or are identified with extremely well-known places or individuals, however, as you advance, the playing board grows to whatever is left of the world and gets more challenging.

Guide Race is number four on the rundown. The thought behind it is to demonstrate to you a satellite photo of an area and four possible answers. The challenge is to choose the right answer at the earliest opportunity. In the event that you guess the wrong city, you'll get more opportunities to fathom it, which is terrible.

Number five is MapsTD. MapsTD is a pinnacle barrier game that utilizes Google Maps to create levels from any area over the world. Your undertaking is to safeguard your palace from assailants by deliberately putting and dealing with your guard towers. It's a truly standard pinnacle protection setup, yet the delight originates from doing it crosswise over true lanes and areas.

Number six on the rundown is Build. It is an impact of the coordinated effort of Google and LEGO to exhibit potential outcomes of Google Chrome. It let clients build anything they can envision with virtual LEGO, put it on Google Maps, and offer their manifestations to the world. As the name suggests, it only works in Google Chrome.

Geo Guns is a tank shooting game and is number seven on our rundown. The diversion takes a full preferred standpoint of Google Maps' 45° (Bird's Eye) satellite view. It overlays a few tanks on the satellite picture. Your assignment is to crush the enemy tanks. You can browse various preset war zone areas for your tank battle, yet you can choose any area by entering an area on the highest point of the screen.

Find Street is a StreetView-based game and is number eight. It gives you a progression of irregular Street View scenes. Your assignment is to make sense of the area of each picture and pick the right test reply. As you can see, you can very easily utilize GIS, georeferencing, and AR in your games all at the same time, or by utilizing various aspects of each of these to create them.

The key things to keep in mind and remember are as follows:

- Map design and the player interactions with maps are an essential part of the undertaking of creating a video game.
- The game's appearance, graphics-wise, therefore sets its tone just as much as the control experience, insecurity, exploration, or plot do.
- In competitive titles, the map represents the playing field. Every corner, every little modification, is crucial, as the players take their positions based on that. Monitoring this positioning is a must for the winning team.
- In open map titles, the game experience often exceeds the information provided by the maps.

These items are critical for determining which approach best fits the idea and structure you want to implement.

Summary

In this chapter, we discussed the history of GIS, how GIS data is collected, how GIS data is used, GIS applications, GIS games, and how to incorporate GIS into augmented reality applications and games. There were many more interesting bits of information provided, such as the data formats and how they changed with time; we learned that GIS has many applications, both in the past and in the present for statistics and analysis, that will most likely continue to be used in the future here on Earth and on other planets, as we are starting to see with Mercury, Venus, Mars, and our Moon.

GIS is a broad field that has the ability to be applied in many different ways and for a variety of purposes, and in learning the basic fundamentals of GIS and its history, we can now apply that information to the games and applications we create. In the next chapter, we will learn about sensors and plugins with Unity.

12
Censored - Various Sensor Data and Plugins

In this chapter, we will discuss the various sensors that we can access through the various SDKs provided to us. This includes ARKit, Vuforia, ARCore, Swift API, and the Java API. Now, the reason we will be going with this route is that there are some things in the core APIs that are not exposed in the SDKs provided to Unity but that we can leverage using native plugins with wrapper calls in C#. To break this up, to be a little more succinct without going outside of the bounds of this book, I will not be teaching the syntax of the Java or Swift programming languages; there are already some fantastic books that have been written by other Packt authors that cover this material, such as *Beginning Swift* (https://www.packtpub.com/application-development/beginning-swift) and *Java Programming for Beginners* (https://www.packtpub.com/application-development/java-programming-beginners).

This chapter will be broken down into several main sections, as follows:

- Leveraging sensors with Plugins
- Writing Unity Plugins
- C# Language Plugin
- C++ Language Plugin
- Swift Language Plugin
- Objective-C Language Plugin
- Java Language Plugin

By breaking the chapter down into these distinct sections, we can make it much easier for you to find the specific section you want.

Project overview

We will create basic plugins in C#, C++, Swift, Objective-C, and Java. Each one will be an implementation of a basic mathematical return value. Writing the plugins in their native code should take no more than 10 minutes to complete for each native code snippet. You must have a working test in Unity.

Getting started

When dealing with AR Applications and games, there are bound to be prerequisites. The following are the requirements for an Apple Mac computer:

- macOS 11
- Xcode 9
- Mono Framework **5.14.0**
- Unity 2017
- ARKit

 It is suggested that you have a 2013 or later model Mac computer, as older versions do not support the Metal API for graphics.

When you install Unity on a Mac, it will install Visual Studio for Mac as well; the catch is it requires Mono Framework to run, so be sure to download and install everything.

Here are the requirements for a Windows computer:

- Windows 10
- 8 GB of RAM or more
- Unity
- ARCore
- JDK 8 or higher
- Visual Studio
- Android Studio

For more information, click on these links:

```
https://store.unity.com/
https://developer.apple.com/arkit/
http://www.mono-project.com/download/stable/#download-mac
https://www.visualstudio.com/
https://developer.Android.com/studio/
```

Sensors

First things first, we need to get a good grasp of what sensors are and what they can be used for before we get into the various mini-projects that will coincide with each of the SDKs we will be using. This list of sensors is by no means a complete list and are some of the most common ones that we can leverage in AR applications and games:

- Fingerprint Sensor
- Radiation Sensor
- Heart Rate Monitor
- Pedometer
- Air Humidity Sensor
- Thermometer
- Barometer
- Light Sensor
- Proximity Sensor
- Magnetometer
- Gyroscope
- Accelerometer
- Ambient Light Sensor
- Iris Scanner
- IR Blaster
- Touch Sensor
- Microphone
- Camera
- GNSS
- NFC
- Laser
- Air Gesture Sensor

- Signal Receiver
- LiFi
- Clock

In this section, we will describe what each of these sensors is and what they can be used for, besides their native functions.

Proximity Sensor: The proximity sensor can detect when the cellphone is within a certain range of objects and manipulate software or hardware to react in a certain way, once the sensor's trigger has been tripped. It is generally used to reduce the total amount of battery consumption by dimming the backlight of the cellphone when it reaches a certain range of the user's ear or pocket. Theoretical usage in AR games and applications requires a little bit of thinking outside the box. We know that a proximity sensor can't detect the difference between objects, so what we could do is detect whether there are multiple objects near the device and register an event based on that.

Gyroscope: The gyroscope is a sensor designed to read and output the direction of a cellphone or device with the sensor installed. It is generally used to power apps and detect the orientation of the device to determine whether the UI should be displayed in landscape or portrait mode. Theoretical usage in AR games and applications could be to use the device to act as a compass for traversing the game world.

Fingerprint scanner sensor: The fingerprint scanner sensor is a sensor designed to detect whether the pressure has been added to a special plate and to read the input data from the plate.
It is generally used to add an additional layer of security over a login password. It is much more secure and harder to bypass than most standard passwords, even with AES encryption with salting.

Camera: The camera is itself a sensor. It is able to able to digitize waves of light and the electromagnetic radiation emitted so that a device can interpret the information and display it in a way that is understandable to the user. It is generally used to take pictures to store and retrieve.

Barometer: The barometer sensor is designed to detect changes in the atmospheric pressure, which in turn means it can effectively act as a means of forecasting the weather. It is generally used to determine the weather in the general vicinity where the user is located.

Thermometer: The thermometer sensor is a sensor used to detect changes in temperature and store/send that information to be displayed or acted upon. It is generally used to keep track of and measure the temperature of sensitive components in the device.

Accelerometer: The accelerometer is a sensor designed to detect the momentum of the device, and, by extension, detect the momentum of the user. It is generally used to determine the speed in which the user is traveling while in possession of the device.

Pedometer: The pedometer is a sensor that is designed to take the user's momentum within the confines of human speed limits and convert it into steps walked. It is generally used to calculate the user's daily step count and display it at a specific time for the user to review.

Touch sensor: The touch sensor is designed to detect when a user's finger touches the device's screen and return the position and length of time the finger was in that location. It is generally used to activate and manipulate all the basic and advanced usage for the device.

Microphone: The microphone is a sensor designed to detect sound waves and convert them into digital information that the device can understand and store. It is generally used to pick up the sound waves during a phone call and transmit that data to a connected device remotely.

Ambient light sensor: The ambient light sensor is designed to react to a variety of light conditions in such a way that it mimics how the human eyes would perceive and react to those different light scenarios. It is generally used for power saving by adjusting the backlight intensity levels (lighten or darken the screen), based on the lighting of the area around the device.

Iris Scanner sensor: The iris scanner sensor is designed to create high-resolution images of the eye. It is used mainly for security purposes. It is considered a form of biometric security, as it will only accept data from a specific eye for unlocking the device.

Air gesture sensor: The air gesture sensor is able to detect via infrared sensors — movements from hands in front of the device's screen. It is generally used to add basic control of the device without needing to use the touch screen, for example, activating the screen or applications.

Heart rate monitor sensor: The heart rate monitor sensor is a sensor designed to be able to track someone's heartbeat using a combination of algorithms, green LEDs, and the accelerometer to measure blood flow, and store this information. It is generally used to accurately measure your heartbeat during exercise.

Air Humidity Sensor: The air humidity sensor is a thermal conductivity sensor that utilizes aspects of the temperature sensor to be able to detect humidity.

Light sensor: There are many different types of light sensors that could be photoresistors, photodiodes, or even phototransistors. They are designed to detect whether there is light in a given area and, if so, how much light is available. A light sensor generally works in tandem with the ambient light sensor to give an accurate light assessment for taking pictures.

Magnetometer: The magnetometer is a sensor designed for measuring magnetic forces. Magnetometers are generally used for treasure-finder apps.

IR Blaster sensor: The IR Blaster sensor is a sensor designed to emulate an infrared remote control. It is generally used to create a universal remote control app for a variety of devices.

GNSS (Global Navigation Satellite System): GNSS is a sensor designed to pick up signals from multiple satellites for better accuracy, availability, and redundant data collection. It is generally used to poll for a user's location in order to give more accurate results in a GPS app.

NFC (Near-Field Communication): NFC sensors are designed to be wireless data transferers for proximity-based communication. They are generally used for using services such as Apple Pay and Apple Wallet payments.

Signal receiver sensor: The signal receiver sensor is a sensor designed to receive radio waves and convert them into a digital form that the device can understand. It is generally used for telephone calls or for playing music from the radio.

LiFi sensor: LiFi sensors, also known as *Light Fidelity Sensors*, use **Light-emitting diodes (LEDs)** to transmit data. They are generally used for areas that cannot use Wi-Fi, such as power plants, to send and receive data.

Clock: The **Real-Time Clock** or **RTC** is designed to accurately keep track of the time. It is a clock that shows the exact time.

Leveraging sensors with plugins

As previously stated, we can access the information provided by any exposed piece of hardware and send that information to our applications and/or games we create within Unity. The catch is that if there isn't an implementation within Unity or the SDKs we are using for AR applications, we will need to create a plugin with a wrapper to access that sensor.

This is also heavily dependent on which devices we want to target and whether we want to target both iOS and Android-based devices without any implementations done for us. If so, then we need to create the plugin ourselves. We can't just write a plugin in C#, though; we would need native plugins to call upon these sensors to do our bidding. This means that we will need to utilize the Java and Swift languages for their respective operating systems. For Android, the native-level code would be Java or C++, and for iOS, the native-level code would be Swift, Objective-C, or C++.

It is extremely important that we first understand how the sensor values are returned to us from the JDK and Apple SDKs. The JDK breaks all of the sensors down into specific categories. The accelerometer, the gyroscope, and the pedometer are all in the motion sensors category; the temperature sensor is located within the environment sensors category.

There is an imperative distinction to be made between the categories that need to be fully understood. The environment sensors category returns a single sensor value for each sensor event; meanwhile, the motion sensors category will return a multi-dimensional array of each sensor event that occurs. With this tidbit of information out of the way, let's move on to the next section, where we will learn how to write and dissect basic plugins for Unity in C++, C#, Java, Swift, and Objective-C.

Writing unity plugins

The first thing we need to do is gain an understanding of what a plugin is for Unity before we can create and dissect a very simple plugin for Unity.

What is a plugin?

A *plugin* is a dll file that stores code written in a different programming language that is a base implementation of some event that needs to be executed or in the same language that gives the base implementation of core code that functions as a library or non-changeable event.

Now, this is a very simplistic definition, but we can do better by explaining what they can do for the developer or a developer who wants to utilize code you have written. Plugins allow a developer to extend existing code without having to trudge through the source library by accessing methods and properties that are made public to them, which adds new features to the game engine that is not natively present, separates operating system-specific code, and they can reduce the size of an application.

For Unity specifically, plugins allow us to directly interface with native calls and use them as we wish in our application or games. Many developers tend to create plugins with native system calls to extend the render pipeline or for enhancing shaders.

It is important to note that there are two very distinct plugin types available to use in Unity. Those two types are **Native Plugins** and **Managed Plugins**. A very simplified explanation of the difference between native and managed plugins is that native plugins are for low-level calls, and managed plugins are an easy way to hide source code.

There is, however, a more nuanced differentiation between them than this old adage.

A managed plugin can and will easily hide source code from prying eyes when a developer wants to sell something in the asset store. It can also be used to include libraries and frameworks that are not otherwise readily available to Unity. For example, a developer could import the Entity Framework dll files into Unity and utilize the Entity Framework to create, manage, and handle database code with Unity. The final thing that a managed plugin can do is allow a developer to utilize some .NET languages and compilers that are not supported by Unity, such as F#, JScript, IronPython, ClosureCLR, or even Powershell. For example, a developer could create a plugin for Unity that allows for scripting in IronPython, or they could write game code using IronPython and import it as a plugin and use it without issues.

A native plugin, on the other hand, is profoundly more powerful. A native plugin normally consists of using Java, Swift, Objective-C, or C++ to access the direct hardware of their respective devices and provide functionality that a developer could otherwise not have access to within Unity. Let's say a developer is working with a device that connects to a smartphone that is not normally present in smartphones; in this case, we will go with the **BACtrack Mobile Pro** as our example.

The BACtrack Mobile pro is a police-grade breathalyzer that can check a user's blood alcohol content and send that information to a device via Bluetooth connections. This developer wants to make a drinking-style AR game, and they want to make the game harder, the higher the end user's BAC level is. This developer would need to use a native plugin to gain access to the BACtrack device's sensors' results.

Now that a firm understanding should have been gained from this explanation, we can finally start looking at the structure of a plugin for C++, Swift, C#, and Java. What we will do is create a very simple plugin that will simply add two numbers together. This is to keep things simple and allow for the flow of steps for the overall workflow to be much more easy to follow.

There is a list of file types that Unity will automatically recognize as plugins. It is very important that we familiarize ourselves with these file formats:

- `.dll`
- `.winmd`
- `.so`
- `.JAR`
- `.aar`
- `.xex`
- `.def`
- `.suprx`
- `.prx`
- `.sprx`
- `.rpl`
- `.cpp`
- `.cc`
- `.c`
- `.h`
- `.jslib`
- `.jspre`
- `.bc`
- `.a`
- `.m`
- `.mm`
- `.swift`
- `.xib`

Then there are also folder types that are treated as single plugins; they are as follows:

- `.framework`
- `.bundle`
- `.plugin`

With native plugins for Unity, you can run into C linkage issues that will cause a phenomenon called **Name Mangling**. Name mangling is also called *name decoration,* which is essentially a process that gives each function in a program a unique name; this is so that the linkers can separate common names in the language. The issue comes from the fact that there is no standard for this, and they typically don't work well with C compilers.

C# language plugin

Let's get started by creating our first plugin with C#:

1. We need to begin by opening Visual Studio and creating a new project. This new project type will be inside the **Windows Desktop** subfolder of **Visual C#** and will need to be a **Class Library (.NET Framework)**:

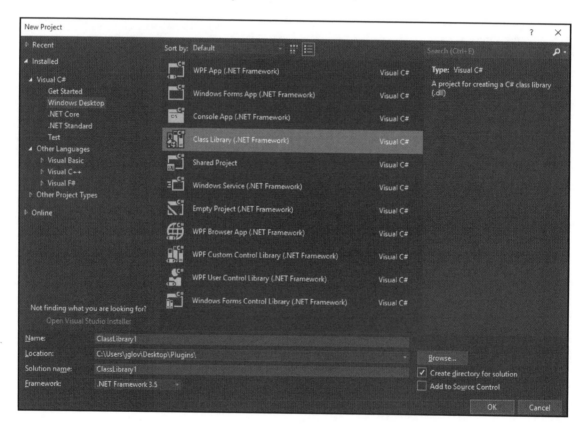

Project type

2. The project name will be `CSharpManagedPlugin`, and the Framework version will be `.NET Framework 3.5`. Select the **OK** button:

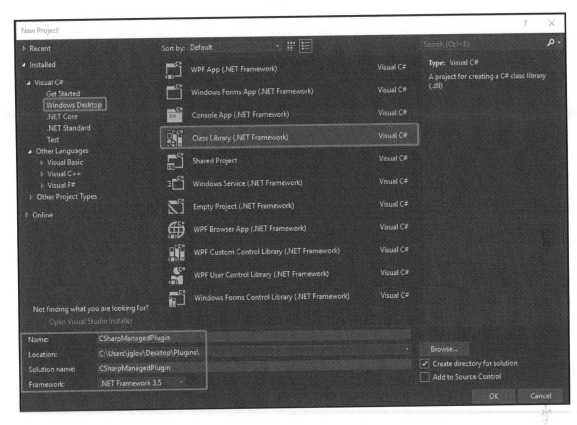

Project setup

Making sure to change the Framework version to 3.5 is extremely important, as we need to make sure that Unity can utilize our plugin without experimental support.

3. Now that we have created our solution, we can change the class name from `Class1` to `Addition`. Now, add an integer method called `addify` with the parameters of `a` and `b`, and then return `a` plus `b`. Your code should look as follows:

```
namespace CSharpManagedPlugin
{
    public class Addition
    {
        public int Addify(int a,  int b)
        {
            return a + b;
        }
    }
}
```

We can now build the solution that will generate the dll file we need. We can now open Unity and see how we can utilize this plugin with Unity:

1. Load Unity, and let's begin by creating a new project. The project will be of type 3D, and the name I will give it is `Packtpub`. I will start by creating two folders; the first one will be called `Plugins`, and the other will be called `PluginWrappers`. This will allow us to keep our project organized:

Project setup

2. We will start by taking the C# dll file we created and dragging it into the `Plugins` folder. I named my dll file `CSharpManagedPlugin` to make it a bit easier to differentiate between the different plugins we have at the end:

Plugin added

3. If you click on the `CSharpManagedPlugin`, in the inspector, you will see more information:

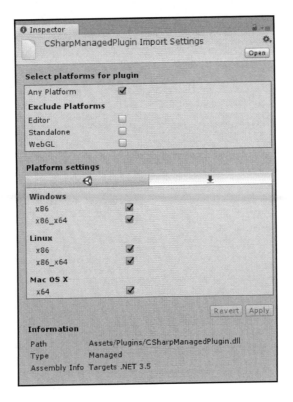

Inspector

4. As long as the target version of .NET is the same or lower than that of Unity, you should receive no errors and should be able to use it in the editor, standalone, in WebGL, Linux, Windows, and Mac OS.

5. What we can do now is move over to our `PluginWrappers` folder and get this bad boy up and running.

6. Create a new script; mine will be called `CSharpWrapper`. We can now open the script in Visual Studio:

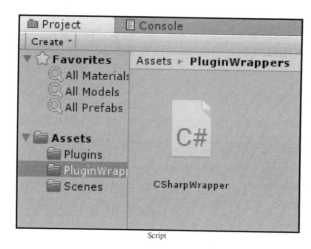

Script

7. Managed plugins are the easiest, and all we need to do is call our plugin directly, just as if it were a non-monobehavior script. Your code should look as follows:

```
using UnityEngine;
public class CSharpWrapper : MonoBehaviour
{
    private void Start()
    {
        var addition = new CSharpManagedPlugin.Addition();
        var add = addition.Addify(5, 2);
        print(add);
    }
}
```

As you can see, we called our plugin as if it were just another namespace in the assembly. We can now attach this Unity class to a GameObject, and we will see the results of step 7 appear in the console window of the Unity Editor.

C++ language plugin

Moving on to C++, we will use Visual Studio once more to create this project:

1. This project type will be in **Visual C++ | Windows Desktop | Dynamic-Link
   Library (DLL)**:

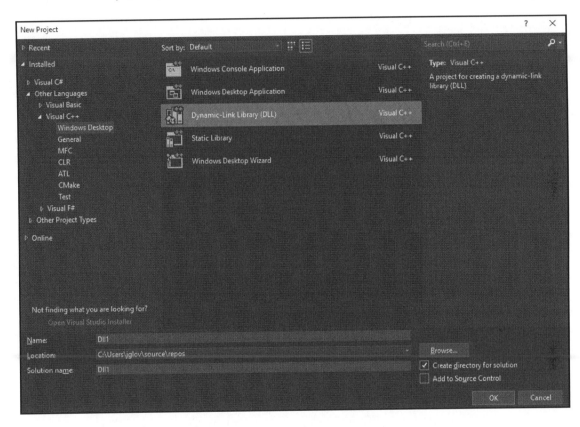

2. The name of this project will be `NativeWindowsPlugin`, and C++ will be slightly
   different than the managed plugins, due to name mangling, which we will learn
   how to avoid next.

3. So, to get around this problem of name mangling, we need to create a header and
   cpp file. Take a look at this code:

   ```
   The header will have the extern c and a preprocessor win32 define
   along with __declspec, dllexport functions to make sure that name
   mangling does not occur. Again, we will define our public function
   of addify, which will be our addition function. Your header should
   look like this.
   ```

```
#pragma once
extern "C" {
#if (defined(WIN32) || defined(__WIN32__))
        __declspec(dllexport) int addify(int a, int b);
#else
        int addify(int a, int b);
#endif
}
```

4. Essentially, what is happening when we use the `__declspec, dllexport` call is that we are avoiding the usage of a `.def` file.

5. Now that our header has been created, we need to fill out the information in our cpp file.

6. Make sure to include the header for the native windows plugin, and fill out the function details of `addify` here. Your code should look as follows:

```
#include "stdafx.h"
#include "NativeWindowsPlugin.h"
int addify(int a, int b)
{
        return a + b;
}
```

7. Click on **Build Solution**, and we will be ready to jump into Unity.

Load Unity, and let's open our `Packtpub` project:

1. Like we did previously, we will be using our `Plugins` and `PluginWrappers` folders for keeping things organized. Copy the `CPlusPlusPlugin` into the `Plugins` folder:

Folder structure

If you take a look at the plugin in the inspector, you will notice that it is only available for Windows. That is because we only had our if directive set for Windows and no other operating system. This is something you should keep in mind when wanting to work with multiple operating systems with C++.

2. Now, we can create a new C# class in the `PluginWrappers` folder called `CPlusPlusWrapper`:

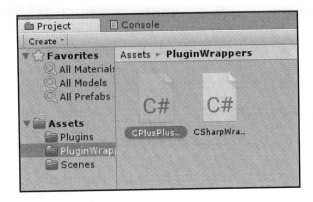

CPlusPlusWrapper

3. The code here will be different than what we used for the native plugin. We will need to import the dll file using a very special attribute called `DllImport`. This attribute requires the string name of the plugin we used and then underneath the attribute, we need to make sure it is a **Public Static Extern Method**.

4. Public static extern method types designate that the method call we want to use will be static, public, and loaded from an external assembly. To use the DLL Import attribute, we need to use the System.Runtime.InteropServices namespace. Your code should look as follows:

```
using System.Runtime.InteropServices;
using UnityEngine;
public class CPlusPlusWrapper : MonoBehaviour {
    [DllImport("CPlusPlusUnManagedPlugin")]
    public static extern int Addify(int a, int b);
    private void Start()
    {
        var add = Addify(2, 4);
        print(add);
    }
}
}
```

After we do that, the call is essentially the same from there on out. It is a little bit different, and a little more involved, but, overall, it is very easy once you understand how it works. You can now attach this C# script to a GameObject and run it to test the results.

Swift language plugin

Swift Language Plugins have the extension of .swift and have a completely different structure than C#, Java, and C++, which is to be expected, as Swift is only available on macOS devices. The language itself has elements from a variety of sources, and while I will not go into greater details of the finer points of the language, I will say that I like the methodologies they incorporated into the language structure.

Swift and Objective-C require the usage of Xcode, and while the basic setup is very similar, there are some key differences. Swift plugins require you to utilize both Objective-C and Swift to create a plugin that boils down to the implementation in Swift and you call that Swift code in Objective-C. This exceeds the parameters of this section, as the nuances of both languages need to be explored further.

Objective-C language plugin

Objective-C plugins are similar in some ways to Swift plugins and many of the basic steps are the same. Objective-C has been around for quite a long time and was Apple's version of the C language family. While Swift has been designed to be Objective-C's successor, Apple has not depreciated the language and is still a powerful tool to use and know:

1. To start, open Xcode, and get ready to have some fun:

2. Click on **Create a new Xcode project** and we'll have a big list of items to choose from.

3. Go over to **macOS** and select **Library**.

Although the **Library** is not available with iOS projects, you can also go with Bundle or Cocoa Framework Library types as well for this.

4. Select **Library** and click **Next**:

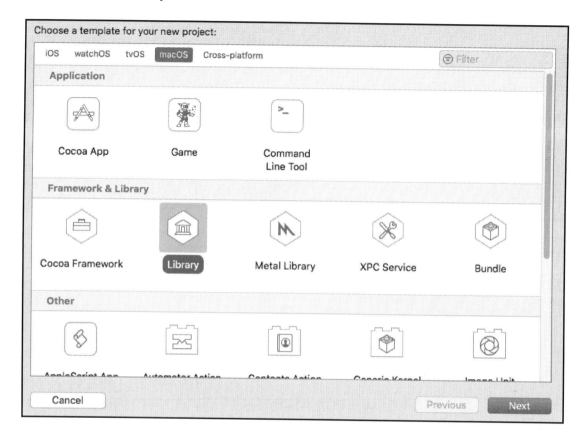

5. Set the product name to `ObjectiveCPlugin`; this keeps us in line with how the projects have been developed thus far:

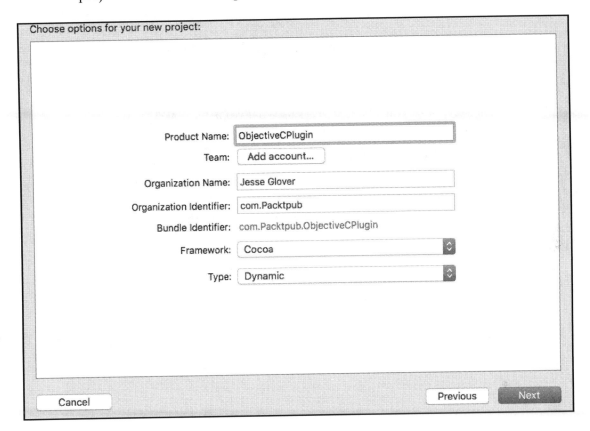

6. Now, before we continue, let's look at the various Frameworks that are available for us in the drop-down menu:

We have **Cocoa**, **STL**, and **None**. Cocoa gives us what we need for Objective C and Swift, **STL** is the **Standard Template Library** for C++, and None is a blank C++ and C project, with no Standard Libraries attached to it. We will stick with Cocoa.

Next, we should take a look at what is available to us with **Type**:

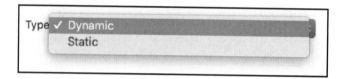

Type gives us the choice between Dynamic and Static, which would be a **Dynamic Library** or a **Static Library**. A static library is a library that is resolved at compile time and copied into a target application that produces an object file and an executable. A dynamic library is an opposite. It is resolved at runtime and only produces the header and source file that can be called in another application or program. We will stick with dynamic here:

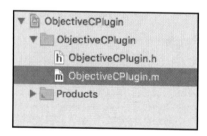

1. Our base Library file has a .h and .m file already created for us, so all we have to do is fill in the code that is needed. Let's go ahead and fill in the header file. Look at this code:

```
#import <Foundation/Foundation.h>
@interface ObjectiveCPlugin : NSObject
int Addition(int a, int b);
@end
```

2. Right away, we can see that it looks very similar to C++, with the slight difference of syntax. Next up, let's take a look at the .m file:

```
#import "ObjectiveCPlugin.h"
@implementation ObjectiveCPlugin
int Addition(int a, int b)
{
  return a + b;
}
@end
```

3. And, again, it's pretty much the same as C++, where we just fill in what the method actually does. We can now build the project and get ready to import it into Unity:

4. Now, we can open Unity after the project has been built and get ready for the fun part. Inside the `Plugins` folder that we previously created, create a new folder called `iOS`:

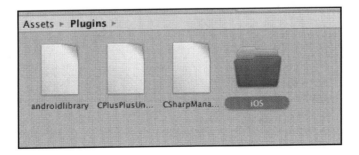

5. Inside the iOS folder, copy the .h and .m files that were created:

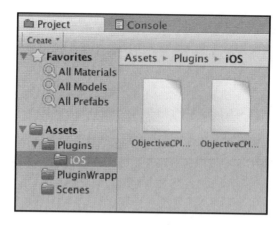

6. Now, go over to the PluginWrappers folder and create a new script called ObjectiveCWrapper:

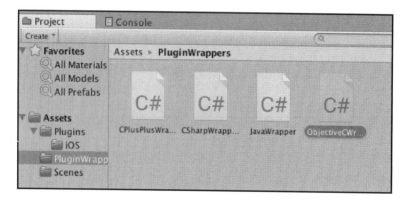

7. We can now open the class in C# and add our code:

```
using System.Collections;
using System.Collections.Generic;
using System.Runtime.InteropServices;
using UnityEngine;
using UnityEngine.UI;
public class ObjectiveCWrapper : MonoBehaviour
{
 private Text text;
#if UNITY_IOS && !UNITYEDITOR
```

```
   [DllImport("__Internal")]
   public static extern int Addition(int a, int b);
#else
   [DllImport("ObjectiveCPlugin")]
   public static extern int Addition(int a, int b);
   #endif
private void Start()
   {
   text = GetComponent<Text>();
   text.text = Addition(1,5).ToString();
   }
   }
```

The nice thing about Objective-C is that it does not have the name mangling issues that C++ has, so we don't need to worry about doing the `extern` method before. Instead, due to the way code is compiled for iOS devices, we have to call __internal, instead of the name of the plugin.

To finish, we would have to build this for iOS and open it in Xcode to finish the compile process and either run it on an iPhone or the iPhone Simulator to test the results.

Java language plugin

For the Java language plugin, we have two choices that work just fine. We have the Java Library, which compiles to a JAR file, and the Android Library, which compiles to AAR format. To access Android-specific functions, we need to create the Android Library, and for pure Java language usage, we would create the Java library.

There is a major distinction between the two, and this should be discussed. Consider the following:

- Android Library projects contain native and Java code along with resource files and an Android Manifest. They will include the .class files and .jar files that need to be precompiled into the Android Studio project, before being imported into Unity.
- Java Library projects are built directly to be JAR files, and they can be imported into Unity.

Both of these plugins need to be run on an Android device; this means you cannot test them in the editor; you must build and run on an emulator or on an actual device. If you want to get the best from plugins, using the Java Language. Android Library projects offer the most bang for your buck.

With that being said, let's open Android Studio and create our basic library:

1. Click on **File**, highlight **New**, and locate **New Module**. The Module options window will open in a new window:

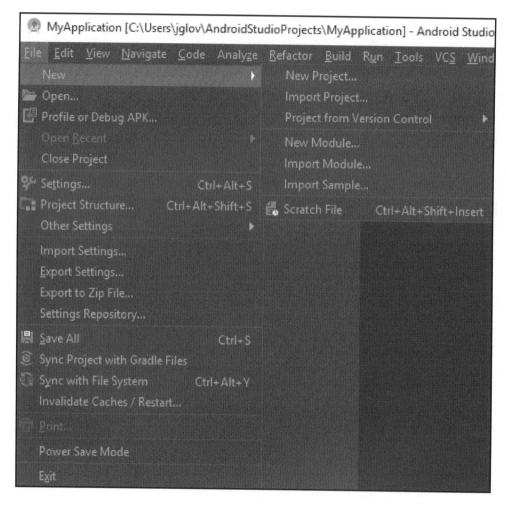

Android Studio

2. Here, we have the option of selecting a **Java Library** or **Android Library**. As discussed previously, it is much more advantageous to use the **Android Library**, so select that one and click **Next**:

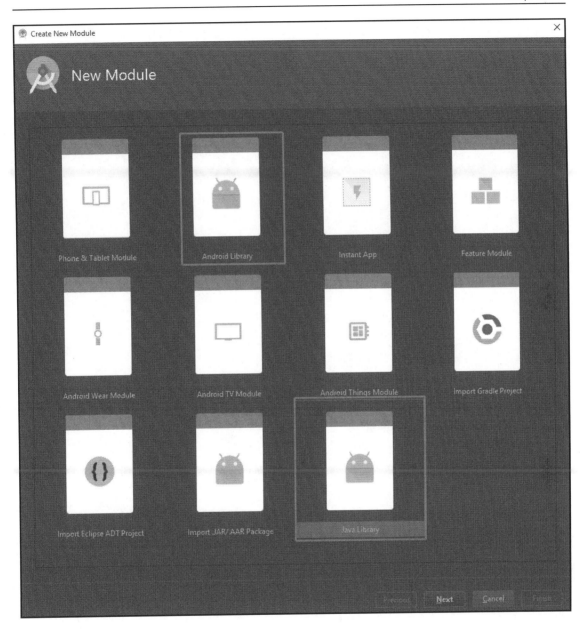

Library choices

3. Now, we can name and configure our module. I will set the library name to be `AndroidLibrary`; the module name will automatically be made to be the name of the library in lowercase.

4. The package name will be changed to `com.packtpub.Androidlibrary`, and the Minimum SDK version will be `API 21: Android 5.0 (Lolipop)`:

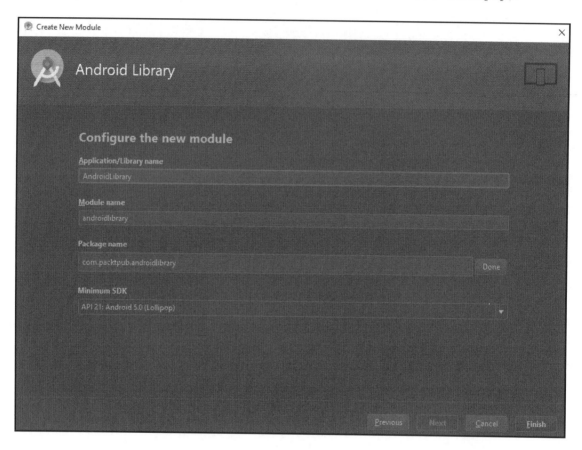

Module setup

5. Once that has been set up, click **Finish**.
6. On the left-hand side of the Android Studio Editor, we can see the layout of the project:

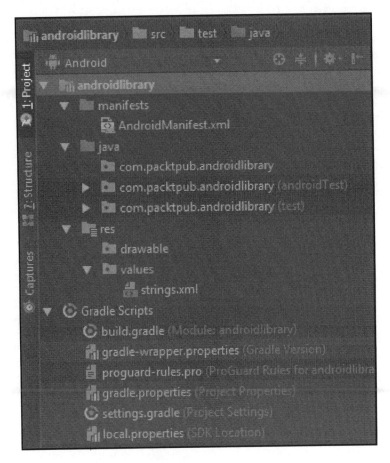

Layout

7. The main area we want to focus on is the `java` folder with the name of `com.packtpub.Androidlibrary`. We need to right-click on this specific one and add a new Java class to it. This will open a brand-new window to set up the class:

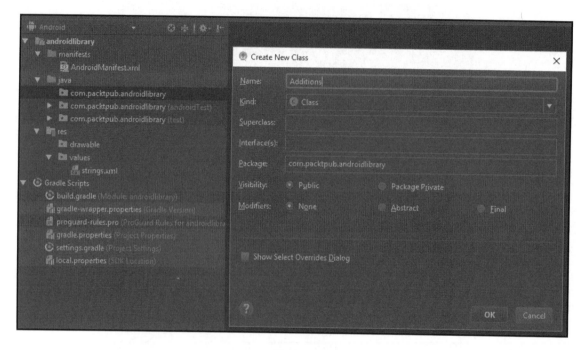

New class

8. I will name the class `Additions` to specify that we are just making a simple math library and then select the **OK** button.

9. The procedure is the same for C#: we will just add a public `int` with the name of `AddMe` with the parameters of `int a` and `int b`, with the return being `a + b`. Your code should look as follows:

```
package com.packtpub.Androidlibrary;
public class Additions {
    public int AddMe(int a, int b)
    {
        return a + b;
    }
}
```

10. Click on the **Build** button at the top of the editor window, and click on **Make Project**. This will build the project for us.

11. Let's take a quick look at the output folder of the project:

Building the project folder

We can see here that we have quite a few folders and other miscellaneous files. The AAR file we need is located in the `AndroidLibrary` folder. The exact location would be Android library, Build, Outputs, AAR.

The AAR file is technically a zip file, so you can unzip and look at its contents by using "7zip"; however, this is the exact file we need to use in Unity. Now, it is time to open Unity and see how we can get Unity to interact with this file.

Load up Unity, and let's open our `Packtpub` project:

1. Like we did previously, we will be using our `Plugins` and `PluginWrappers` folders for keeping things organized. Copy the AAR file into the `Plugins` folder:

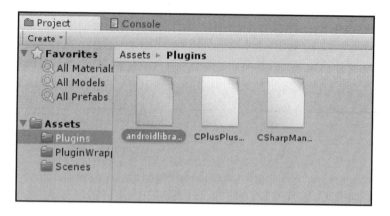

Plugins folder

2. In the `PluginWrappers` folder, create a C# class called `JavaWrapper`, and then open it in Visual Studio.
3. The code is slightly different than the C# and other native implementations. We will need a preprocessor directive to check whether this code is being executed in Android.
4. Then, we will create a new Android Java Object with the string name of the class we created in Java.
5. We will follow that up with a call of that class with the string value of the method we want, followed by the parameters. Your code should look as follows:

```
using System.Collections;
using System.Collections.Generic;
using UnityEngine;
public class JavaWrapper : MonoBehaviour
{
        // Use this for initialization
        void Start () {
#if UNITY_Android && !UNITY_EDITOR
        var javaClass = new AndroidJavaObject("Addition");
        javaClass.Call("Addification", 2, 9);
#endif
    }
  }
```

Now, we can't test this code in the Unity Editor, but we can build the project out and test it on an Android device, after attaching it to a game object to run.

Creating a sensor driver in Java

Now, what if we wanted to implement our own sensor from the hardware provided? As it turns out, Google has already thought of that and has a very in-depth tutorial on creating and registering your own driver which can be viewed at `https://developer.Android.com/things/sdk/drivers/location`. I will go over a few of the items specified, but it is best to read what they wrote.

In short, we will just look at the sample code provided that will make it so that we can convert GPS data as a plugin. The basic structure is exactly the same as the one we used to create our basic plugin in Java. The next step will be to write our code so that it returns the data so that it can be passed from the native plugin to Unity. Take a look at this:

```
// Convert latitude from DMS to decimal format
private float parseLatitude(String latString, String hemisphere) {
 float lat = Float.parseFloat(latString.substring(2))/60.0f;
 lat += Float.parseFloat(latString.substring(0, 2));
 if (hemisphere.contains("S")) {
 lat *= -1;
 }
 return lat;
}

// Convert longitude from DMS to decimal format
private float parseLongitude(String longString, String hemisphere) {
 float lat = Float.parseFloat(longString.substring(3))/60.0f;
 lat += Float.parseFloat(longString.substring(0, 3));
 if (hemisphere.contains("W")) {
 lat *= -1;
 }
 return lat;
}

// Return a location from an NMEA GPRMC string
public Location parseLocationFromString(String rawData) {
 // Tokenize the string input
 String[] nmea = rawData.split(",");

Location result = new Location(LocationManager.GPS_PROVIDER);
 // Create timestamp from the date + time tokens
 SimpleDateFormat format = new SimpleDateFormat("ddMMyyhhmmss.ss");
 format.setTimeZone(TimeZone.getTimeZone("UTC"));
```

```
try {
Date date = format.parse(nmea[9] + nmea[1]);
result.setTime(date.getTime());
} catch (ParseException e) {
return null;
}

// Parse the fix information tokens
result.setLatitude(parseLatitude(nmea[3], nmea[4]));
result.setLongitude(parseLongitude(nmea[5], nmea[6]));
result.setSpeed(Float.parseFloat(nmea[7]));

return result;
}
```

Now, all you need to do is compile the plugin as specified in the previous section and add it to Unity in exactly the same way.

Summary

In this chapter, we have discussed various sensors that are generally available to us from mobile market devices. We have discussed how to create a basic plugin in the major languages for the different platforms at our disposal, and we now have all of the basic knowledge we need to get started making AR applications and games with Unity.

In the next chapter, we will take what we have learned so far and create a prototype project that will allow us to incorporate sound as the basis for an AR application.

The Sound of Flowery Prose

13

In this chapter, we will design and create our first AR application with macOS and utilize ARKit. This will be an application that utilizes a touch sensor and camera sensors in tandem to initiate sound clips from various literary sources. This will serve as a fantastic introduction to programming and setting up Unity to work with the AR tools available to us. This will also allow us to utilize the built-in functions provided for using the camera sensor and the touch sensor.

In this chapter, we'll cover the following topics:

- Conceptualizing the project
- Setting up the Unity project
- Code implementation details
- Working with XCode

Project overview

The concept of this application is to be able to select anywhere in the video feed of the camera, and it will read a random passage from a poem or book based on the lighting of the area. The build time is approximately 30 minutes.

Getting started

The following are the software prerequisites:

- XCode
- Unity 2018 for Mac
- ARKit
- Visual Studio for Mac
- MonoFramework

The software can be downloaded from the following websites:

- https://store.unity.com/
- https://developer.apple.com/arkit/
- https://www.visualstudio.com/
- http://www.mono-project.com/download/stable/

The following are the minimum hardware requirements:

- 2011 or newer Mac computer
- 8 GB of RAM

Conceptualizing the project

Before building any game or application, it should always be a first step to know exactly what you want to build. You don't have to know the exact implementation details, just what you want to build and how you want to go about building it. This should include the following:

- Basic idea/concept
- Programming language to use
- Platform to release on
- Game engine or libraries/frameworks to use
- Design document/design outline
- Written or code implementation prototype for proof of concept

Now, why are these points so important? They are important because it helps solidify the idea, gives a clear path for what you want to accomplish, and most importantly, proves that the project is possible to build. Let's dive into each point and use them to build our first AR application.

Basic idea/concept

The basic idea or concept of an application or game should not be any more than a paragraph explaining what you want to create. It isn't meant to explain the full features or everything you want that to be in the application or game. Rather, it is only meant as a basic starting point that says that this is the overall idea that you want to work on.

This is important because it is the core of the application or game idea, and you can define what the main features of the app or game are and give a clear point of reference for researching.

Our basic concept is to be able to select anywhere in the video feed of the camera and it will read a random passage from a poem or book based on the lighting of the area. Now, this doesn't go too much into depth on what the application will do, but we can use this as the basis for the fourth step to expand upon the basic idea to create a fully functional and detailed explanation of the application.

Choosing the right programming language

This choice is not always obvious when developing an application or a game. While your own knowledge does play a major role in choosing the language to use, so do the requirements of the application or game and your team's knowledge. This step should be done in tandem with the next step before finalizing the decision, as your research may determine that the language that you prefer doesn't have the proper libraries or capabilities for developing the particular game or application you want.

Luckily for us, our example will be using C#.

Choosing your release platform

This one is rather straightforward. Do you want to release on Android, iOS, Windows, or some other platform? This will determine which language to select to use as well as which game engine or libraries/frameworks we need – which leads us to the next section.

Choosing your game engine, libraries, and frameworks

As stated previously, this step should be done in tandem with the previous steps as they are intrinsically tied together. This step requires you to do in-depth and highly detailed research into what you wrote for the basic idea/concept. Not only are you looking to see if what you want to do is possible, but also whether or not the language, game engine, or library/ framework you want to use supports it. This also requires you to know which platform you want to release on.

With the basic idea of this application, we know that it would require utilizing the camera and having touch events to detect whether something is lit well enough or not to determine whether or not it should play the audio file.

Developing the game design and application design document

The design document is more of a design specification document that describes the application in its entirety. That means that all of the data-, architectural-, interface-, and component-level design is described for it. The following example showcases how the documentation would look. You can download a copy of the template from http://ec. europa.eu/idabc/servlets/Doc7e17.doc?id=18632:

TABLE OF CONTENTS

Technical design template

For game design, the design document can be a bit more involved than it is for applications. A typical game design document will require the sections described to be filled out in as much detail as possible. You can download a copy of the template from `https://docs.google.com/document/d/1-I08qX76DgSFyN1ByIGtPuqXh7bVKraHcNIA25tpAzE/edit`:

Overview
    Theme / Setting / Genre
    Core Gameplay Mechanics Brief
    Targeted platforms
    Monetization model (Brief/Document)
    Project Scope

    Influences (Brief)
      - <Influence #1>
      - <Influence #2>
      - <Influence #3>
      - <Influence #4>
    The elevator Pitch
    Project Description (Brief):
    Project Description (Detailed)
What sets this project apart?
    Core Gameplay Mechanics (Detailed)
      - <Core Gameplay Mechanic #1>
      - <Core Gameplay Mechanic #2>
      - <Core Gameplay Mechanic #3>
      - <Core Gameplay Mechanic #4>
Story and Gameplay
    Story (Brief)
    Story (Detailed)
    Gameplay (Brief)
    Gameplay (Detailed)
Assets Needed
    - 2D
    - 3D
    - Sound
    - Code
    - Animation
Schedule
    - <Object #1>
    - <Object #2>
    - <Object #3>
    - <Object #4>

Game design template

Now, you might be thinking that this is a lot of work for applications or games. The key to success is never wrought from laziness or pure luck. In creating documentation that has as much depth as this, you are ensuring that you know exactly what you need to do and why you need to do it, and if you bring on team members, they will be able to read the document and fully understand your goals and intentions with little input from you.

This also means that you can keep yourself firmly in line with the project, forcing you not to add little pet features except as extra milestones after the project has reached the completion mark.

Bonus – UML design

Unified Modeling Language (UML) is a great way for visualizing the design of your application or game. NClass is a free UML editor that you can download and use.

You can preplan all of your methods, attributes, properties, classes, and enums – pretty much everything related to programming – with UML. UML really helps for the next phase, which is actually to implement the prototype:

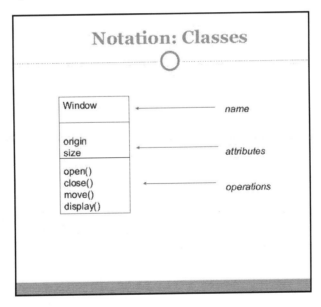

Further planning of implementations can be seen in the following screenshot:

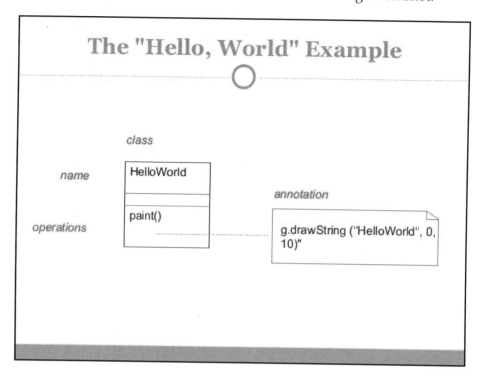

Prototyping

Now, our proof of concept will actually be the full project, although for your own projects in the future, run a small-scale implementation to make sure the features that are 100% necessary are able to be implemented and work appropriately.

The reason for this is that, if for any reason you are unable to implement the main feature of the app or game, you haven't wasted as much time or money on the project as you would have done by implementing on a larger scale.

Setting up the Unity project

The very first thing we are going to do is set Unity up on our Mac computer to be able to create our project. Since we know we will need ARKit, which only works on macOS, we will have different projects for the different chapters, as we don't want any compilation issues:

1. Let's create a new project, and we will call it `Chapter4` or `Sound of Flowery Prose`:

2. Next up, we need to click on the store and search for ARKit to download and add it to our project:

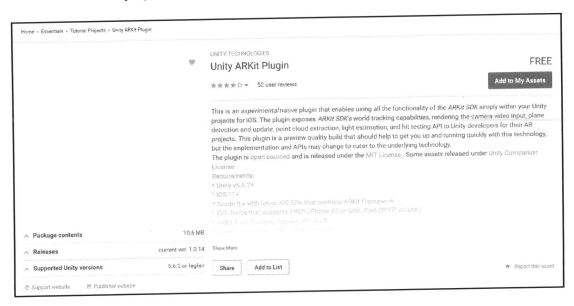

3. I am a bit of a stickler for organization, so we have to make sure to set up all the empty game objects we need to keep things organized. So, we will have four empty game objects called `CameraParent`, `ARKitControl`, `ARCameraManager`, and `HitCubeParent`. Your project should look like the one in the following screenshot:

4. Drag the camera into the `CameraParent` empty game object:

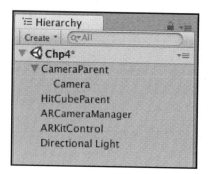

5. Create a `Cube` and drag the `Cube` into the `HitCubeParent` object:

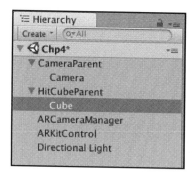

Now that we have Unity basically set up as required, we can move on to creating and attaching the scripts we need for the project:

1. Click on the **Camera** component – we have two scripts we need to add to it. The first script is **Unity AR Camera Near-Far**, and the second is **Unity AR Video**.

2. The **Unity AR Video** also needs a clear material, so let's set that to be
   `YUVMaterial`:

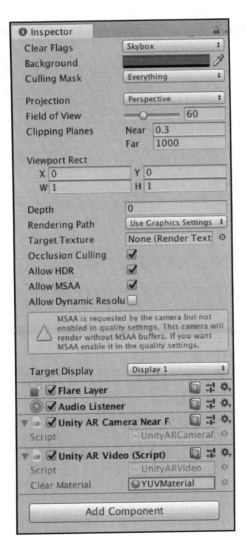

3. `ARCameraManager` needs the appropriate script attached to it – in this case, it is called the **Unity AR Camera Manager**:

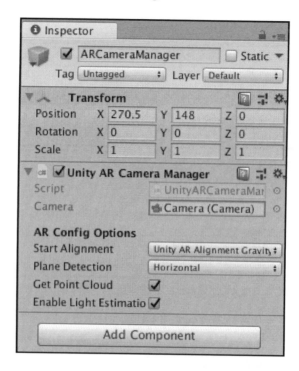

4. `ARKitControl` also needs a script attached to it, and it is called **Unity AR Kit Control**:

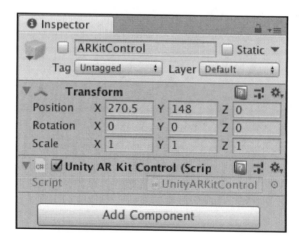

5. The final thing we need to do is set up our `Cube` from inside the `HitCubeParent` object to have a brand new script created for it.
6. Click on the `Cube` object and select **Add Component** I **Script** I **New Script**. The name should be `ARHitCube`:

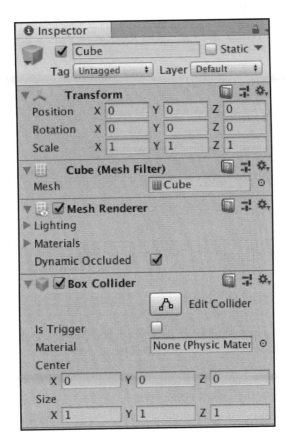

Code implementation details

Obviously, the most important part of any project is actually to implement what we want to accomplish. We want this project to play a literary quote from a list of audio samples automatically. To do this, we need an audio source and audio clips. We also want this project to take advantage of ARKit to run, so we need to write a C# class that utilizes features from the ARKit plugin that is exposed from the Objective-C and C++ libraries.

Let's open up the `ARHitCube` class, fill in the details, and explain what is happening at the same time. I should note that very similar code is already provided in the script file called `UnityARHitTestExample`; I created this script to be able to show only what is needed and to be able to explain the workflow/thoughts necessary for creating the functionality we need:

```
using System;
using System.Collections.Generic;
```

1. As per usual, we will only call the specific namespaces we need for our project. In this case, it is `System` and `System.Collections.Generic`:

```
namespace UnityEngine.XR.iOS
```

2. Our namespace will be used to organize our code to make sure it stays separate from ARKit and Unity's API, which will avoid naming collisions:

```
public class UnityARHitTestExample : MonoBehaviour
{
        public Transform m_HitTransform;
        public AudioClip[] clips;
        public AudioSource source;
```

3. Our class will inherit from `MonoBehavior`, as we want to be able to use it directly from the object (as well as make sure it can be attached to the game object).

4. We create a public transform to allow us to track locations and a public array of audio clips more easily:

```
bool HitTestWithResultType (ARPoint point, ARHitTestResultType
resultTypes)
{
    List hitResults =
UnityARSessionNativeInterface.GetARSessionNativeInterface
().HitTest (point, resultTypes);
```

5. We create a `Boolean` method type that has the parameters of `ARPoint` and `ARHitTestResultType`. Both of these are exposed by ARKit, and you can read the documentation for them or look at the source in Unity to gain a better understanding of it. The simplified explanation is that `ARPoint` is a point coordinate derived from a Vector 3 value, and `ARHitTestResultType` is an enum with the possible results being `ARHitTestResultTypeFeaturePoint`, `ARHitTestResultTypeEstimatedHorizontalPlane`, `ARHitTestResultTypeEstimatedVerticalPlane`, `ARHitTestResultTypeExistingPlane`, `ARHitTestResultTypeExistingPlaneUsingExtent`, and `ARHitTestResultTypeExistingPlaneUsingGeometry`.

6. We create a list called `hitResults` which is going to be set to be `UnityARSessionNativeInterface`. `GetARSessionNativeInterface().HitTest` with the parameters being point and result types filled in. What this does is create a list every time a native interface hit test is registered and stores the values:

```
if (hitResults.Count > 0) {
    foreach (var hitResult in hitResults) {
        Debug.Log ("Got hit!");
        m_HitTransform.position = UnityARMatrixOps.GetPosition
(hitResult.worldTransform);
        m_HitTransform.rotation = UnityARMatrixOps.GetRotation
(hitResult.worldTransform);
        return true;
    }
}
return false;
}
```

7. Next up, we do an `if` check to verify that the count is greater than 0. If it isn't greater than 0, return as false, otherwise proceed to the `foreach` loop. Inside of the `foreach` loop, we check all of the hit results and log the results. The `HitTransform` position will always be set to be `UnityARMatrixOps.GetPosition` with the parameter being the `hitresult.worldTransform`.

8. The `HitTransform` rotation will also always be set to be `UnityARMatrixOps.GetRotation` with the parameter being the `hitresult.worldtransform`. We end by returning true. Essentially, all this function does is detect whether a hit is registered or not and passes information to the correct areas that need the information:

```
void Update () {
```

```
/* Let's start the update method as it is probably the second most
important aspect of the code.
*/
if (Input.touchCount > 0 && m_HitTransform != null)
{
var touch = Input.GetTouch(0);
```

9. The first thing we want to do is check whether or not the `input.touchcount` is `0` and the `HitTransform` is not equal to null. If either of these checks fails, then we aren't going to be able to retrieve the information we need.

10. We set a touch variable to be `input.gettouch` with the parameter being `0`. `0` is the basic tap gesture:

```
if (touch.phase == TouchPhase.Began)
{
var screenPosition =
Camera.main.ScreenToViewportPoint(touch.position);
```

11. The `if` touch phase statement here is a check to see which touch phase is being initialized. The began touch phase is what we want, as it is the starting location of touch events.

12. We created a screen position variable and set it to be the camera screen to viewport point, with the parameter filled out being the touch position:

```
ARPoint point = new ARPoint
{
    x = screenPosition.x,
    y = screenPosition.y
};
```

13. ARPoint point is set to be a new ARPoint, and we want the x value to be the screen position's x value and the y value to be the screen position's y value:

```
ARHitTestResultType[] resultTypes = {
ARHitTestResultType.ARHitTestResultTypeExistingPlaneUsingExtent,
    ARHitTestResultType.ARHitTestResultTypeHorizontalPlane,
    ARHitTestResultType.ARHitTestResultTypeFeaturePoint
};
```

14. `ARHitTestResultType` is an array called result types. We want to make sure that the hit test result types are understood, and in this case, we have three types to use: `ExistingPlaneUsingExtent`, `HorizontalPlane`, and `FeaturePoint`:

```
foreach (ARHitTestResultType resultType in resultTypes)
    if (HitTestWithResultType (point, resultType))
        {
```

```
source.PlayOneShot(clips[Random.Range(0, clips.Length)]);
source.Stop();
return;
}
```

15. We can now do a final `foreach` loop on the `ARHitTestResultType` and create an `if` statement to check the `HitTestWithResultType` with the parameters filled with the point and `resultType`. This essentially just checks to see if the proper touch events have occurred, and if they have, then it activates the play method. Upon another touch event, it will stop the media that was playing. Following that, we return to break from the loop.

16. We can go back to the Unity Editor and look at the cube object's attached script:

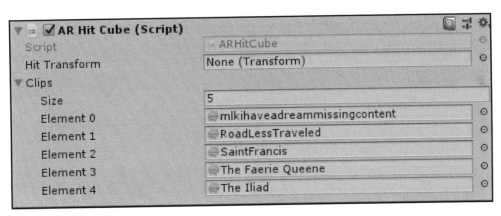

17. We can attach our `Cube` to be the **Hit Transform** as when we tap, this will be the registered object to read the information:

We can now build this project:

1. To do this, click on **File** and **Build Settings**. We will be utilizing iOS as the platform:

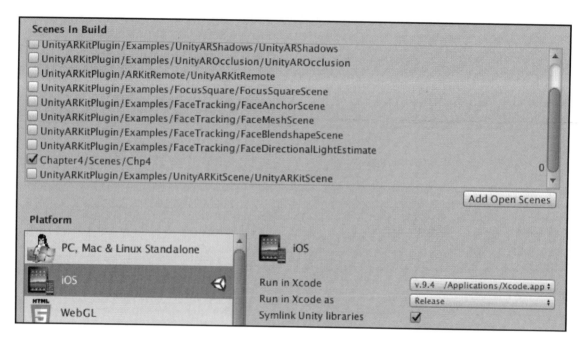

2. In **Player Settings**, we need to change our app's name in the **Bundle Identifier** area and write a small description in the camera usage description.

3. I will name the app com.rpstudios.arkitscene, and the description will be AR BABY:

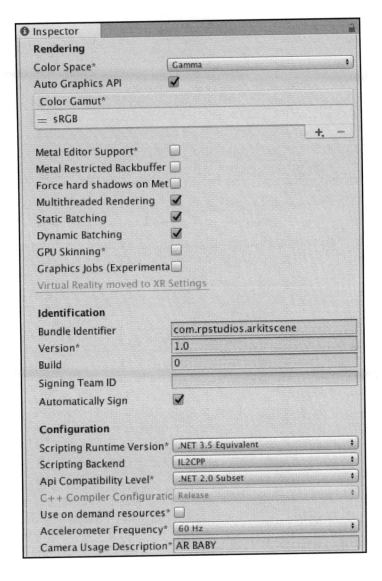

4. Once we select **Build** app, Unity will create an XCode project, which is the main difference between building for Android, Windows, and Linux:

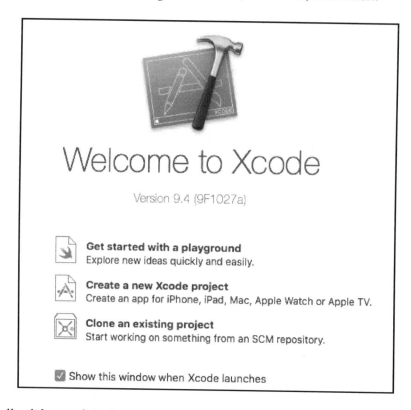

The main bulk of the work is done; now we just need to get familiar with XCode and finalize the build process there.

Working with XCode

We can navigate to the `Build` folder of our application here and click on it to open our XCode project:

1. On the left-hand side of the screen, you should see **Unity-iPhone** as one of the items you can select. Click on it and you should see **Unity-iPhone** in the center and **Identity and Type** on the right:

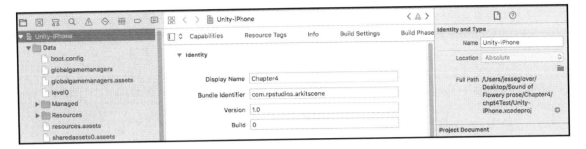

2. Check to make sure the Identity is correct. **Display Name** for me is Chapter4, with the **Bundle Identifier** as com.rpstudios.arkitscene:

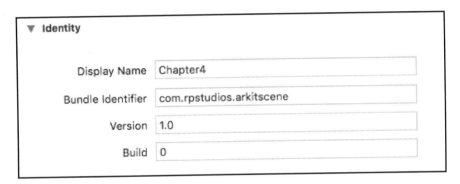

3. Now, on **Signing,** you need to look and make sure that the **Automatically manage signing** checkbox is checked and your **Team** has your email address attached to it. The **Signing Certificate** is extremely important, as you will not be able to compile or send to the simulator properly. If you don't, you have to register for an Apple Developer account at developer.apple.com:

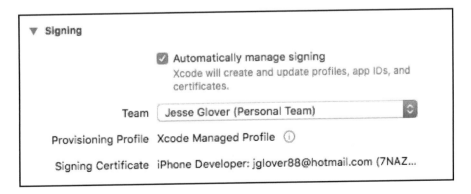

4. Scroll down and look for **Linked Frameworks and Libraries**. **AVFoundation** should be set from **Optional** to **Required**. I've noticed that when it is set to **Optional**, the linker fails to work properly:

Name	Status
▼ Linked Frameworks and Libraries	
Security.framework	Required ↕
MediaToolbox.framework	Required ↕
libiPhone-lib.a	Required ↕
CoreText.framework	Required ↕
AudioToolbox.framework	Required ↕
AVFoundation.framework	Optional ↕
CFNetwork.framework	Required ↕
CoreGraphics.framework	Required ↕
CoreLocation.framework	Required ↕
CoreMedia.framework	Required ↕
CoreMotion.framework	Optional ↕
CoreVideo.framework	Required ↕
Foundation.framework	Required ↕
MediaPlayer.framework	Required ↕
OpenAL.framework	Required ↕
OpenGLES.framework	Required ↕
QuartzCore.framework	Required ↕
SystemConfiguration.framework	Required ↕
UIKit.framework	Required ↕
libiconv.2.dylib	Required ↕
libil2cpp.a	Required ↕
Metal.framework	Optional ↕
ARKit.framework	Required ↕

5. Locate **Architectures**, because we need to change from the default to **Standard**. This is due to there being different architectures and iOS doesn't utilize ARM anymore:

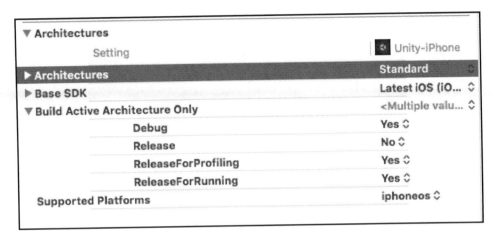

6. Now, you can click on **Build** and attach your iPhone 6 or above to your Mac computer. Build and then run it on the device. It will ask you to trust the app on your phone, so follow the instructions to give trust.
7. Click on the app on your phone and voila! It will load and you can play with the app.

Summary

In this chapter, we learned how to work with ARKit and Unity to build an AR application for Mac devices. While this was a very simple implementation, it should definitely pave the way for you to incorporate different aspects of sound into your own AR games and applications.

Learning the foundations of dealing with AR is possibly the most difficult part, as well as figuring out why building for different devices doesn't work as you intended initially. Debugging and testing is something that should be integral to every aspect of development. I would suggest either having someone test every build, or run automated testing at every chance you get.

In the next chapter, we are going to create an educational-style game prototype aimed at children, which will challenge their cognitive reasoning skills by means of a puzzle.

Picture Puzzle - The AR Experience

14

In this chapter, we will create another AR-based application. This time, the focus will be a puzzle that could be used in education to teach languages or word recognition. The reason for this is that AR-based applications and games are also very viable sources for inspiration, and target audiences.

This chapter will introduce you to the following:

- How to update an existing installation of Unity to add Vuforia support
- Unity Hub
- How to build an education-based AR app for Windows, Android, and iOS

Let's dive right in and get into the background of this project and why it is relevant to AR.

Project background

As with any other project, it is always best to start with an idea. When I first thought of this project, I wanted to showcase AR applications and games to also reflect education. I have educated children on the English language and know the frustrations of learning a new language intimately.

Game and application development should also teach something to the users; it doesn't always have to be history, mathematics, language, science, or geography; it can also be something innocuous, such as reflex training or hand–eye coordination. We, as developers, have a unique place in the world, being able to incorporate learning something in an engaging way, without it seeming like something the user *has* to do.

This doesn't mean that we have to mull over this and try to incorporate it into our apps and games; it could, and generally is, something that just happens. With this project, though, I have specifically targeted the learning aspect, to show how easily it could be incorporated into AR projects.

Project overview

This project is based on the idea of being able to teach children word association and spelling by creating a really simple puzzle for them to solve in the real world, which they can then check with this app, to find out whether they solved the puzzle.

The build time for this project is 15 minutes at the most.

Getting started

Here are the system requirements for Unity Version 2018.1.5:

- **Released:** 15 June 2018
- **OS:** Windows 7 SP1+, 8, 10
- **GPU:** Graphics card with DX9 (shader model 3.0) or DX11 with feature level 9.3 capabilities.

 Check out the following:

```
https://unity3d.com/
https://www.turbosquid.com/FullPreview/Index.cfm/ID/967597
```

Installing Vuforia

To install Vuforia on both macOS and Windows, the steps are quite simple; however, I want to show you a different method of acquiring the Vuforia software and Unity.

Unity has another type of installation you can do called the Unity Hub, which you can get from the Unity website in lieu of the 2018 installer file. What Unity Hub does is allow you to have multiple installations of Unity in a single location, a way to set your preferred Unity Editor, consolidation of your projects into a single launcher, an easy way to update components you want installed, and it also gives you access to templates for project preset types. Follow these steps:

1. Navigate to the Unity website and click on **Get Unity**:

2. You will be presented with an option for **Personal**, **Plus** or **Pro**. Click on **Try Personal** if that fits you and what you need:

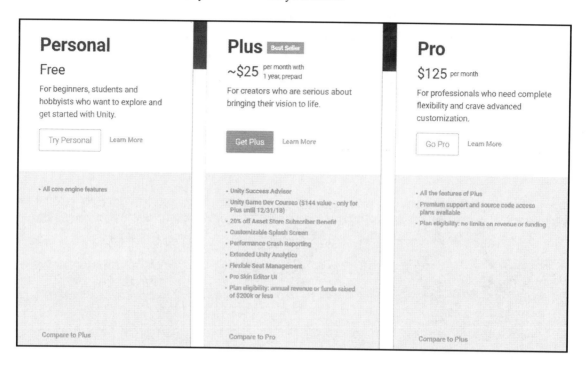

3. That will lead you to the download page, in which you need to put a check mark to accept the terms and give you the option to download the Unity application itself or the Unity Hub that is in Preview. We want the Unity Hub:

Accept terms

☑ **By clicking, I confirm that I am eligible to use Unity Personal per the** Terms of Service, **as I or my company meet the following criteria:**

- Do not make more than $100k in annual gross revenues, regardless of whether Unity Personal is being used for commercial purposes, or for an internal project or prototyping.
- Have not raised funds in excess of $100K.
- Not currently using Unity Plus or Pro.

If you are not eligible to use Unity Personal, please click here to chat with our team about what product is right for you.

Download Installer for Windows   Download Unity Hub (Preview)

Looking to download the installer for Mac OS X?
Choose Mac OS X

4. Once you have downloaded and installed the Unity Hub, you can open it, and it will give you an option for **Projects**, **Learn**, or **Installs**. Click on **Installs** to look at the available versions:

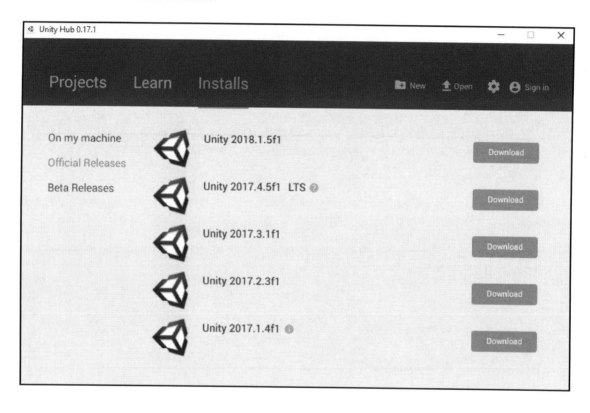

5. We want to install the latest version of Unity, which is 2018.1.5f1:

6. Once you click to install the version you want, click on the **Components** you want and press **Done** to install the Unity Editor:

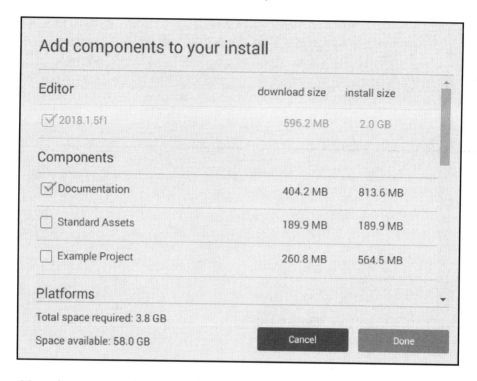

Now, let's say you forgot to select to install Vuforia during this step when you installed Unity—no problem; you can skip the previous points and just follow along from here on out.

7. Open a project in Unity; it could be a dummy project that you don't want, or it could be the basis for this chapter's project.

8. Click on **Build** from the file menu that opens the build menu:

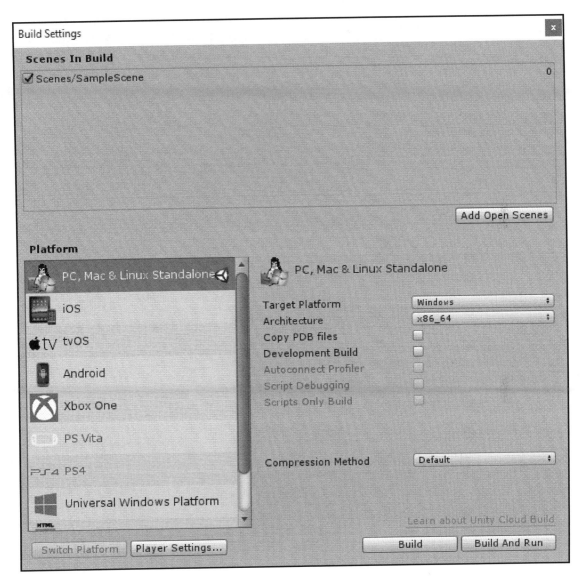

9. We want to select **Player Settings** from this window:

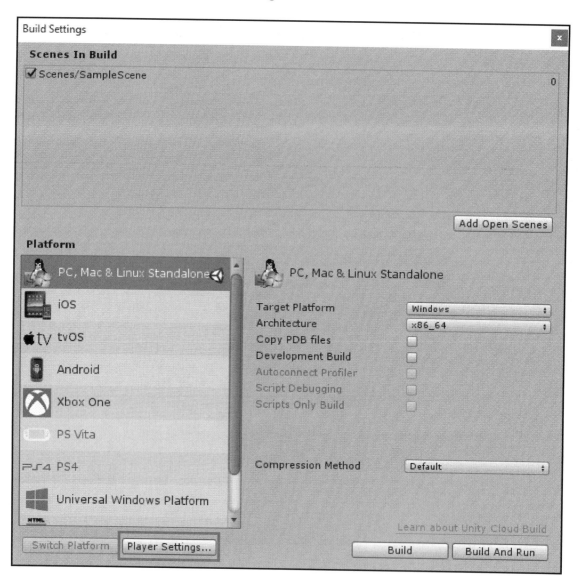

10. The **Player Settings** window should open up where the inspector pane normally is. Locate **XR Support Installers** and click on **Vuforia Augmented Reality**:

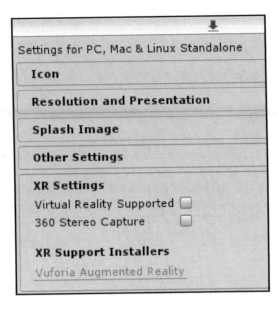

11. This will open your browser and ask you to download a file. Click **Save** to download the file:

12. Close the Unity Editor and install this file. This will add Vuforia support to your Unity installation without having to reinstall the entire editor.

Now that this has been completed, we can move on to creating this project in Windows.

Differences between macOS and Windows setups

There is very little difference in the basic setup between macOS and Windows prior to building for their respective platforms. I have set up the projects in the exact same manner so as to make the flow easier to follow. If you own both a macOS and a Windows computer, then when you go to the macOS portion, you can skip to the building section. If you only own Windows, then you can just follow the instructions there. Conversely, if you only own a macOS device, then you will have the full set of instructions there and you can skip the *Windows project setup* section.

Windows project setup

Navigate to the Vuforia Developer Portal and log into your account. Now follow these steps:

1. In the Vuforia Developer Portal, click on **Develop**, and make sure the submenu has **License Manager** selected. We need to create a new **Development License Key** with the app name of Chapter5 or Picture Puzzle:

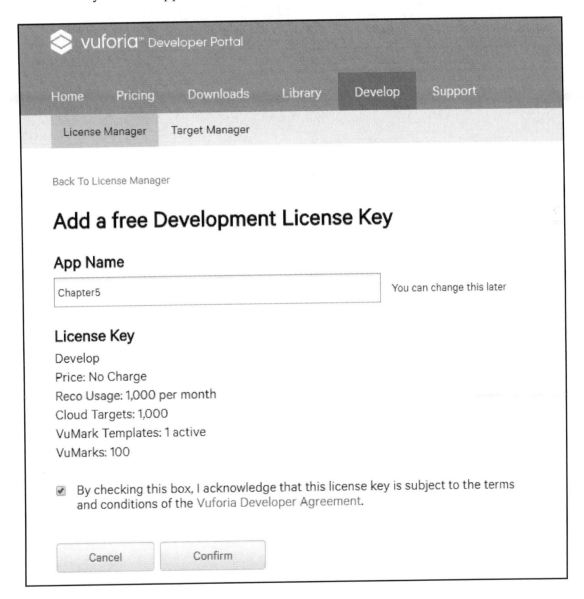

2. After the new key has been created you should see the **License Manager** show the `VuforiaIntro` and the `Chapter5` keys we have created:

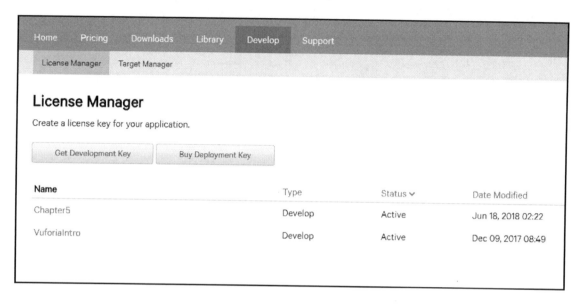

3. Click on `Chapter5` to gain access to your license key. You should copy and paste this into Notepad or Notepad++ for later use:

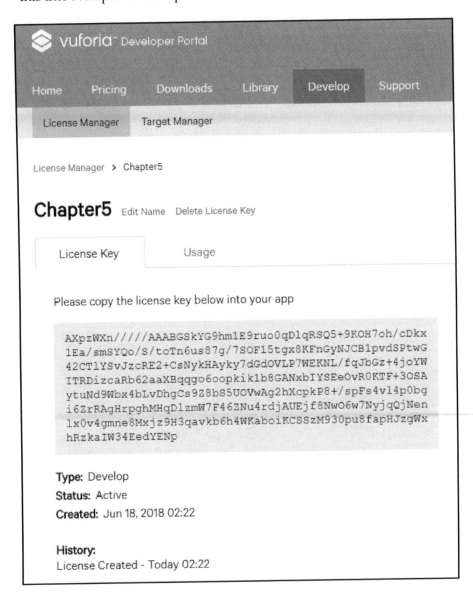

4. Click on **Target Manager**, as we are going to create our own image target for this project:

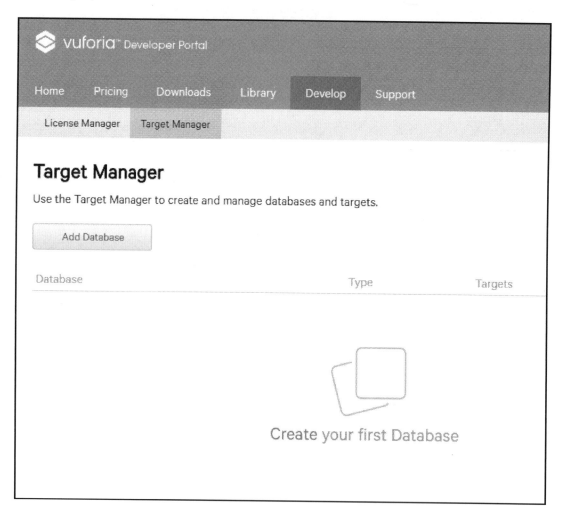

5. Click on **Add Database** to create the brand-new database that we will be utilizing in our project:

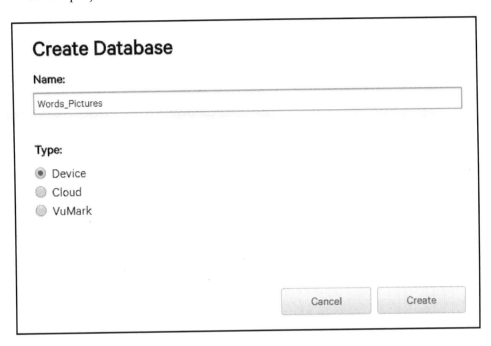

6. You can name the database whatever you want; in my case, I will call it Words_Pictures, with the **Type** being **Device**, and click **Create**:

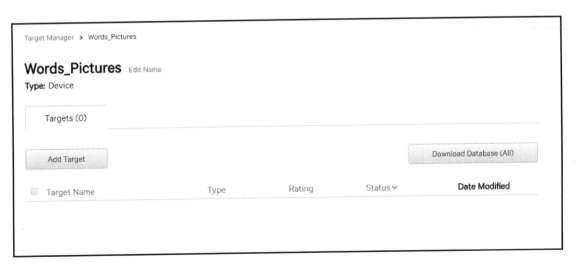

7. It should take us back to the **Target Manager** page and showcase our new `Words_Pictures` database:

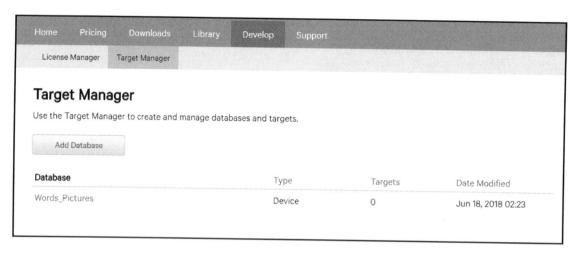

8. Click on `Words_Pictures` to gain access to the database, and then click on **Add Target** when you see it:

9. We will now be able to add a brand-new target to the database. In this case, we want a single image.

I strongly advise you to create and use a JPG format, as a PNG format requires an 8-bit greyscale image or a 24-bit RGB.

10. The width should be set to the same width as your image. The name should reflect what the image is:

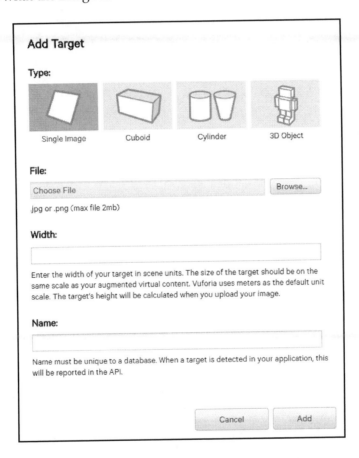

11. Open up Microsoft Paint, and we can begin to create the file that we will use for the target:

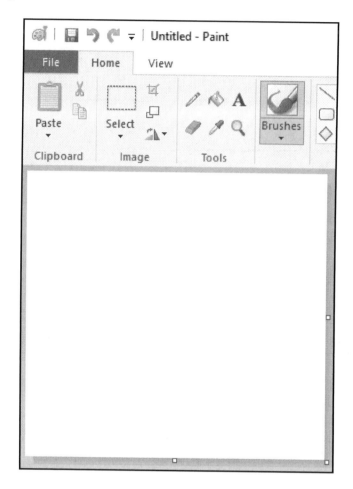

12. The next step is to find the exact size we want to use for this image, and I find the best way to do that is to know what the image is we are going to use. In our case, it will be a **72** in font size, have a font name of **Bastion**, and display the word TREE:

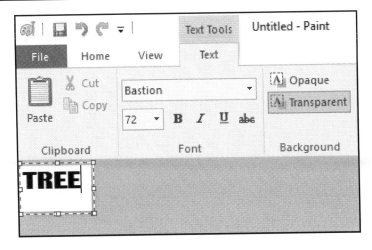

13. Resize the proportions to be close around the edges of the word:

14. Save the file as a JPG and call it `Tree`:

15. If you look at the bottom of the Paint menu, it will tell you the dimensions of the file we just created. In this case it is 253x106, which is the size we want.

16. Navigate back to the **Add Target** web page and choose the `Tree` file we just created:

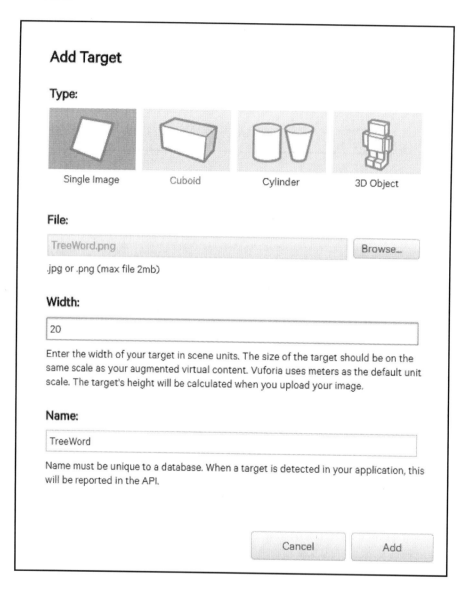

17. Set the width to be `253` and the name to `Tree`, and then click **Add**:

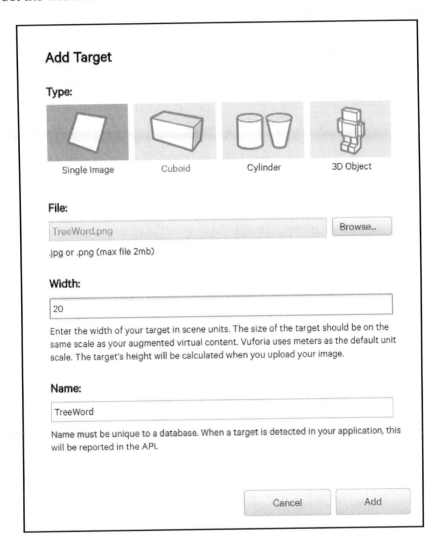

18. It will take you back to the database, and you should see the `TreeWord` with `Tree` as the name. The type should be **Single Image**, and there should be a three-star rating:

Target Name	Type	Rating	Status ⌄	Date Modified
TREE Tree	Single Image	★★★☆☆	Active	Jun 19, 2018 02:57

19. The rating system is designed to tell you whether it is of the proper size to be read correctly by your AR device. We currently have a three-star rating, which means that it should be good, but it could be much better. What can we do to fix this? We can enlarge the image.

20. Let's delete the image from the database. To do this, click on the little checkbox next to `Tree`, and above it will appear a very small **Delete** button:

21. Let's go back to Paint and resize the image. `680` by `480` should be perfect, although `500x300` will work as well:

22. Upload the new target, and the results should have a five-star rating:

	Tree	Untitled		Single Image	★★★★★		Active		Jun 18, 2018 02:38

23. Click on **Download Database (All)**:

24. This will open a new window that will ask us which development platform we want to utilize this with. We want Unity Editor. Click **Download**:

Words_Pictures

It will download a Unity file that we will need to import into our Unity Project—which, now, we can begin to work with in Unity, without having to leave the editor to do any other work. Open Unity, and let's begin building our project.

Building the Windows project

Create a new Unity Project, if you haven't already, and call it Chapter5 to begin with. Then load the project.Now follow these steps:

1. The Words_Pictures file that we downloaded now needs to be located and imported into the project:

Words_Pictures

2. Before we dive in and create the project, let's have a look at the folders that were created upon import.

3. Our main `Assets` folder will now have an `Editor` folder, a `StreamingAssets` folder and a `Scenes` folder:

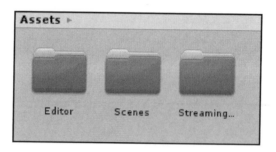

4. Inside the `Editor` folder, it will have another folder called `Vuforia`:

5. Inside the `Vuforia` folder will be another folder called `ImageTargetTextures`:

6. Inside the `ImageTargetTextures` folder, there will be a folder called `Word_Pictures`:

7. The `Word_Pictures` folder will contain our tree image sprite:

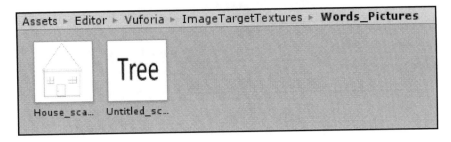

8. Go back to the main `Assets` folder, and let's take a look, starting with `StreamingAssets`:

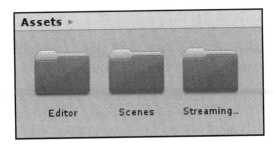

9. Inside the `StreamingAssets` folder will be a `Vuforia` folder:

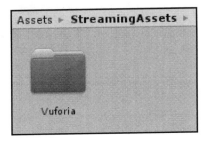

10. Inside the `Vuforia` folder will be two files: `Words_Pictures.xml` and `Words_Pictures.dat` file:

11. Let's take a look at the XML file in depth to see what exactly is in it. Take a look at this code:

```
<?xml version="1.0" encoding="UTF-8"?>
<QCARConfig xmlns:xsi="http://www.w3.org/2001/XMLSchema-instance"
xsi:noNamespaceSchemaLocation="qcar_config.xsd">
  <Tracking>
    <ImageTarget name="Tree" size="680.000000 480. 000000" />
  </Tracking>
</QCARConfig>
```

The XML file has the default schema for it set up, with the main tag being `QCarconfig`.

The next tag, which houses our image, is `ImageTarget`. It has the name, which we set to `Tree` and the size written in floating-point values.

The XML file is very short and to the point. This file is specifically for housing the data that Vuforia needs to know, the size of the images we are using, and to be able to reference the proper file if we were to have multiple images. Continue to follow the steps:

12. Go to the TurboSquid website and download the free `Tree` model that we will be using:

13. You will need the `Tree_FBX` and the `Tree_textures` files for this next portion:

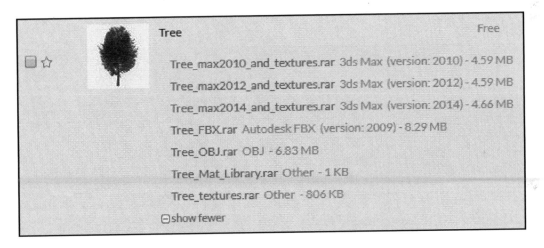

14. Navigate back to the main `Assets` folder and create a new folder called `Models`:

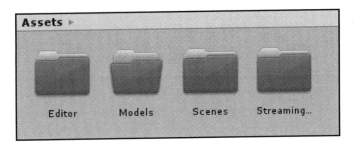

15. Extract both the tree model and the textures. Copy and paste the model and textures into the `Models` folder inside Unity:

16. Delete the standard camera from the hierarchy pane.
17. Right-click in the hierarchy pane and navigate to **Vuforia**; click to add an **AR Camera**:

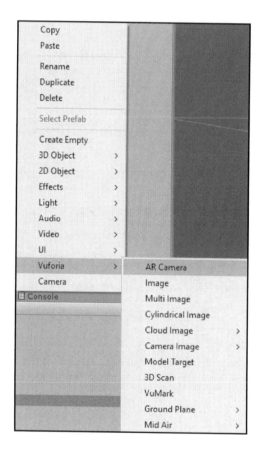

18. Click on the `AR Camera` in the hierarchy pane. Look over to the **Inspector** pane and click on **Open Vuforia Configuration**:

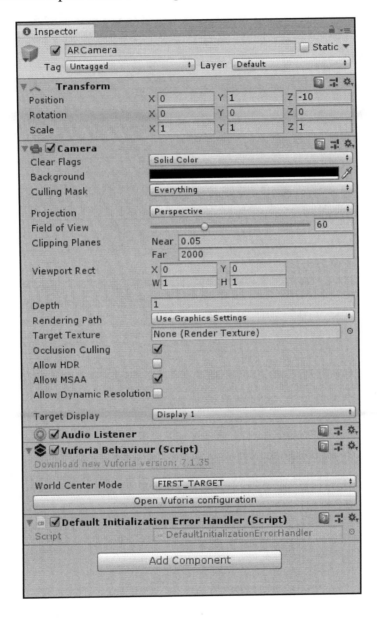

19. Unity should ask for you to import and download more items for Vuforia and accept the Vuforia license:

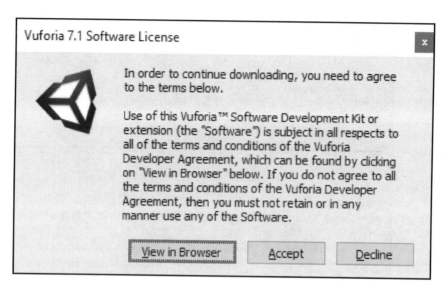

20. Copy and paste your app license key into the **App License Key** section:

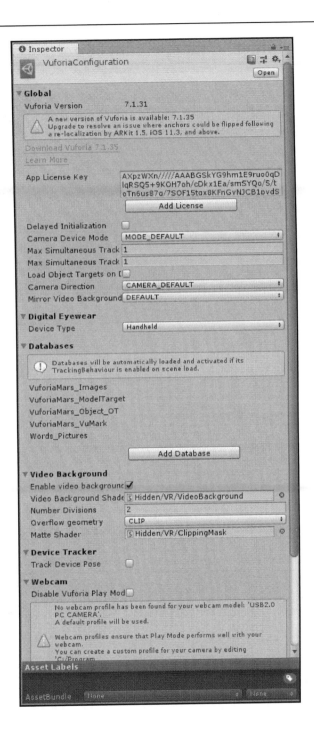

21. Right-click on the hierarchy pane and create an empty game object called `ImageTarget`.

22. Right-click on the `ImageTarget` object and highlight **Vuforia** and click on **Image**:

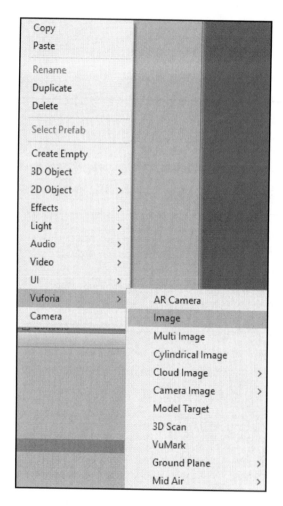

23. Click on the **Image** object and look at the **Inspector** pane. **Image Target Behavior** should have the type be **Predefined**; the **Database** should be **Words_Pictures**, and the **Image Target** should be **Tree**:

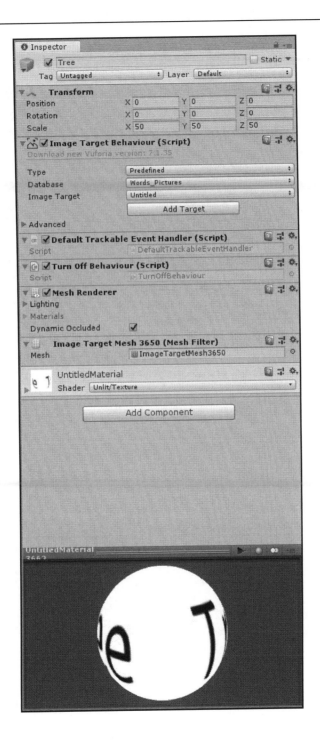

Now we need to add our model. I am assuming you know how to set up materials for the model, so I will not go over it here.

24. Drag and drop the model on to the scene. Set the *x*, *y*, and *z* positions to be 0,0,0, with the scale being 0.09 for the *x*, *y*, and *z* coordinates. The last thing to do is make it a child of the image inside the **ImageTarget** object:

25. Print out the Tree text and cut the paper into four strips.

26. Build the project for a **PC, Mac & Linux Standalone** or **Android** by clicking on **File | Build Settings**, and click on **Build**:

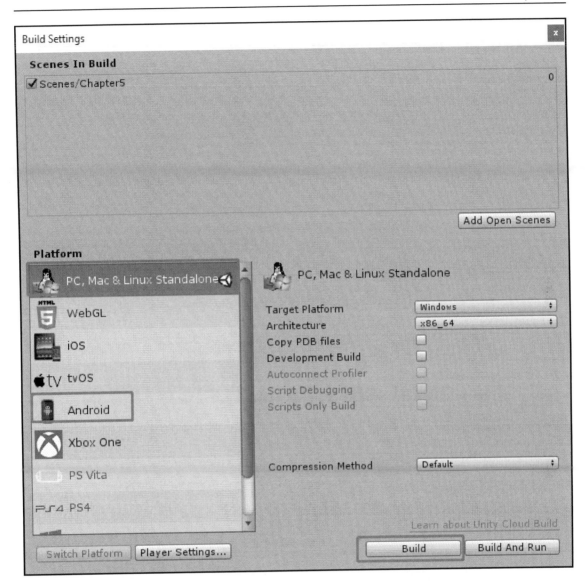

Now with your Android device or PC camera being utilized, put the strips together in the proper order, and the `Tree` model will appear over the top of the paper.

macOS project setup

The steps for setting up the project in Mac are nearly identical, with the difference mainly being the software we will use to create the text file, but, nonetheless, this should be gone over, as I expect Mac users will not want to read the Windows section of this chapter. We will need it, as we will be using Vuforia to create this project. Navigate to the Vuforia Developer Portal and log into your account. Now follow these steps:

1. In the Vuforia Developer Portal, click on **Develop**, and make sure the submenu has **License Manager** selected. We need to create a new **Development License Key** with the app name of Chapter5:

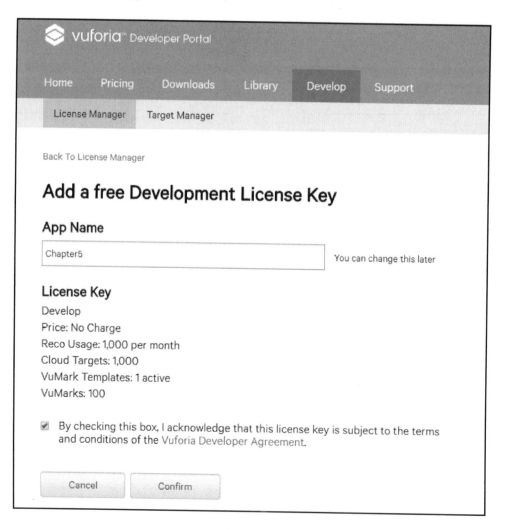

2. After the new key has been created, you should see the **License Manager** show the `VuforiaIntro` and the `Chapter5` keys we have created:

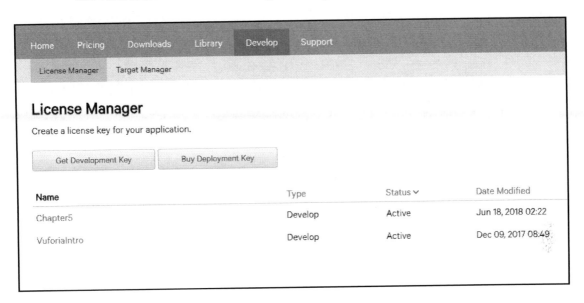

3. Click on `Chapter5` to gain access to your license key. You should copy and paste this into Notepad or Notepad++ for later use:

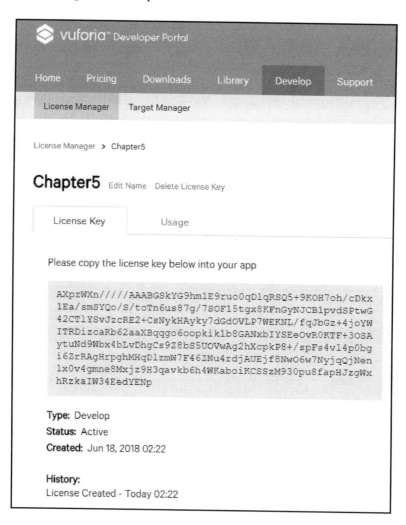

4. Click on **Target Manager**, as we are going to create our own image target for this project:

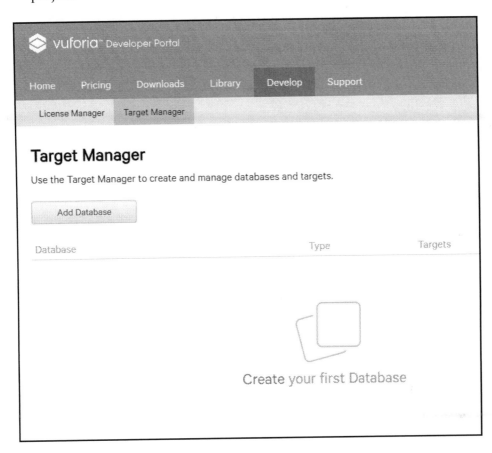

5. Click on **Add Database** to create the brand-new database that we will be utilizing in our project:

6. You can name the database whatever you want; in my case, I will call it `Words_Pictures`, with the **Type** being **Device**, and click **Create**:

7. It should take us back to the **Target Manager** page and showcase our new
   `Words_Pictures` database:

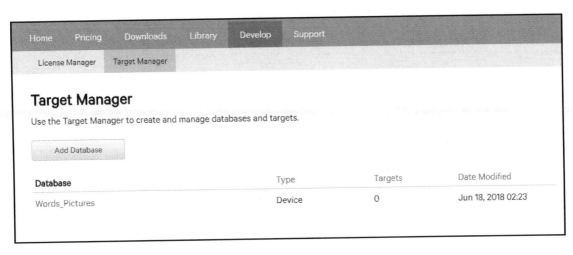

8. Click on `Words_Pictures` to gain access to the database, and then click on **Add Target** when you see it:

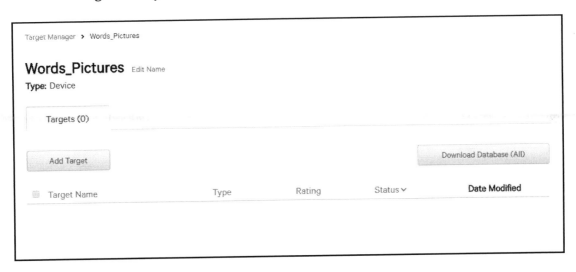

9. We will now be able to add a brand-new target to the database. In this case, we
   want a single image.

I strongly advise you to create and use a JPG format, as a PNG format requires an 8-bit greyscale image or a 24-bit RGB.

10. The width should be set to the same width as your image. The name should reflect what the image is:

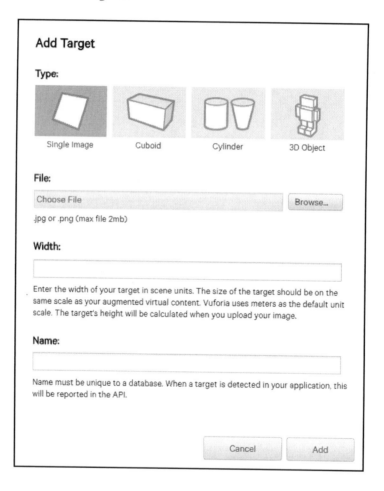

11. Open Microsoft Paint, and we can begin to create the file that we will use for the target:

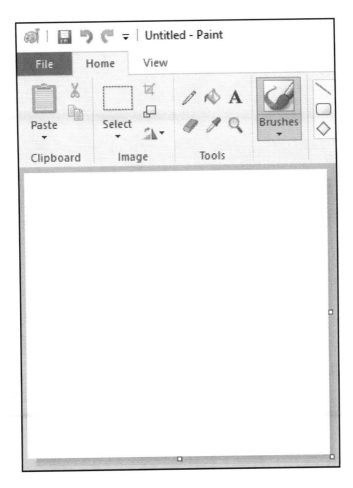

12. The next step is to find the exact size we want to use for this image, and I find the best way to do that is to know what the image is we are going to use. In our case, it will be **72** in font size, have the font name of **Bastion**, and display the word `Tree`:

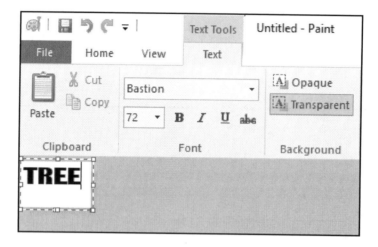

13. Resize the proportions to be close around the edges of the word:

14. Save the file as a JPG and call it `Tree`:

15. If you look at the bottom of the Paint menu, it will tell you the dimensions of the file we just created. In this case it is `253x106`.

16. Navigate back to the **Add Target** web page and choose the `Tree` file we just created:

17. Set the width to be 253 and the name to be **Tree**, and then click on **Add**:

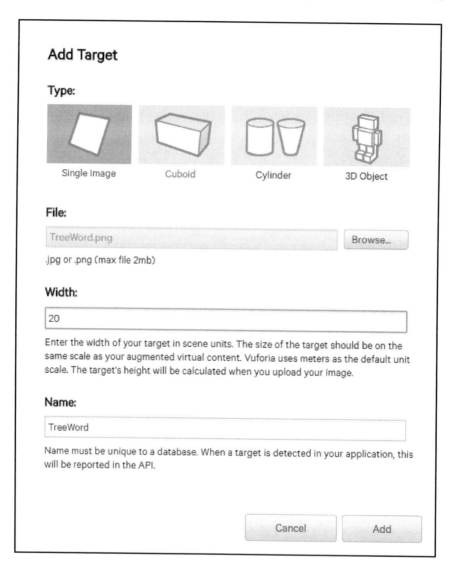

18. It will take you back to the database, and you should see the word `Tree`, with the **Name** as `Tree`, **Type** as **Single Image**, and there should be a three-star rating:

	Target Name	Type	Rating	Status ∨	Date Modified
☐ TREE	Tree	Single Image	★★★☆☆	Active	Jun 19, 2018 02:57

The rating system is designed to tell you whether it is of the proper size to be read correctly by your AR device. We currently have a three-star rating, which means that it should be good, but it could be much better. What can we do to fix this? We can enlarge the image. Let's continue following the steps:

19. Let's delete the image from the database. To do this, click on the little checkbox next to `Tree`, and above it will appear a very small **Delete** button:

20. Let's go back to Paint and resize the image. `680` by `480` should be perfect:

21. Upload the new target, and the results should have a five-star rating:

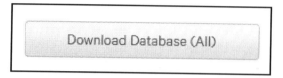

22. Click on **Download Database (All)**:

23. This will open a new window that will ask which development platform we want to utilize this with. We want Unity Editor. Click **Download**:

It will download a Unity file that we will need to import into our Unity Project—which, now, we can begin to work in Unity, without having to leave the editor to do any other work. Open Unity, and let's begin building our project.

Building the macOS Project

Create a new Unity Project, if you haven't already, and call it `Chapter5` to begin with. Then, load the project. Now follow these steps:

1. The `Words_Pictures` file that we downloaded now needs to be located and imported into the project.
2. Before we dive in and create the project, let's have a look at the folders that were created upon import. Our main `Assets` folder will now have an `Editor` folder, a `StreamingAssets` Folder, and a `Scenes` folder:

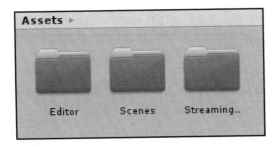

3. Inside the `Editor` folder, it will have another folder called `Vuforia`:

4. Inside the `Vuforia` folder will be another folder called `ImageTargetTextures`:

5. Inside the `ImageTargetTextures` folder, there will be a folder called `Word_Pictures`:

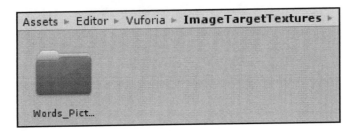

6. Inside the `Word_Pictures` folder, we will have our tree image sprite:

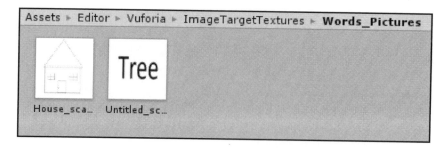

7. Go back to the main `Assets` folder and let's take a look, starting with `StreamingAssets`:

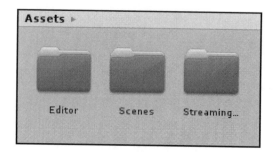

8. Inside the `StreamingAssets` folder will be a `Vuforia` folder:

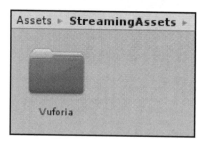

9. Inside the `Vuforia` folder will be two files: `Words_Pictures.xml` and `Words_Pictures.dat`:

10. Let's take a look at the XML file in depth to see what exactly is in it:

```
<?xml version="1.0" encoding="UTF-8"?>
<QCARConfig xmlns:xsi="http://www.w3.org/2001/XMLSchema-instance"
xsi:noNamespaceSchemaLocation="qcar_config.xsd">
   <Tracking>
      <ImageTarget name="Tree" size="680.000000 480. 000000" />
   </Tracking>
</QCARConfig>
```

The XML file has the default schema for it set up, with the main tag being `QCarconfig`.

The next tag, which houses our image, is `ImageTarget`. It has the name, which we set to `Tree`, and the size written in floating-point values.

The XML file is very short and to the point. This file is specifically for housing the data that Vuforia needs to know, the size of the images we are using, and to be able to reference the proper file if we were to have multiple images. Let's continue with the steps:

11. Go to the TurboSquid website and download the free `Tree` model that we will be using:

12. You will need the `Tree_FBX` and the `Tree_textures` files for this next section:

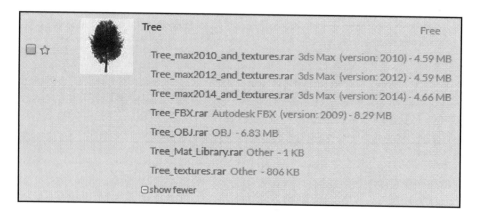

13. Navigate back to the main `Assets` folder and create a new folder called `Models`:

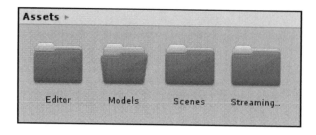

14. Extract both the tree model and the textures. Copy and paste the model and textures into the `Models` folder inside of Unity:

15. Delete the standard camera from the hierarchy pane.
16. Right-click in the hierarchy pane and navigate to **Vuforia**; click to add an **AR Camera**:

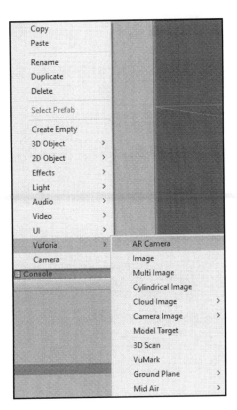

17. Click on the `AR Camera` in the hierarchy pane. Look over to the **Inspector** pane and click on **Open Vuforia Configuration**:

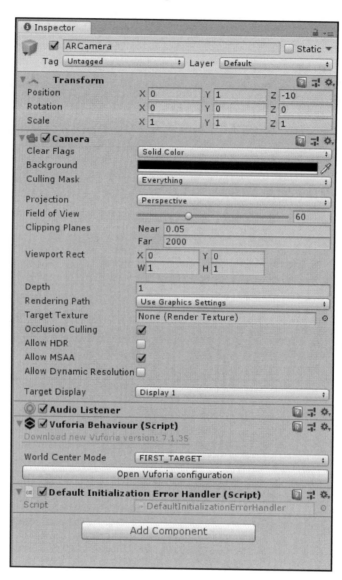

18. Unity should ask for you to import and download more items for Vuforia and accept the Vuforia license:

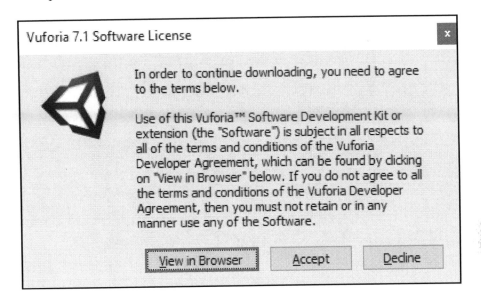

19. Copy and paste your app license key into the **App License Key** section:

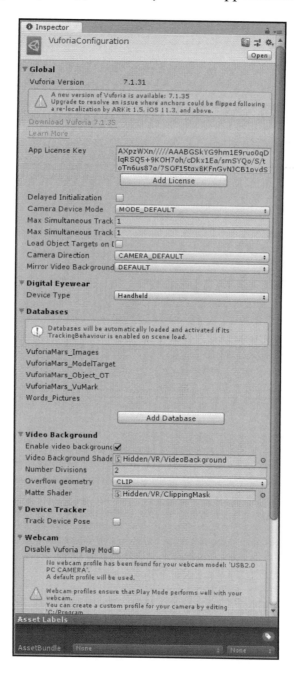

20. Right-click on the hierarchy pane and create an empty game object called `ImageTarget`.

21. Right-click on the `ImageTarget` object and highlight **Vuforia**, and click on **Image**:

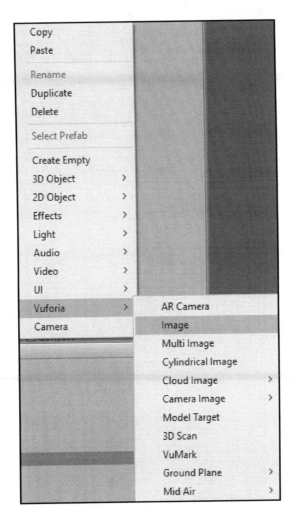

22. Click on the `Image` object and look at the **Inspector** pane. **Image Target Behavior** should have the **Type** as **Predefined**. Database should be **Words_Pictures** and **Image Target** should be **Tree**:

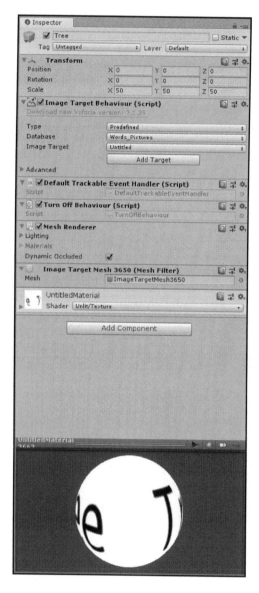

Now we need to add our model. I am assuming you know how to set up materials for the model, so I will not go over it here. Let's continue with the steps:

23. Drag and drop the model on to the scene. Set the *x*, *y*, and *z* positions to be 0,0,0, with the scale being 0.09 for the *x*, *y*, and *z* coordinates. The last thing to do is make it a child of the image inside the **ImageTarget** object:

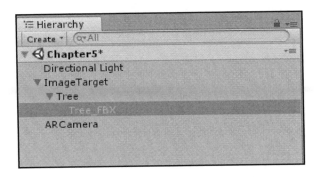

24. Print out the Tree text and cut the paper into four strips.

25. Build the project for **iOS** by clicking on **File | Build Settings**. Make sure to select the **Development Build** check mark:

Working with Xcode

We can navigate to the Build folder of our application here, and click on it to open our XCode project. Follow these steps:

1. On the left-hand side of the screen, you should see Unity-iPhone as one of the items you can select. Click on it and you should see **Unity-iPhone** in the center and **Identity and Type** on the right:

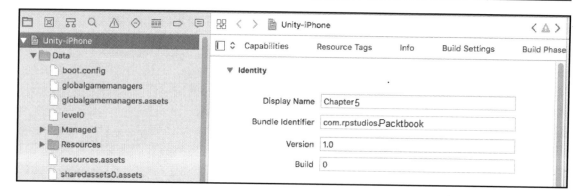

2. Check to make sure the **Identity** is correct. The **Display Name** for me is Chapter5, with the **Bundle Identifier** as com.rpstudios.Packtbook:

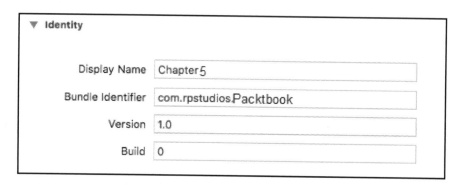

3. Now, on **Signing**, you need to look and make sure that the **Automatically manage signing** checkbox is checked and that **Team** has your email address attached to it:

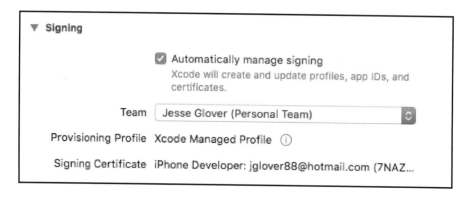

4. Scroll down and look for **Linked Frameworks and Libraries**. AVFoundation should be set from **Optional** to **Required**. I've noticed that when it is set to **Optional**, the linker fails to work properly:

▼ **Linked Frameworks and Libraries**

Name	Status
Security.framework	Required ⌄
MediaToolbox.framework	Required ⌄
libiPhone-lib.a	Required ⌄
CoreText.framework	Required ⌄
AudioToolbox.framework	Required ⌄
AVFoundation.framework	Optional ⌄
CFNetwork.framework	Required ⌄
CoreGraphics.framework	Required ⌄
CoreLocation.framework	Required ⌄
CoreMedia.framework	Required ⌄
CoreMotion.framework	Optional ⌄
CoreVideo.framework	Required ⌄
Foundation.framework	Required ⌄
MediaPlayer.framework	Required ⌄
OpenAL.framework	Required ⌄
OpenGLES.framework	Required ⌄
QuartzCore.framework	Required ⌄
SystemConfiguration.framework	Required ⌄
UIKit.framework	Required ⌄
libiconv.2.dylib	Required ⌄
libil2cpp.a	Required ⌄
Metal.framework	Optional ⌄
ARKit.framework	Required ⌄

5. Locate **Architectures**, because we need to change from the default to **Standard**. This is due to there being different architectures and iOS doesn't utilize ARM anymore:

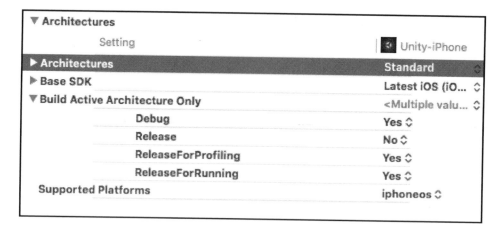

6. Now you can click on **Build** and attach your iPhone 6 or above to your macOS computer. **Build** and then run it on the device. It will ask you to trust the app on your phone, so follow the instructions to give trust.

7. Click on the app on your phone and—voila!—it will load, and you can play with the app.

Now with your iOS device being utilized, put the strips together in the proper order, and the Tree model will appear over the top of the paper.

Summary

In this chapter, we learned how to create an educational game for children so they can learn what objects are in relation to the words for them. We learned how to develop using Vuforia, for both macOS and Windows for Android and iOS devices. We also learned that the basic building blocks for building on Windows and macOS devices are fairly similar code-wise, the only major difference being the extra steps required to compile to iOS or macOS, using XCode.

In the next chapter, we will build a prototype of a fitness application designed to allow the user to randomly select the location of where they want to walk, for fun.

15
Fitness for Fun - Tourism and Random Walking

In this chapter, we will utilize Mapbox to create an AR fitness application prototype. The reason for this is that the main focus will be utilizing GPS, geolocation, and the Android/Apple device hardware to communicate with satellites and receive that data. Mapbox is an SDK designed to utilize the geolocation features of both Android and Apple devices within Unity. The software we will use in conjunction with Unity to make this happen much more seamlessly is Mapbox. Mapbox takes care of a lot of the most difficult portions of the work, so we only have to focus on our games and applications that utilize the software. We will learn how to use Mapbox with Unity to create a fitness application that promotes walking around the area in which you live. Basically, the user will tap on a random location and it will set the destination as that location. The user will then have to walk to that location, which will trigger the destruction of that marker.

In this chapter, we will cover the following topics:

- Learning about Mapbox
- Integrating Mapbox into Unity
- Implementing Mapbox data into an AR application

Background information on Mapbox

Mapbox allows you to create Location Based, City Simulators, TabletopAR and WorldScaleAR applications and games. For any project you have that might require geolocation, Mapbox is the software to utilize. Mapbox was built from the ground up to be compatible with Unity, Android, and iOS.

Mapbox is free for web and mobile SDKs for up to 50,000 map views, geocode requests, direction requests, and matrix elements per month. After reaching the 50,000 limit, there is a charge of 0.5 cents per 1,000 web map views, geocode requests, direction requests, and matrix elements per month for mobile SDKs and web apps. The free version also includes 5 GB of dataset storage for satellite and street maps, an unlimited amount of styles for Mapbox Studio, and access to create public and free web/mobile apps.

Now, it should be noted that there is a commercial option that is required when you have a paid web app or website that is free or subscription-based, a private web app or website with restricted access, or an app or website that tracks assets / monitors people or things. The commercial plan includes private or paid apps for up to 250 seats, asset tracking for up to 1,000 different assets, and turn-by-turn navigation apps for up to 50 seats. The cost is the same as the free plan in addition to $499 per month:

Project overview

We will be creating a small application that allows the user to select the location they want to walk to and it will set the destination. The build time will be around 20 minutes.

Getting started

The technical requirements for this application are as follows:

- Android device with kernel version 24 or above
- Unity 2018
- Mapbox (`https://www.mapbox.com/`)

Setting up Mapbox

We will now see how to set up Mapbox:

1. The very first thing we need to do is sign up for Mapbox. This requires a username, email address, and password:

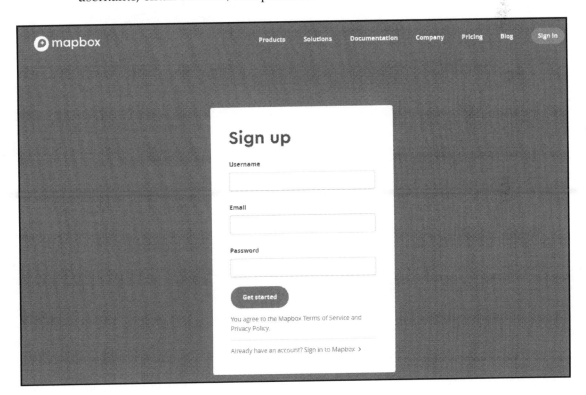

2. After you have signed up and verified your email address, it will take you to a page to find out which version of Mapbox you need. You have the option of **iOS**, **Android**, **Web**, and **Unity**:

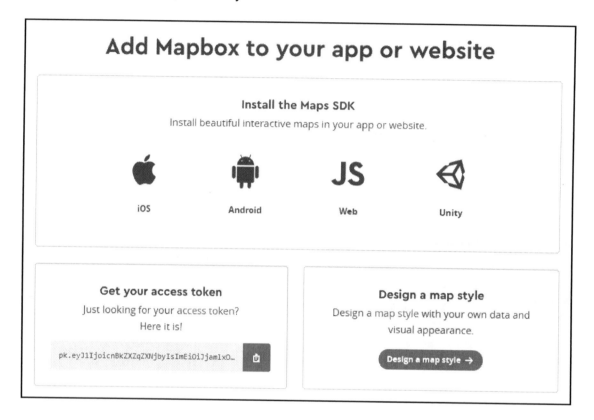

3. The version we want will obviously be the Maps SDK for Unity, so be sure to download the Unity package before proceeding:

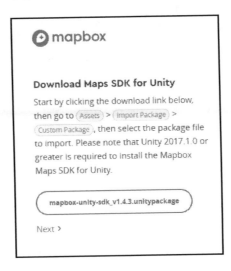

4. As per the following screenshot, you will be given an access token, which will be required to utilize the Mapbox software. Be sure to copy this key and paste it into Notepad for later use:

5. Create a new Unity project and call it `Chapter6` or `Fitness for Fun`:

6. Import the Mapbox Unity asset file into the project:

7. This will probably take some time to install:

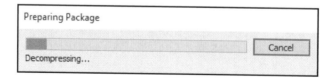

8. Right away, after the installation, you should notice a new menu item called **Mapbox**. This opens up quite a few new features that are exposed for us to play with:

9. **Mapbox** gives us **Atlas Template Generator**, **Clear File Cache**, **Setup**, and **Map Editor** options:

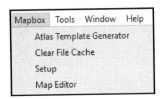

10. The **Mapbox Atlas Template Generator** is a tool that allows you to create and test custom map atlases:

 For every item we look at in this section, exit from it immediately after taking a look at it so we can continue. We will revisit the items we need when building the project.

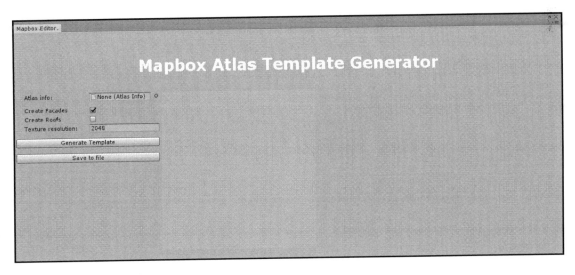

11. The **Map Editor** allows you to visualize the underlying data structure of the maps you create and use:

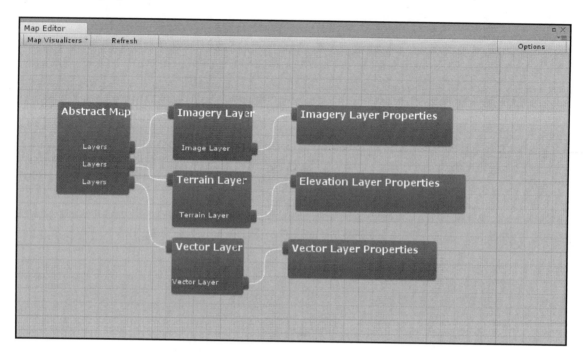

12. In addition to that, the Map Editor's data is tied directly to the Map object's **Abstract Map Script**. Any changes you make to the **Abstract Map Script** data is reflected in the **Map Editor**, and any changes you make in the **Map Editor** are reflected in the Abstract Map Script's data:

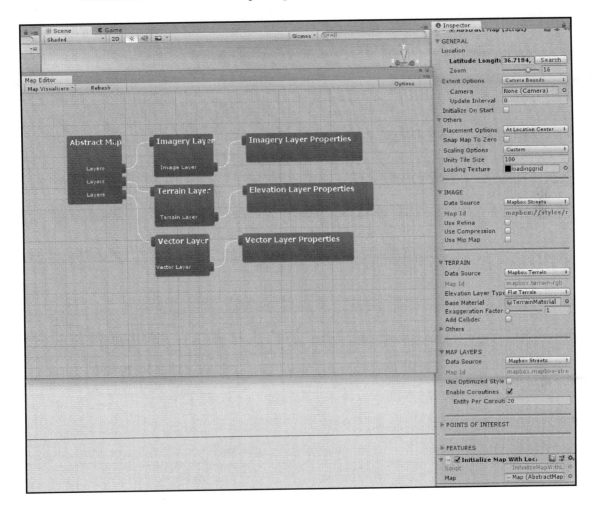

13. The **Mapbox Setup** option allows you to select **Example** scenes or **Map Prefabs**, however, this can only be accessed after you copy and paste your **Access Token** and submit the information. This will require you to be connected to the internet for verification:

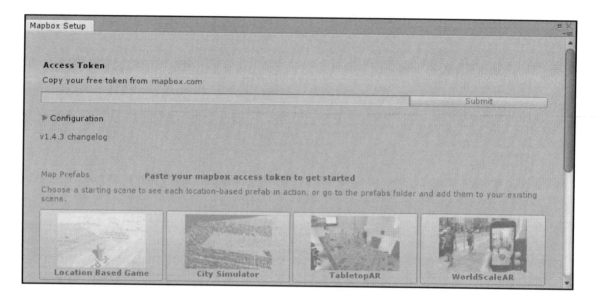

Important items to note

With different project types, you will have prefabs that will automatically be added to the active scene. In this section, we will go over the main object that is added to any template type, which is the Map object.

The Map is the most important object that is added to with any of our templates and has many extremely important items within the script that we should go over:

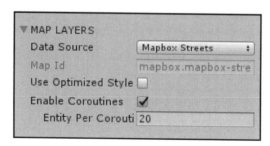

The first item within the Map object is the **Abstract Map** script. The most important items within are **MAP LAYERS**, **GENERAL**, **Location**, and **Others**:

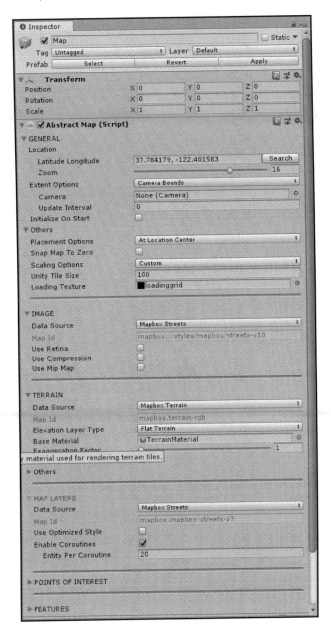

Within the **GENERAL** tab, we have:

- **Latitude Longitude**: If you click on **Search**, you can set this by typing in an address, or country and city, or even city and state, depending on the location you want to utilize. It will automatically convert it to be latitude and longitude values.
- **Zoom**: This is specifically set for how close and far away the map can be drawn; be advised that the zoom function will only work appropriately if you have the proper tilesets generated for it.
- **Extent Options**: These are how far you want the map to be drawn. By default, it is set to the bounds of the camera.
- **Camera**: This is the camera you want to use, whether it is an AR camera with Vuforia, ARCore, ARKit, or even the regular Unity camera.
- **Update Interval**: This is how long the program should wait before updating positions and drawing.
- **Initialize On Start**: This is a Boolean value for whether or not you want the map to immediately be drawn upon the start of the scene:

In the **Others** tab, we have a few options as well:

- **Placement Options** allows you to choose between **At Location Center** and **At Tile Center**. This controls the center or root placement of the tiles. Location center is able to be defined by you, whereas the tile center is the center of the tile.
- **Snap Map To Zero** is a Boolean value that specifies whether or not the map's root should be snapped to 0,0,0.

- **Scaling Options** allows you to choose whether you want a custom or world scale. **Custom** is defined by Unity using a Mercator conversion factor. **World scale** means that the actual scale is rendered and the Mercator conversion is ignored.
- **Unity Tile Size** is the size of the tiles used in Unity units.
- **Loading Texture** is the texture used when the textures are loading.

The next tab is the **IMAGE** tab:

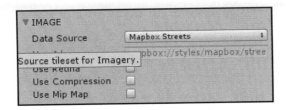

- **Data Source**: This is the source of our maps. We can use **Mapbox Streets**, **Mapbox Outdoors**, **Mapbox Dark**, **Mapbox Light**, **Mapbox Satellite**, **Mapbox Satellite Street**, **Custom**, or **None**. These are essentially theme options for the map you want to use.
- **Use Retina**: This is a Boolean that allows you to choose whether you want to enable the usage of larger texture maps and better visual quality for retina displays.
- **Use Compression**: This is a Boolean that allows you to choose to use Unity compression for the tile texture.
- **Use Mip Map**: This is a Boolean that lets you choose whether to use Unity-generated mip mapping.

The next tab is **TERRAIN**, which gives us the ability to modify the terrain of our Mapbox maps:

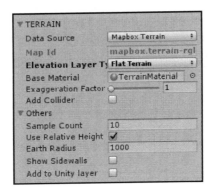

- **Data Source**: This is the first option available, and it lets us choose between using **Mapbox Terrain**, **Custom**, or **None**. **Mapbox Terrain** provides us with digital elevation with worldwide coverage. **Custom** allows us to use a custom elevation model. **None** is a flat terrain.
- **Map Id**: This is the Id of the corresponding tileset that we want to use.
- **Elevation Layer Type**: This gives us the choice between **Flat Terrain**, **Terrain with Elevation**, **Low Polygon Terrain**, and **Globe Terrain**. This allows us to render our terrain with the specified elevation type. **Flat Terrain** renders a flat terrain with no elevation. **Terrain with Elevation** renders terrain with elevation from the source specified. **Low Polygon Terrain** renders a low polygon terrain with elevation from the source specified. **Globe Terrain** renders a terrain with no elevation for a globe.
- **Base Material**: This is the material used to render the terrain tiles.
- **Exaggeration Factor**: This multiplies the factor to vertically exaggerate elevation on the terrain, however, it does not work with the **Flat Terrain Elevation Layer Type**.
- **Add Collider**: This is a Boolean that lets us add Unity physics colliders to terrain tiles for detecting collisions.

The **Others** tab within the **TERRAIN** tab has a few options available to us as well:

- **Sample Count**: This gives us the resolution for our terrain, with the result being an *n* x *n* grid.
- **Use Relative Height**: This is a Boolean that lets us use a world-relative scale for scaling the terrain height.
- **Earth Radius**: This is the radius of the Earth we want to use in Unity units of measurements, which is meters.
- **Show Sidewalls**: This is a Boolean that adds side walls to terrain meshes, which reduces visual artifacts.
- **Add to Unity layer**: This adds the terrain tiles to the Unity layer. Upon checking the checkbox, you will get the choice of which layer you want to add them to—**Default**, **TransparentFX**, **Ignore Raycast**, **Water**, **UI**, **Postprocessing**, and **Add Layer**.

Next is the **MAP LAYERS** tab:

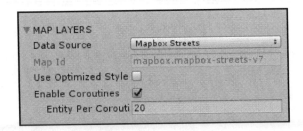

- **Data Source**: This is the source dataset for the vector data.
- **Map Id**: This is the Id of the map we are using.
- **Use Optimized Style**: This is a Boolean that allows us to use Mapbox-style-optimized tilesets that remove any layers or features in the tile that are not represented by a Mapbox style. Style-optimized vector tiles are smaller, serve over the wire, and are a great way to reduce the size of offline caches.
- **Enable Coroutines**: This is a Boolean that allows us to use coroutines.
- **Entity Per Coroutine**: This specifies how many entities can be grouped together in a single coroutine call.

POINTS OF INTEREST is the next tab. Here you can create special markers for important locations in your application or game:

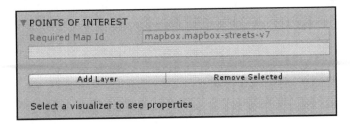

- **Required Map Id**: This is the map Id of the tileset we are using and cannot be empty.
- **Add Layer**: This allows us to add points of interest layers.
- **Remove Selected**: This allows us to delete a layer.

The last tab is **FEATURES**, which gives us **Vector Layer Visualizers** with the options to add or remove visualizers. **FEATURES** allow us to modify how certain features look in relation to the point of interest we create:

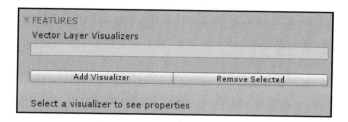

- **Add Visualizer**: This allows us to change how we visualize a points of interest layer
- **Remove Selected**: This allows us to delete the selected visualizer

Finally, we have another script, called **Initialize Map With Location Provider**, which only has the option to add an **Abstract Map object** to it. This script does what the name states—it registers if you are on an iOS, Windows, or Android device, and selects the **Location Provider** that is most relevant for it.

Setting up the project

It's now time to set up our project:

1. Let's create a new scene and call it FitnessFun:

2. Click on **Mapbox** and then **Setup**. This will open a setup menu where you need to paste your **Access Token** in order to gain access to the **Map Prefabs** template:

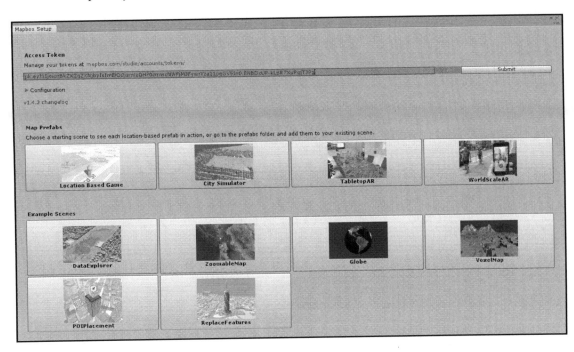

3. The **Map Prefabs** template we want to use is **Location Based Game**:

4. It will add a prefab onto our scene, which will have what looks like a pawn in the scene edit tab:

5. If you look over in the **Hierarchy** pane, you will notice a LocationBasedGame prefab added there, and if you drill down to look at the objects inside, you will see a **Map**, **Player**, and **LocationProvider** inside. You will also notice a **Canvas** and **EventSystem** automatically added to the **Hierarchy**:

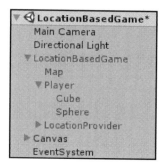

6. Inside the `Scenes` folder, create a `Scripts` folder:

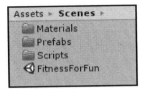

7. Inside that `Scripts` folder, create a C# script called `TargetLocationController`:

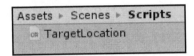

8. Create another script called `DestroyTargetLocation`:

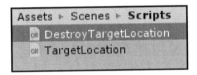

9. Go back to the **Hierarchy** pane and make a copy of the **Player** component:

10. Remove the **Immediate Position** and **Rotation with Location** scripts along with renaming it to `targetLocation`:

11. Inside the `Scenes` folder, create a folder called `Prefabs`:

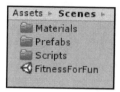

12. Drag and drop the `TargetLocation` object into the `Prefabs` folder:

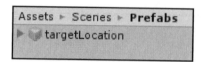

13. Navigate to our `Scripts` folder and open the **TargetLocationController** script.

We need to write our script to create a new instance of the `TargetLocation` object and to destroy the object when something happens.

Scripting the project

In this section, we'll see how to script our project:

1. We will first make sure to utilize Unity Engine, as we need access to MonoBehaviour:

   ```
   using UnityEngine;
   ```

2. Our public class will be called `TargetLocationController`, which is the same name as the script file we named in the Unity Editor. We will also inherit from MonoBehaviour:

   ```
   public class TargetLocationController : MonoBehaviour
   {
   ```

3. We will create a public `GameObject` called `targetObject`; this is so that we can drag and drop our prefab onto this object to set a reference to it:

   ```
   private GameObject targetObject;
   ```

4. We will create a `Start()` method at this point. We want to find the object in the project with the tag of `targetLocation`, as we will be creating it upon a touch event instantiating it:

```
private void Start()
{
    targetObject =
GameObject.FindGameObjectWithTag("targetLocation");
}
```

5. We will need to create a `SetLocation` method and instantiate a new raycast to utilize the touch event the way we want for reading finger presses on the screen:

```
private void SetLocation()
{
RaycastHit hit = new RaycastHit();
```

6. We need to loop through to check on our input via touch events:

```
for (int i = 0; i < Input.touchCount; ++i)
```

7. We check to see if the touch count is greater than 0, and if our touch phase is moved:

```
if (Input.touchCount > 0 && Input.GetTouch(0).phase ==
TouchPhase.Moved)
{
```

8. Now, we will construct a ray from the current touch coordinates on the screen:

```
Ray ray = Camera.main.ScreenPointToRay(Input.GetTouch(i).position);
```

9. We need to do a check to see if the raycast hits anything:

```
if (Physics.Raycast(ray, out hit))
```

10. If the raycast hits anything, then we will create a new instance of our prefab with the position based on our touch event:

```
Instantiate(targetObject, new Vector3(Input.GetTouch(i).position.x,
4.23f, Input.GetTouch(i).position.y), Quaternion.identity);
    }
}
```

11. In our `Update()` method, we call our `SetLocation` script:

```
private void Update()
{
SetLocation();
}
}
```

12. Now, we just need a simple collision check script to check if the player object collides with the `targetlocation` object. We want to destroy our `targetLocation` object if the player object collides with it.

13. Open the `Destroy Target Location` script.

14. We will need the `UnityEngine` namespace as usual, since we want to inherit from `MonoBehaviour`:

```
using UnityEngine;
using System.Collections;
```

15. The name of the class is the same as the name we gave the C# script file and inherits from `MonoBehaviour`, so we can attach it to a game object in the Unity Editor:

```
public class DestroyTargetLocation: MonoBehaviour
{
```

16. We create an `OnCollisionEnter` method with the parameters of `Collision col`:

```
void OnCollisionEnter (Collision col)
{
```

17. We will do a simple `if` check to see if what we are colliding with is the `targetLocation` object via the object's tag name:

```
if(col.gameObject.tag == "targetLocation")
{
```

18. If the simple `if` check returns true, then we will destroy the `targetLocation` object:

```
Destroy(col.gameObject);
}
}
}
```

We have everything we need to finalize the project.

Finalizing the project

We will now finalize our project:

1. Navigate back to the Unity Editor, attach the `targetLocation` script to the player object, and set the object to be the `targetLocation` object:

2. Attach the `DestroyTargetLocation` script to our object called `LocationBasedGame`:

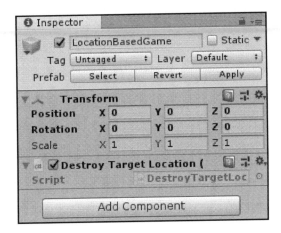

3. Now we can click on **File** | **Build**:

4. Set the project type for **Android**:

5. Make sure the only scene added for building is the `Chapter6` scene. If the scenes list is empty, click on **Add Current Scene**:

6. Now, build the project and install it on your Android device to run the program.

Summary

In this chapter, we conceptualized and created a fitness application prototype that encourages walking to different locations for the user's enjoyment. We learned about Mapbox and what it does, and we learned how to integrate it into Unity. We then leveraged Mapbox to create a viewable AR map that is able to use geolocation technology to track the user's position and destination.

In the next chapter, we will go over creating an application/game that facilitates learning for children by creating a picture puzzle.

16
Snap it! Adding Filters to Pictures

In this chapter, we will create an application that will allow us to add an overlay over a person's head. If this application sounds familiar, that is because there are many applications that are on the market that do just this, and today, you will learn how to do so as well.

In this chapter, you will learn about the following:

- OpenCV
- Setting up OpenCV
- Incorporating OpenCV into Unity
- Creating a prototype project using OpenCV and Unity

Project overview

This project makes heavy use of facial recognition-and-detection algorithms, which requires knowledge of OpenCV.

Build time: two hours

Getting started

In this section, we will cover a few things that you will need and some optional items for more in depth building from source requirements.

- OpenCV 3.4.1, which you can find at `https://opencv.org/releases.html`, is the library itself in pure source form or in library form. If you want the Unity specific plugin, you can purchase it from `https://assetstore.unity.com/packages/tools/integration/opencv-for-unity-21088`, along with the sister library file at `https://enoxsoftware.com/dlibfacelandmarkdetector/`.
- Unity 2018 can be download from `https://store.unity.com/`.
- Visual Studio, a requirement for writing or compiling source code, can be downloaded from `https://visualstudio.microsoft.com/downloads/`.
- CMake, which you can download from `https://CMake.org/download/`, is required when building your own version of the library, the plugin, and the source for OpenCV.
- Python, which is a requirement if you need to build your own library for OpenCV, can be downloaded from `https://www.python.org/getit/`.

What is OpenCV?

OpenCV stands for **Open Computer Vision**. OpenCV is an open source computer vision and machine learning software library that was built with C++ and has C++, Python, Java, and Matlab interfaces to support Windows, Linux, Android, and macOS.

OpenCV mainly focuses on real-time vision applications, although it can be used for machine learning very nicely. The library has many optimized algorithms and functions to compose or support such algorithms for state-of-the-art computer vision and machine learning, with roughly 2,500. To break down the ratio here, there are roughly 500 algorithms, and the rest are functions to compose or support these algorithms.

Talking about algorithms is fun and all, but I'm sure you are more interested in knowing what these algorithms are capable of doing. The algorithms are designed to be used to detect faces, recognize faces, identify objects, detect and classify human actions in video feeds, track camera movements, move object tracking, extraction of 3D models from objects, produce point clouds from stereo cameras in 3D, stitch images together for high resolution images, quickly find the same or similar images from an image database, red-eye removal, eye tracking, detect scenery, and establish markers for augmented reality overlay, and so much more.

OpenCV can work with TensorFlow, Caffe, Torch, Yolo, Vuforia, ARCore, and ARKit with ease. OpenCV can be used for **Augmented Reality (AR)**, **Virtual Reality (VR)**, and **Mixed Reality (MR)**. You can use visual scripting options, such as PlayMaker, and have access to all methods available in OpenCV. OpenCV also works with tons of different hardware, such as HoloLens, Oculus Rift, Telepathy, Kinect, and Raspberry Pi, to name a few.

We have two different options for gaining access to OpenCV. The first one is to build from source and create our own wrappers to create a Unity plugin for OpenCV. The second option is to purchase OpenCV for Unity from the Unity Asset Store.

If you want to go the easy route and purchase the Unity extension, it will cost 70 dollars, unless you have a Unity Plus/Pro membership, which will decrease the cost to 56 dollars. The good news is that it supports Unity Version 5.6 or greater and is based on OpenCV 3.4.1.

There are sample assets packs that you can download from the Unity Asset Store or from GitHub that will give you prebuilt examples for working with HoloLens Face Detection Overlay, FaceLandmark Detection, Facemasking, Real-time Face Recognition, Markerless AR. Face Swapping, Kinect with OpenCV, Facetracking, working with Vuforia and OpenCV, and marker-based AR.

Now, the other option, in other words, the cheap route, because, let's be honest, the Unity plugin is rather pricey, especially for younger developers or those who just want to try out OpenCV to see whether it is a good fit, is to build from source. What benefits do we gain from build from source, besides the low cost?

We get to decide which aspects of the library we need, for one. This is a huge bonus, as we can remove bloat to reduce the file and compile size. However, even when doing this, you can have the same features, or even more than the Unity plugin, since you are building from source.

The downside is that there are many things you need to get the full compilation of the source taken care of, which is dependent on whether you want to use prebuilt binaries or building your own library from scratch.

To build from scratch, you will need Visual Studio with C++ modules installed, CMake, Python Version 2.7 or later, Numpy, **Intel Threading Building Blocks (TBB)**, **Intel Integrated Performance Primitives (IPP)**, Intel IPP Asynchronous C/C++, Eigen, CUDA Toolkit, OpenEXR, OpenNI Framework, and Doxygen.

Creating the project with paid assets

In this section, we will use the Unity asset files, as they are a bit shorter to set up. The Dlib FaceLandmark Detector costs 40 dollars, and OpenCV for Unity costs 70 dollars. That means to build this project, you will need to have spent 110 dollars. Sadly, there are no free alternatives in the Unity Asset store, and if you want to build the project without purchasing the assets, you will need to build the wrappers and implementations on your own. Now, follow these steps:

1. Create a brand new Unity Project. I will call mine `Snap`:

2. Make sure your `Assets` directory is completely empty:

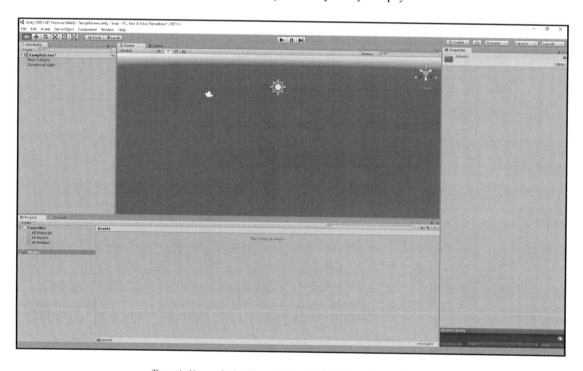

The text in this screenshot is not important. It indicates that the Assets directory is empty.

3. We will start by importing OpenCV into Unity. This will take some time to complete:

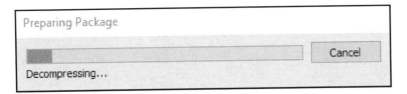

4. You will have many examples that include some very nice shaders that can be used in other projects, so import everything:

5. Your `Assets` directory should have an `OpenCVForUnity` and a `Realistic_Water_Fountain` folder:

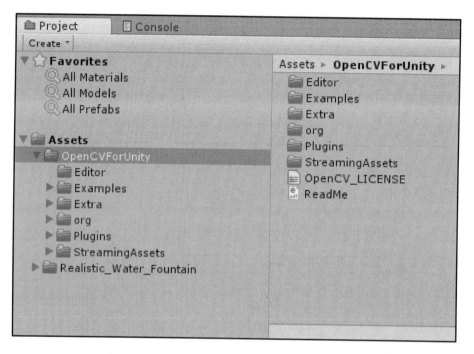

6. Now, we will need to import the Dlib Facelandmark Detector.
7. The last asset we will need is the **FaceMask Example**. Click on this link: `https://assetstore.unity.com/packages/templates/tutorials/facemask-example-79999`.
8. This package contains some additional scripts, as well as some examples of how to apply face masking to the camera, to be able to record videos or take a picture.
9. Use the **FaceMask Example** scene, and this will create our basic prototype.

We now have a working prototype for Snap it. You can add more features such as different items to cover the face, cover only a small portion of the head, add shader effects to the scene, and so much more to create your own feature-rich AR application based on OpenCV and the Dlib Facelandmark Detector.

Installing and building OpenCV

Now, what if you don't have the funds to build this project with paid assets that would make your life easier? Well, the option is to build from scratch. It is much more involved and is generally a rabbit hole that more experienced developers tend to go down than beginners.

This isn't to say that beginners can't follow along and build from scratch themselves; in fact, I suggest that if you are a beginner, follow along, as there are many new things to learn from this exercise, from dealing with other people's source files, to incorporating them into your own projects with an understanding of that code base.

To get OpenCV set up to run with Unity, we have a few steps we need to go through. We need to download OpenCV and CMake. OpenCV is the library we will be heavily utilizing, and CMake is the software that allows us to manage the build process in any given operating system and compiler with independence in mind.

Downloading OpenCV

Let's get started by first downloading OpenCV. We could go down the route of getting the pure source files or by getting the prebuilt binaries, both of which have their own pros and cons associated with them. For example, the pure source files version would require us to have every library used within OpenCV and language associated installed and configured to be able to build our own binaries. We will simplify the process just a hair, by going with the prebuilt binaries approach. Follow these steps:

1. To get started with building OpenCV from prebuilt binaries, we first need to download the files we need. There are two possibilities for this, `https://opencv.org/opencv-3-3.html` or `https://sourceforge.net/projects/opencvlibrary/`:

2. We need to choose the installation version we want; in this case, I am going to go with the latest version, which is 3.4.1, as it is the same as the Unity extension version:

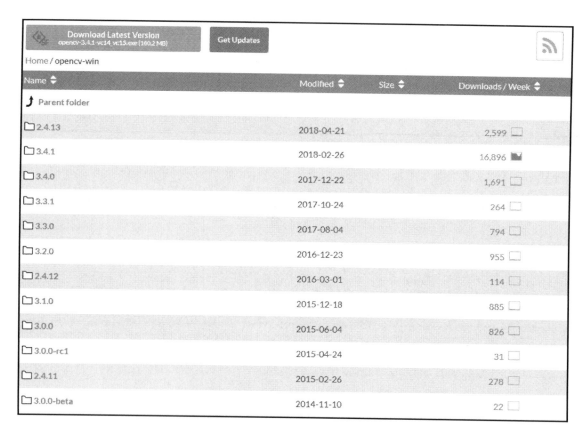

3. The executable file is 172 MB in size, so, depending on your internet connection speeds, you could have a long download time:

4. Create a new folder to house the extracted OpenCV files:

5. Now, we have our OpenCV self-extracting file:

6. Right-click on the installer file, and select **Run as administrator**. We need to have elevated privileges to make sure the project extracts correctly:

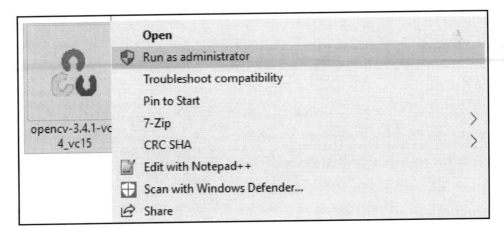

7. Select the folder you created as the installation location:

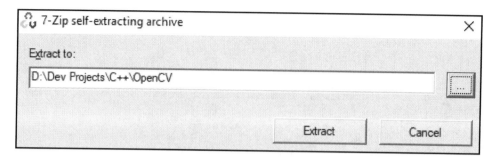

8. Extracting the files should not take long:

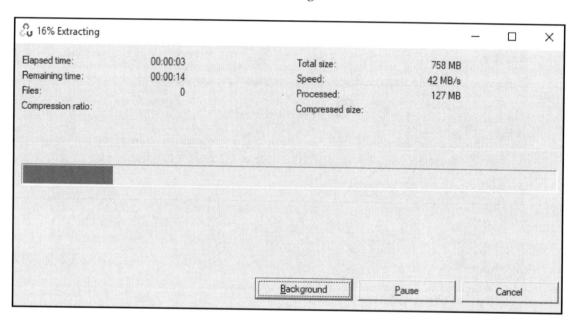

9. Now, we have extracted OpenCV.

Downloading CMake

Now that OpenCV has been download, it is time to do the same for CMake, as both of these files are integral to continuing properly.

This is only the case if you decided to go with the source direction instead of the binaries method, so I will touch on these steps a little as well.

Downloading CMake is a rather quick and painless process, regardless of whether you are using Linux, macOS, or Windows. Since I want to build with Windows, I will showcase the steps with that particular OS in mind.

1. Go to `CMake.org`; click on download latest, and scroll down to latest release to download CMake:

 CMake   About ∨   Resources ∨   Developer Resources ∨   Download   🔍

Latest Release (3.11.4)

The release was packaged with CPack which is included as part of the release. The .sh files are self extracting gziped tar files. To install a .sh file, run it with /bin/sh and follow the directions. The OS-machine.tar.gz files are gziped tar files of the install tree. The OS-machine.tar.Z files are compressed tar files of the install tree. The tar file distributions can be untared in any directory. They are prefixed by the version of CMake. For example, the Linux-x86_64 tar file is all under the directory cmake-Linux-x86_64. This prefix can be removed as long as the share, bin, man and doc directories are moved relative to each other. To build the source distributions, unpack them with zip or tar and follow the instructions in Readme.txt at the top of the source tree. See also the CMake 3.11 Release Notes. Source distributions:

Platform	Files
Unix/Linux Source (has \n line feeds)	cmake-3.11.4.tar.gz
	cmake-3.11.4.tar.Z
Windows Source (has \r\n line feeds)	cmake-3.11.4.zip

Binary distributions:

Platform	Files
Windows win64-x64 Installer: **Installer tool has changed. Uninstall CMake 3.4 or lower first!**	cmake-3.11.4-win64-x64.msi
Windows win64-x64 ZIP	cmake-3.11.4-win64-x64.zip
Windows win32-x86 Installer: **Installer tool has changed. Uninstall CMake 3.4 or lower first!**	cmake-3.11.4-win32-x86.msi
Windows win32-x86 ZIP	cmake-3.11.4-win32-x86.zip
Mac OS X 10.7 or later	cmake-3.11.4-Darwin-x86_64.dmg
	cmake-3.11.4-Darwin-x86_64.tar.gz
Linux x86_64	cmake-3.11.4-Linux-x86_64.sh
	cmake-3.11.4-Linux-x86_64.tar.gz

Download verification:

Role	Files
Cryptographic Hashes	cmake-3.11.4-SHA-256.txt
	cmake-3.11.4-SHA-256.txt.asc

---

2. Double-click on CMake to run the setup wizard:

3. Put a check mark in the *License Agreement* block and click **Next**:

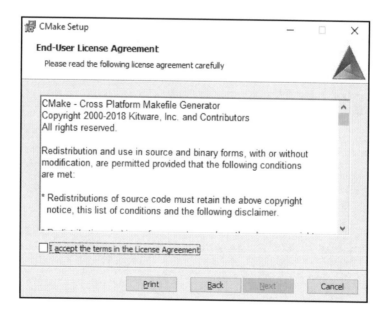

4. Make sure to **Add CMake to the system PATH for current or all users**, depending on your preference. Just make sure that it is set to the system path before clicking **Next:**

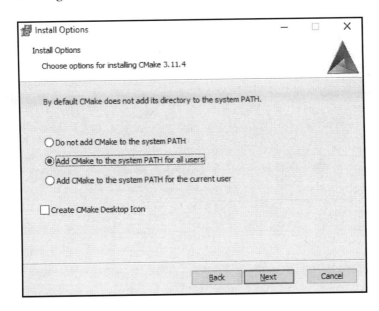

5. Click **Next** to install CMake to whatever folder you want:

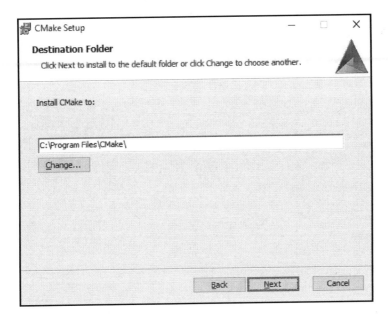

6. To install CMake, it requires elevated privilges, so if you have UAC enabled and don't have admin rights, make sure you have someone nearby that can give you access to install:

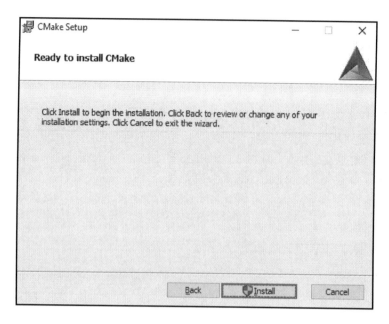

7. Installation will take a few minutes to complete:

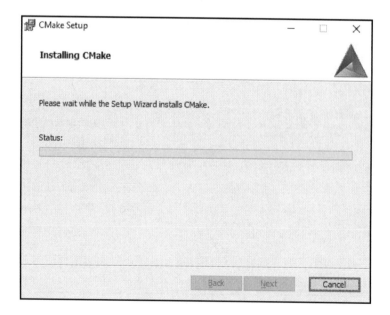

8. Click **Finish** to complete the installation process:

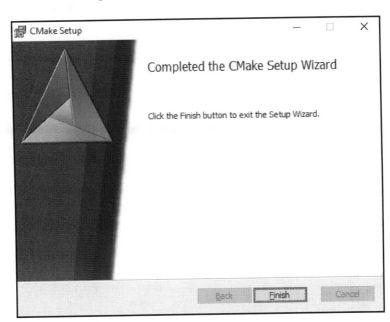

Configuring the CMake and OpenCV source files

Now, we can move on to configuring CMake and getting everything set up to build OpenCV as a library to utilize within Unity. Now, to do this, you need the full-on source code of OpenCV, instead of the binaries, which you can grab from `https://github.com/opencv/opencv/archive/3.3.0.zip`. or `https://github.com/opencv/opencv/archive/3.3.0.zip`.

Start *CMake* (`CMake-gui`). You may again enter it in the start menu search or get it from **All Programs** | **CMake 2.8** | **CMake** (`CMake-gui`). First, select the directory for the source files of the OpenCV library (1). Then, specify a directory where you will build the binary files for OpenCV library (2).

Press the **Configure** button to specify the compiler (and the IDE) you want to use. Note that you can choose between different compilers for making either 64 bit or 32 bit libraries. Select the one you use in your application development.

CMake will start based on your system variables and will try to automatically locate as many packages as possible. You can modify the packages to use for the build in the *WITH* ▸ *WITH_X* menu points (where *X* is the package abbreviation).

Select all the packages you want to use, and again press the **Configure** button. For an easier overview of the build options, make sure the **Grouped** option under the binary directory selection is turned on. For some of the packages, CMake may not find all of the required files or directories. If it doesn't find all of them, CMake will throw an error in its output window (located at the bottom of the GUI) and set its field values to not-found constants.

Press the **Configure** button again and ensure that no errors are reported. CMake will create the project files by pushing the **Generate** button. Go to the build directory and open the created OpenCV solution. Depending on just how many options you have selected, the solution may contain quite a lot of projects, so be tolerant on the IDE at the startup. Now, you need to build both the **Release** and the **Debug** binaries. Use the drop-down menu on your IDE to change to another of these after building for one of them.

In the end, you can observe the built binary files inside the bin directory.

To collect the header and the binary files, which you will use during your own projects, into a separate directory (similarly to how the pre-built binaries ship), you need to explicitly build the **Install** project.

To test your build, just go into the Build/bin/Debug or the Build/bin/Release directory and start a couple of applications, such as contours.exe. If they run, you are done.

For more in-depth information on this, go to https://docs.opencv.org/3.0-beta/doc/tutorials/introduction/windows_install/windows_install.html. The OpenCV documentation will go into this in more detail, along with the other tools you will need to install to go down this route.

OpenCV with Unity

We can now move on to importing our dlls into Unity and writing our wrapper classes to handle interfacing with OpenCV and Unity. That way, we can then create our scripts to build our project:

1. Create a folder. I will call mine ConfigureOpenCV:

2. We need to create a new empty C++ project in Visual Studio. I will call mine
   `ConfigureOpenCV`, with the location being set in the `ConfigureOpenCV` folder:

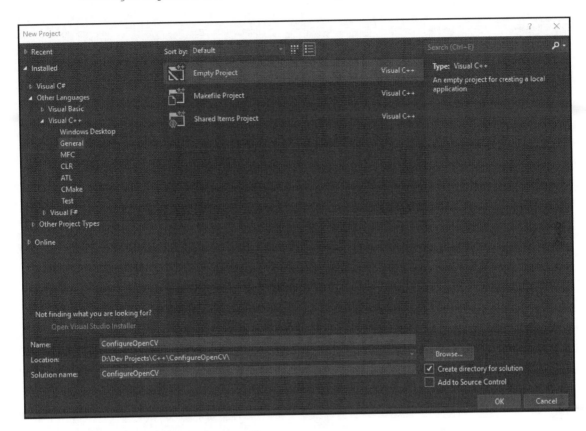

3. Set the platform to be **x64** in Visual Studio:

4. Right-click on the project properties file and select **Properties**:

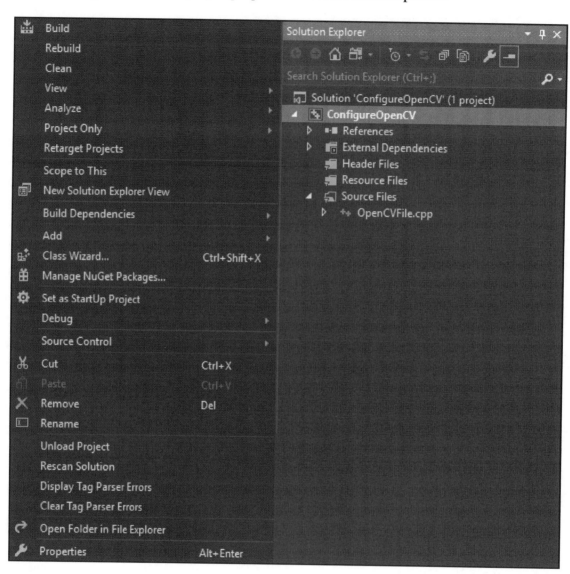

5. This will open our properties window:

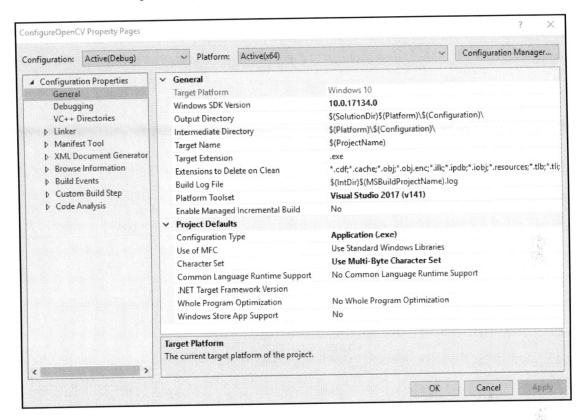

6. The first thing we need to do is change **Target Extension** in the **General** tab from
   .exe to .dll:

7. We need to change the **Configuration Type** from **Application (.exe)** to **Dynamic Library (.dll)**:

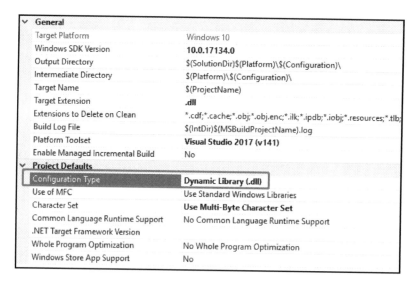

8. Over in **VC++ Directories**, add our `OPENCV_DIRs` to include it in **Include Directories**:

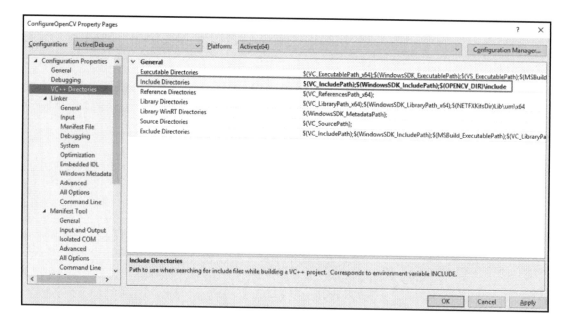

9. Over in Linker's **General** Tab, add `$(OPENCV_DIR)\lib\Debug` to the **Additional Library Directories** option:

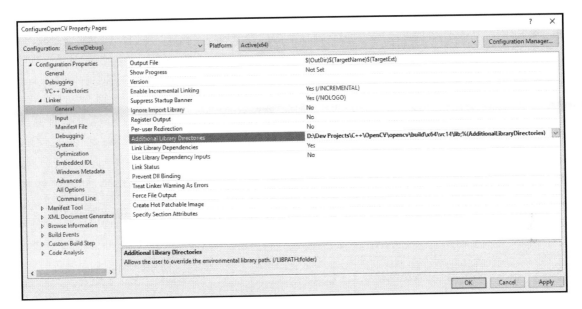

10. Finally, in the Linker's **Input** tab, we need to add a few items to the **Additional Dependencies** option. Those items will be the following:

- `opencv_core310.lib` (or `opencv_world330.lib`, depending on your OpenCV version)
- `opencv_highgui310.lib`
- `opencv_objdetect310.lib`
- `opencv_videoio310.lib`
- `opencv_imgproc310.lib`

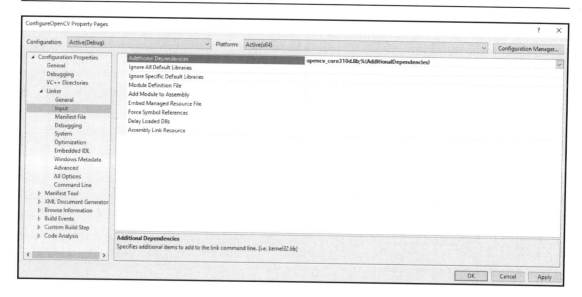

Figure shows the location of Additional Dependencies in the Linker's Input tab with opencv_core added.

11. Now, we can create a new CPP file:

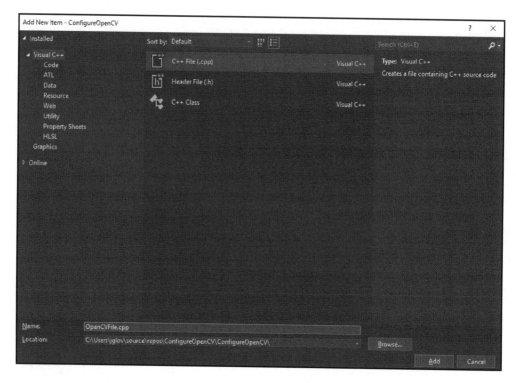

We will now incorporate the headers and namespaces we absolutely need here:

```
#include "opencv2/objdetect.hpp"
#include "opencv2/highgui.hpp"
#include "opencv2/imgproc.hpp"
#include <iostream>
#include <stdio.h>
using namespace std;
using namespace cv;
```

1. Declare a `struct` that will be used to pass data from C++ to Mono:

```
struct Circle
{
Circle(int x, int y, int radius) : X(x), Y(y), Radius(radius) {}
int X, Y, Radius;
};
```

2. `CascadeClassifer` is a class used for object detection:

```
CascadeClassifier _faceCascade;
```

3. Create a string that will serve as the name of the window:

```
String _windowName = "OpenCV";
```

4. Video Capture is a class used to open a video file, or capture a device or an IP video stream for video capture:

```
VideoCapture _capture;
```

5. Create an integer value to store the scale:

```
int _scale = 1;
```

6. `extern "C"`, as a refresher, will avoid name mangling from C++. Our first method is `Init` for initialization:

```
extern "C" int __declspec(dllexport) __stdcall  Init(int&
outCameraWidth, int& outCameraHeight)
{
```

7. We will create an `if` statement to load the LBP face `cascade.xml` file that is part of `CVFeatureParams`; if it cannot load, then it will exit with a return code of −1:

```
if (!_faceCascade.load("lbpcascade_frontalface.xml"))
return -1;
```

8. Now, we will open the video capture stream:

```
_capture.open(0);
```

9. If the video stream is not opened, then we will exit with a return code of −2:

```
if (!_capture.isOpened())
return -2;
```

10. We will set the camera width:

```
outCameraWidth = _capture.get(CAP_PROP_FRAME_WIDTH);
```

11. And we also need to set the camera height:

```
outCameraHeight = _capture.get(CAP_PROP_FRAME_HEIGHT);
return 0;
}
```

12. Now, we need to make sure that we create a method to close the capture stream and release the video capture device:

```
extern "C" void __declspec(dllexport) __stdcall  Close()
{
_capture.release();
}
```

13. The next step is to create a method that sets the video scale:

```
extern "C" void __declspec(dllexport) __stdcall SetScale(int scale)
{
_scale = scale;
}
```

14. Next up, we will create a method that allows us to detect an object:

```
extern "C" void __declspec(dllexport) __stdcall Detect(Circle*
outFaces, int maxOutFacesCount, int& outDetectedFacesCount)
{
Mat frame;
_capture >> frame;
```

15. Next up, if the frame is empty, we need to guard against possible errors from this by exiting from the method:

```
if (frame.empty())
return;
```

16. Create a vector called `faces`:

    ```
    std::vector<Rect> faces;
    ```

17. We will create **Mat**, which is one of the various constructors that forms a matrix with the name of `grayscaleFrame`:

    ```
    Mat grayscaleFrame;
    ```

18. We then need to convert the frame to grayscale from RGB colorspace for proper cascade detection:

    ```
    cvtColor(frame, grayscaleFrame, COLOR_BGR2GRAY);
    Mat resizedGray;
    ```

19. The next step is to scale down for better performance:

    ```
    resize(grayscaleFrame, resizedGray, Size(frame.cols / _scale,
    frame.rows / _scale));
    equalizeHist(resizedGray, resizedGray);
    ```

20. Next up, we will detect the `faces`:

    ```
    _faceCascade.detectMultiScale(resizedGray, faces);
    ```

21. We will now create a for loop to draw the faces:

    ```
    for (size_t i = 0; i < faces.size(); i++)
    {
    Point center(_scale * (faces[i].x + faces[i].width / 2), _scale *
    (faces[i].y + faces[i].height / 2));
    ellipse(frame, center, Size(_scale * faces[i].width / 2, _scale *
    faces[i].height / 2), 0, 0, 360, Scalar(0, 0, 255), 4, 8, 0);
    ```

22. Now, we will send this information to the application:

    ```
    outFaces[i] = Circle(faces[i].x, faces[i].y, faces[i].width / 2);
    outDetectedFacesCount++;
    ```

23. Since we have a matrix, we need to make sure that we don't exceed the limits of the array. To do this, we will break if the faces count is equal to the max amount of faces count we have allocated; if it is, exit from the loop:

    ```
    if (outDetectedFacesCount == maxOutFacesCount)
    break;
    }
    ```

24. The last thing we need to do is display the debug output:

```
imshow(_windowName, frame);
```

25. Now, build the `dll` file, and we can now begin to work in Unity.

OpenCV and Unity

Now, we can finally start working in Unity in this section. This is the easier part, where we just need to create our wrapper and our `MonoBehaviour` script to attach to an object.

Navigate to the `dll` file that we created. This should be in the **x64 | Debug** folder of the source project:

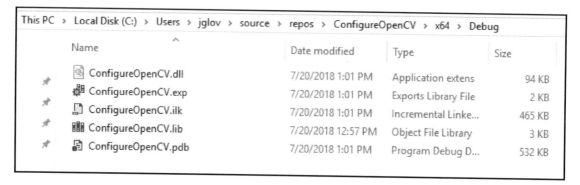

Create two folder called `Plugins` and `Scripts` in Unity, just as we did in `Chapter3`.

Now, we will create two scripts. One for our `Wrapper` class, and the other for our `MonoBehaviour`. The `Wrapper` class will be called `OpenCVWrapper`, and the `MonoBehaviour` class will be called `OpenCVFaceDetection`.

Open the `OpenCVWrapper` class in Visual Studio. It is time to write some more code.

We only need to use the `InteropServices` namespace for this class:

```
using System.Runtime.InteropServices;
```

We will create an `internal static class` this time around:

```
internal static class OpenCVWrapper
{
```

We will import the `Init` function that we created in the last step, and we need to make sure that we reference the parameters. The `ref` keyword is very similar to the `&` keyword in C++:

```
[DllImport("UnityOpenCVSample")]
internal static extern int Init(ref int outCameraWidth, ref int
outCameraHeight);
```

We will import the `Close` function, which closes the connection and will avoid memory leaks when we use the functions that we've created:

```
[DllImport("UnityOpenCVSample")]
internal static extern int Close();
```

We will import the `SetScale` function we created, along with keeping the parameters that we required in C++:

```
[DllImport("UnityOpenCVSample")]
internal static extern int SetScale(int downscale);
```

We will import the `Detect` function, and this one is a bit different, as we are actually using a pointer; this will be very important very soon, as this deals with unsafe code in C# and Unity. If you aren't familiar, the `*` keyword denotes a pointer, which is the address of the object in memory:

```
[DllImport("UnityOpenCVSample")]
internal unsafe static extern void Detect(CvCircle* outFaces, int
maxOutFacesCount, ref int outDetectedFacesCount);
}
```

Lastly, we will create a structure that needs to be sequential and with the correct byte size (3 ints = 4 bytes * 3 = 12 bytes) for CvCircle:

```
[StructLayout(LayoutKind.Sequential, Size = 12)]
public struct CvCircle
{
public int X, Y, Radius;
}
```

This takes care of the wrapper class, and we can now move over to our `MonoBehaviour` class.

We need a few namespaces, as they will be fully utilized in this script:

```
using UnityEngine;
using System.Collections;
using System.Collections.Generic;
```

We have our class named the same as the file in the Unity Editor and inherit from `MonoBehaviour`:

```
public class OpenCVFaceDetection : MonoBehaviour
{
```

The main thing to notice here is that I have a reference to the camera and a `WebCamTexture`. This is because we will feed the data from the webcam to the camera:

```
public Camera camera;
public static List<Vector2> NormalizedFacePositions { get; private set; }
public static Vector2 CameraResolution;
private const int DetectionDownScale = 1;
private bool _ready;
private int _maxFaceDetectCount = 5;
private CvCircle[] _faces;
private Quaternion baseRotation;
private WebCamTexture webCamTexture;
```

In this `Start` method, we get everything set up and running. We also check to make sure that the `cascades.xml` file is able to be found (more on that in the next section):

```
void Start()
{
int camWidth = 0, camHeight = 0;
webCamTexture = new WebCamTexture();
Renderer renderer = GetComponent<Renderer>();
renderer.material.mainTexture = webCamTexture;
baseRotation = transform.rotation;
webCamTexture.Play();
camWidth = webCamTexture.width;
camHeight = webCamTexture.height;
int result = OpenCVWrapper.Init(ref camWidth, ref camHeight);
if (result < 0)
{
if (result == -1)
{
Debug.LogWarningFormat("[{0}] Failed to find cascades definition.",
GetType());
}
else if (result == -2)
{
Debug.LogWarningFormat("[{0}] Failed to open camera stream.", GetType());
}
return;
}
CameraResolution = new Vector2(camWidth, camHeight);
_faces = new CvCircle[_maxFaceDetectCount];
```

```
NormalizedFacePositions = new List<Vector2>();
OpenCVWrapper.SetScale(DetectionDownScale);
_ready = true;
}
```

This method will make sure that the connections are closed to the webcam. This will free up the resources and make sure that we don't leak any memory:

```
void OnApplicationQuit()
{
if (_ready)
{
OpenCVWrapper.Close();
}
}
```

This Update method makes sure that the orientation of the webcam is corrected, checks whether the camera is read or not, and actively tracks for face detection:

```
void Update()
{
if (!_ready)
{
return;
}
transform.rotation = baseRotation *
Quaternion.AngleAxis(webCamTexture.videoRotationAngle, Vector3.up);

int detectedFaceCount = 0;
unsafe
{
fixed (CvCircle* outFaces = _faces)
{
OpenCVWrapper.Detect(outFaces, _maxFaceDetectCount, ref
detectedFaceCount);
}
}

NormalizedFacePositions.Clear();
for (int i = 0; i < detectedFaceCount; i++)
{
NormalizedFacePositions.Add(new Vector2((_faces[i].X * DetectionDownScale)
/ CameraResolution.x, 1f - ((_faces[i].Y * DetectionDownScale) /
CameraResolution.y)));
}
}
}
```

Save the script and go back to the Unity Editor. You will immediately notice that Unity will show an error along the lines of *unsafe code needs to be allowed*. Let's go ahead and enable this feature. To do this, go to your **Player Settings**, which is located inside the **Build Settings.**

Inside the **Player Settings**, look down at the configuration inside **Other Settings**, and there is a checkbox called **Allow 'unsafe' Code**. Make sure that it is checked:

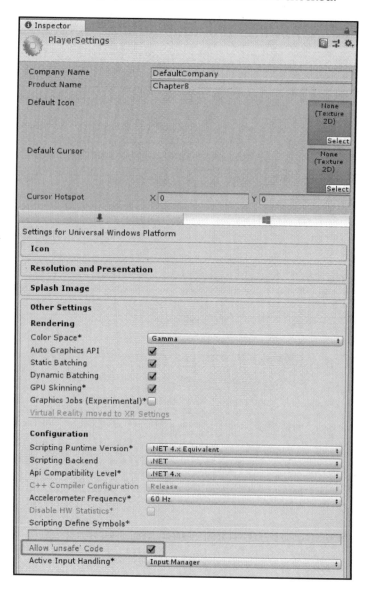

In the `Scripts` folder, you need one more file to be added; in my example file that you can download, I have quite a few more `.xml` files than what I am going to tell you to add. The reason for this is to allow you to play around with the different `.xml` files to see their results. You will have to update the C++ plugin to account for the proper `.xml` file you want to use; alternatively, you can update the `Init` function to take a string parameter to be able to change the `.xml` file in the Unity Editor.

In your `OpenCV` folder, navigate to `OpenCV\opencv\build\etc\lbpcascades`:

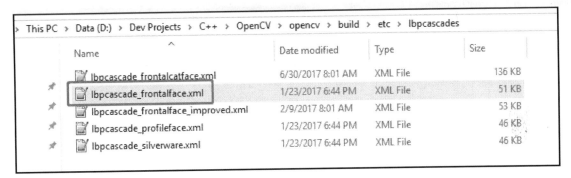

You want to copy `lbpcascade_frontalface.xml` into the scripts folder in Unity. (My project has everything in an XML folder, as I have many more `.xml` files to play with.)

Finally, we just need to create a plane to face the camera.

The last step is to attach the `OpenCVFaceDetection` script to the plane.

Now, the project will compile and run appropriately (if you get a dll import error, make sure you have the dll set to **x86-x64** and that the project is built for **Windows**):

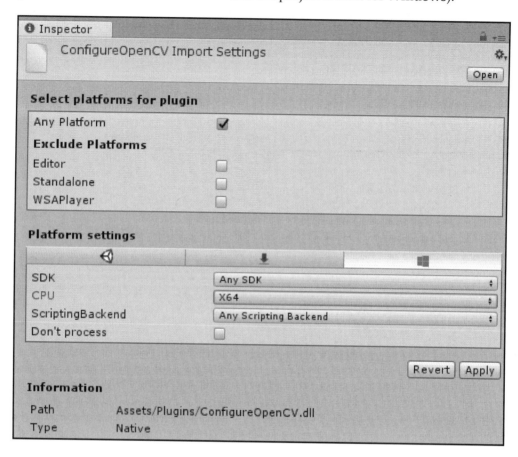

Summary

In this chapter, we learned how to use CMake to build OpenCV from source, to import it into Unity, and create an AR application similar to many on the market that are able to add images over a person's face and track their movements reliably, by using OpenCV and DLib FaceLandmark Detector, using Dlib C++Library.

In the next chapter, we will look into building for MR devices such as HoloLens. As a short teaser, MR incorporates elements from AR and VR into a single game or application, which can prove to have massive and interesting effects.

17
To the HoloLens and Beyond

In this chapter, we will look into how we can work with HoloLens to understand how to make **Mixed Reality** games and apps. The main focus will be to code with the HoloLens device in mind but be able to use the simulator for both the HoloLens and the Mixed Reality viewer. This will allow us to be able to test and view what is happening, regardless of whether we have the actual HoloLens device.

The learning objectives of this chapter are as follows:

- Learning what Mixed Reality is
- Understanding how Mixed Reality works
- Implementing a basic Mixed Reality prototype

What is Mixed Reality, and how does it work?

Mixed Reality is known as **MR** or **XR (extended reality)** and can refer to Augmented Reality, Virtual Reality, a combination of AR and VR into a single application or game, or it can be a reference to the game world being driven and modified by the real world. There are many ways to incorporate aspects of both **Augmented Reality (AR)** and **Virtual Reality (VR)** and by extension XR into a single application or a game.

It should be noted that Microsoft exclusively uses the MR for Mixed Reality; however, the terms XR and MR can be used interchangeably, with people being able to understand what you are referencing.

Let's take a look of a few notable examples of Mixed Reality games by Gbanga Millform Inc and dissect why they are Mixed Reality instead of just AR or VR games. Two games that I feel are very notable are Smart Urban Golf (`https://gbanga.com/gameography/smart-urban-golf/`) and Urban Hunt (`https://gbanga.com/gameography/gross-stadt-jagd/`).

Urban Hunt

Urban Hunt is an iOS and Android platform real-time game where players have to run and escape from a car that is hunting them throughout the city of Zurich. The game lasts anywhere from 90 minutes (one-and-a-half hours) to 150 minutes (two-and-a-half hours). The winner receives a Mercedes-Benz CLA Shooting Brake car in real life. Look at this screenshot:

The text in this image is not important. It's an image of Urban Hunt in use

The game incorporates GPS and location-based data to build the game world. The game is built to be played by everyone in the city of Zurich. The game has an AI that you the player have to run away from in real time.

Now, let's break down what is AR, VR, and MR about this game.

Right away, we can see that there are no elements of VR added to this game at all. So, we don't have to worry about that aspect of MR. It utilizes GPS, location data, and the city map of Zurich in the game. This means the game has some aspects of AR built into it by design. Moving on, it has MMO elements; this is neither AR or VR specific, but rather just massively multiplayer-online-game specific. Finally, the AI is what you the player have to run away from. This is where XR or MR comes into play. The reason for this is you don't control the character with button prompts; you are the character, and it is based on your real-life walking and running movements. This is the aspect of augmenting the game world with real-world interactions or, conversely, augmenting the real world with a game world.

Now, you might be thinking, *that last sentence is the literal definition of AR*, but let's break it down further. The game is not projecting into the real world, nor is the real world being fully projected into the game. The AI solely lives in the game world and you (the player) are simultaneously in the game world and the real world. You still have to pay full attention to the rules and the AI of the game world, in addition to the rules and struggles of real life. This is how it is Mixed Reality, instead of just Augmented Reality.

Smart Urban Golf

Smart Urban Golf is a game where you play golf using your cell phone as the club, and you hit golf balls in the game world. You can practice by playing the driving-range mode, which makes the game generate random courses based on your current position, or you can play in a live tournament mode where you compete with others for the highest score on the online leaderboards.

Look at this screenshot:

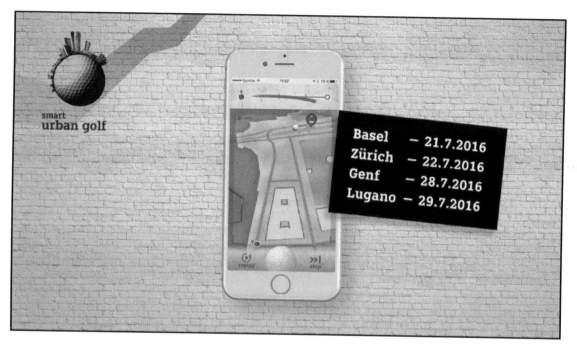

Smart Urban Golf

Breaking down the elements of the game, we can see that the golf club being the phone automatically places AR as one of the technologies being utilized. The location-based random courses means that Geolocation and GPS are being heavily utilized, which is mainly found in AR applications. Competing with others is a standard game mechanics. The ball is living in the game world only but is affected by the golf club (your cell phone), so the game is XR or MR.

XR applications in media

With these two example games being showcased, we should have a better idea of what XR or MR is. But I think we can go a bit further—what about using VR and AR together? There are certain people on YouTube who utilize the mixture of AR and VR together so the viewer can see what they see in the game as well as their body positions at the same time as using VR applications. Take a look at this:

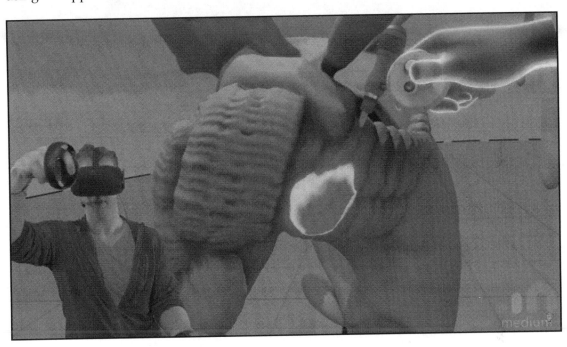

Jazza

Here we see Jazza from Draw with Jazza is sculpting a model in a VR application with Oculus Rift. We can see what he is sculpting along with him working from outside the application. This is an example of utilizing XR to enhance the viewing experience of a third party.

But let's also take a look at an XR video for gaming as well. Take a look at this:

Brometheus

Brometheus is playing a game called Nevrosa Prelude with the HTC Vive, and it is also a VR game but has AR projected to enhance the viewing experience of a third party.

XR with HoloLens

This is all well and good, but let's take one more look with a HoloLens example this time around. Take a look at this:

Minecraft

During the E3 demo of the HoloLens and Minecraft in 2015, we saw an AR projection of the game in the real world along with the person using the HoloLens in VR mode.

One last example with the HoloLens and **Windows Mixed Reality (WMR)** should suffice, as I think all of these examples combined into one really exemplify the MR or XR full experience. Let's take a look at this:

The text in this image is not important. It gives you an example of Mixed Reality with fragments

The game in this screenshot is called *Fragments*, which is an adventure-style detective game. What makes this MR or XR over pure VR is that the game will scan where you are and allow the objects and characters in the game interact with it seamlessly. As you can see from the screenshot, the character is sitting on the player's sofa.

What we have learned in this section is that XR or MR is essentially taking VR and AR elements and incorporating them into real-world environments and situations with seamless integration. This is the backbone of how we can take AR or VR to the next level for a proper Mixed Reality integration.

Getting Mixed Reality ready

The HoloLens requires your computer to meet a couple of requirements; this includes the requirements for supporting Hyper-V and being VR-ready. This is also true for utilizing the HoloLens emulator. So, what requirements do we need to meet? Take a look at the following:

- 64-bit Windows 10 Pro, Enterprise or Education editions.

 If you are using Windows 10 Home edition, it does not support Hyper-V or the HoloLens emulator.

- 64-bit CPU
- CPU with four or more cores, or multiple CPUs with a minimum total of four cores
- 8 GB of RAM or more
- GPU with support for DirectX 11.0 or later
- GPU with **WDDM (Windows Display Driver Model)**, 1.2 driver or later

We also need a bios that supports the following features, and have them enabled:

- Hardware-assisted virtualization
- **Second-Level Address Translation (SLAT)**
- **Hardware-Based Data Execution Prevention (DEP)**

Microsoft has a handy list of specifications to meet, for both laptop and desktop computers, for minimum and recommended settings. Alternatively, you can use software on the Microsoft Store to run a PC check for compatibility (`https://www.microsoft.com/en-us/p/windows-mixed-reality-pc-check/9nzvl19n7cnc`).

	Minimum	Recommended
Processor	**Notebook:** Intel Mobile Core i5 7th generation CPU, Dual-Core with Hyper Threading **Desktop:** Intel Desktop i5 6th generation CPU, Dual-Core with Hyper Threading **OR** AMD FX4350 4.2Ghz Quad-Core equivalent	**Desktop:** Intel Desktop i7 6th generation (6 Core) **OR** AMD Ryzen 5 1600 (6 Core, 12 threads)
GPU	**Notebook:** NVIDIA GTX 965M, AMD RX 460M (2GB) equivalent or greater DX12 capable GPU **Desktop:** NVIDIA GTX 960/1050, AMD Radeon RX 460 (2GB) equivalent or greater DX12 capable GPU	**Desktop:** NVIDIA GTX 980/1060, AMD Radeon RX 480 (2GB) equivalent or greater DX12 capable GPU
GPU driver WDDM version	WDDM 2.2 driver	
Thermal Design Power	15W or greater	
Graphics display ports	1x available graphics display port for headset (HDMI 1.4 or DisplayPort 1.2 for 60Hz headsets, HDMI 2.0 or DisplayPort 1.2 for 90Hz headsets)	
Display resolution	Resolution: SVGA (800x600) or greater Bit depth: 32 bits of color per pixel	
Memory	8 GB of RAM or greater	16 GB of RAM or greater
Storage	>10 GB additional free space	
USB Ports	1x available USB port for headset (USB 3.0 Type-A) **Note: USB must supply a minimum of 900mA**	
Bluetooth	Bluetooth 4.0 (for accessory connectivity)	

Microsoft specs

Hyper-V must be enabled on your system. Let's follow these steps:

1. To enable Hyper-V, go to the **Control Panel**:

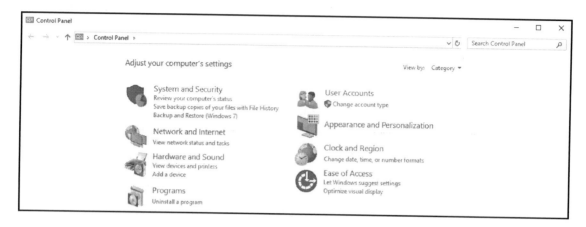

2. Select **Programs**:

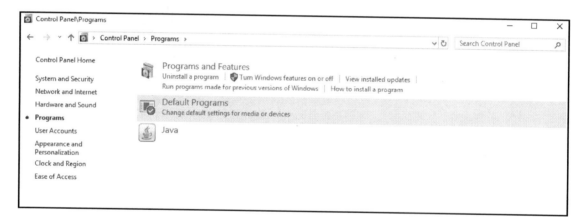

3. Select **Programs and Features**:

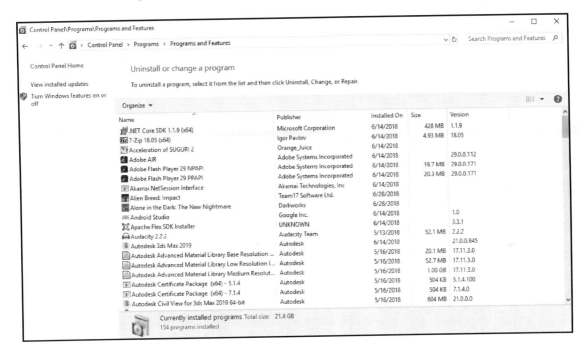

4. Select **Turn Windows features on or off**:

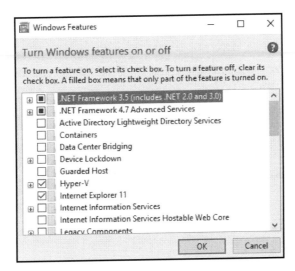

Windows features

5. Select all Hyper-V features by putting a check mark in and clicking the **OK** button:

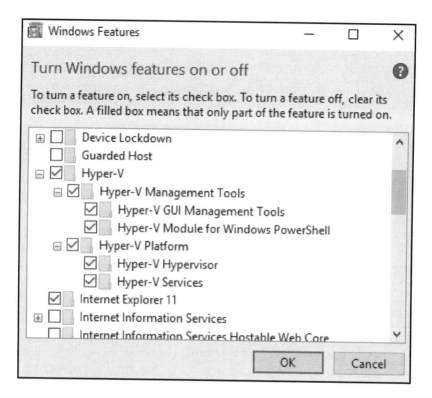

Enable Hyper-V

Next up, we need to be absolutely certain that we have Visual Studio set up in the proper manner. Follow these steps:

1. Open Visual Studio Installer from your Start menu. If you have the Visual Studio Community edition, it will work too:

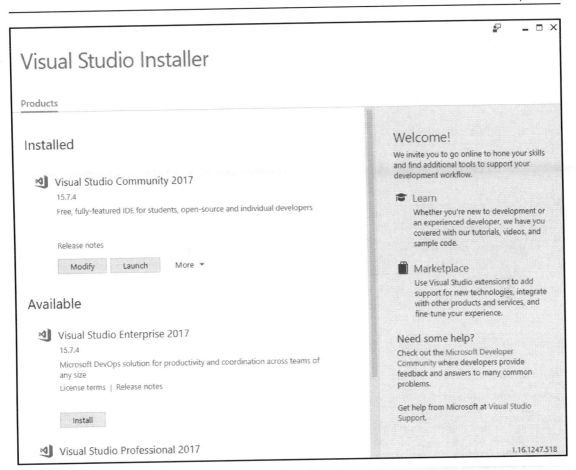

Visual Studio Installer

Products

Installed

Visual Studio Community 2017

15.7.4

Free, fully-featured IDE for students, open-source and individual developers

Release notes

Modify | Launch | More ▾

Available

Visual Studio Enterprise 2017

15.7.4

Microsoft DevOps solution for productivity and coordination across teams of any size

License terms | Release notes

Install

Visual Studio Professional 2017

Welcome!

We invite you to go online to hone your skills and find additional tools to support your development workflow.

🎓 Learn

Whether you're new to development or an experienced developer, we have you covered with our tutorials, videos, and sample code.

📖 Marketplace

Use Visual Studio extensions to add support for new technologies, integrate with other products and services, and fine-tune your experience.

Need some help?

Check out the Microsoft Developer Community where developers provide feedback and answers to many common problems.

Get help from Microsoft at Visual Studio Support.

1.16.1247.518

VS Installer

We need to make certain that we have the most up-to-date version of Visual Studio. So, if it tells you to update instead of modify, do the update first.

2. Now we need to click on **Modify** and, then, once things are ready, click on **Individual components**:

Modifying — Visual Studio Community 2017 — 15.7.4

Workloads | Individual components | Language packs | Installation locations

Individual components

3. Scroll down until you see the list of Windows 10 SDKs. We need the latest one, which is 10.0.17134.0, and also the Windows 10 SDK for UWP C#, which is version 10.0.16299.0:

Windows 10 SDK

4. The last thing we need to do, if you haven't followed any other chapter in this book, is to make sure your minimum version of Unity is 2017, although we will be using the latest version of Unity, which is 2018.1.6f1. If you don't have it, make sure to update using the Unity Hub:

Latest Version of Unity

5. We also need to make sure we have the **Windows Store .NET Scripting Backend, Windows Store IL2CPP Scripting Backend**, and **Windows IL2CPP Scripting Backend**, to make sure we can translate from Unity specific code over to Windows code effectively:

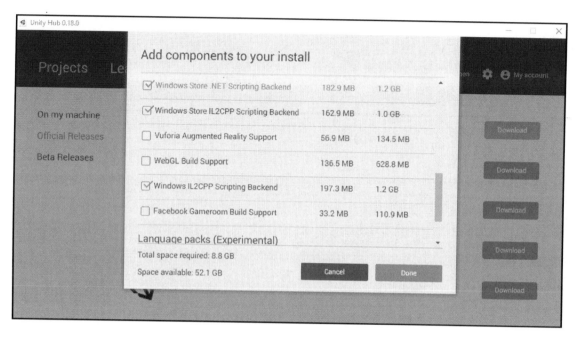

Unity Components

It will require a total of 8.8 GB in size on your hard disk.

Project overview

This project will be a basic prototype that will make sure that we can simulate a basic model can be displayed when viewed in HoloLens.

Playing with Mixed Reality

Let's begin by first downloading the model we will be using with this project. Once again, let's follow these steps:

1. Go to `turbosquid.com` and type `scifi` as the search parameters:

2. Next, change the pricing to **Free**:

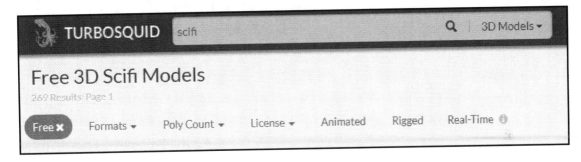

3. Find one you like. I like robots and I use FBX format, as I find it easy to use with multiple projects and game engines. So, I will select this one:

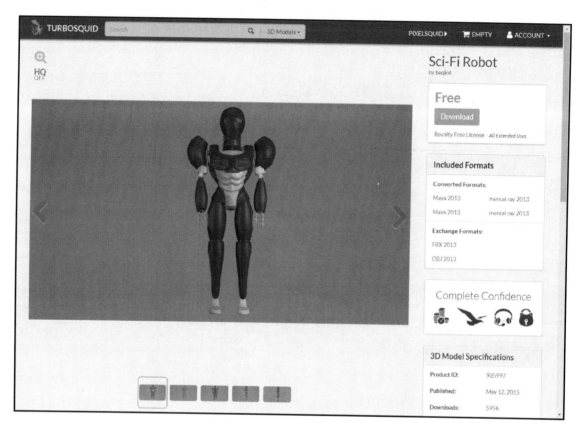

4. It will take you to a download page, so make sure you select the correct file you want and if it has a `textures` folder, download that as well:

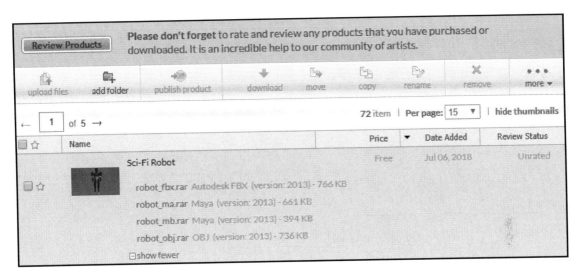

Download robot

5. Go to the folder where you downloaded the zip file and extract it:

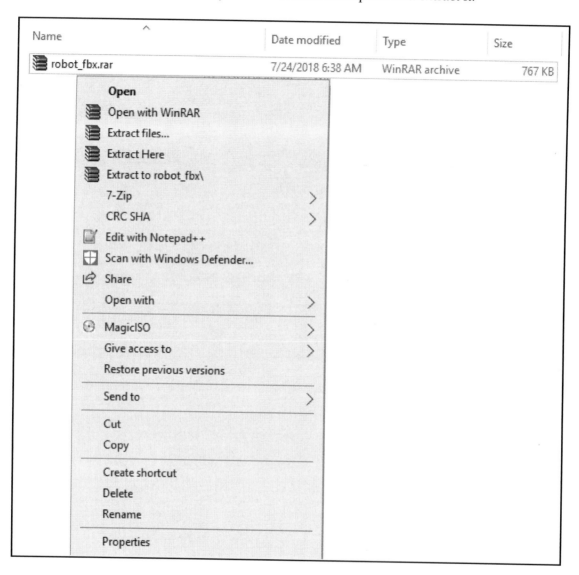

6. Now we can jump into Unity. Create a new project and I will call this one
   `Chapter8`:

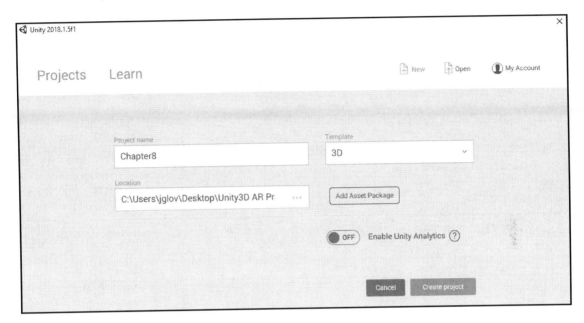

7. Create a new folder called `Models`:

8. Import the model into the project:

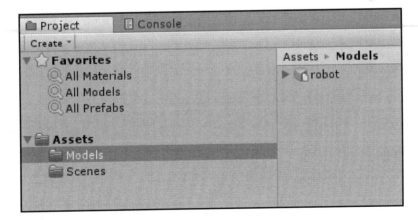

We now need to go through the steps to install the HoloLens Emulator. I should note that this will only work for Visual Studio, 2015 edition. If you have Visual Studio 2017 or later, you can use the Mixed Reality simulator that is built into the Windows 10 SDK. Let's follow the steps:

1. Go to `http://go.microsoft.com/fwlink/?LinkID=823018` to download the simulator.
2. Click on the installer to begin the installation process:

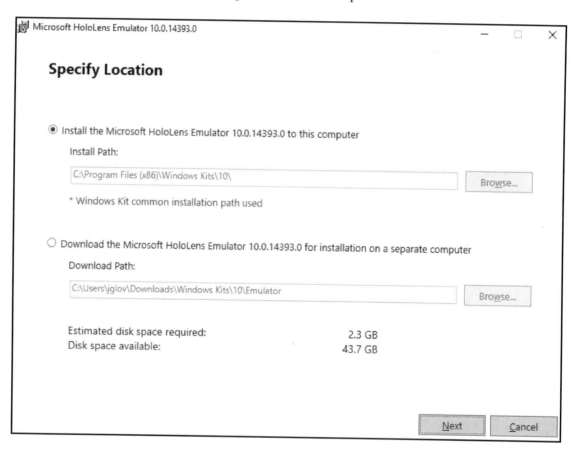

3. It will ask you if you want agree to using the CEIP program; choose your answer and click **Next**:

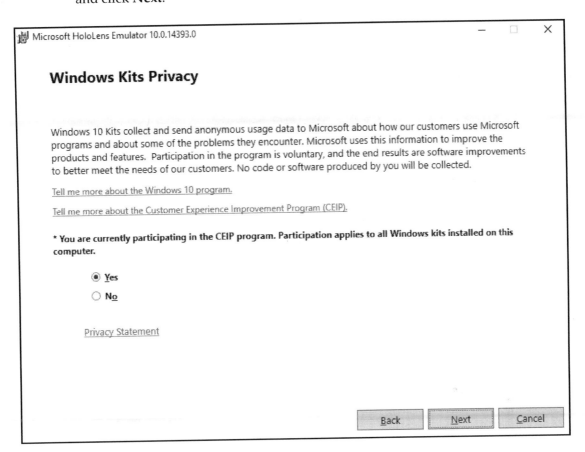

4. Next up will be the standard **Microsoft License Agreement**; I would suggest reading it to know what you are agreeing to, and then click **Accept** afterward:

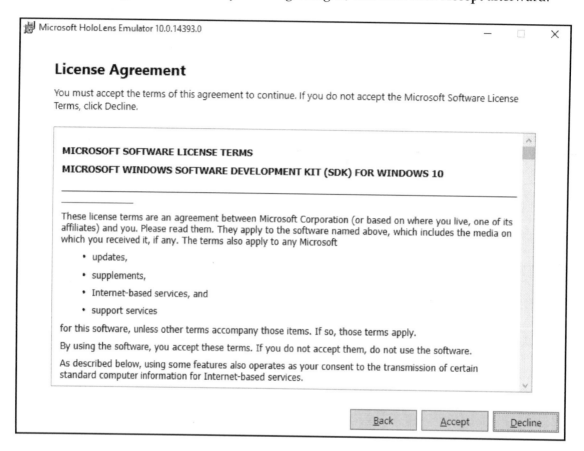

5. Select the features you want to install; I would suggest getting both the emulator and the templates for future reference. Click **Install**:

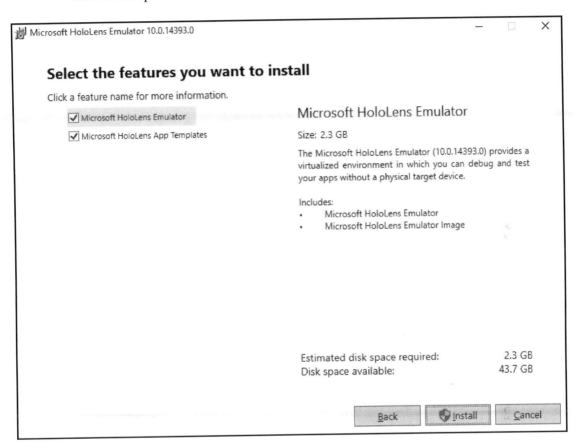

Now we can begin to set up the remaining portions of the project.

Setting up the camera

Since we or the user are using the HoloLens, we will be the first-person camera; it is important to remember that our starting position should always default to the Vector 3 values of x being 0, y being 0, and z being 0. Everything else should always be offset according to that knowledge.

1. So, the first thing to do will be to click on the camera in the **Hierarchy** pane:

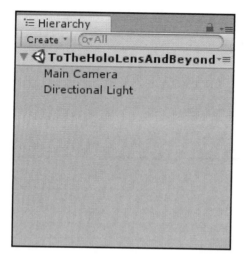

Camera selected

2. The default values for the camera are set to **X** being 0, **Y** being 1, and **Z** being
   -10:

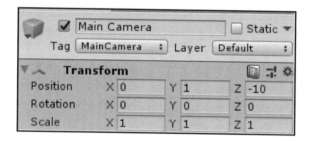

Default camera values

3. We need to change this to **X** being 0, **Y** being 0, and **Z** being 0. Look at this screenshot:

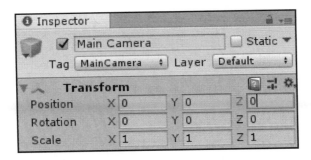

Modified camera values

4. With this being made for HoloLens, we don't need a Skybox texture; we want everything the camera renders. To do this, we need to change the **Clear Flags** from the default values.

5. The default values for the **Clear Flags** is **Skybox**:

Default Clear Flags

6. We are going to change it to **Solid Color**:

Clear Flags modified

7. Next, we need to click on the background option underneath **Clear Flags**, which will open a color-picker window and change the RGBA values set to this: 0,0,0,0:

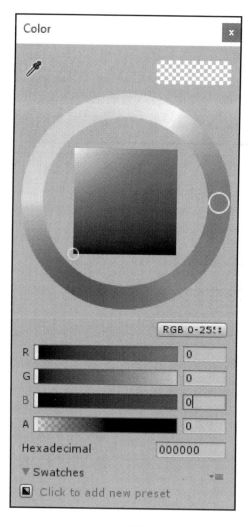

Background Color

If you are going for Mixed Reality applications targeted to immersive headsets, you can keep the default settings that the Unity camera provides for the **Skybox** being used.

Performance and quality control

As with any other game or application, performance is a very important thing to keep in mind. We need to maintain a high frame rate for Mixed Reality headsets and the HoloLens. As these headsets don't have many years of being on the market and aren't upgradeable like PCs, Android phones, iOS devices, or consoles yet, it is best to keep the Quality Settings set to the lowest values possible.

1. To do this, click on **Edit** and look for **Project Settings**:

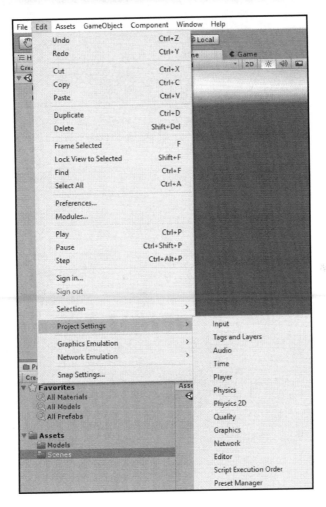

Project Settings

2. Click on **QualitySettings**:

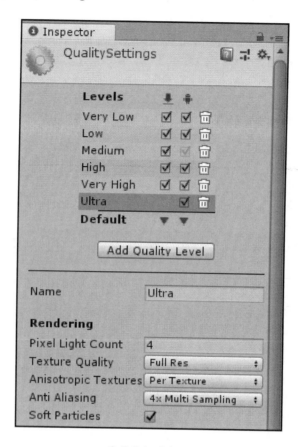

QualitySettings Defaults

3. Change the **QualitySettings** from **Ultra** or whatever your default values are to **Very Low**:

QualitySettings

4. The last thing to do is click on the arrows next to **QualitySettings** and set those defaults to be **Very Low** as well. Look at this screenshot:

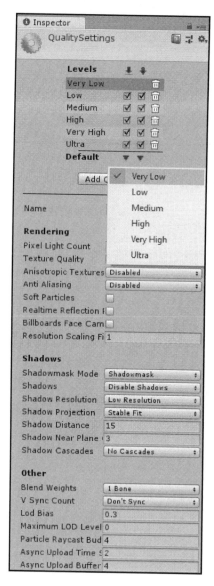

Set QualitySettings

Targeting the Windows 10 SDK

The next step is to make sure we set the target we need for building, in this case, the Windows 10 SDK. First things first, we need to change the scripting backend. Let's follow these steps:

1. To do this, open the **Build Settings** menu:

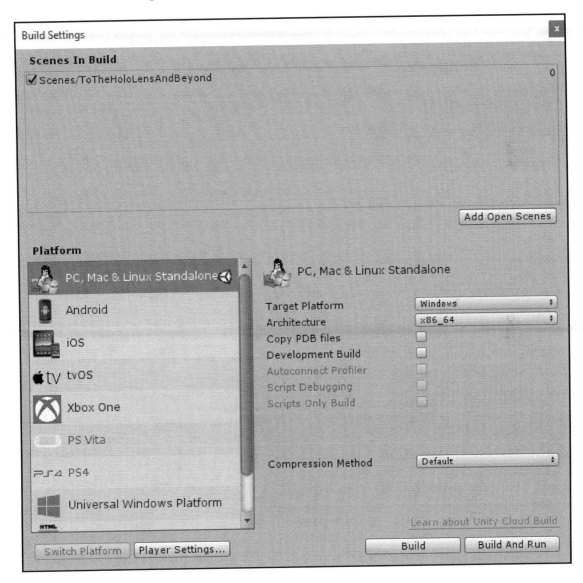

2. Now change the target from **PC, Mac & Linux** to **Universal Windows Platform**:

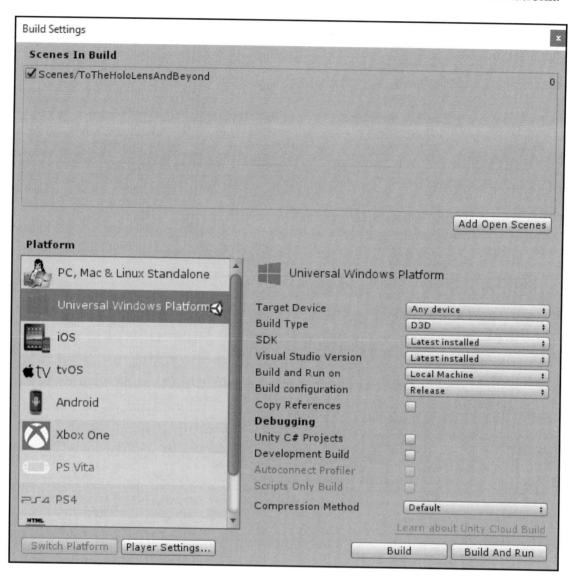

3. Click on **Player Settings** and look for **Configurations**. Your **Scripting Runtime Version** should be set to **.NET 4.x Equivalent, Scripting Backend** should be set to **.NET**, and **API Compatibility Level** should be set to **.NET 4.x**:

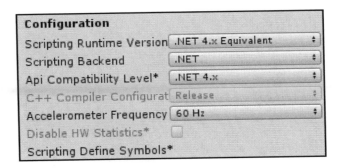

4. Now scroll down and select **XR Settings**:

5. Click on the box to put a check mark into the **Virtual Reality Supported** box to enable it; **Windows Mixed Reality** should automatically be there with **Stereo Rendering Method** defaulting to **Multi Pass**:

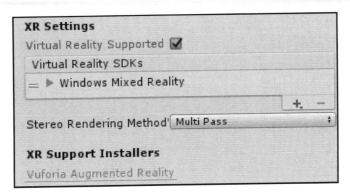

Do the robot

We are getting down to the final steps of this prototype project. So, let's add and configure our robot into the scene to get going into the home stretch. You know what to do—follow these steps:

1. We need to add the **robot** to the scene:

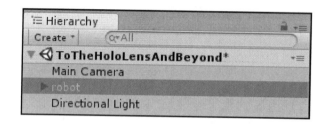

Add robot

2. There are a few values we need to change, the first of which will be the position from the **Inspector** pane, then the rotation, and finally the scale. The default values place it to be at the origin of the player and is too big to be of any use currently:

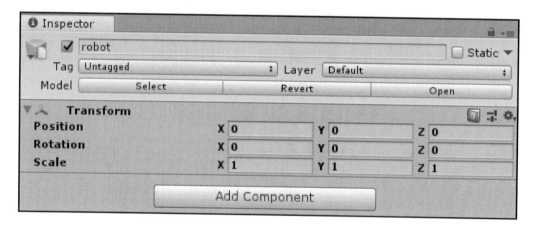

Robot Inspector

3. The **X** position should be set to 0.26, to account for the slight offset that we have from the groupings. The **Y** position should be set to 0, and the **Z** position should be set to 2:

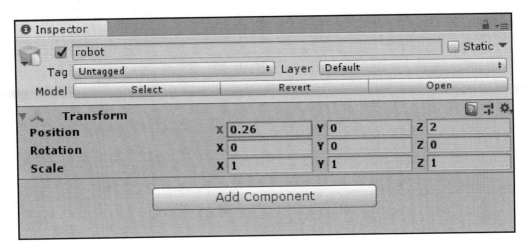

Position

4. Next up is the rotation; we will set the **X** rotation to be 45, the **Y** rotation to be 45, and the **Z** rotation to be 45:

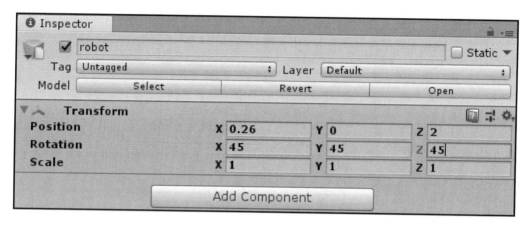

rotation

5. Last, but certainly not least, is the scale. The **X** scale will be set to 0.6, the **Y** scale set to be 0.6, and the **Z** scale to be 0.6:

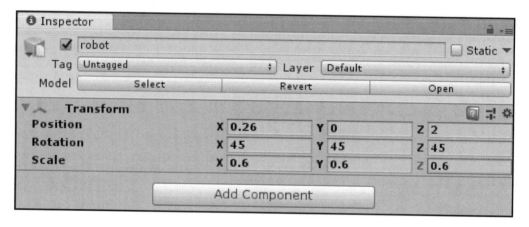

scale

Now we are ready to build and finish this off.

Building and deploying from Visual Studio

OK, this is the last bit, so follow these final steps:

1. Click on **Build Settings** in Unity:

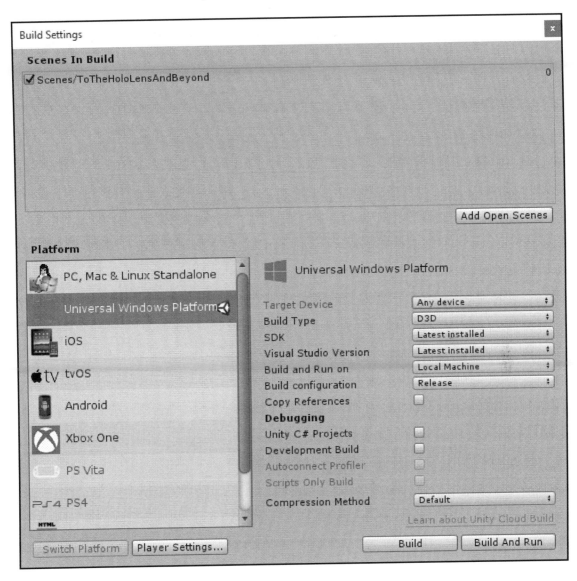

Build Settings

2. Make sure that **Unity C# Projects** has a check mark in it; everything else should have everything pre-setup appropriately:

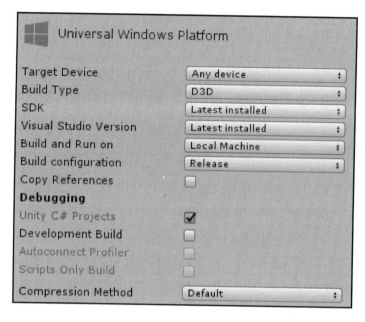

Configuration

3. Click on **Build**:

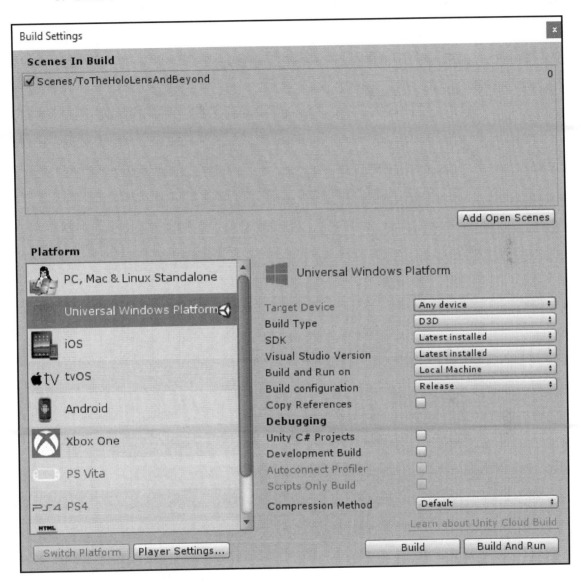

Build

4. It will ask you for the folder you want to build to; create a new folder called `App`, and select it:

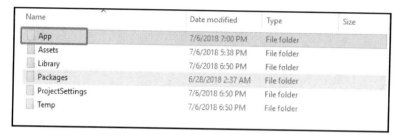

create folder

5. It will take quite a few minutes to finish building, so be prepared for a wait:

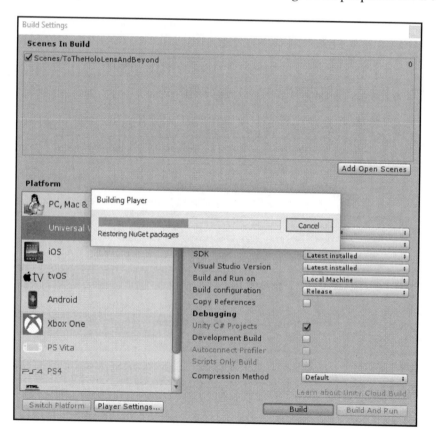

Building

6. Once complete, the folder should auto open; select the App folder, to have a look at it:

Name	Date modified	Type	Size
Chapter8	7/6/2018 7:02 PM	File folder	
Unity	7/6/2018 7:02 PM	File folder	
Chapter8.sln	7/6/2018 7:02 PM	Microsoft Visual S...	3 KB
UnityCommon.props	7/6/2018 7:02 PM	Project Property File	1 KB
UnityOverwrite.txt	7/6/2018 7:02 PM	Text Document	2 KB

App Folder

7. Click on the Chapter8.sln file to open it in Visual Studio:

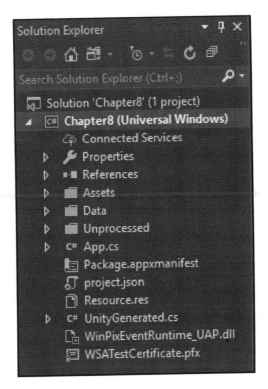

Visual Studio

8. Change from **Debug** to **Release**:

Debug

9. Change from **ARM** architecture to **x64**:

64 bit

10. Change from **Device** to the **HoloLens Emulator**:

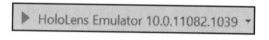

HoloLens

11. Click on **Debug,** and **Start without Debugging**:

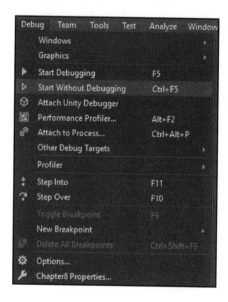

No Debugging

It will display in the simulator now. You have made your first prototype of a Mixed Reality program.

Summary

We learned about how Mixed Reality works and a few different techniques we can apply from the theory to practical use. We looked at some examples of Mixed Reality and set up our computers to build for Mixed Reality, using the HoloLens Simulator.

Other Books You May Enjoy

If you enjoyed this book, you may be interested in these other books by Packt:

Getting Started with Unity 2018 - Third Edition

Dr. Edward Lavieri

ISBN: 9781788830102

- Set up your Unity development environment and navigate its tools
- Import and use custom assets and asset packages to add characters to your game
- Build a 3D game world with a custom terrain, water, sky, mountains, and trees
- Animate game characters, using animation controllers, and scripting
- Apply audio and particle effects to the game
- Create intuitive game menus and interface elements
- Customize your game with sound effects, shadows, lighting effects, and rendering options
- Debug code and provide smooth error handling

Unity Artificial Intelligence Programming - Fourth Edition

Dr. Davida Aversa, Aung Sithu Kyaw, and Clifford Peters

ISBN: 9781789533910

- Create smarter game worlds and characters with C# programming
- Apply automated character movement using pathfinding and steering behaviors
- Implement non-player character decision-making algorithms using Behavior Trees and FSMs
- Build believable and highly efficient artificial flocks and crowds
- Create sensory systems for your AI with the most commonly used techniques
- Construct decision-making systems to make agents take different actions
- Explore the application of machine learning in Unity

Leave a review - let other readers know what you think

Please share your thoughts on this book with others by leaving a review on the site that you bought it from. If you purchased the book from Amazon, please leave us an honest review on this book's Amazon page. This is vital so that other potential readers can see and use your unbiased opinion to make purchasing decisions, we can understand what our customers think about our products, and our authors can see your feedback on the title that they have worked with Packt to create. It will only take a few minutes of your time but is valuable to other potential customers, our authors, and Packt. Thank you!

Index

Made in the USA
Columbia, SC
22 October 2020